SCIENCE, LANGUAGE
AND THE
HUMAN CONDITION

SCIENCE, LANGUAGE

AND THE

HUMAN CONDITION

REVISED EDITION

Morton A. Kaplan

PARAGON HOUSE
New York

First paperback edition, 1989

Published in the United States by

Paragon House Publishers
90 Fifth Avenue
New York, NY 10011

Library of Congress Cataloging in Publication Data

Kaplan, Morton A.
Science, language, and the human condition.

Bibliography: p.
Includes index.
1. Knowledge, Theory of.   2. Languages—Philosophy.
3. Science—Philosophy.   4. Ethics.   5. Marx, Karl,
1818–1883.   6. Social sciences—Philosophy.   I. Title.
BD161.K265   1984   191   84-1141
ISBN 0-913729-01-9
1-55778-147-8 (pbk.)

Manufactured in the United States of America

Contents

Acknowledgments

I wish to thank the following readers of this book for helpful comments: Wayne Booth and Peter Dembowski reviewed the chapter on Derrida; Lev Dobriansky, the section on Marxian economics; Lloyd Eby and John Andrew Sonneborn, a late draft of the book; Franco Ferrarotti, Part One; David Greenstone and Pat Suppes, an early draft of what became chapters 1, 2, 5, 6, and 7; Russell Hardin, early drafts of Parts One and Two; Ira Katznelson, early drafts of Parts One and Four; Leonard Linsky, the chapters on meaning and Wittgenstein; Karl Pribram, Andrew Reck, and Nathan Tarcov, an early draft of the book. My manuscript editor, Isabel Grossner, made many helpful suggestions. Subsequent manuscript editing by Lynn Musgrave also was extremely helpful.

I am grateful to Marnie Berkowitz, Cassie Richard, and Susan Reno, who typed the text of this book from tapes and transcribed numerous revisions.

I am indebted to Georg Süssman for his comments on my discussion of issues in physics in the revised edition.

M.A.K.

Preface to the Revised Edition

At one time a graduate of a good university would have absorbed a synoptic view of the world and of the place of moral values in that world. Philosophy played a major role in that enterprise. Two developments helped to erode that state of affairs: the development of professionalism within disciplines and the rise of positivism in philosophy. In addition, the sharp split between the analytic and the continental philosophers has ruptured dialogue within philosophy.

I am a professional in a discipline other than philosophy and I both value and appreciate the power that professionalism has brought to the understanding of the various aspects of knowledge. However, I deplore the loss of our ability to place specialized knowledge in perspective, the devaluation of this task in the academy, and the failure of most professionals to understand what philosophy can teach them.

In my opinion, the increasing tendency of other disciplines to regard the philosophic enterprise as a quaint anachronism, except perhaps in the area of mathematical logic, stems in part at least from the tendency among philosophers to treat such subdisciplines of philosophy as the philosophy of science, epistemology, language theory, and ethics almost without reference to each other. As a consequence, philosophy has become an arcane subject that plumbs a particular area of inquiry without showing either how it contributes to other areas of knowledge or how other aspects of knowledge contribute to the understanding of philosophy.

I believe that philosophy does have a synoptic subject matter, the understanding of which can place particular academic disciplines outside of philosophy, and subdisciplines within philosophy, in a perspective that modifies them in important ways.

When Plato or Aristotle discussed ethics, they may not have derived their ethical position from their metaphysics but it was consistent with their physics, their concepts of essence, their understanding of language, and their epistemologies. Although more than one system of metaphysics is consistent with a concept of natural law, for instance, there are understandings of the natural world that are, at least apparently, inconsistent with such a concept.

If relativity theory and quantum theory are inconsistent with a strongly and transitively ordered world, as I shall argue, then attempts to revive natural law on Aristotelian or neo-Thomist grounds are implausible in the absence of a sustained argument that meets the objections. The belief that one can make the case without an inquiry into physics and epistemology, even if only to show why the objections do not hold, is faulty.

The idea that we can discuss justice without some concept of the nature of the good seems implausible to me and I shall show why some major attempts to do this necessarily fail. I shall argue that the nature of the world in which we live and the dispositional nature of man are relevant to inquiries about ethics. If one doubts this, I believe that better arguments will be needed to meet the case I have made than have so far been presented in the literature.

Science, Language, and the Human Condition represents my attempt to contribute to synoptic understanding. Several distinguished readers of the first edition of this book suggested that it may help to relegitimate a synoptic approach to philosophy. Although I am too aware of my own status as an outsider to believe that I can play this role, none the less these comments encouraged me to produce this revised and corrected edition.

The preface to the original edition stated my purposes in producing this book. I will use this opportunity to state more succinctly a few of the conclusions I reached that contribute to a synoptic view. I affirmed the objectivity of knowledge but denied that the concept of "nearer to the truth" is meaningful except in reference to particular frames of reference. I show that the world is weakly ordered and that statements about it are dependent on frames of reference. I state that two techniques of inquiry—theory and assessment—temper each other. Confirmation and falsification, thus, also are seen as complementary rather than as foundational techniques of investigation. The acquisition of knowledge is objective and neutral between widening bodies of investigators as part of a spiral process that produces reinterpretations and redefinitions.

These conclusions are related to language. I argue that language is correlative in its character and that literal language and metaphor are not such as such. These conclusions allow me to distinguish between structure and disposition and to show that neither is such as such. This permits me to develop an approach to values, which I show are primarily dispositional and dependent on frame of reference. But I also show how one can advance from particular frames of reference to more inclusive frames and how this invokes conceptions of obligation and justice.

I make use of Niels Bohr's concept of complementarity: the concept that different and incompatible techniques of investigation reveal different aspects of the world that cannot be reduced. This also supports the view that the world is weakly ordered.

The concept of objectivity used in this book does not commit one to the Greek metaphysics against which Heidegger and Derrida railed. However, I find their approach obscurantist. In effect, then, I try to deal with the problems raised by both the analytic and the continental traditions and to find a synoptic solution, one that also responds to some of the insights of Asian thought.

I hope that even those readers who disagree with my particular solutions to problems will value an enterprise that I believe contributes both to professional knowledge and to a humane or liberal understanding of the world in which we live and act. What we believe about ourselves and the world will strongly influence the kind of world we make for ourselves and our children.

MORTON A. KAPLAN

Introduction

My choice of a title for this book does not require much explanation. Part One deals with the philosophy of science. Part Two deals with language. In Parts Three and Four, my concern is with the human condition: in Part Three, specifically with theories of value; in Part Four, with Marxian and neo-classical economic theory as they affect the human condition and, to this extent, with philosophical problems of the social sciences.

This book had been formerly tentatively titled *Man in the World: Glimpses into the Unity of Knowing and the Relatedness of the Known*, a title that is equally relevant, for I hope to show, through an inquiry into science and language, that the human race has a meaningful place in the world, that similar general methods of inquiry are appropriate to the sciences and the social sciences, and that the method of *praxis*, or assessment, relates neighboring realms of knowledge.

The position that the human race has a natural place in a natural universe is apparently a discredited one. It is widely believed that chance elements in evolution, the Freudian discovery of the unconscious, Einstein's discovery of relativity, Heisenberg's principle of uncertainty, and more recently discovered natural singularities, such as black holes, have invalidated the idea of an orderly and rational world, and, especially, of a world in which people have a natural place.

To understand that we are related to the world in a natural way, we must first understand how we know things; how the physical, social, and moral realms, although radically different in content, are brought within the realm of knowledge by similar general methods; and how the ways in which we know the world illuminate our relationship to it, a relationship that is neither simple nor hierarchical.

To develop this world view, I shall use part-system analysis, interpret language as basically correlative, sharply distinguish proof and assessment, emphasize the disjunction between external and internal criteria, and stress the complementarity of definitional and dispositional investigations. These tools will enable me to integrate the philosophy of science with the analysis of language and to show how and why moral investigations are objective. They will also enable me to utilize the strong points in, and to understand the weaknesses of, such opposing positions as those of Thomas Kuhn and Karl Popper, Willard Quine and Saul Kripke, Ludwig Wittgenstein and Jacques Derrida, and Karl Marx and Milton Friedman. In previous books, because of its integration of pragmaticism and the systems approach, I have called my world view systemic pragmaticism. Analytical pragmaticism or, more felicitously, analytical pragmatism also would be an appropriate designation. And, of course, the correlative approach to language is central to my analysis.

The two general ways in which we know the world are those of theory, or demonstration; and assessment. Although one or the other of these methods may be emphasized in any discipline, no discipline, whether in the physical or the social sciences, can advance without employing both methods either explicitly or implicitly. To understand these two methods, we must understand how they employ language and symbols, that is, *signs*, in inquiry.

To begin with, I will try to show how profoundly the understanding of signs has changed, but will not explore the details of particular philosophical or scientific positions. For this purpose, I shall sketch the position of the alchemists of the sixteenth century; of the great skeptic, Descartes, as the model of seventeenth-century scientific philosophy; and of Hegel, as representative of the organismic view of the nineteenth century. Admittedly, the following account is only schematic and leaves out of account competing approaches.

In the sixteenth century, nouns, i.e., signs, were believed to be natural and to reveal the nature of things directly. This belief accounts for the formulas of the alchemists, who thought that they could unlock the secrets of nature by finding the correct wording. In their view, nature consisted of qualitative identities and differences. Everything that was possible was accounted for in fixed form in a fundamental table of possibilities. Thought proceeded by analogies that revealed similarities in things. Therefore, resemblance was their primary criterion.

The Cartesian revolution turned nouns, or names, into signs that represented things, and it based measurements on ordering principles. Mathematics was employed to order those things that had simple natures, and qualitative categories were used to account for complex aspects of the world. Cartesians were also interested in the genesis of things. These techniques were thought to permit an exhaustive ordering of the world. Thus, the Cartesiam position had in common with the sixteenth-century position the belief that reality fell into a unique and coherent pattern and that the correct signs could represent this natural and unique whole.

In the nineteenth century, with the breakup of the Hegelian system that attempted to integrate new organic and functional theories into a coherent whole, the conception of reality as a uniquely ordered whole began to disintegrate. Organisms and their structures and functions became the foci of independent analyses. The positivists reintroduced relativism into philosophy. The growing understanding that cognition was interest-oriented resulted in a subjectivist view that emphasized will, intentionality, and utility. Instrumentalism seemed an attack on the very idea of objectivity. Hermeneutical philosophers hoped to supersede scientists as seekers of wisdom. Although representationalism was fighting a rear-guard action, Peirce, and later Wittgenstein, found meaning in use. If this notion of meaning is combined with the notion of partly independent and often weak orders and second-order discourse, as I combine them in Part One of this book, the unity of knowing can be restored and the natural place of man in the world understood.

This position combines a number of ideas: for instance, that reality is not uniquely ordered. Different interpretations of reality may be equally valid, provided their uses are not inconsistent. Wave and particle interpretations of the photon, for instance, are not inconsistent, because the investigations proceed within incompatible, but not contradictory, frameworks of inquiry. There are no contradictions in quantum theory.

Definitions, which are correlatively linked to dispositional concepts, are relevant only within limited, stable structures of inquiry and may change when the frame of reference is changed. A dispositional analysis of concepts, as I shall show in chapter 4, is necessitated by such shifts in the frame of reference. In some aspects of inquiry, the loci of the observers lead to different first-order statements of fact but not different second-order statements. The concept of "fit," which is essential to the praxical framework of inquiry, determines how neighboring realms of knowledge and the theories appropriate to them accord with each other. Because these realms are often weakly ordered, particularly if they relate to complex aspects of natural and social reality, reality does not have a single, unique structure. There is a complex structure, however, the elements of which fit together.

This framework will be seen to characterize not merely the physical but also the social and the moral realms. Knowledge is objective. Thus, the place of the human race in the universe is not determined by will or by language.

What are the topics of the individual parts of the book? In Part One, I shall discuss theory and praxis, or assessment, and show that they are correlatives. I shall discuss that the relationship between metaphor and literal statement and show that the literal language of science serves as the arbiter for metaphor. I shall also discuss meaning.

In carrying out this task, I attempt to show how the argument for the circularity of theory goes wrong and how agreement can emerge from different initial theories or world views in a manner that is both objective and neutral. Part of this task will be to show that knowledge is not a highly integrated system but one that consists of at least partly independent systems.

In Part Two, some of the topics of Part One are discussed in the light of the writings of two antithetical philosophers: Wittgenstein and Derrida. Wittgenstein's reliance on language games is an alternative to the position stated in chapter 4. Although much in his position is valid, I will argue that his treatment of description, of the insularity of language games, of the concept of the "I," and of psychological processes is misleading.

Jacques Derrida's approach to human knowledge is one of the most important anti-scientific philosophies. It is a powerful challenge to the entire scientific tradition, not merely to the position taken in this book. I will attempt to show where what Derrida had to say is valid and where he went wrong. The earlier discussion of metaphor, literal language, and sign theory (in chapter 4) is essential to the understanding of my critique of Derrida and can be applied by the reader to all mystical positions.

Many modern logicians are infuriated by Hegel's concept of contradiction. Michel Foucault and Jacques Derrida talk puzzlingly of the Other, glances, and caesuras. The reader will see that in many ways this book deals, in the literal language of science, with the problems to which these metaphors allude. Metaphor may be a necessary trigger for science. But science requires literal language.

Derrida argued that the road to knowledge began in the pre-Socratic period, before metaphysics contaminated thought. In chapter 10, I shall argue that this is incorrect. Although Leo Strauss immersed himself in the Socratic view—and, hence, according to Derrida, in metaphysics—my readers can determine for themselves, by extrapolation, how the same objections would apply to Strauss's arguments that the route to knowledge began in Socrates' Greece and that modern science can be understood only by understanding seventeenth-century science. I cannot deny that the history of concepts, particularly the more recent history, is useful in decoding a text or in understanding why a position was developed; I do deny, however, that the history of concepts is necessary, or even always important, in finding truth.

As Derrida's problems arose from his dialectical involvement with the phenomenologists and existentialists, the discussion of the phenomenologist movement in chapters 4 and 10 informs appendix 1. The reader may contrast my claims in appendix 1 with the writings of the phenomenological authors by applying the framework that is developed in Part One.

In Part Three, I attempt to show that, by a proper application of the techniques described in Part One, we can restore the field of morals to the real world and to the arena of objective statements. I shall also argue that approaches that are exclusively rule-oriented or consequence-oriented misrepresent the character of the moral world. Aspects of the characteristics of self-organizing systems that are relevant both to the analysis of systems described in chapter 3 and to the concept of "transfinite stability" that is important to my account of moral behavior in Part Three are treated briefly in appendix 2.

The same methodology will be used in Part Four to show that, despite the plethora of recent attempts to show that Marx was not a determinist, Marx failed to make an adequate distinction between theory and praxis. By attempting to unite the two, rather than using them correlatively, Marx was wedded to a determinism that not even his qualifications could eliminate. This error, I shall argue, invalidates Marx's specific conclusions as well as some aspects of neo-classical economic theory. I shall show that modern Marxists fall victim to this same confusion. The reader who applies the discussion of signs in chapter 4 to Marx's use of concepts will see how Marx's neo-classical understanding of signs contributed to the ultimate failure of his theory.

Marxists, in my opinion, raise important questions but handle them badly. Neo-classical economists offer a method for dealing with some economic questions but foreclose consideration of more important questions. They also mistake the appropriate use of theory. Finally, I offer my own theory of international relations to illustrate what I consider the proper use of theory and praxis. The epilogue is a reprise intended to show how and to what extent the book illuminates the place of humanity in the world.

The organization of this book responds strongly to my belief—for which I argue strongly in chapters 1 and 2—that real and intellectual systems are composed of partly independent and partly interdependent part systems. Hence, the topics of each part of the book are related in a web rather than in simple sequence. This necessitates some repetition—a repetition that is intended to deepen and to widen our understanding of individual topics. The web of relationships that binds together the arguments of this book has fewer strands between than within the parts. Different parts of the book deal with topics that are less closely connected than are the elements of each part. Yet, the careful reader will see that the web is present and that it helps to illuminate our understanding of the individual parts.

On the whole, I have tried to dispense with technical argument. In some places, particularly in chapter 4, this has not been entirely possible. Still, what technical discussion remains is largely illustrative and I hope the reader will bear with it for the sake of following the argument.

Although I have attempted to be fair and accurate in discussing the positions of the authors whose works I examine, I have not attempted an exegesis of their works, even of Karl Marx, to whom two chapters are devoted. Interpretations are always subject to controversy; in my own defense, I may say only that the interpretations I accept are accepted by many and that they have at least enabled me to explore and evaluate the alternative positions that I consider it important to discuss.

Thus, for example, if I am wrong about the naiveté of the supporters of the concept of the ''selfish gene,'' it would not affect my argument for identification and relevance. That argument should be able to stand even if my *ad hominem* charge cannot. The issue is not whether the gene is selfish, but whether I am correct about identification and relevance, their role in praxical reasoning, and their place in the position developed in this book.

My intellectual debts will be apparent to the reader. My pragmaticism, with variations, is derived from Charles Sanders Peirce, my view of systems theory from Ross Ashby. I learned much from reading Morris Cohen; in particular, his occasional references to the polarities of language almost surely stimulated some of my thinking about meaning. Occasional insights were derived from John Dewey. Despite my harsh criticisms, I regard myself as a neo-Hegelian and neo-Marxian. As Morris Cohen has said, Aristotle is the source of this tradition. It is well known that Pierce was strongly influenced by Hegel; and those familiar with F. H. Bradley's *Appearance and Reality* will perceive the pragmatic elements in this avowedly idealistic philosophy that derive from those aspects of Hegel's system that also influenced Marx.

With respect to oriental thought, Lao Tzu is reputed to have said that the Tao is not the Tao, that the way is not the way. Hindu philosophy, which provided a foundation for Buddhist doctrine, contains an argument resembling that in the Tao. Events are described as representing a concatenation of causes and consequences, a thesis which is, in some respects, similar to the transactional approach developed in this book. However, when oriental philosophers speak of things as illusions and of ultimate reality, or the One, as hidden by the veil of Maya, they employ metaphors that lack meaning except as correlatives. I shall attempt to show, in chapter 4, what is licit and illicit use of metaphors and correlatives.

There is a glossary. Except as otherwise specified—or occasionally when talking about the positions of other authors whose use of language is different —the terms are defined as I use them in this book. I urge the reader to pay close attention to the glossary. Because the definitions are adapted to my philosophical position, several differ in important ways from some more usual definitions. Like all lexicons, this glossary inevitably contains definitions that are circular. The glossary will, I hope, help the reader to understand particular statements in the book and, in its entirety, will make clearer my own world view.

Glossary*

Abstraction. A *concept*; a *sign* in its role as a sign.

Analytical. Formally related, related by inner criteria (see *truth, logical*); alternatively, related in an abstract *system*.

Analyze, to. To separate into components.

Assessment. An *abstract sign system* that *mediates concepts* and *referents* and that employs the methods of *praxis*.

As such. As things are in their *essence*.

Bracket, to. To suspend judgment concerning the status of the appearance under examination (Husserl).

Centrality of logic. The more a definition or theorem is crucial to the logic of a *theory* or mode of inquiry—that is, the more that variance in it would produce radical change in the theory or mode of inquiry—the more central it is to its logic.

Characterize, to. To make a *concept* embodied in a pair of *correlatives* relevant to a *particular* by means of a *sign*. Characterizing is hypothetical in two senses. First, whether a particular *entity, process*, sign, or *quality* thereof exists: the concept "ether" in physics, e.g., has no *referent*. Second, whether the attribution is correct: green, e.g., may be experienced as red by a color-blind person. These problems are solved by *praxical assessment*.

Coding. An explicit or implicit routine for *characterizing perceptions* or *signals*.

Coherence theory. A *theory* that the *elements* of the world are *internally related* and that they *fit* together in a *strongly ordered, univocal* fashion.

Complementarity. Aspects of an object, *event*, or *process* that contribute to *knowledge* of it but that require incompatible techniques for their determination are in a state of complementarity. According to Niels Bohr, the positions and momenta of quanta are in a condition of complementarity. The measurement of

---

*Terms in italics are defined separately in this glossary.

one requires rigid instruments; of the other, instruments with moving parts. "*Mind*" and "*body*" are also *concepts* whose *analysis* requires incompatible techniques.

Concept. A *universal* or cluster of universals in their relationships. For example, the concept is "lightness," the *sign* is "light," and the *referent* is light. Clusters of concepts are *theories* or *assessments* and refer to *events, processes, structures*, and *systems*. Signs that *mediate* them include "ape," "scholar," "relativity," "revolution," and "fusion." There are external standards for the correct use of a concept: there must be an actual referent; there is none for unicorn, e.g., except in fiction. Internal standards also govern the use of a concept: these may be set by definitions or by theories.

Concrete. Pertaining to a manifest *entity, process*, or *event*.

Concrete particular. See *Particular, concrete*.

Consciousness. The state of *knowing*, of having *experiences*.

Conventional. Artificial, chosen, not constrained by nature.

Copy theory. A *theory* that there is a descriptive correspondence between *ideas* and *concrete entities* or *processes*.

Correlatives. Qualitative pairs of *concepts* that *characterize* aspects of *experience*, such as "warm" and "cool." Because the *referents* of correlatives are always *particulars*, their use is always constrained by context and a frame of reference that produces inner connectedness.

Correspondence theory. A *theory* that there is an invariant association between *signs*, the *concepts* they *mediate*, and *concrete particulars*.

Covering law. See *Law, covering*.

Danda. Products of interpretations that rest on *world views* or "worldwide structural hypotheses," e.g., organicist philosophies that distinguish between appearances and realities, the natures of which depend on the philosophy, e.g., the *meaning* of Idea in Plato's theory depends on other elements of his theory (Pepper).

Deconstruction. A critical method designed to show how culture, including writing, inevitably produces incoherence in the presentation of the real world. Every signifier invokes an infinite sequence of signifiers, no one of which has a firm presence. Each produces its own gap or absence, in an infinite sequence. An example of deconstruction is the tearing apart of a text in an effort to find the one book that all existing texts hide (Derrida).

De dicta. A non-univocal relationship between *sign, referent*, and *concept*. How things are spoken of (cf. *de re*).

De re. How things are in themselves. A *truth* that will not vary from world to world.

Describe, to. To *characterize*. Description is always hypothetical.

Designation, rigid. The univocal relationship of *concept, sign,* and *referent* in all possible worlds. How things are *de re*.

Dispositional. A *concept* that cannot be defined, recognition of which depends on its manifestations under different circumstances, e.g., electric charge.

Ego. The *self,* or the *conscious* subsystem thereof, to which all *first-order transactions* have reference.

Element. Member of a set.

Entity. A *structure*; occasionally used as a synonym for *system*.

Epistemology. The *assessment* of the standards for and the possibility of *knowing*.

Equilibrium, homeostatic. A characteristic of a *system* in which changes in one or more *elements* keep another element at a constant *value*: e.g., when the room cools, the heater is automatically turned on.

Equilibrium, mechanical. A state of equality to which independent measures and *covering laws* apply.

Equilibrium, transfinitely stable. Refers to the ability of a *system* to adjust a complex *structure* of rules, goals, and *values* to circumstances, to substitute new rules, goals, and values for old ones, to develop new rules, goals and values and to relate its behavior to its understanding of itself and its world.

Equilibrium, ultrastable. Refers to the ability of a *system* to correct its code of behavior to keep at least one of its *elements* at a constant *value*: e.g., if the coded behavior does not turn on the heat, the system will search for a new response that will.

Essence. That which underlies appearance and determines its character; underlying or basic character.

Event. An occurrence to which the concept of "space-time" applies and the *elements* of which are externally connected: e.g., *praxical assessment* is an event.

Existential. *Concrete,* manifest.

Existentialism. A *theory* that the world is meaningless or that *meaning* is introduced into a meaningless world by human will. Existentialists may find meaning in the fear of nonexistence or in anxiety and often share with philosophical *phenomenology* a belief in Being.

Experience. Awareness of *entities, processes, events, signs, concepts, thoughts,* and feelings.

Explanation. An account that can be derived from a *theory* or *covering law* and applied directly to the real world when the boundaries of the theory or law are explicit.

Extension. Reference by pointing.

External Relations. See *Relations, external*.

Fact. An empirical *truth*.

Feedback. Produced by a control *system* in which the behavior of a *system* is monitored, modified or compensated for, and then returned to the system: e.g., as by an automatic passenger elevator.

Feedback, negative. *Feedback* that controls output by reducing excess: e.g., the control of distortion in a sound amplifier.

Feedback, positive. An amplification of the content of a *signal* after internal monitoring.

First-order reference. The locus of reference of an observer, actor, or *system*.

Fit, to. To be consistent with, to complement; a *metaphor*; therefore, the criteria for *fit* must be stated each time the *concept* is used.

Function. The role an *element* plays in controlling *equilibrium* or change in a *system*.

Game theory. A mathematical *theory* that prescribes *optimal* strategies to be used in games in which players take into account the strategies of the other players (von Neumann).

Hermeneutics. The principles by means of which a text is *analyzed*; a set of *concepts* and *signs* divorced from real *referents*.

Homeorhesis. Maintenance of a direction of flow or of development in a *system* (Waddington).

Idea. See *Concept*. The *meaning* of idea that sustains idealistic *theories* differs from my definition; e.g., *danda*.

Idealism. A *theory* that the reality underlying matter is *Idea*.

Idealism, objective. A *theory* that the world is the appearance of *essences* and, therefore, of *Idea*, but also that essences are inferred from existence; compatible with contingency in the temporal world.

Idealism, subjective. A *theory* that the world is phenomenal only or that it is, or consists of, *ideas* in the *mind*.

Idiosyncratic. Personal; dependent on the history of individuals, persons, or groups and variability in their environment.

Information. A *signal* that conveys *knowledge* to a *transceiver*: e.g., the *characteristics* of an *entity* or *process*, the *signs* stored in a computer.

Intensional. Having significance or *meaning*.

Internal Relations. See *Relations, internal*.

Invariant. Deterministic; constant under specified conditions; the quantum equations are invariant although quantum *events* are probabilistic.

Justice, procedural. A *process* intended to produce *substantive justice*.

Justice, substantive. A condition in which each actor, role, or *organization* obtains that outcome or participates in that state of affairs that it ought to obtain or participate in (cf. *Society, just*).

Knowledge. *Concepts* and *reals mediated* at least implicitly by *signs*, a triadic relationship that involves two *correlative pairs*: "*concept*" and "*sign*" and "*sign*" and "*referent*," as well as relationships between *perceptions* of referents and *systems* of concepts; awareness of features of the world or of relationships among them. See *Mind*.

Knowledge, transactional. The *characterization* of a *referent* by a *transceiver* or perceiver.

Law, covering. A *system* of *signs* that specifies an *invariance* among defined *entities* or *processes* and that *mediates concepts* and *reals*. Requires independent measures.

Literal. Use of a *concept* that *fits* its *referent* exactly. A one-to-one relationship between concept, *sign*, and referent.

Locator terms. Terms that designate a qualitative or quantitative ordering of one of a pair of *concepts* that are *correlatives*.

Macrophysics. The domain in which mass points interact with force fields. Mechanics, field physics, and phenomenological thermodynamics.

Materialism. A *theory* in which the *real* is equated with the material and in which *mind* is held to be either epiphenomenal or physical.

Meaning. Meaning is given by the scope of the use by a *transceiver* or perceiver of the *sign-mediated* application of a *concept* (in its *correlative* aspect) or of a *system* of concepts (in their correlative aspects) to *referents*. As *reflexive* referents, signs in their relations to other signs can have intra-systemic *meaning*. There are external (and also internal) criteria for these applications; and, thus, the concept of empirical *truth* is applicable.

Mediate, to. To occupy an intermediate position in a *transaction*.

Message. A *signal* or signal set; a communication that conveys *meaning*.

Metacorrelatives. *Correlative signs* whose *referents* are other correlatives.

Metalanguage. A language within which another language is *analyzed*; language used to discuss language.

Metaphor. A *sign* that is complexly related to *concepts* and *referents*, that is, that does not *fit* them in some respects: e.g., his elephantine walk, which can resemble the concepts or referents of "elephant" and "walk" only in some respects. External criteria are used to determine that a fit is not *literal*.

Metaphysical system. A systematic hypothesis of the nature of the world. As Pepper has shown, if it were genuinely worldwide, it would be circular.

Metaphysics. The fundamental principles that govern the world; the *danda* that shape the interpretation of data.

Metatheory. The principles that *characterize* relationships in the world; e.g., *part systems, first-order* and *second-order references*. These principles are not *a priori* principles and, as part-systems within a *world view*, they are not circular.

Microphysics. Quantum physics. Quantum mechanics is the field in which we cannot assign location or velocity without reference to specific experimental contexts. In quantum field theory the quantification of fields yields particles. In quantum theory, the non-Aristotelian logic of complex probability amplitudes leads to *objective* probabilities.

Mind. A *system* that uses and transforms *concepts, signs*, and *perceptions* of *referents*; and the states and organization of which are affected by its processing of them.

Mysticism. The belief that there is a fundamental reality that is ineffable and inexpressible, certain aspects of which can be partly discerned through *metaphor* or intuition.

Name. An identifier of a *concrete particular* or a *system*; a noun.

Natural. Produced by the *potentialities* of the *transactional process*; the opposite of *conventional* or artificial.

Natural kind. *Entities* that *fit* within a scientific classification; according to Kripke and Putnam, a natural kind is determined by a *necessarily true* definition.

Necessary. *Internally related*; deductive or *correlative*.

Neutral. A *second-order invariance*.

Nominalistic. Existing only as *particulars*.

Normative. Pertaining to criteria that guide, or are intended to guide, judgment.

Objective. The state of being a *referent*; hence, in the object language. It connotes *invariance*, at least at a *second-order* level of reference, and includes thoughts and relationships insofar as they are the objects of *knowing* or *thinking*.

Ontology. The study of the nature and *relations* of being.

Optimal. Best under the circumstances of choice.

Order, strong. An order that is determinate and *univocal*.

Order, univocal. An order in which each state of the world, *entity*, and *process* is associated with a specific locus that belongs to it alone.

Order, weak. An order that is indeterminate and not *univocal*.

Organization. A *system* in which participants have goals or tasks.

Paradigmatic. *Fitting* a *concept literally*: e.g., a paradigmatic example of a free market economy would be one in which *information* is free, assets can be transferred without loss, and products are indistinguishable.

Particular. Distinguishable from other *entities, processes, events*, or *signs* of the same kind or classification; a member of a class that can be denoted by "this" or "that": e.g., this apple.

Particular, abstract. A *sign* or *sign set* that qualifies a *concrete particular*: e.g., "green" is an abstract particular that qualifies a concrete particular. "Greenness" is the *concept*, that is, the universal.

Particular, concrete. An *entity, process, event*, or *quality*: e.g., the White House, World War II, or that green baseball.

Part system. A *system* of sufficient stability and independence so that it can be studied while changes in related systems are ignored, at least tentatively; a subsystem.

Perception. A holistic, analog process of *minds* that *codes* neural *signals* and inputs from the environment. See *prehend*.

Personal. Not *subjective*, but related to the individual (cf. *idiosyncratic*).

Phenomenology. As a method, the *analysis* of *experience*; as a philosophy, the attempt to penetrate to the *essences* that underlie appearances by analyzing appearances. Its emphasis is on human psychology, and it is often *characterized* by the thesis that Being has a *meaning* beyond *particular* beings or types of being.

Positivism. The claim that science starts from sensory data and that *theories* are built from this ground up.

Potentiality. The capability of becoming manifest or of producing or contributing to the production of manifest *entities, processes, events*, or *properties*.

Practice. How things work or how they are done; e.g., how pilots fly planes rather than what the regulations specify (cf. *praxis*).

Pragmaticism. Charles Sanders Peirce's *theory* that the *meaning* of a *concept* is inferred from the infinite totality of its *relations* and effects. Peirce rejected the notion of *essences*, but accepted the *idea* of a *telos*. He coined the term "pragmaticism" to distinguish it from William James's misuse of the term "pragmatism."

Praxical assessment. An account that is not entirely deductive and that employs *concepts* such as *fit, centrality of logic*, and *relevance*. My employment of praxical assessment includes *second-order* and *part-system analysis* and, therefore, takes observers into explicit account. I drop the concept of an infinity of tests in favor of sustained comparative testing.

Praxis. A reasoning *process* in which the explicit or implicit employment of *concepts* such as *fit, centrality of logic*, and *relevance* are used in the evaluation of *theories*, propositions, and data; thus, the *practice* of scientific method as distinguished from the construction and testing of formal theories provides an external standard for theories. Not, however, practice in the ordinary or the Marxian sense.

Preconscious. *Potentially conscious.*

Prehend, to. To grasp by means of the senses. See *perception*.

Process. The regular changes that *functions* produce in a *structure*.

Quality. The *referent* of a *concept* that *characterizes* an *element* of an *entity*, *process*, *event*, or *sign*.

Rational. In accordance with internal and external criteria.

Real. An *event, entity*, or *process*; the *potentiality* of a *particular* entity or process; the properties of particular entities, events, or processes. To Hegel, *essences* were real.

Referent. A *particular*, including *relations; signed*.

Reflexive. *Self*-referring.

Reify, to. To treat an *abstract concept* as *concrete*; to treat a *process* as an *entity*; to treat a *function* as the whole; to treat a relational concept as independent; e.g., the concept of class in Marx and of wants in neo-classical economic *theory*.

Relations, external. Relations among *concepts* or their *referents* when they are *mediated* by *assessment* rather than a *theory*; relations between concepts that are not *correlatives*.

Relations, internal. The relations among *correlatives* or among the *concepts* or *referents* of concepts in a *theory* or in the theoretical subcomponent of an *assessment*; a *necessary* relationship. "*Mind*" and "*body*" are correlatives and thus are internally related. The *meaning* of mass depends on the theory in which it is imbedded and, to this extent, is internal.

Second-order reference. A reference standpoint that is independent of the locus of particular observers, actors, and *systems*: e.g., relativity *theory* provides a *neutral* perspective for observers on independent inertial systems.

Self. The *reflexive* subject that experiences the world; the housing of the *ego*.

Self-consciousness. *Knowledge* of *consciousness; reflexive* consciousness.

Sign. A symbol or word that is associated with a *referent*.

Signal. The content of a transmission from a source to a *transceiver*.

Signal source. A *referent*; a *real*.

Signed. The *referent* of a *sign*.

Sign set. Related *signs*; the signs of the *real elements* associated with a *name*.

Society, just. A society in which a good way of life, good *values*, and individual and *organizational* virtues are manifest.

Structure. The static relationships between *elements* of a *system*.

Subjective. The *correlative* of *objective; consciousness*.

System. *Abstractly*, a set of *elements* and *functions*; in *real* terms, an *entity* and its *processes*: e.g., this man, that telephone network.

System, definitional. A *system characterized* by an *invariant structure* and by invariant *processes* carried on within or by that structure.

Telos. A direction of development (Peirce).

Test-in-principle. A *thought* experiment to test *values*.

Theory. An *abstract sign system* that *mediates concepts* and *referents* and that employs undefined terms, definitions, axioms, and theorems in a deductive way within explicit boundaries. In addition to the two senses in which *characterization* is hypothetical, there is a third sense in which characterization of the real world by a theory is hypothetical: there are internal standards for judging whether its predictions are accurate and, therefore, whether the theory adequately *characterizes reals*.

Theory sketch. A reasoned account, the *elements* of which are only loosely or plausibly related, although there may be occasional instances of strict deduction. It differs from Hempel's "explanation sketch" insofar as Hempel assumes that a *potential theory* always underlies a sketch.

Thinking. A *process* in which *concepts* are *mediated* by *signs* in theorizing about or assessing interrelationships in the world.

Thought. An *element* in *thinking*; a single proposition, express or implied.

Transaction. A *process* the outcome of which is produced by relations between *entities*.

Transceiver. A *system* that characterizes *entities, events*, and *processes* by *coding signals*. *Minds*, that is, perceivers, are transceivers but not all transceivers are minds.

Transmission. A *process* involving a *transceiver*, a *signal* set, a medium, and a *signal source*.

True. Something is true if it follows from internal criteria, if it *fits* external criteria, or if it is axiomatic.

Truth, empirical. The *fit* between an *entity, event*, or *process* or a *theory, assessment*, or proposition and external criteria. As applied to theories and the theoretical aspects of *assessments*, it meets internal criteria as well.

Truth, logical. An axiom, deduction, or inference that satisfies internal criteria. (cf. *analytical*).

Universal, abstract. A *concept* that *characterizes* an *entity, event, process*, or *quality* thereof. *Mediated* by a *sign*, but one that does not name a *particular*. Greenness but not green.

Universal, concrete. *Concrete* and generic; that is, its concreteness actually or *potentially* invests more than one *particular* of the same kind. To Hegel and Marx, the *essence* of something: e.g., humanity or the working class. Whitehead's "eternal objects" are universals, but they are *real* and not *essences*.

Univocal. See *Order, univocal*.

Values. Goals, rules, or criteria that guide judgment.

Verisimilitude. A *first-order univocal* mapping in which each prediction of a *theory* corresponds with a descriptive position or *relation*. The concept of *fit* is *literal* and different types of theories can be compared with respect to fit.

World view. Includes *metatheoretical* principles, *concepts*, and an *assessment* of how things and *processes fit* together. Although it includes "*internal relations*," it is *characterized* even more by their *correlative*, "*external relations*."

PART ONE
SCIENCE: PRELIMINARY CONSIDERATIONS

THE FAILURE OF positivism produced a crisis in accounts of how we know, and relate to, the world. In Part One, I shall attempt to deal with some of the major issues that have arisen out of this crisis.

If all knowledge involves interpretation, how do we escape circularity in our claims to knowledge? We cannot doubt the power of physics. If, however, its methods are circular, how can we account for its power? Alternatively, does truth in physics rest on fact and truth in the human sciences on intentionality? What does it mean to make this distinction? Is it even possible to talk of truth if all experience and all knowledge involve interpretation?

In chapter 1, I argue against the view that the methods of science are circular. After clearing this ground, I shall develop, in subsequent chapters, a position that is consistent with objectivity and neutrality, but not in the form in which these concepts are usually employed. Instead, I shall argue that the process of knowing is not circular but is spirally progressive. It employs some part systems (relatively independent areas of knowledge) in the interpretation of others; and, in this process, no phase has ultimate priority.

The discussion of *metatheoretical principles* (that is, principles that describe relationships in the world) in chapter 2 will provide the scaffolding for my position. Here I discuss *first-order* and *second-order references* (i.e., those that depend on the locus of the observer and those that are neutral with respect to the observer) and show how the distinction helps to resolve apparent contradictions. Here also, the reader is introduced to part-system analysis and the concept of weak orders, ideas which play an important part in my position.

Chapter 3 is devoted to a consideration of systems and the scope of theory. The two are distinguished, and the term "systems theory" shown to be misleading. The meaning and limitations of covering laws, so well-accepted in our scientifically oriented society, are discussed. The differences between the applicability of theories in the physical and the social sciences are considered.

Chapter 4, an extended discussion of meaning, science, and reality, contains an analysis of the relationship among concepts, signs (words and symbols), and referents. It will be seen that meaning is essentially conveyed by correlatives, paired concepts such as "light" and "dark," which help to characterize the world but for which no absolute standards exist. It follows that our perceptions, as well as the theories and knowledge we derive from them, are dependent upon the context in which we frame them. Once this is understood, many ambiguities and apparent paradoxes can be resolved. An examination of some logical propositions serves to illustrate this conclusion. Special attention is given to the correlatives "definitional" and "dispositional." This leads to a preliminary discussion of problems of morality and rationality.

In chapter 5, the techniques of praxical assessment and of theoretical explanation are defined and illustrated. The criteria of fit, category, relevance, and centrality of logic are shown to validate theories in the physical and social sciences, sometimes more so than experimental tests of theories.

In chapter 6, I examine some alternative accounts of theory and theory testing, explore their strong and weak points, relate them to the concepts of theory and praxis employed in this book, and discuss the implications of these concepts in respect to a realistic view of the world. In part, this chapter contains an assault on the concept of verisimilitude, but it is an assault that does not dispose of truth with a small "t" or of an adequate concept of objectivity but, instead, supports them meaningfully.

Chapter 7, on indeterminacy, intentionality, and consciousness extends the critique of other philosophical theories. The differences between the social and the physical sciences are again explored, and the intentionality (meaning) of language is considered.

Chapter 1
The Problem of Circularity

A number of modern writers have challenged, or at least have appeared to challenge, the concept of objectivity in science and have argued that scientific method is circular. It is the general idea that scientific method is circular that I am disputing. I shall emphasize the work of Thomas C. Kuhn because of his prominence in this respect.*

Kuhn brought the term paradigm into wide play. By paradigm Kuhn meant either a global set of shared commitments of a scientific group, including rules and criteria for their application, or a particularly important scientific commitment which, thus, is a subset of the first. He emphasized shifts in paradigm in what he calls scientific revolutions. How and why scientists shift from one mode or paradigm of analysis to another—for instance, from Newtonian mechanics to Einsteinian principles—is indeed interesting. From the standpoint of a general philosophy of science, however, it becomes a big problem only if one denies that there are neutral or objective grounds for justifying the shift.

Kuhn has denied that the views attributed to him were accurate interpretations of what he wrote. Nevertheless, his concept of scientific revolution gained its major currency from what appeared to be his claim that scientific reasoning is "circular" and that choices among paradigms are determined by "persuasion."

I shall proceed by showing what Kuhn did say that legitimately gave rise to an interpretation he now rejects, although my analysis will make use of a more general claim for the same position: the now little known, but philosophically more cogent, argument of Stephen C. Pepper.

---

*Thomas C. Kuhn, a student of the history of science and of the philosophy of science, came to general notice with *The Scientific Revolution* (Chicago: University of Chicago Press, 1962). Among his opponents are Gerard Radnitzky and Imre Lakatos.[1]

KUHN'S POSITION

Before I characterize Kuhn's recent position, let me outline his initial position. Kuhn stated:

> The decision to reject one paradigm is always simultaneously the decision to accept another, and a judgment leading to the decision involves the comparison of both paradigms with nature *and* with each other.[2]

This sounds reasonable enough, although some may have wondered exactly how he defined "nature" and "paradigm."

However, Kuhn went on to argue:

> When paradigms enter, *as they must*, into debate about paradigm choice, their role is necessarily circular. Each group uses its own paradigm to argue in that paradigm's defense. The resulting circularity does not, of course, make the argument wrong or even ineffectual. . . . Yet, whatever its force, the status of the circular argument is *only* that of *persuasion*.[3] [Italics added.]

This is what led to the charge that Kuhn's position was merely subjectivistic. Logic and evidence may be involved in persuasion, but in the last analysis, its force is gained on other grounds.

The view that Kuhn's approach is subjective is reinforced by his discussion of gestalt psychology. He pointed out that one may see a figure on a card either as a duck or a rabbit. One can see either form, he said, by making a conscious choice and can then relate these observations to the card. There is, he wrote:

> . . . an external standard with respect to . . . a switch of vision [that can] be demonstrated [and in the absence of which] no conclusion about alternate perceptual possibilities could be drawn. With scientific observation, however, the situation is exactly reversed. The scientist can have no recourse above or beyond what he sees with his eyes and instruments.[4]

In effect, Kuhn claimed that to change one's scientific paradigm is close in character to a religious conversion.

Later, Kuhn wrote that there are indeed grounds for preferring one paradigm over another. Such judgments may be based on such scientific values as accuracy, consistency, scope, simplicity, and fruitfulness.[5] Although he argued that these values are not so well-defined that they can dictate the choice between two theories, he regarded this as a virtue because they do not cause a premature choice between competing theories and thus they permit a rational consensus to evolve.[6]

Much of what Kuhn says can be accepted by reasonable scholars. However, because Kuhn has not yet renounced the circularity argument—a position I reject—it is important to stress the differences in our positions. If one insists on the literal meaning of "prove," it is true that one cannot prove one theory to be true and its adversaries to be false. But this has nothing to do with so-called incommensurabilities or circularities. And there are objective standards for assessing decisions in favor of a theory over its adversaries. Before I develop this argument, however, I want to deal with the issues of incommensurability and circularity.

PEPPER'S POSITION

Let me turn to a well-formulated and philosophically deeper argument for circularity than Kuhn's, that of Stephen C. Pepper. I believe that the claims made for the coherence, scope, and justification of the worldwide hypotheses Pepper analyzes justify his contention that they are circular.

In his argument with the positivists—which was merely a particular exercise of his general argument that different structural world views cannot be adjudicated within a common framework—Pepper argued:

> In order to assemble data so as to drive out alternative danda,* a positivist must make a structural hypothesis, and a worldwide one, such that fact corroborates fact throughout and every fact is a single "datum." Then, and only then, can no alternative danda squeeze in but then this positivist has developed a structural world hypothesis, and his "data" become actually danda of a certain sort.[7]

Therefore, they cannot be criticized except within their own framework.

In essence, Pepper was saying that metaphysical world views establish an interpretative framework that cannot be criticized from competing frameworks. Therefore, he concluded, differences in world views cannot be adjudicated, although a world view may fail because its own criteria are not satisfied.

Pepper was aware that metaphysical systems had been challenged and superseded. If their danda are circular in their formulation, how did he explain this? The root metaphors of metaphysical systems—that is, the metaphors that permit their characterization as mechanistic, for instance—cannot be disproved, he said, because the assumptions that characterize them as such, and that shape their danda, are present in their formulation. However, the particular metaphysical system that embodies the root metaphor may be inadequate in its own terms.

Pepper cited Thales, within whose materialistic system water was the metaphysical basis of all that is, and noted that subsequent philosophers pointed out that earth, air, and fire cannot be reduced to water. Although it is true that these philosophers, like Thales, were materialists, he does not show how they argued within Thales' framework.[8] After all, any significant change in a theory will also change its danda, as we shall soon see. Moreover, could not an idealist have come to the same conclusion? In what sense was the argument inadequate in its own terms? The closest that Pepper came to an answer to this question lies in his distinction between data and danda.

Data, Pepper says, permit us to evaluate alternative versions of a metaphysical

---

Danda are products of interpretation that rest on worldwide structural hypotheses. Plato's Idea is a dandum because its meaning depends on his philosophical position.

system but not alternative systems. Does this follow for scientific theories also? Or does the claim fail in both cases?

If their production of incommensurable danda is the necessary and sufficient condition that precludes the comparative evaluation of competing worldwide structural hypotheses—and this is Pepper's claim—then it should not be possible to evaluate comparatively different scientific theories if they produce incommensurable danda. Therefore, if of two competing scientific theories that produce incommensurable danda, one can be shown to be false and the other to be supported by the evidence, serious doubt is cast on Pepper's conclusion; and we shall soon see the reason for his error.

Let us take an example from mechanics rather than from philosophy to explore this issue because mechanics can be discussed with greater precision. If Newton's theory is correct, light emitted from a moving source, if reflected, will return to the source more quickly in the direction of its motion than away from it. If, however, light returns simultaneously regardless of the direction of motion of the source, the theory needs to be reformulated. This is but one instance of a lack of fit between Newton's formulation of the laws of mechanics and the data.

Note how this circumstance introduces a serious difficulty into Pepper's argument on circularity. To explain the data that could not be accommodated within Newton's theory, one would look for a new theory, like Einstein's, the major assumptions of which were different and, hence, the meanings of some of whose major concepts—for instance, "mass"—were different. These concepts, in Pepper's terms, constitute danda. The interpretative frameworks of the two theories were different, even though both were mechanistic, as Pepper uses that concept. Yet there are grounds for preferring Einstein's theory to Newton's.

The previous example is one that exemplifies Kuhn's account of incommensurability, an account that does not rest on the concept of a worldwide hypothesis, as does Pepper's. In effect, Newton's language and Einstein's express different cognitive commitments. The concepts of space and time are absolute in Newton's system and relative in Einstein's, for which the velocity of light is an absolute. The geometries of the two systems are different as are the concepts of mass. There will be imperfections in translations from one account to the other. Yet, as I have argued here, and as I shall show in more detail as this same example is employed in other contexts in this and subsequent chapters, we can find adequate grounds for choice and, in this case, we can make clear the respects in which Einstein's theory is superior to Newton's.

In principle, metaphysical systems and their danda can be adjudicated by similar methods, although their looseness of construction may make the assessment difficult in practice. This does occur to some extent. The power of theories in physics did give a boost to philosophical materialism in the modern age. And contemporary quantum mechanics has made it difficult to support materialism in any recognizable form. Thus, it would seem that we must reject Pepper's argument about circularity.

However, before we do so, let us note a problem in Pepper's account of how metaphysical systems are shown to be inadequate. Insofar as the resolution of the problem of circularity rests on Pepper's distinction between data and danda, where do the data come from that refute a theory? Pepper called such data ordinary common sense, an evasion that does contain a kernel of truth. Let us now see what that kernel of truth is.

There are data that are not accommodated in particular theories or world views. These include, but are not restricted to, ordinary common sense. They may in fact involve highly sophisticated concepts. And they are not independent of interpretation.* Let us first show that this is so and then why such data can be used non-circularly.

Consider, for instance, the problems that I. Langmuir had with the Davis-Barnes experiment. The properties at issue were defined by physical theory—not merely by simple observation—and the supposed identifications were unlikely according to a specific accepted theory, Bohr's theory of the hydrogen atom. Thus Langmuir was led by theoretical considerations to a rejection of observational identifications that had been made by Davis and Barnes and to an explanation of their mistake.** Now let us see why interpreted data can be used to critique theories non-circularly.

No world view or "worldwide structural hypothesis," as that term was used by Pepper, has ever been constructed by any philosopher, except in elliptical form. It seems obvious that a philosophical theory that has not been (and in my view could not have been) formulated in detail, cannot be used systematically. We formulate only aspects of any philosophy, except in elliptical form. We organize theoretically only aspects of experience, not the whole, even with respect to a field of science. It is easy to see that this is true of the history of

---

*As the position that all data involve interpretation is commonly accepted, I shall not give the reasons for this even more general position now. However, they will be made clear in the discussion of germane topics in chapters 4 and 6.

**"Well, in the discussion, we questioned how, experimentally, you could examine the whole spectrum; because each count, you see, takes a long time. There was a long series of alpha particle counts, that took two minutes at a time, and you had to do it ten or fifteen times and you had to adjust the voltage to a hundredth of a volt. If you have to go through steps of a hundredth of a volt each and to cover all the range from 330 up to 900 volts, you'd have quite a job. (Laughter) Well, they said that they didn't do it quite that way. They had found by some preliminary work that they did check with the Bohr orbit velocities so they knew where to look for them. They found them sometimes not exactly where they expected them but they explored around in that neighborhood and the result was that they got them with extraordinary precision. So high, in fact, that they were sure they'd be able to check the Rydberg constant more accurately than it can be done by studying the hydrogen spectrum, which is something like one in the 10^8. At any rate, they had no inhibitions at all as to the accuracy which could be obtained by this method especially since they were measuring these voltages within a hundredth of a volt. Anybody who looks at the setup would be a little doubtful about whether the electrons had velocities that were fixed and definite within 1/100 of a volt because this is not exactly a homogeneous field. The distance was only about 5 mm in which they were moving along together." I. Langmuir, *Pathological Science*, edited and transcribed by R. N. Hall, General Electric, *Technical Information Series*, report no. 68-C-035 (Schenectady, New York: General Electric Research and Development Center, April 1968), pp. 2, 3. Quoted by permission.

philosophy, of the history of science, and of human experience. That all lexicons are circular and that all theories use undefined terms is additional evidence of this position.

There is a great overlap between the methods and interpretations of theories. If this were not so, it would not be possible for opposed philosophical formulations or scientific theories to grow out of the same cultural base. They would be excluded by virtue of an existing interpretative framework that would determine the kinds of observations that could be reported and the interpretations to which they could be subjected.

If one has a world view that is not strongly ordered, that is, not complete and systematic in Pepper's sense, then the argument about incommensurablity is deficient because external criteria can now be brought to bear on the problem that, at least in principle, can decide the case. Some specific instances have already been given.

But even the claim that a worldwide structural hypothesis is possible is unconvincing. We do not even know how to program a computer to distinguish faces as well as a child can, let alone how to formulate an algorithm that will account for our assessment of all of reality. Our most sophisticated analytical procedures are extremely restricted devices. It is highly probable that the search procedures of the brain employ a more reliable but less precise logic than our formal procedures of proof, as John von Neumann speculated in his posthumously published Silliman lectures.[9] It is likely that the two hemispheres of the brain use different coding systems. In the absence of prelinguistic coding, how else could we explain how infants perceive events or acquire language? Most likely prelinguistic and non-linguistic codes coexist with a variety of interpretative considerations in the adult mind. These may be partly compartmentalized and partly interactive in ways we do not yet understand, but it is difficult to understand how we have survived as a species unless this or something like it is so. Thus, the argument for circularity is inherently specious.

The evolutionary argument in the previous paragraph that suggests more than a single coding system also works against an analytically precise and hierarchical grammatical structure.

THE LIMITS OF COMMUNICATION

Human information-processing systems are characterized by an inherent ability to restructure themselves. However, what can be done well can also be done poorly. Some individuals may insulate or compartmentalize information in such a way that connections and relationships are lost or gravely distorted. Others may restructure their thinking into a caricature of unitary danda-programmed perceivers, a situation similar to the resistance generated in psychotherapy. Although it is extremely unlikely that even that marvelously complex and sophisticated information-processing system, the human mind, is capable of producing uniformity among all its subroutines, it may, for all practical purposes, do so in some situations.

Although it can be demonstrated how error-reinforcing information systems develop and operate and although they can be compared to error-correcting information systems, I admit that the likelihood of communication between the two is minimal. In most societies, there is likely to be an overlap of information processing that makes scientific communication fruitful. It is one thing to recognize that some areas of science are sufficiently uncertain that alternative interpretations of particular areas are defensible, or even to argue that at any stage of scientific development there will be uncertain areas, even though these will change over time. It is quite another to suggest that, in principle, there necessarily will be theories and methods between which reasoned choices cannot be made.

There is a deep but mistakenly presented element of truth in arguments for circularity. All knowledge and reasoning is circular in one sense. Without initial systems for coding information, no perceiver can exist. Without systems for processing information, the elements of the realm of knowledge cannot be related to each other in a productive manner: a manner that produces new information. Locke's *tabula rasa* could not generate or use information.

In the paragraph quoted earlier, Pepper refers to positivism, yet virtually all former positivists now admit that positivism will not account for science. Instead, they refer back to a wider realm of knowledge (this is apparently what Gerard Radnitzky means by background information)[10]—which they continued to possess despite their avowal of positivism—to evaluate positivism. There are criteria for assessing these judgments.

ASSESSMENT

We do not prove all conclusions; we assess some. However, precisely because these are *not* proofs in the deductive sense, there is not a vicious circularity: the dependence of whole to element, of element to whole, and of element to element, is limited. Non-circular assessments—for instance, whether light bends when it passes a gravitational field—are common in science. Kepler, Newton, and Einstein would have agreed on what they meant by "planet," "perihelion," "curvature," and "light" for the purpose of the relevant experiments, although they might have disagreed in other respects. Kepler and Newton would have been unfamiliar with certain techniques of measurement, but their science would not have precluded such understanding. The three would have disagreed on what they meant by "mass," "time," and "space"; but this would not have been relevant to tests that compared the competing theories in this respect. Such assessments are not circularly dependent upon the theory to be tested. Nor do they depend on the absence of interpretation.

Note that the interpretations and applications of physical concepts by Newton and Einstein in this imaginary world would be shaped by common problems. Different problem orientations might well lead to different theories and rules of application. This would cause a scandal only for someone who believed that the world is strongly ordered and that our scientific accounts of it must at least correspond with it in some relatively simple and univocal fashion. We shall see in the next chapter why these assumptions are without warrant.

Notice how this position links knowing to history without falling prey to historical relativism. The state of knowing is linked intimately to both contemporary historical conditions and the paths by which they have been reached. Yet the method of assessment permits a critical examination of these linkages. Although absolute neutrality of perspective is a chimera that would require taking a position extrinsic to and independent of all frameworks of inquiry, we can acquire relatively neutral perspectives and we can do this with greater and greater power as knowledge increases.

Are there any limits to communication? Any profound circularities? There are limits; but there are no profound circularities with respect to problems that can be stated in specific form.

To illustrate the problem of communication more simply, let us turn to a non-conscious and relatively simple information-processing entity: the computer. We cannot derive the output of the computer from its circuitry, unless we already know the operations the computer can make with data, the program, and the data that have been fed into it.

However, the problem is even more fundamental than this. The performance of the computer depends upon the exact correspondence of the programmed instructions used and the form of the data entered with the information already stored with the computer. Thus, even at this level of information processing, the computer "recognizes" the meaning of the symbols if the prescribed language and format are used precisely by the human operator. Even so, we still do not know how to relate the output symbols with observations. To do this, we must have knowledge of their use and, hence, of their meaning in practice. But this always refers to something external.

Are there ways of acquiring information other than the ways we know? Completely different ways of processing it? Only an agnostic stance can be offered. Even to formulate such questions, we would have to be radically different types of systems. Still, we can analyze such cases speculatively. Consider Josiah Royce's example of a creature with a span of perception of 10,000 years. It would perceive the stars as moving and the planets as circles. It could not experience our existence let alone hypothesize that we are reasoning creatures. A limitation of this type would make communication between these species concerning a possible common world impossible.

A brief reference to the position I shall develop may be in order. Whereas Pepper, and perhaps Kuhn, see world views or paradigms as circular—that is, as dependent on initial assumptions—I see them as spiral.* That is, scientific reasoning is never independent of the assumptions that are employed or of the

---

*Although I have come into possession of it too late to refer to it in the body of the book, a remarkable manuscript by Gerhard Vollmer, "On Supposed Circularities in an Empirically Oriented Epistemology," also uses a spiral concept.

tests and uses that are open to scientific workers. Conceptions of absolute neutrality and of verisimilitude are at best misleading. Still, the absence of a closed set of codings and of closed systems permits of expanded assumptions, novel conceptions, and at least a relatively neutral approach to competing positions.

As we use, alternatively, one area of the realm of knowledge to assess others, and so on, and as we advance to second-order evaluations, the neutral and objective realm of knowledge progresses in a spiral fashion. The elements of this process are examined in the following chapters.

NOTES

1. See Imre Lakatos and Alan Musgrave, editors, *Criticism and the Growth of Knowledge* (Cambridge: Cambridge University Press, 1970), for a symposium in which Kuhn confronts many of his major critics.

2. Thomas S. Kuhn, *The Scientific Revolution* (Chicago: University of Chicago Press, 1962), p. 77.

3. Ibid., p. 93.

4. Ibid., p. 113.

5. Thomas S. Kuhn, *The Essential Tension* (Chicago: University of Chicago Press, 1978), p. 322.

6. Ibid., p. 331 ff.

7. Stephen C. Pepper, *World Hypotheses* (Berkeley: University of California Press, 1942), pp. 67–69.

8. Ibid., pp. 92 ff.

9. John von Neumann, *The Computer and the Brain* (New Haven: Yale University Press, 1958).

10. Gerard Radnitsky, "Progress and Rationality in Research," in *On Scientific Discovery*, edited by M. D. Grmek, R. S. Cohen, and G. Cimino (Dordrecht, Holland: D. Reidel Publishing Co., 1980).

Chapter 2
Metatheoretical Considerations

In this chapter I shall state a number of metatheoretical considerations that will provide the intellectual scaffolding for the resolution of the problem of circularity and objectivity. By *metatheoretical* is meant the conditions that describe inter-relationships in the world. These conditions include first- and second-order discourse, strong and weak orders, and part-system analysis, concepts which will be used extensively throughout the book. Whereas a metaphysical system would be circular, were it actually a systematic worldwide hypothesis, the metatheoretical principles developed in this chapter are non-circular and revisable, for reasons that will become clear during their exposition.

SECOND-ORDER REFERENCES

A *first-order reference* is dependent on the locus of the observer, actor, or system; a *second-order* one is independent of the locus of particular observers or actors or systems, including systems of thought, although it is not independent of all reference. For instance, observers on different inertial systems will agree (in the same phase of science), in terms of second-order analysis, on Einsteinian theory as a neutral focus of analysis, even though they will disagree on the first-order question of which system is moving with respect to which.

Niels Bohr's principle of *complementarity*, i.e., aspects of something are complementary if they contribute to knowledge of it but require incompatible techniques of inquiry,[1] shows in effect that quantum theory is a second-order theory because it subsumes results from the incompatible first-order (or direct) experiments with respect to position and momentum and shows that they complement each other. This is a limiting case, for most second-order accounts are expressed as assessments and not as theories, e.g., the porosity of a table to a gamma ray but not to a fist or the analysis of a system in equilibrium and in process. The latter second-order reconciliation is not theoretical but it is complementary, while the second-order reconciliation of the clock paradox in Einsteinian theory is theoretical but not complementary in Bohr's sense (unless with respect to the almost marginal consideration that the observers are on independent inertial systems).*

The correlative pair, first-order and second-order, may also constitute a bridge between Kuhn, who sees no way of asserting that Einsteinian theory is "nearer to the truth" than Newtonian, and his opponents, who regard the latter concept as meaningful.[2] I agree in part with Kuhn: the concept "nearer to the truth" implies verisimilitude, a one-to-one mapping between concepts, signs, and states of the world that cannot be substantiated. However, second-order discourse permits conclusions that are neutral and objective, i.e., invariant, with respect to wider webs of considerations and tests, as in the paradox of the clock. Thus, claims of greater adequacy and progress in science can be justified. Second-order reference systems may not be completely or systematically translatable in first-order terms but they can produce objective and relatively neutral conclusions.

Let us now apply second-order considerations to the problem of communication that was illustrated in the last chapter by Josiah Royce's example of a creature with a 10,000 year span of perception. It could not experience us let alone hypothesize that we are rational creatures. Yet the very speculation that at first seems to deny the possibility of a potentially common universe implicitly affirms it; for it posits a neutral second-order assessment in which the failure of communication is related to constituent differences in the creatures. It does not undermine this position to hypothesize a creature so different that we cannot even imagine its characteristics. The assertion of this possibility implicitly depends on a neutral second-order assessment that relates this failure of communication to ontological differences. It is no more vague than the speculation to which it is a response.

PART-SYSTEM ANALYSIS

A *part system* is a system, more accurately subsystem, of such independence and regularity that changes in related subsystems have little, if any, effect on it. Information about part systems is tentatively held constant during analysis while information about others is revised, and so on. It is this that produces the spiral effect. Acceptance of a revision in part-system information depends in part upon recognition of a fit between the revision and its relevant surround. This recognition depends upon the contemporary coding of the transceiver and, thus, has implicit, and not entirely explicit, elements. Communication requires sufficient overlap in the codings of the transceivers for convergence to be possible in their spiral reasoning processes; and agreement within this framework depends upon supporting, objective evidence and praxical grounds.

---

*The paradox of the clock refers to the fact that each observer correctly believes that it is the *other* system that is moving with respect to his, and on which time is passing more slowly.

The process is not really different from Kuhn's example of a picture that can be seen either as a rabbit or as a duck (discussed in chapter 1), despite Kuhn's belief that it is. When we view that equivocal picture, we compare aspects of the ambiguous picture with a picture of a duck or rabbit, or with real creatures, and learn how and why we can perceive first one and then the other when presented with the duck-or-rabbit picture.

In a similar way, if the argument is over whether the earth is flat or globular, we can compare models of both hypotheses and evaluate what we would perceive from different positions. If this process is like a religious conversion, it is so with respect to those aspects of the conversion process in which matters of fit and objectivity in reasoning are involved, rather than with those aspects that our faith refuses us to allow to question.

STRONG AND WEAK ORDERS

The concept of a weak order is not intuitively clear, although most real orders are weak. In some early views, the world constituted a simple strong order such that God, if He knew the starting state of every atom, could predict all of history. Newtonian physics is also strongly determinate, in the sense that every mechanical state of affairs has a pre-determined outcome. However, as Max Born has pointed out, any uncertainty in measurement—and all measurement is subject to some uncertainty—implies a future that is unpredictable at some distant time.[3] Classical physics involves a residual weakness that is obscured by ignoring the residual effects of instruments upon predictions: a stance that is justifiable in practice, but philosophically somewhat misleading. In the statistical mechanics of Willard Gibbs, the relative weakness of the order is inherent in the conceptual design.[4]

Soon, we are in the arena of really weak orders. There is an infinity of weak orders; and I shall adumbrate various of their aspects at various times in this book. Let us here consider a few types of weak orders. Although both position and speed are meaningful concepts in subatomic physics, we cannot speak meaningfully of both simultaneously. The relative measurement of motion from the framework of different inertial systems is only weakly ordered in relativity physics.

In economics, price in a perfectly competitive system is strongly ordered. In Edward Chamberlin's theory of monopolistic competition, however, price is weakly ordered within a region created by the overlap of bands of supply and demand.[5] And von Neumann's solutions to coalition problems are weakly ordered.[6] The characteristics of a dominant solution can be discovered, but different partners can coalesce in an actual coalition within this constraint.

Evolutionary advantage is a weakly ordered concept. Some of the criteria that determine it may involve ease of reproduction, survivability of progeny, adaptability to changes in the environment, ability to escape predators, and so forth. Because the criteria are different, no simple or strongly ordered measure is possible although it may be relatively easy in respect to particular species to distinguish some evolutionary changes that are clearly inferior, some that are probably inferior, some that are probably superior, and some that are clearly superior—at least in particular environments.

Different problems in physics require formulations that function under different boundary conditions and different frameworks of assumptions; say, those of macrophysics and those of microphysics. Even in theories in the "hardest" segments of physical science, crucial tests are rare; furthermore, alternative formulations of similar theories may imply different ranges of tests. As long as these differences do not create problems in the larger realm of knowledge by giving rise to genuinely, and not merely apparently, inconsistent notions about reality, the weakness of the relationships within the realm does not create a major scientific problem, even though it may affect decidability in particular cases. The weakness of the relationship increases as we move to biology, sociology, psychology, and so forth. The conceptual systems are very different, as are the techniques of investigation, the axiomatic assumptions, and the environmental constraints. Whether an order is strong or weak is not an absolute, but depends upon the relationships among the elements in question.

Suppose, for instance, that the existence of mental telepathy were to become firmly established. This would affect strongly ordered aspects of the world. We would be required either to adjust our notions about energy and the transmission of information or to challenge the evidence for telepathy. Suppose that the ability to predict the future in detail were validated. Either we would have to challenge the evidence or reconstruct the present notion of space-time. In either event, we would operate by appealing to tentatively uncontested features of the wider realm of knowledge while constructing new tests for this purpose.

On the other hand, there are many different capacities of the human mind and body that might be discovered without any need for a change in existing theories of biology or of physics. A new drug might tap vastly greater mental powers or open up a much wider range of perceptions. The relationships that would be affected are weakly ordered.

There is, it must be admitted, a way of assessing the proof of telepathy such that its impact on the realm of knowledge might be regarded as weakly ordered. It is well known that minds can affect physical things. For example, the atom bomb could not have been constructed in the absence of a relevant theory of physics. However, this situation affects only the initial conditions of an experiment and, hence, a physical outcome, not the rules, or laws, that one uses to explain physical outcomes. In this sense, the laws of physics are dominant over beliefs; and we have no evidence sufficient to challenge their dominance. The laws of physics do not mention beliefs: they are neutral concerning them. Even statements about what produces changes in initial conditions refer to the force exerted by the body, not the decision to move the body. In fact, what we mean if we say that beliefs do not affect physics is that the rules of physics determine the physical results in any given set of initial conditions.

Should evidence accumulate that beliefs can affect the rules of physics, we would not change the rules; we would, instead, include the absence of such an effect as a boundary condition of their statement. The assumption of a vacuum in Newtonian physics could serve as a metaphor here, but only as a metaphor. It is unlikely that we could accommodate perturbations from the state of equilibrium in the same regular way as in the case of the vacuum, and we would likely state different rules for different boundary conditions.

The idea that beliefs can affect the laws of physics is no more absurd than the idea of virtual particles or than the contemporary hypothesis that a proton might be created in a vacuum near a superheavy atomic nucleus if a powerful electromagnetic field were applied to the vacuum—that is to say, that something can be created out of nothing. However, if thoughts and physical reality represent techniques of comprehension that, in Niels Bohr's terms, are in a state of complementarity, that would be the wrong hypothesis to pursue. In that case, their relationship would not be causal, parallel, or reducible. Instead, they would be independently valid, and non-contradictory products of incompatible techniques of inquiry.

Because weak orders constitute much of the realm of knowledge, it is possible to entertain different theories, even about the same things, that do not completely mesh. There need be no conflict between a theory that treats a Portuguese man-of-war as a single organism and one that treats it as a collectivity of organisms, for the definition may depend upon the types of tests and the types of outcomes that lie at the focus of the investigation.

In other instances, theories may be in conflict, but the theoretical neighborhoods that are affected may be small. Some contrasting interpretations of the red shift (the shift toward the red spectrum of a star that is receding from us), some different theories concerning the origin of the universe, and some different interpretations of nuclear forces are compatible with the theory of relativity and, even more so, with particular theorems such as $E = mc^2$. Whether or not changes in the money supply constitute the key factor in inflation is relatively unrelated to theories about the conditions under which industries tend toward monopoly.

Whether a particular tax policy affects the money supply in a given way may depend upon the evaluation of data, the instruments of interpretation, the methods of analysis, and the theoretical "neighborhoods" employed in the analysis. Even what a neighborhood is, in terms of the relevance of data, theory, and instruments of analysis, must itself be referred back to other elements of the realm of knowledge.

There may be competing objective, but weak, solutions to some problems: e.g., whether dinosaurs were ectotherms or endotherms, whether a crystal is living, the astrophysical implications of the red shift, the first-order disagreement and second-order agreement about which system is moving with respect to which, the best of several workable ways to design an air-warning system, and so forth. Sometimes, more information will produce a unique answer, whether about a proposition or competing theories. In other situations, common first-order but not second-order agreement is ruled out. There may sometimes be solutions that are objectively logical or empirical equivalents, and sometimes not.

Because much of the world is weakly ordered, the effect upon assessment of other elements of the world may be only local and perhaps minor as well, even when the consequences of theories contradict each other in some essential fashion—as for example, interpretations of the red shift, of the effect of changes in money supply, and so forth. The concept of weak order is closely linked to that of "fit." Einstein's theory of relativity, for example, fitted the general realm of knowledge of the early twentieth century. In my discussion of relativity in chapter 5, the reader will see that although the order was then weak, the criterion of fit was satisfied; even in the absence of critical tests, to believe in Newtonian physics would require a major act of faith in the twentieth century. Moreover, by comparing the worlds of Newton and Einstein, we can understand both why Newton made the assumptions he did about space and time and why they cannot be made now.

NOTES

1. Max Born, *Physics and Politics* (Edinburgh: Oliver & Boyd, 1962), pp. 55 ff.

2. M. D. Grmek, R. S. Cohen, and G. Cimino, editors, *On Scientific Discovery* (Dordrecht, Holland: D. Reidel Publishing Co., 1980).

3. Born, *Physics and Politics*, pp. 49 ff.

4. Josiah Willard Gibbs, *Elementary Principles in Statistical Mechanics* (New York: Charles Scribner and Sons, 1902).

5. Edward H. Chamberlin, *The Theory of Monopolistic Competition* (Cambridge: Harvard University Press, 1933).

6. Morton A. Kaplan, *System and Process in International Politics* (New York: John Wiley & Sons, 1957), pp. 203 ff.

Chapter 3
Systems and the Scope of Theory

In this chapter, I shall draw upon the available evidence to show how and why different types of systems respond differently to theoretical investigation, why the range of useful generalization varies with the type of system and problem, and why the identification of the relevant generalization, rather than its falsification or confirmation, is the more fruitful technique in the social sciences.

The term "systems theory" is misleading. The analysis of systems instead of being considered a theory, should be considered an approach that calls for the development of theories or for the explicit recognition of those characteristics of systems about which useful propositions can be framed. Thus, the initial task, in an inquiry into a system, is to define the term "system."

A *system* is a set of interrelated elements sufficiently distinctive to serve as a focus of inquiry. A system may consist of points, numbers, roles, organizations, and so forth. A person is a system; so is a network of telephones; so is a society. The elements may be analyzed in terms of authority, wisdom, wealth, strength, or any other characteristic.

Systems include both elements and functions. The heart pumps blood and the lungs process air. Priests provide absolution, legislatures pass laws. An alteration to a system that changes its characteristic behavior is called a *step function*. Opium changes the characteristic optic behavior of the biological organism. A successful revolution changes the values and the characteristic behavior, that is, the essential rules, of a political system.*

The choice of a system is, in effect, a choice of a subject matter. In principle, the same reality may be analyzed by a variety of models or theories; then, which elements are internal or external depends upon which theory is used. This choice also determines whether a statement within a theory is axiomatic or derived. Complementary aspects of that reality may be explored by different types of theories. It follows that there is no single correct first-order method of investigating the universe and that the realm of knowledge, as a whole, is not strongly

---

*For a discussion of essential and transformation rules and their relationship to internal and external system conditions, see Morton A. Kaplan, *System and Process in International Politics* (New York: John Wiley and Sons, 1957), pp. 9, 10, and 23 ff.

ordered. All systems and theories are closed; and no theory or system, therefore, can capture the full potentiality of the open world for producing new self-organizing states of systems or systems.

EQUILIBRIUM AND STABILITY

Systems analysts and theoreticians make wide use of the concept of equilibrium. By *equilibrium*, I mean that two sets of properties are in an unchanging relationship with each other. Mechanical equilibria are usually classified as stable, static, and unstable. A ball at rest on a flat surface, for instance, is in static equilibrium with the surface, for it will not move of itself. A ball in a valley illustrates stable equilibrium; on the top of a narrow ridge, it is unstable.

Whether an equilibrium is stable or not depends on our perspective. Biological life on earth looks stable to relatively short-lived human beings and even to nations, with longer lives, but it is unstable from the standpoint of the astrophysicist, for eventually the sun will die. There is no contradiction here, or any retreat into subjectivity, for, given an adequate statement of the character of the inquiry, there are objective—and publicly communicable—standards by which to determine their accuracy.

Although in principle we could construct dynamic models in disequilibrium, there are so many different ways in which we could do so that the probability that we would hit upon a model useful for analyzing any actual social system in disequilibrium is remote. Equilibrium is a much more productive concept in social science investigations than disequilibrium.* Moreover, the differences in types of equilibria manifested by different types of systems provide us with important information about the behavior of systems.

Mechanical Equilibria

The best-known type of equilibrium is *mechanical equilibrium*. We say that an automobile resting on a flat surface is in mechanical equilibrium. By this we mean that the physical force that might move it is cancelled by the force that keeps it at rest. These forces are not merely inferred from the resting state of the car. They can be measured independently. And their cancellation, in this instance, can be derived from Newton's laws.** Many concepts are used with a common meaning in mechanics, thermodynamics, optics, and astrophysics. Their measurement, in experiments, is generally made according to a common scale. We can define and identify these concepts independently of more complex variations in systems. And we can, therefore, employ them in physical laws.

The absolute independence of these concepts, however, is questionable. They are not independent as such but, like the zero-sum game (to be discussed shortly), in which the utility schedules of the opposing players are assumed not to vary

---

*This topic is explored further in appendix 2.

**They can be derived provided that initial conditions are taken into account.

with boundary conditions or interactions among the players, permit relatively independent measurement and the use of covering laws.

A *law* or *covering law* is a universal relationship between sets of properties that can be expressed as a set of equations the terms of which are independently measurable and generally invariant in all applications. In this limited sense, all mechanical equilibria can be explained by covering laws. Although a law expressing the conditions for a mechanical equilibrium does not convey much significant information—far more information is conveyed by the other specifics of particular theories—the concept of mechanical equilibrium implies the existence of laws conveying information that can be put into the form of propositions.

Homeostatic Equilibria

Homeostatic systems of equilibrium, such as thermostatically controlled heating systems or the mechanism that controls the temperature of human blood, do not imply the existence of laws, even though all homeostatic systems operate within boundaries set by some mechanical system.

No such independently measurable system of equalities applies to the thermostatic system, however. For instance, the term *homeostatic equilibrium* tells us, by definition, that the system is one in which one key element is held at a near-constant value by compensating changes in the values of other elements as the environment changes. This definitional element, this label, is all that the temperature-maintaining systems of the human body have in common with the thermostatic properties of a house-heating system or the error-control system that keeps one's hand on course when it moves to pick up a pencil. The label does not tell us how or under what conditions any one of the systems operates to maintain this homeostatic equilibrium: that is, it is not a theory of the system.

We have just seen that the operation of a thermostatic control system for a residence is not accounted for by the laws for mechanics. No biological or social system is accounted for by mechanical laws even though all homeostatic systems are consistent with the laws of mechanics.

To make this point as strongly as possible, consider a thermostatic system for a residence: a system the individual elements of which are mechanical. If my conclusion applies here, *a fortiori*, it applies to biological and social systems also.

For instance, if one knows the size of the area to be heated, the efficiency of the engine and fuel, and so forth, the laws of mechanics will account for the amount of energy required to raise the temperature of the area by one degree. Moreover, each physical aspect of the thermostatic system obeys mechanical laws. A change in a boundary condition such as the temperature of the room changes the level of mercury in the thermometer; a change in one internal physical aspect of the system changes another, e.g., a change in the level of mercury trips a relay; and so forth. However, the homeostatic system—that is, the system that maintains the temperature of the room by producing intrasystem changes in response to boundary changes—cannot be derived from mechanical laws. The laws of physics and the physical characteristics and responses of the elements of the homeostatic system are only boundary conditions of its operation. A second-order account may be used to coordinate the physical and the homeostatic accounts; but they are not identical and the categories of one do not reduce to the categories of the other. The systems have non-identical internal elements and boundaries. Let us examine the consequences of these facts.

The biological system is homeostatic and the blood temperature system is thermostatic. The temperature of the blood may be adequately measured by a thermometer, but that temperature is not equal to anything else in the system. Moreover, although the temperatures of blood of different biological systems are measured by a common scale, what is normal in one system will not necessarily be normal in another system; for instance, the normal human temperature differs from the cat's. And what constitutes a significant deviation from normal may be quite different in the two systems.

Furthermore, whereas mechanical properties such as the energy contained in a unit of a fuel are measurable independently of the efficiency of particular engines—and this, of course, implies that the efficiency of all engines can be measured—the values of the properties of homeostatic systems on the other hand, for instance, demands and supports, cannot be measured independently. A political protest march by West Point cadets would not likely alter the United States' system of government, but the protest march by Turkish cadets in 1960 was a clear sign that the Menderes government was going to be brought down.

Covering laws of the type available to physicists in the area of mechanics depend upon the independence of the measurement of the variables in the system. Because independent measures are not available for non-mechanical systems and because all social systems are of the non-mechanical variety, covering laws are not available in social science.

Generalizations that apply to systems with carefully stated boundary conditions may be possible but they will differ from covering laws in several respects. For instance, my "balance of power" theory is applicable to many different historical circumstances, but the level of capability that makes for essential actor (great power) status will differ from case to case. Furthermore, even for a given system, the degree of interdependence between an intrasystem factor and boundary conditions may produce intrasystem variations in that factor. Thus, the minimal military capabilities required to become an essential actor in a "balance of power" system, for instance, would not have been the same in the seventeenth and nineteenth centuries. The proportional differences between essential and non-essential actors would not have been the same in the two centuries. Moreover, even within similar periods of time, these capability requirements might shift with technology, economic conditions, and other boundary factors in ways that can be determined only on an *ad hoc* basis, and even then not with exactitude. Thus, although it may be possible to reach some informative conclusions about the macrorelationships within a particular type of international system under standardized boundary conditions and to extrapolate from these for changes in

boundary conditions, it is important to recognize the important differences between these types of qualitative assessments and the use of covering laws.

As is the case for all types of homeostatics systems, attempts to assess their
macrostructures and processes must be restricted to particular types of systems.
Important information is lost as attempts are made to generalize even about
different subtypes of similar systems. Thus, although it is considered a truism
that democratic systems require popular support if they are to function, this
conveys little information about the conditions necessary for popular support in
any particular democracy. Moreover, democratic systems often function well
without much popular support, and the proposition tells us nothing about how
to distinguish situations in which it is relevant from those in which it is not
relevant. Indeed, even undemocratic systems require support.

As the level of abstraction is raised to statements that apply to all political
systems—for instance, "Political systems are in equilibrium when demands and
supports are in balance"—we no longer have even a weak truism. In the absence
of independent measures that are generally applicable, the statement is vacuous.
This does not mean that demands and supports are themselves vacuous concepts,
but only that their qualitative manifestations in concrete circumstances differ in
major ways from system to system. The strength of these manifestations does
not have a measure that is independent of experience, either practical or theoretical, with particular types of political systems. Therefore, if statements are to
be relatively meaningful, their application must be restricted to subtypes of
systems.

When lower-level generalizations are used in a qualitative theory or theory
sketch, with specified boundary conditions and specified actors, they do convey
useful—although not necessarily precise—information. This level of theoretical
development can be, and often is, sufficiently articulated for comparisons to be
made among different types of social systems. By looking at similarities and
differences among the different systems and within the individual systems, one
may be able to generate hypotheses as to the conditions that foster different types
of social systems, that enable them to function more effectively, or that enable
them to satisfy different types of demands effectively. Even so, the varying
meanings of social concepts in different environments can mislead us.

It is an interesting parallel that the only area of game theory for which there
is a general solution is the *zero-sum game*. In this game, the gains of the winners
and the losses of the losers add up to zero. This would not be possible if the
opposing players did not place identical values on identical outcomes and if,
additionally, the value of the gain were not the exact opposite of the loss.
Although, of course, no real-world game can be a precisely zero-sum one, some
games may approach it sufficiently to make the model a reasonable approxi-
mation.

This shows that values, called *utile numbers*, are independent of context in
zero-sum games in virtually the same way in which the units in mechanical
physics are independently measurable. Thus, the general solution of the zero-
sum game—the *minimax strategy*, which guarantees the best of the worst out-

comes that an opponent can inflict upon one—constitutes a kind of equivalent to the covering laws of physics. For the non-zero-sum game, however, no general solution has ever been found; particular solutions apply only to particular types of non-zero-sum games. The zero-sum case is at best asymptotic even in card games. It is irrelevant in the analysis of complex social systems.

The failure of rules or common formulations to hold across different types of non-mechanical systems is sometimes misunderstood by incautious students of so-called general systems theory. They note, for instance, that the growth curves of populations within city limits and of bacteria within enclosed cultures are similar. They then infer that general trans-system laws have been found.

Their mistake is that of reference. The growth curve, in this example, is a constant that applies to systems with certain characteristics. To the extent that these specific characteristics are dominant—and this will be true only of specific systems and within specified boundary conditions—a particular interpretation of the formula will explain only the relevant facets of the real world. It will not explain other closely connected facets of behavior.

Thus, such formulas may explain certain features that some political units have in common with some non-political units. They are not general theories but particular theories, such as theories of population growth in an enclosed area. And they function only as boundary conditions in studies of political systems *qua* political systems or of bacterial systems *qua* bacterial systems. That is another reason why general theories cannot explain the behavior of different varieties even of the same general type of non-mechanical systems. When they appear to do so, they will be either vacuous or even consistent with *contradictory* predictions.

My last example illustrates the methodological principle that is developed and justified in Part One: that there is no simple hierarchical organization of the world to which any one theory ought to correspond. Instead, there is a crazy quilt, the structure of which is dependent on problems and research purposes. Consequently, the assessment of theories and propositions, as will be shown, resonates to this cross-cutting complexity and defeats simple-minded notions of "closer to the truth." The more complex concept that a theory is better than its rivals, however, is defensible; and consequently so is the concept of progress in science.

Chapter 4
Meaning, Science, and Reality

Because a theory employs *signs*, i.e., words and symbols, and because the relationships among the systems of signs employed, concepts, and reality are intrinsic to the meaning and realistic implications of a theory, this chapter is vital to those that follow. In this chapter, therefore, I shall discuss meaning. I shall also draw upon the conclusions of chapter 3 with respect to the absence of covering laws and the consequent absence of independent measures in non-mechanical systems to support the claims I shall be making about the role of signs in inquiry. I shall show that concepts are correlative in character and that they necessarily have non-explicit and non-conscious penumbra.

The analysis up to this point has set the stage for the subsequent chapters of Part One of this book and, in particular, for this chapter.

John Dewey argued that our knowledge of "red" is not derived from a red sensation. The theory that perceptions are produced by sensations* itself stems from and depends on experience.[1] Yet physiology reveals the inadequacies of naive empiricism as surely as does epistemological theory. Because the pupil of the normal eye is in continual motion, no message, that is, signal or sets of signals, can present a stationary object as stationary to the brain. The message is first transformed by the nerves that transmit it and then further transformed by the brain. And this statement can be confirmed by experiment. Thus, experience always requires the active participation of the perceiving system, or transceiver.

Messages, thus, require transceivers. Meaning is a product of a transaction between a transceiver and a world; experience is not a simple or automatic display of incoming signals. The transceiver codes, or produces, data in transactions with referents within a milieu. In addition to interpreting sensory inputs, the transceiver also selects inputs that fit with the expectations, hopes, and fears of the system. Thus, for instance, it is less likely that the psychological mechanism of projection involves a biased interpretation of specific incoming data

---

*It is not clear what empiricists mean by "sensation." The feel of a tingling or of warmth? The angstrom wave patterns that are transmitted to the eye? Or the content of the message that is carried by nerves from the optic receptor to the brain?

than that it involves a selection of data that accord with expectations and the censorship of incoming data that conflict with those expectations.

Thus, the processes involved in perception do not link a discrete coding element or sign to a discrete signal or signal pattern in any simple fashion. Stimulus-response theories, in which such discrete elements are assumed, may be good enough for a sufficiently stable world and a sufficiently stable organism, or even for simple aspects of a more complex organism. But such a discrete conception of physiological coding reifies concepts, by appearing to give a color like red, for instance, a meaning that is independent of the transceiver, the source of light, and the character of the referent.[2]. The correlative terms "solid" and "porous" also do not characterize as such, but only with reference to a transceiver and a context. The table is solid when I hit it, but porous to an electron.

There is no simple correspondence between a transceiver's implicit or explicit codes and external things, events, and processes. Indeed, external things, events, and processes are experienced only as interpreted phenomena, and beliefs about their character are revised by implicit or explicit part-system analysis. The difference between perceptual coding and linguistic coding is that the former is continuous, non-serial, and analog whereas the latter is discrete, serial, and digital.

CORRELATIVES

In my opinion, the correlative concept of pair is the basic unit of language. It bridges the transaction between the perceiver and the object, process, and arena of action or perception. It functions by means of contrast. For example, the contrast between light and dark produces meaning for a perceiver. It does not merely match a sign to an external datum as the English empiricists and the positivists believed. Instead, a correlative concept is mediated by a sign with respect to an aspect of experience, an application that involves a judgment and, thus, one that invokes other elements of the realms of knowledge.

Correlative sign pairs depends upon each other for their meaning. Their use produces clear conceptual distinctions, e.g., "light" or "dark." However, whether something is light or dark depends upon the context and a frame of reference that produces inner connectedness. It is not such *as such*, i.e., things are not, in essence, either light or dark. Consider "determinism" and "indeterminism" in quantum theory. Quantum theory is indeterministic with respect to a particle's momentum or position, but deterministic with respect to the dynamic state transformations signified by the quantum equations.

It is not difficult to understand why language is correlative. The communication theorists have taught us that the bit, a binary element, is the smallest unit of information. The bit is a quantitative unit in computers and measures the distinction between one (positive) and zero (negative). However, the sentence in which I make that claim uses qualitative concepts: positive and negative. Their contrast alone permits qualitative knowledge, the qualitative bit. This is easy to see in pairs such as positive–negative, deterministic–indeterministic, and so forth.

Characterization, that is description, requires contrasting concepts. They need not be binary in an analysis, but it is not surprising that they often are, for dichotomizing concepts are powerful. Locator terms—to be discussed shortly —permit finer distinctions in an analysis containing many (binary) dichotomies. They also function through contrast. Thus, for instance, when we learn to distinguish shades of a particular color, we do this by contrasting them to their neighbors. The discussion in this chapter of the relational character of knowledge makes characterization the key concept. We shall see that knowledge operates through correlative axes that are used to characterize the objects, processes, or events that are the referents in experience of signs and concepts.

The argument that language is correlative is an assessment, not a deductive proof. Many of the subsequent discussions in this book will provide corroborating evidence that treating language as correlative assists in the assessment of philosophical problems.

Willard van Orman Quine's well-known argument against an absolute distinction between the analytic and the synthetic[3] may hold only because it is an instance of the correlative character of language. The analytic can be distinguished from the synthetic. However, no proposition is either analytic or synthetic as such; an issue to which I shall return.

Thus, correlatives are fundamental building blocks of language: pairs, the meaning of each of which involves the other. And often, as in pairs such as "determinism" and "indeterminism" or "solid" and "porous," the same real-world entity or process can be characterized by either aspect of a pair, depending on the aspect of the world to which one is referring or the frame of reference.

METACORRELATIVES

If correlatives are the basic units of language, *metacorrelatives* are employed in analyzing their use and significance. "Sign" and "signed," for instance, comprise a metacorrelative concept that is used in the production of meaning itself. For example, "solid" and "porous" are correlatives. They provide meaning. "Solid" has as its referent a solid entity. The former is the sign and the latter is the signed. "Sign" and "signed" are metacorrelatives, for they raise the level of abstraction.

LOCATORS

Locators, i.e., terms that help us to locate an object, process, or event, are limited to only one aspect of a correlative pair, and they permit distinctions within that aspect of the correlative pair. For instance, the correlative relation between "space" and "time" is irrelevant to geographic surveys. If a correlative concept (e.g., "bright," "heavy," "finite," or "analytic") exhausted the object or event to which it referred, we would not need locators.

Moreover, for practical purposes, locators function in a multiple, rather than a binary, fashion. We know that our system of arithmetic is based on ten's but that a binary base is used in computers. The accident of ten fingers and toes almost surely played a role in determining our choice of an arithmetic base of ten. The connections within an electronic circuit, which can be turned only on or off, produce the zero-one base of electronic arithmetic.

At least implicitly, paired concepts are used in language to determine meaning. Almost surely some highly practical determinant of language—perhaps the fact that paired terms are particularly powerful in clarifying types of meaning while locators function primarily within a typology and with respect to circumstances in which the influence of the polar elements is vanishingly small—produced these differences. "Types" and "locators" are themselves metacorrelatives, and their meaning depends on their use.

LANGUAGE AND MEANING

Let me now encapsulate the view of language and of meaning that has been presented. Certain kinds of words, signs that mediate concepts, enable us to characterize and to locate aspects of the real. Sentences, expressions, and longer and more complex formulations are constructed according to rules that permit the particular meaning—as distinguished from the general meaning—of words to be understood within an exposition that employs a system of concepts.

Language has meaning because it uses signs to relate concepts to referents. Although some types of rules for its use, such as grammar, can be specified, many people can speak intelligibly without knowing all the rules of grammar. Meaning depends upon a host of cues to which people have become acculturated. The meaning of a word may be tacit or private, but it is usually fairly commonly recognized, more commonly in specific subcultures and less in the general culture.

FICTION AND REALITY

To write that a unicorn met a lady is to write fiction, although meaningfully so, because we can specify the unicorn's characteristics even though there is no evidence of its existence. Moreover, a unicorn may not be a fiction in a fictional realm; that is, it satisfies the criteria appropriate to that realm. An irrational number is not a fiction in the worlds of mathematics or physics.

Perhaps some readers have experienced bright spiralling lines under anesthesia. When we say that they were "tuning in" on a process that transforms sensory elements into perceptions, we do not mean that the formulas by means of which these processes can be characterized exist as "things" in the human organism. But neither are they fictions.

Was Newton's theory a fiction? Newton's theory was disproved. It was, however, a useful although incorrect account of the cosmos. Newton's laws have been shown to be not fictional, but marginally incorrect within solar distances. From the standpoint of relativity, Newton's theory is a good *metaphor*.

The foregoing statements require qualification. The appropriate application of theories treats their boundary conditions as if they are fully known. This assumption is a fiction, but a vanishingly small one in many cases.

WORDS AND SENTENCES

I agree with Quine that the meaning of an element, or a term, bears a relationship to the set, or sentence, within which it is used.[4] I agree with Hilary Putnam that terms in a sentence have a meaning that is independent of the sentences in which they are used.[5] At least I agree in part. I know, for instance, what I mean by "eye," at least partly independently of a theory of vision or of particular sentences employing the term.

One need think only of "eye of the needle," "eye of the storm," "human eye," or "eye of the bee" to see that neither element nor sentence has absolute priority in the analysis of the meaning of eye. We do not know the precise meaning of eye except within the sentence. And yet we cannot know its meaning within the sentence unless we already have an initial set of meanings of the word to choose among, at least some of which depend for their meanings upon their contrasting characteristics. This is a part-system problem; and neither Quine's position nor Putnam's can be defended if pushed to an extreme.

CONCEPTS AND TRUTHS

Concepts are validated both internally and externally. They are validated internally by definitions or by relations to other concepts either in a theory or in part-system codings of the mind. "Eye of the camera" and "eye of human" carry with them, among other concepts, those of inorganic and organic respectively. On the other hand, criteria such as "metal," "mechanical," "neurological tissue," and so forth also have meanings that are independent of the particular concepts, "eye of camera" and "eye of human." Thus, they serve as external criteria for empirical truth: in this case, correct application of the concept. It is this interplay between "inner" and "outer" concepts and the use of part-system analysis that permits a theory of meaning and a theory of empirical truth to be reconciled. And it follows from this that one may know, at least partly, the meaning of something without knowing how to apply it, for the external criteria may not yet be understood. And vice versa, for its meaning may not yet have been refined.

A *theory* is a system of concepts mediated by signs, and the elements of a theory have meanings that depend upon their inner, that is, their within-the-theory relationships. "Mass," for instance, has at least partly different meanings in Newtonian and Einstenian physics. And "line," for instance, has at least partly different meanings in Euclidean and non-Euclidean geometries. The application of a theory to the concrete world involves both inner meanings, meanings that are constrained by the system of signs, and meanings that are external, that is, that are constrained by other signs or systems of signs and the concepts they mediate; and, thus, ultimately by empirical assessment.

SIGNS AND REFERENTS

The previous discussion leads me now to a brief examination of Gottlob Frege's position on sign, sense (i.e., concept), and referent.[6] Frege was in error, as I shall attempt to show, in holding that the same referent may have more than one meaning.

Frege's distinctions among a sign, its sense, and its reference contain hidden ambiguities. He argued that "morning star" and "evening star" have different senses, but the same reference: Venus. However, this independence of sense and reference is artificial, for Venus is the referent of "Venus," and is a planet in the solar system, according to a first-order astronomical theory. The "morning star," "the evening star," and "Venus" have not yet been related. This matter can be clarified only by a second-order analysis, that is, one that is neutral with respect to the different frames of reference.

The argument that the terms "Venus," "the morning star," and "the evening star" have the same reference, the planet Venus, requires the use of second-order discourse to correlate the sign systems of astronomy and of ordinary common sense. There is an identity in meaning in the three signs in second-order discourse, but not in first-order discourse.

Einstein's theory of relativity accounts for differences in interpretation of first-order space–time phenomena by observers on different inertial systems. One of the remarkable achievements of his theory of relativity is to integrate seemingly contradictory first-order frameworks within a single set of second-order equations, a feat also accomplished in quantum theory. To use another example, second-order procedures make possible the translation of English into, say, Russian or Japanese. However, we cannot encompass the second-order reconciliation within a metalanguage that produces one-to-one relations between words or concepts. And this is the usual case.

LOGIC AND REALITY

Quine is often accused of having denied that there is a distinction between analytic and synthetic propositions or even of having failed to accept the existence of analytic propositions. Hilary Putnam, for instance, defended against Quine the utility of regarding "No bachelors are married" as analytic.[7] I do not read Quine as having denied the existence of analytic truths. There is, however, a question as to the conditions under which an analytic truth is an empirical truth. Consider a culture in which all males are married at birth but remain bachelors until the marriage is ceremonially consummated at the age of 13. The quoted proposition is not an analytic truth in that culture, for the analytic form, No $A = \bar{A}$ (no A equals not A), is not met. Even with respect to the form, however, Morris Cohen's argument—that $p \supset p$ (if p, then p) holds only if the p's are identical—is valid. That this is not a mere quibble is illustrated by the difficulty of programming computers to read. How much variation in form can be permitted if the identity is to be recognized? That the human mind can solve most simple problems of this kind readily does not mean that no problem is present. "*P*'s" do not exist as such.

There is both *intension*, i.e., meaning—and *extension*, i.e., examples, in these cases. *P* is only a sign. The problem becomes more complex when referents and concepts are involved, as in the "blue-colored" example below and even more complex in more sophisticated problems.

I don't doubt the existence of analytic truths. They are the correlatives of synthetic truths. Although the meaning of each depends upon the other, there is a clear distinction between the concepts. Whether "all blue objects are colored" is a logical truth depends on the inner relationship between "blue" and "colored." "All blue objects are colored is a logical truth" follows from the inner relationship between "blue" and "colored." That "all blue objects are colored" is true. But this last assertion of truth is not of logical truth. The judgment that the proposition is an analytic truth in this world—and possibly in all other worlds as well—depends upon external criteria that govern use and, hence, is its contingent correlative. Neither is such as such.

Logical truth invokes a world in which meanings are given and relationships are inner. A synthetic proposition invokes a world in which the relationships between referents and between concepts depend also on external criteria. For instance, the theorems of Euclidean and of non-Euclidean geometry are logical truths. But the meanings of analogous concepts, such as "line," differ in the two theories because of their relationships to other concepts. And differences in these analogous concepts are understood partly in terms of external criteria, including comparison.

For a long time it was believed that astronomical space was Euclidean. Now it is believed that space is non-Euclidean. Although Euclidean geometry provides fairly accurate approximations within solar distances, it is not believed to be true of any real space. On the other hand, "all bachelors are single men" may be a logical truth in some usages and not in others. (The arguments by Kripke and Putnam for *a posteriori* necessary truths will be considered subsequently.)

A more interesting argument—but also misleading and for the same reasons—is over which logical postulates are truly necessary. Take the principle of contradiction for instance.

Even a multi-valued logic translates into the principle of contradiction; for the argument that *x* is neither A nor not-A means that it is like A in some respects and not like A in others. On the other hand, every two-valued use can be translated into a multi-valued one for an appropriate statement of a problem. These systems of logic are correlatives. Which system of logic should be employed in a particular case can be determined only by part-system analysis.

In logic, the rules of the notational system determine what statements are true. To determine whether a system is useful, its set of rules must be tested against experience. No set of general rules avoids problems. In Bertrand Russell's notational system, "Santa Claus lives at the North Pole" is a false statement.[8] But surely there is a sense in which this sentence is true. Contrast it with "Santa Claus lives at the South Pole." Frege's notational system avoids this problem but permits statements with empty names, that is, names without denotation.[9] The problem created is obvious. Alexius Meinong avoids the problem of both Russell and Frege by recognizing that existence is not a quality.[10] However, his notational system permits statements such as "The circle is square" and "Bismarck has both a fat and a thin mother." Because Meinong does not assert that a round square exists or that both mothers exist, he avoids contradiction. Bismarck may, in fact, have had a fat and a thin mother; she may have gained weight or lost it. In this book we have seen that many apparently contradictory statements are not contradictory when properly interpreted in second-order discourse. Thus a table may be both solid *and* porous, depending upon whether we are referring to a human being or a gamma ray. A sweater may be both yellow *and* green, depending upon the light. And Sirius may be moving with respect to the sun *and* the sun may be moving with respect to Sirius, depending upon the inertial system from which the reference is made. What notational system works for a domain, or how it needs to be adapted to make it work, is determined by assessment at a literal level of analysis.

Systems of logic determine only analytical truth. According to formal logic, an antecedent, if false, entails the truth of any consequent. "Franklin Roosevelt was queen of England" entails "Harry Truman was the archbishop of Canterbury." This particular type of entailment, which logicians call material entailment, is not what we mean when we assert that one aspect of the world produces another; such as "When the sun rises, it will become day on earth." We have no difficulty in distinguishing such logical entailment from real-world connections. And, thus, we have no difficulty in knowing when *not* to use such logical entailment. Logic is merely a tool to be used. The failure of formal logic to deal with real-world relations says more about the nature of some systems of logic than it does about the world.[11]

Once we move past the basic postulates of logic—and, to some extent, even within them—we can vary our use of language. But we do this legitimately only to elucidate aspects of experience. Language and reality always condition each other, although not always in the seemingly simple and limited ways of the basic postulates of logic.

In effect, I reject formalism and all attempts to base logic on a single, correct axiomatic system. Although it might appear that my position then must be intuitionist, this is not the case, either. Systems of signs are merely tools for dealing with the signed world. I deny the existence in real time of infinite sets. I accept them as mathematical entities and also as potentialities in the real world.

DIALECTICS

Recently there have been attempts to formalize dialectical logic in both the Greek and Marxian senses. The classical Greek usage, in which dialectics involves the use of arguments generally believed to be true, is not inconsistent with the positions taken in this book. But Marxian dialectics is.

Some of those who have attempted to formalize dialectical logic have also attempted to justify the use of negations of negations and the appropriate non-use of the principle of the excluded middle. Although the following is not an instance of what a Marxist means by a "negation of a negation," it is easy to see that two-valued logic has its limitations. "He is not unintelligent" is not the same as "He is intelligent." It would be easy to show that the Marxian concept of a negation of a negation is as metaphoric as arguing that "He is not unintelligent" is a negation of "He is not intelligent." In such sentences, the negation of a negation is a metaphor: the meaning of negation in two-valued logic is being employed when one of the negations is not two-valued. For instance, one Marxist position is represented by the following: the division of labor is the negation of craft work; in turn, it is negated, as the result of its dialectical contradictions, by work in the state of Communism where intellect and labor would be combined non-restrictively. However, whether the projected transition is possible in whole or part depends on the possibilities of both technology and social organization. Recent Swedish experiments do cast serious doubt on the continued efficiency of mechanistic work division, but work environments incorporating new modes of worker organization are being adopted in the new General Motors Saturn plant, a prime example of capitalism. In short, however work becomes organized in the future, the Marxist analysis is abstract and formulistic. The empirical truth value of its formulations is attested to not by its internal logic but by its adequacy of analysis, a factor that is not dependent on those formulations. The problem is that most Marxists have turned metaphors into verbal magic and employed them in the absence of that literal analysis that alone makes concepts applicable to a particular case. There undoubtedly are genuine phenomena to which the metaphor "negation of a negation" may be partly applicable. Conceivably the concept may have some heuristic value in orienting one to the possibility of reversals in the real world. However, scientific knowledge is transmitted only by literal language.

I suspect, although he wrote in too packed a way for one to be sure, that it is this error that underlies Jürgen Habermas's concept of dialogic* as well as many hermeneutical analyses.[12] These metaphors are more dangerous than those that give rise to the paradoxes of class or language discussed by Bertrand Russell and Alfred Tarski,[13] to which I now turn; for the Marxian metaphors pile uncontrolled use on top of uncontrolled use. Formalization of a concept is not a sufficient, or often a necessary, condition for controlled use. It is the *literal* understanding of a problem that provides the justification for both formalization and application.

LEVELS OF LANGUAGE AND TYPES OF PROPOSITION

The previous discussion complements Tarski's concept of "levels of language." A sign always has a referent, even if the referent does not exist as an experienced

---

*To the extent that Habermas's concept of linguistic competence draws upon Anglo-Saxon language philosophy, the discussion in chapter 9 answers it.

event, object, or process. In principle, a sign is non-self-referring in its function as a sign, although by successive use in a *metalanguage*, that is, a language in which the prior language is discussed, it may refer to itself in its signed aspect; but, even then, only formally by the assertion of identity.

When a sign is used successively, it becomes the referent of a formally identical sign but not of itself. Thus, the metastatement may be a metaphor, an analogy by proportion—"x" as a sign is to x as signed as "x as a sign as signed" as a sign is to "x as a sign" as signed—if x as signed is not identical to, e.g., "x as a sign" as signed. There is often a significant shift in meaning as signs are used successively in an argument. Whether this is the case is a factual matter in which external criteria are employed.

Although Aristotle's position, which is still generally accepted by rhetoricians and logicians, is that the analogy by proportion is a metaphor, an equation involving proportions is not necessarily a metaphor: for instance, in mechanics, an area in which independent measures and covering laws exist, a proportional equation is literal. However, the problems addressed by Tarski's concept of levels of language and Russell's theory of types are in fact metaphors when their use of signs is correctly analyzed.

Thus, if the only sentence on a blackboard is "The first sentence on the blackboard is false," it might appear to create a paradox. If it is true, it is false. And if it is false, it is true. However, if the sentence is treated as a sign system, no paradox ensues. The sentence is neither true nor false, for there is not a properly constructed referent. "The first sentence on the blackboard" is a nounal clause; "is false" completes the sentence, and, therefore, can refer neither to the nounal clause nor to the complete sentence. However, a second sentence, "The first sentence on the blackboard is true," is neither true nor false. For it to be true or false, the first sentence on the blackboard would have to make a claim that is true or false, and it does not do so. Only if the first sentence on the blackboard referred to itself without a distinction between its sign and its signed aspects would a problem arise.

Consider an envelope paradox: "The next sentence I am going to write is true," followed by "The previous sentence is false." This is a variant of Tarski's level-of-language problem. It has implications that bear on my earlier discussion of logic and reality. In the standard case, the second sentence or sign system would have a signed referent that is the indirect referent of the first set of signs. The paradox arises because mutual implications of the envelope type are not restricted in this system of logic. I am not arguing that this is necessarily true of every Gödelian-type problem.[14] Kurt Gödel's conclusion—that for any mathematical system, there are true propositions that cannot be proved within it—is correct. By incorporating information from part systems not included in the system of logic that produces the paradox, we can see that a restriction on mutual implications is required in the envelope type of argument. The logical system must be adapted to the realm of knowledge, not vice versa. Would it be a problem if the second sentence on the board read, "The previous sentence is not the first sentence"?

Consider Russell's problem: the class of all classes that are not members of themselves.[15] Is it a member of itself? If it is, it isn't. But if it isn't, it is. This, however, holds only if "sign" and "signed" are identical. It is a member of the class in its signed aspect, but not as a sign. If the use of the sign and the signed are not identical, and if they are correlative aspects of language, the paradox does not arise.[16]

Many statements at different levels of language that appear to be true turn out to be metaphors when the distinction between sign and signed is assessed. Even in mechanics, the meaning of measurements that appear to be entirely literal and concrete can become metaphoric. As Max Born noted, over a sufficiently long period of time predictions become impossible because of measurement "error."[17] There is no such thing as an absolutely precise measure or a fully determinate world.

KRIPKE, PUTNAM, AND "NECESSARILY TRUE" DEFINITIONS

More than fifty years ago, Morris Cohen argued that definitions are not arbitrary, that elements of definitions are factually connected: refined sugar, for instance, is "both white and sweet," because nature connects things in this way.[18] Saul Kripke and Hilary Putnam, however, argued that true definitions are necessary and true in all possible worlds.[19] This position is ultimately related to Kripke's rejection of connotational meaning for common and personal names.[20] Personal and proper names, according to Kripke, are rigid designators *de re* in all possible worlds, that is, they refer to things as they are in themselves and not as they are *de dicta*, that is, from a particular point of view. Thus, Aristotle would be Aristotle even if Plato had not been his teacher and gold would be gold even if it were not yellow. We may be mistaken that gold is yellow, according to Kripke, but scientific analysis will clarify that problem.

Kripke, thus, believed that there are no ambiguities of scope in modal logic. Leonard Linsky has shown at length why this position fails to hold.[21] For instance, in modal logic, if it is true that "Sir John wants to know whether Hesperus and Phosphorus are identical," and if it is true that Hesperus and Phosphorus are identical, then "Sir John wants to know whether Phosphorus is identical to Phosphorus" is also true. But this is clearly false. All we know of Ste. Anne is that she was the grandmother of Jesus. Thus, there could be no world in which Ste. Anne could be Ste. Anne unless she were the grandmother of Jesus. Hence, as Linsky noted, sense is essential to identification.

The concept of rigid designation in all possible worlds is too restrictive. Should Socrates have suffered brain damage as a child, would he still have been Socrates? Is the man the boy? The tree the tender shoot? What does it mean to say that two electrons are different electrons or that one electron at one time is the same as, or different from, that electron at a different time? When an amoeba splits, are both the new and the old amoeba the former amoeba? One? Neither? Is a second personality of a schizophrenic the same person as the first personality, or a different person? In what sense would Aristotle remain Aristotle in all possible worlds if no *de dicta* elements are specified? Suppose his parents had been different? His language? If he had not been a philosopher? What does it mean to say Aristotle is Aristotle in all possible worlds *de re*? How do we determine what is *de dicta* and what *de re*?

Denotation *always* implies some connotative elements, if only to clarify that we are pointing to the same thing. The concept of denotation in logic is egregiously underdetermined and covertly borrows the concept of sense. Understanding sense and pointing, re-understanding sense and re-pointing, and so on are correlative techniques. Neither can be eliminated. And neither has priority.

The difficulties in the position of Kripke and Putnam are even more profound than Linsky asserted when he noted that their position requires logical and metaphysical omniscience. In an earlier section of this chapter, I pointed out that a statement may be a logical truth but that the assertion that it is a logical truth is not a logical truth. I shall use this mode of analysis now to show why the claim that a definition, if true, is necessarily true misstates in principle the ways in which we can know and speak about the world.

A logical truth is necessarily true as a consequence of internal criteria, but the assertion that it is empirically true, that is, that it applies correctly to a real-world domain, also depends upon external criteria, that is, upon criteria from other part systems or domains.

But the crux of the sleight-of-hand by means of which Kripke and Putnam seemed to satisfy their claim lies in their illicit use of the "if true" stipulation in a context in which its meaning has varied. We have seen how variance of meaning affects Russell's type problem and Tarski's level-of-language problems. Does the stipulation "if true" overcome those difficulties? Or is this characterization of "true" different from the logical "true"? The problem is whether logical truths, if true, become truths as such, and hence metaphysically necessary, or whether they function as correlatives in characterizing aspects of the world.

Consider tautologies in which a substitution occurs in one of the elements of the tautology. For instance, for mammal $\supset$ mammal (if mammal, then mammal) substitute dolphin $\supset$ mammal. Or take a definition: water $=$ H$_2$O. Here, Kripke's and Putnam's position requires rigid correspondence between the elements of the proposition or definition, a correspondence that is neutral and independent of all contexts and frames of reference. Putnam's argument to sustain this position rests, in addition, on the use of extensional logic, which gives absolute priority to the independent use of signs.

The preliminary answer to Kripke's and Putnam's claim, however, is that "sentence" and "words" are true correlatives and that neither can take absolute priority over the other. The importance of the sentence as the context of the signs has been confirmed repeatedly by experiments that show that an isolated word that cannot be understood, when it is heard alone, can often be understood when the other words of the sentence in which it occurs are heard. The earlier example of "the human eye" and "the eye of a storm" are evidence of the role of context in interpreting signs. Thus, the meaning of "truth" in "truth table" and in "truth of theory" are not necessarily the same. Perhaps, though, Kripke and Putnam would answer that the types of eye need to be distinguished *a posteriori* and that the correct use of signs would permit their rigid designation. Let us, therefore, carry on the analysis.

If, as Kripke argues, a table is not the same if it has been replaced by an identical duplicate (and how could this be known unless the substitution were observed?), what does it mean to deny that they are the same? Heraclitus argued that a river is never the same river, for different water is flowing. Most of the cells in the human body are replaced in seven years. Is it then the same body? What does "same" and "not same" mean in these examples?

"Same" and "not same" are correlatives, not truths as such. Something may be the same in one frame of reference and not the same in another. Second-order discourse eliminates the apparent contradiction. The river may be both the same and not the same, depending on the frame of reference. The body may be the same with reference to form and genetic characteristics, and different from the standpoint of cellular material.

Just as the "as such" concepts of "changing" and "unchanging" or "same" and "not same" are reifications, so is the idea of rigid designation or correspondence as such. Consider "yellow." How did Kripke handle this problem? Kripke argued that yellow is a manifest, and not a dispositional, property because if we had different neural structures, all this would mean is that yellow objects would not produce yellow sensations in us.[22] (By the way, no one ever had a yellow sensation. We see yellow objects.) However, yellow is a product and what becomes manifest as yellow depends on the lighting and the transceiver as well as upon its source. Furthermore, there are shades of yellow.

Can we resolve this problem by resorting to physics, as Kripke attempted to do with the problem of molecular motion? Suppose we define yellow by an angstrom number. But there is no yellow in physics. And, if we change the optic system, the angstrom pattern will no longer produce yellow. Is this difficulty perhaps why Kripke conceded that molecular motion may not be heat *de re*: because molecular motion might not produce heat in the physiological system? Nevertheless, he thought that this rigid relationship exists and said that "molecular motion is molecular motion" in all possible worlds.[23] However, molecules and motions are also products, and we are no better off than with yellow; for what counts as a molecule and what counts as motion is not entirely independent of transceivers, context, and frame of reference, and thus upon meaning in some respects. In any event, what varies with what is the rate of movement of atomic particles with temperature on a Kelvin scale.

I must admit that I do not know why Kripke regarded yellow as manifest *de re*, whereas he said that it is possible that heat is *de dicta*. The transactions that produce angstrom wave counts and temperature readings involve transactions with laboratory transceivers, whereas the experience of warm and yellow involves transactions with physiological transceivers. Angstrom waves are inferred entities, and degrees of temperature, or heat, are inferred quantities. Their meanings are not entirely independent of the range of transactions and of the theories that permit their existence or character to be asserted. However, angstrom wave production and color are not rigidly related, nor are heat production and hot. The same temperature is sometimes perceived as warm and sometimes as cool. "Hot" and "heat" are different concepts.

Would we not immediately spot something wrong if it were argued that human motion ⊃ human motion? That is a logical truth. However, what counts as human motion? A corpse's motion? A reflex? An intended motion? These questions have no answer as such; they can be answered only when the schemata of investigation and the problems to be solved are given.

Consider a well-known theoretical identity: water = H_2O. This definition is permissible (1) because by experiment we can show that two atoms of hydrogen and one of oxygen will result when water is vaporized and (2) because we will refuse to call anything water of which (1) is untrue even if it looks and behaves like water.

Hilary Putnam used the same example, H_2O, to attempt to make Kripke's point. If in another world, he wrote, people drink a substance that is not H_2O, it is not water.

> Once we have discovered that water (in the actual world) is H_2O, nothing counts as a possible world in which water isn't H_2O.[24]

This, he said, is a logical and metaphysical, even if not an epistemic, necessity. Whereas Kripke retreated to physics, Putnam refused to count as a possible world one in which water is not H_2O. Neither position withstands analysis. If we ask on what ground can one restrict the definition of water to H_2O, the somewhat different stances of Kripke and Putnam will be seen to have a common defect.

If liquid H_2O on a given world will not satisfy thirst, is it water? Below freezing, is H_2O ice or water? Consider, "He froze to death in a block of water." Solid H_2O and methane are both ice, but solid gold is not. Gold is a metal, but two atoms of gold do not constitute a metal. The relevant distinctions depend not merely upon physics or chemistry, but also upon meaning and the frame of reference. There is no single frame of reference that serves as a foundation for necessary meaning.*

Necessity, in Kripke's and Putnam's thesis, is imbedded (1) in the structure of the logic of a theory, (2) in a decision to give priority to a particular theory, usually physics, and (3) in a decision to let (2) determine the use of names. However, either we can call both U_{235} and U_{238} uranium or we can designate them differently, depending on their atomic structure and on the purpose of the distinction. There is no necessity here, even though Kripke and Putnam draw their best examples from strongly ordered aspects of the world. The truth of a

---

*Although Putman seems to take a similar position on frames of reference, the position developed here excludes his thesis on necessary truth.

theory as a frame of reference and of the identifications within it, as will become clear in chapter 5, is always dependent on assessment. A theory is never true as such. Neither are identifications.

The problem inheres in the important differences of meaning between the concept of truth in logic and the concept of truth in science. To call a theory true is not merely to make an epistemically fallible claim. It cannot be a fully determinate claim. It will always be based to some extent on external criteria that justify it in a specific domain, but that do not necessitate it. And the necessity of its internal logic is always bounded by this correlative non-necessity. Kripke and Putnam offer no arguments for their inference from the identity of the two signs "truth"—the analytical and the empirical—the identity of the concepts and referents the signs mediate. This begs the questions of how language works and how the world is ordered.

The foregoing objections to the thesis of Kripke and Putnam are formidable. Thus, it is not necessary to show whether that thesis implies, as I think it does, that a theory of the world is possible in principle. Such an implication would be inconsistent with Kurt Gödel's famous proof of the incompleteness of mathematical systems, Isaac Newton's critical discovery that the initial conditions are contingent from the standpoint of the theory being applied, and Niels Bohr's complementarity principle. We may someday discover that one or all are wrong, but there is no reasonable ground for believing that to be the case. And each has metaphysical and ontological implications that are inconsistent with the thesis of Kripke and Putnam and consistent with my position.

Furthermore, the concepts "weight of evidence," "confirmation," or "falsification" have no algorithmic determination. There is no necessary order to definitions, theorems, and undefined terms in theories. Thus, what is defined within "true" theories—hence, rigidly designated, according to Kripke and Putnam—can vary with conventional differences in the construction of a theory.

My analysis also is not necessary, for it rests on part-system analysis and assessment. That does not mean that it must be doubted, although any position this complex merits some doubt. However, to clarify this distinction, take two sentences: "It has rained somewhere sometime on earth" and "At least one sentence in this paragraph contains more than three words." No sane person will doubt the first sentence, even though it is theoretically possible that our earthly life is only a dream. And discourse is not even possible unless we accept the truth of the second sentence. Yet we know that people who speak gibberish seem to think that they are communicating, and so perhaps our communication is merely gibberish. Actually, although we cannot doubt either of the two sentences, they are neither necessary nor logical truths.

There are *natural kinds*, that is, there is some sense in which the character of the world determines the classifications that are applied. But I do not mean by the term what Kripke and Putnam do.[25] They believe that only one hierarchical univocal order of classification can be true. In my opinion, an inquiry into what a natural kind is can be answered only by assessments, including theory, but not simply by theory. The classifying and ordering principles will be related to the frame of reference and subject to second-order analysis. The answers are not sharply delineated, at least at their peripheries, and they are not metaphysically necessary.

Thus, where the line is drawn between classifications of beings, for instance, depends upon frame of reference. If the hypothesis of punctuated equilibrium of biological evolution—according to which biological structure is highly resistant to change except when stressed beyond its capacity—is correct, species, as defined biologically, would not change gradually and competitive selection would be between species. The evidence seems to suggest that gradual evolution applies to changes in single-celled organisms and punctuated equilibrium applies to them in more complex organisms. But, the biological framework of reference is not the only framework for classifications. Distinctions can be made according to types of responses to the environment, and beings can be grouped according to whether they are capable of rational behavior, moral understanding, and certain levels of intellectual accomplishment. These groupings might not be compatible with different frameworks, but they would be just as objective as biological designation. Similarly, "carnivorous" and "herbivorous" are classifications that overlap species. Even more cogent examples will be offered in the section on relevancy in chapter 5.

No single ordering principle can be imposed on the concept of natural kinds. Furthermore, the fate of species, as distinguished from that of unions or factories, for instance, depends primarily on external conditions and, apart from procreation, only incidentally on organized relationships among their elements, that is, upon internal characteristics of their systems.

The type of simple but inadequate natural kinds in which Kripke and Putnam believe can be avoided by second-order analysis without giving up the concept of objectivity, or even of natural kinds, provided that one recognizes the limited contexts in which such designations can be used.

In a subsequent section. I shall explore the problem Kripke gets wrong in his discussion of yellow: the correlative character of the *definitional* and the *dispositional*. Whether one or the other governs is not an "as such" matter but one of frame of reference.

STRUCTURE AND PROCESS

The concepts, "structure" and "process," are correlatives. Thus, the decision to use either of the concepts depends on the context and the purpose of analysis. Structure consists of the static elements of a system. Process consists of the regular changes that functions produce in a system.

The sun, for instance, can be defined in more than one way. It can be defined as a luminous heavenly body. It can be defined as the element in the solar system that heats the planets that circle it. It can be defined as a body the heat of which is produced by the process of internal fusion and contraction. We can specify a number of experiments that will permit us to identify the orb in our particular solar system as a sun according to these definitions. Thus, we can employ multiple definitions in identifying structures or entities. A sun is a luminous body that provides heat to the planets that encircle it, and so forth. An ox is a quadruped, horned, cloven-footed, ruminant, and so forth, animal.

However, we can also study the sun or an ox in terms of their internal relations as these relations change. The human body may be subjected to a physiological analysis that is similar. We can study the body either as a structure of parts related to each other in a static fashion or as a process involving growth and decay. The body is both structure and process; and the two modes of analysis are complementary. Statements about the body as structure do not contradict statements about the body as process; they have different referents. Either structure or process may be dominant, depending upon the questions that are asked. And the two modes of analysis differ, even though both employ definitions. Thus the heart of an ox is an organ, and so forth that, in relation to the lungs, etc., has the following functions in producing, and so forth.

The distinction between structure and process takes us along much of the road we need to travel if we are to understand the logic of the statements that will be employed in the remainder of the book and that are essential to the analysis of the problems with which we will be dealing. However, we still appear to have clear definitions when we deal with either structure or process.

DEFINITION AND DISPOSITION

Some concepts cannot be treated strictly definitionally, but only contextually and in complex conditional form. For instance, the term "electric charge" means, among other things, that if one body is placed near another body and is attracted by that second body, then it possesses an electric charge. The ensuing electric current can be inferred from the heat produced in a conductor, the deviation of a magnetic needle, the quantity of a substance separated from an electrolyte, and so forth. Thus, the concept of an electric current cannot be reduced to any one set of terms nor can it be measured simply by measuring a temperature. This is what I mean by a *dispositional concept*.

Dispositional concepts are necessarily employed when the interdependence of the element under consideration and its environment is great. However, this is merely the polar end of a series rather than a dichotomous usage. All manifest properties are products from one point of view as, for instance, the disposition of a type of optic system to produce a perception of yellow when a referent and light source produce given angstrom patterns. That is, they are dispositional in some respects. And all dispositional properties require reference to manifest properties if only to register their production: for electric current, heat and deviation of the needle, for instance. Concepts such as "definition" and "disposition" are correlatives. Neither can be reduced to the other, and part-system analysis enables us to deal with them.

Although "electric current" is a dispositional concept in the area of mechanics, it is indicated on instruments that are considered virtually independent of context. The manifestation of yellow, on the other hand, depends on the conventional standard of sunlight, the chemical composition of referents, the angstrom pattern, and the normal optical transceivers of the human body. Variance in any of these, including the use of filters, would result dispositionally in a different manifest color. Rational and moral behavior are produced dispositionally and there is much greater variance, depending on context, than in color. There is no standard sunlight, chemical composition, or angstrom patterning to narrow the range of contextual variance in the area of moral or rational behavior. Given sufficient specification of transceiver and environment, however, good or rational behavior can be identified.

One of the striking results of von Neumann's development of game theory was the recognition that what was rational depended upon the context in which it was analyzed. Rationality is an extremely strong concept—that is, the criteria that define it are strong—in a situation such as the prisoners' dilemma, in which strictly rational independent behavior produces the worst joint outcome. It is a weaker and more restricted concept in the zero-sum game. The criteria for rationality are weaker still in some other types of games. When one turns to *asymmetric bargaining games*—that is, games in which the maximal outcomes for the players are different and in which they must agree on p, which stands for the proportion of his maximum that one player gets, if the other player gets $1 - p$ of his maximum—it is questionable whether a strategy pair can be picked out as rational, that is, whether there are adequate criteria for defining rationality in this context.[26]

Thus, when we try to analyze what we mean by a human being, our concept of it will depend upon how we structure the analysis and the context that we take into account. A mere examination of what individuals do in specific circumstances provides one framework of analysis. And examination of what they do under a variety of social and environmental circumstances provides another mode of analysis. An analysis of how they attempt to transform their environment in order to transform their alternatives and of how these attempts to change the environment differ in different societies requires still another framework. If we ask what capacities and dispositions they must possess to respond in these ways, we are at a still different level of analysis.

The comparative analysis of different but similar types of systems also can be helpful. We can learn more about human thinking and intelligence by contrasting computer models of computation and problem solving with human thinking and problem solving. We can learn more about human emotions by contrasting different theories of emotion with each other, for instance, Aristotle's, the James–Lange theory, and cybernetic or information-control theories. Such inquiries can also inform us, to some extent, about the interaction between different "housings"—biological in humans, electronic and metal in computers—and their related processes of thinking and problem solving as well as the subjects to which they are directed. In all these ways, we penetrate more and more deeply into the whatness and the meaning of humanity by means of the scientific methods of theory and praxis.

PRAGMATISTIC TESTS

The structure and differentiation of concepts depend not upon abstract conceptual analysis but upon the need to make distinctions that are important in the investigation of problems.

Thus, if we wish to investigate what we mean by "courage," we can do this best not by conceptual analysis but by contrasting varieties of behavior under different conditions. We may contrast the courage required to protect a family from assault by a bandit, the courage to fight for one's country in war, and the courage to think differently, to choose three arbitrary examples. Yet may it not sometimes be more courageous to surrender to the attacker and to limit the damage to one's family? And may it not be foolhardy, on going into battle, to begin a debate about the appropriate technique of attack?

With the aid of examples of this kind, we distinguish courage from foolhardiness or rashness. We may learn that what appears to be courageous is really cowardice: the preference for avoiding the appearance of cowardice regardless of the cost to others. We refine our concepts not only by analyzing them conceptually but by weighing them against the richness of the real world. We learn that different virtues are of different orders of importance in different societies. We learn that certain forms of moral behavior produce better people and better social conditions under existing historical conditions, but not necessarily under all.

The virtues that produce an integrated personality in a medieval society and those that produce an integrated personality in a modern society may be quite different. The values these virtues embody cannot be placed in any simple hierarchy, for their relationships with each other and with historical conditions are highly interdependent. Even the complex balance of values that are judged to be best because they produce the best people under the best possible conditions of one society will not be best in all sectors of the society or in all situations that arise within each particular sector.

To say that some values are more important than others does not mean that the less important values can be derived from the more important values—no system of logic will permit this in a way that accounts for actual experience— but that they will play a more important role in a class of situations or even in a particular situation. Thus, one may lie to save one's brother from the secret police if he is merely a dissident, but not lie to save the brother if he will convey important information to an enemy nation. On the other hand, one may send secret information to the enemy to save one's mother if the information is relatively unimportant or one's own society is not worth preserving. There is always a rich interdependence with other elements of the factual order in these judgments. If we believe that people are by nature selfish—that is, that except under restrictive conditions they will tend to act in their own interest against the public interest or the social good—then we would regard hypocrisy as a virtue, for the wise would be hypocritical and only fools would be taken in by claims to the contrary. Even so, truth-telling may be a virtue, in some situations, even for such selfish and hypocritical persons.

Whatness is revealed by the widest variety of testing possible: a variety that distinguishes between first-order and second-order types of statements and that reveals the dispositional shifts in both the meaning of terms and their relationships. This is similar to the reason the von Neumann utility axioms are insufficiently general, except for limited forms of economic analysis. A value is more important not because it ranks higher in an abstract hierarchy but because it will play a greater role in a decision that is itself more important than others.

This mode of analysis also illuminates the concept of "freedom," for freedom is not abstract, either. For freedom to have meaning, it must refer to the freedom of human beings to act according to their best understanding of what a human is. A drugged person is not free to analyze a problem, for an individual whose information has been severely restricted has lost the freedom to make significant moral decisions. At its deepest level, the understanding of human freedom requires a dispositional analysis. And this understanding will depend upon the facts of particular circumstances, particular societies, particular environmental conditions, particular available alternatives, and particular prospects for transforming those alternatives. Thus, our ability to understand the concept of freedom must be related to a praxical analysis.

IDEAS AND CONCEPTS

My focus thus far, in discussing the problem of meaning, has been from the contemporary theory of signs. In this section, I shall review briefly the same topic in more traditional terms.

"Ideas" and "concepts" are terms that have been used differently by different philosophers. In Plato's philosophy, the *Idea* was a concept by intellection; that is, it was not derived from experience. The Platonic Idea could be applied indifferently to "chair" or "atom." Although the former can be both imagined and sensed, and the latter can be neither imagined nor sensed, both are postulated entities. Aristotle's ideas, on the other hand, depended upon direct apprehension of the sensible, or of the concrete. The only postulates used by Aristotle were logical, and these logical postulates provided form and permanence for the material aspects of the world.

Whereas Plato's sensibles were *nominalistic*, that is, they existed only as particulars, and transitory, Aristotle's sensibles were nominalistic but given immortality by logical form. Not until Hegel did the concept of a *concrete universal*, that is, of essence as concrete and supraparticular, arise. In Hegel's system, the concrete universal connected ideas to reality in a way that avoided Aristotle's reliance upon logic to provide form and permanence and that, instead, substituted a reliance upon the unfolding of history for the ultimate expression of essence. This made some sense in an idealistic system that maintained the objectivity of external facts. Even so, the structure of the argument was insufficient to maintain Hegel's synthesis or to account for science; and this is one of the reasons why the neo-Hegelians had to abandon one or more elements of his philosophy.

F. S. C. Northrop distinguished between concepts derived by intellection, such as electrons which cannot be directly observed, concepts derived by imagination, such as pre-relativistic field physics, and concepts derived by perception, such as tables or chairs. Northrop further distinguished between theories such as those of economics, in which the postulates are directly proven, and the theorems of which are accepted for logical reasons, and theories such as those of physics, that assume elements such as photons that cannot be directly verified. The latter, in his view, depend for their verification upon *epistemic*, that is, observed, correlations between the predictions of the theory and data by perception.[27]

Although it is true that we cannot define an operation or transaction except within the framework of preexisting concepts, it is also true that we cannot delineate the meaning of a concept except within the framework of some manner of use or transaction. Although I reject Northrop's distinction between postulated concepts and aspects of the world that cannot be described independently of perception, there is a metaphoric distinction between the two that implies a genuine, literal difference. The distinction depends upon the structure and content of the relevant realm of knowledge. There are both external and internal standards for the use of particular concepts, or for systems of concepts, as I argued earlier in this chapter. The "ether" of physics has no referent, and is rejected for that reason. The concept of "electron" is modified by the inner standards of the theory in which it is included.

Let us see how Northrop's distinction can be accounted for. There is a tinge of the sensible both in the early analogical conceptions of the electron and in the concept of its performance in a variety of circumstances. The early analogical idea of the atom as a planetary system clearly contains a sensible, although imaginative, core. So does the somewhat different concept of electrons as shells. In our understanding of an electron or photon, however, we treat them as dispositional, that is, as processes, rather than as defined concepts. Thus, there is no idea by intellection of what they are, except as a residual and variable, but there is an idea of what they do. Moreover, these processes may be presented in equivalent notational form. Thus, no particular form expresses uniquely the idea or concept.

In the equations used in quantum mechanics, signs are employed for numbers and other concepts. They are hypothesized to account for experience. They do not develop out of a dialectic of ideas that has no relationship to experience, but out of the failure of previous theoreticians' attempts to account for experience in a satisfactory way. No matter how far removed they are from experience, the very theories that provide part of their meaning have meaning only in use. On the other hand, concepts derived from perception, whether or not they are postulated, are inconceivable in the absence of a coding of the perceiving organism.

How do we characterize these matters properly? Features of the world are universal in their conceptual aspects. They are, however, particular in their signed aspects. They are abstract as concepts and concrete or potentially concrete as particulars. Signs represent ideas or concepts, but only insofar as they are used in the characterization of things, events, or processes. They are not ideas, but the vehicles for the ideas that characterize the world. This is why attempts to reduce ideas to either their extensional or intensional components must fail.

Let me compare this position with Brand Blanshard's. With Blanshard, I would admit of *specific universals* (this particular shade of redness) and *qualitative universals* (those shades of color whose resemblances lead us to call them red). Blanshard uses the term "*this* apple" as the set of qualities "in the relations in which they exist to each other and the things around them."[28] Because these characterizations apply to dispositions as well as definitions, and because they admit the concept of potentiality, they are not merely bundles of qualities at a purely phenomenological level.

Although Blanshard admits that the qualities attributed to particulars, that is, their characterization, can vary somewhat with the perceiver and the environment, he appears—inasmuch as acceptance of the distinction I am making would seem to require discussion by him—to hold to the modern classical position of a fixed system of characterization. I have given reasons for disagreeing with this position earlier in the chapter. One is that I see no necessity in definitions. Different transceivers, different environments, and different research purposes may produce different characterizations at the primary level. Characterizations represent natural kinds only when all the constraints are taken into account, although even then there are some possible indeterminacies. What I do assert, however, is that if the transceiving systems have some things in common, then *some* translatabilities are present that permit *some* degree of objective agreement at a secondary level. It is not an unreasonable hypothesis that there will always be some things in common in the transceivers, that they will not be totally alien to each other.

What I call an idea or concept has a literal basis. However, because the sign and the signed are part of a framework of use that is not sign, signed, or both, ideas also have a penumbra that is not explicated. That penumbra is influenced by the preconscious sets of codes and of stored information that condition the use of signs. Ideas, although not concrete, are part of the world of experience and, therefore, are partly open. They cannot be reduced to, although they may include, the literal.

Thought employing ideas recognizes fit at the literal level because of the influence of the rest of the relevant body of knowledge and perhaps because of the influence of elements of a preconscious and non-linguistic coding system. Recognition of fit is preconscious and is brought to consciousness only as a problem-solving technique. There is a rich interplay between the open concrete world and the open world of intelligence that is merely mediated by the closed world of literal scientific thought. Any philosopher who attempts to reduce this process to one of its elements misrepresents it. This is why the presentation of literal knowledge often excludes much that is essential to understanding it.

NOTES

1. John Dewey, *Experience and Nature* (Chicago: Open Court Publishing Co., 1925).

2. Morton A. Kaplan, *Justice, Human Nature and Political Obligation* (New York: Free Press, 1976), pp. 49 ff.

3. Willard Van Orman Quine, *From a Logical Point of View* (Cambridge: Harvard University Press, 1953), pp. 20 ff.

4. Ibid., pp. 102 ff.

5. Hilary Putnam, *Mind, Language and Reality*, Philosophical Papers, vol. 2, (Cambridge: Cambridge University Press, 1975), p. 52.

6. Gottlob Frege, "On Sense and Reference," in *Translations from the Philosophical Writings of Gottlob Frege*, edited by P. Geach and M. Black (Oxford: Basil Blackwell, Publisher, 1952).

7. Hilary Putnam, *Mind, Language and Reality*, vol. 2, p. 52.

8. Bertrand Russell, "On Denoting," *Mind*, n.s., (1905).

9. Gottlob Frege, "On Sense and Reference."

10. Alexius Meinong, "The Theory of Objects," in *Realism and the Background of Phenomenology*, edited by R. Chisholm (Glencoe, Ill.: Free Press, 1960).

11. For a powerful discussion of this topic see Brand Blanshard, *Research and Analysis* (La Salle, Ill.: Open Court Publishing Co., 1962), pp. 127 ff.

12. Jürgen Habermas, *Theory and Practice* (Boston: Beacon Press, 1973). For a discussion of the neo-Kantian aspects of Habermas's philosophy, see Morton A. Kaplan, *Alienation and Identification* (New York: Free Press, 1976), pp. 29 ff.

13. Bertrand Russell, *Principia Mathematica*, Introduction and chap. 2; Alfred Tarski, *Logic, Semantics, Metamathematics* (Oxford: Oxford University Press, 1956).

14. Kurt Gödel, *On Undecidable Propositions of Formal Mathematical Systems; Notes on Lectures* (Princeton: Institute for Advanced Study, 1934).

15. Bertrand Russell, *Principia Mathematica*, Introduction, chap. 2.

16. A similar conclusion is argued powerfully from a different perspective in Edmond L. Wright, "Logic as an Intention-Matching System: A Solution to the Paradoxes," *Journal of the British Society for Phenomenology*, 10 (1979).

17. Max Born, *Physics and Politics* (Edinburgh: Oliver & Boyd, 1962), pp. 49 ff.

18. Morris Cohen, *Reason and Nature* (New York: Harcourt, Brace, 1931).

19. Saul Kripke, "Semantical Considerations in Modal Logic," *Acta Philosophica Fennica*, 16 (1963); Hilary Putnam, *Mind, Language, and Reality*.

20. Saul Kripke, "Semantical Considerations."

21. See Leonard Linsky, *Names and Descriptions* (Chicago: University of Chicago Press, 1977), pp. 66 ff., for a rigorous refutation of Kripke's view that proper names lack sense, a position that is necessary to Kripke's conclusion.

22. Saul Kripke, "Naming and Necessity," in *Semantics of Natural Language*, edited by Donald Davidson and Gilbert Harman (Dordrecht, Holland: D. Reidel Publishing Co., 1972), p. 326.

23. Saul Kripke, "Semantical Considerations," p. 274, fn. 71.

24. Hilary Putnam, *Mind, Language and Reality*, p. 233.

25. Saul Kripke, "Semantical Considerations"; Hilary Putnam, *Mind, Language and Reality*, p. 233.

26. The reader who is interested further may turn to my discussion, "A Note on Game Theory," in *New Approaches to International Relations*, edited by Morton A. Kaplan (New York: St. Martin's Press, 1968).

27. F. S. C. Northrop, *The Logic of the Sciences and the Humanities* (New York: Macmillan Publishing Co., 1947).

28. Brand Blanshard, *Research and Analysis*.

Chapter 5
Theory and Praxis

In the preceding chapter, I presented my approach to meaning and to the use of signs and concepts. In the present chapter I shall draw heavily on the conclusions reached there to distinguish the methods of theory and praxis and to show why they are correlative methods for arriving at determinations of truth. In the following chapter, I shall indicate why I am dissatisfied with some contemporary alternatives to my position.

By *praxis*, I mean a reasoning process that is not entirely deductive and in which categories such as "fit," "centrality of logic," "range of category," and "relevance" are employed. Praxical assessment will be presented as an alternative to philosophies of science that rest on theory and explanation as *the* exclusive method of science.

I distinguish praxis from "practice," which ordinarily refers to how things are done and not to criteria of assessment. However, praxis, as I use that term, does include the implicit criteria of scientists and, hence, their practice of using such criteria. This approach is perhaps closer to the pragmaticism of Charles Sanders Peirce and to his concept of meaning as use than to any other twentieth-century philosophical position.[1]

THEORY

It is sometimes said that even observational terms such as "green" and "globular" are laden with theory. True, they depend on perceptual coding and, to some extent, on the fit between elements of this coding, at least within any single part system of the code. It is also true that these concepts are transactional and have meanings that are related to transceivers and mediums as well as to the transceived. But to call them theory-laden is to employ a concept of theory different from formal theory. The only similarity is that there are internal standards for concepts, as for theories. The internal standards for concepts are furnished by correlatives and by part-system connections in the coding system.

The Hempelian hypothetico-deductive covering law model[2] is a good account of how theoretical scientists state particular theories, of how they confirm or disconfirm them, and of how they reason from them—including sometimes the prediction of surprising results. According to Hempel, a theory is a deductive system, including theorems or covering laws, and the application of which to the world, if initial conditions are given, will sustain counterfactual conditions. Thus, if all apples are red, and x is a green apple, the axiom fails to explain the anomaly. If, however, a rocket does not fall, the explanation derived from a theory of mechanics is that it would have fallen except for a propellant device. Theories permit answers to "why" questions and, thus, explain.

Thus, the covering law model is not merely an *ex post facto* formalism, although it is not a complete account of scientific reasoning. It comes closest to the actual methods of scientists when the boundary conditions are completely specified and relatively noncontroversial and, therefore, when tests of the formally derived consequences of a theory tend to be conclusive. That is, it accounts for science to the extent that the internal standards provided by a theory require only peripheral supplementation by external standards. It begins to diverge from the real situation somewhat more when external standards, that is, standards from other part systems of the realm of knowledge, are required for the interpretation of results.

The great power of modern science has been produced by formal theory. Still, theoretical scientists begin with a problem, produce a formal theory, test the theory, interpret the test, and then assess the theory against its rivals. Except for the formal theory and its tests, the procedures used are praxical. Praxis comes to the fore even in the presentation of a theory when the boundaries of a theoretical area and the formulation of the theory are so interdependent that the methodologies of theoretical science provide insufficient guidance for choices from among theories.

Theory and praxis are correlative aspects of science. This tends to be obscured by the fact that scientists focus their attention on successful theories and nonproblematic tests, which tend to be well stated, highly confirmed, and located in a surround in which the identification and relevance of the boundary conditions are so well established that assessment appears irrelevant.

Because theory and praxis are correlatives, no actual account is entirely theoretical or praxical. There are rigorous theories, *theory sketches* (partial, loosely connected chains of reasoning), and programs for computers that are devised to explore the consequences of the assumptions imbedded in theory or theory sketch.[3] Hempel's claim that what he calls an explanation sketch is always a stand-in for a possible rigorous theory is too strong.[4] Reasons were given in chapter 3 for believing that rigorous theories are not available in areas that are non-mechanical because the independent measures required for covering laws are not present.

CHANGES IN THEORIES AND PRAXICAL CRITERIA

In theoretical physics, new observations or information, for example, the Michelson–Morley experiment or non-Euclidean geometries, may lead to a reformulation of a theory or to a replacement of one theory by another. The change may be in the meaning of a key concept, for example, mass; in axioms, for example, the constant for light; or in theorems, for example, of the geometry of space. In Newtonian theory, concepts and parameters were treated as givens for centuries, but change, as always, did occur. The methods of praxis come to the fore during periods of transition in which alternative theories become compatible with experimental evidence. Then, the choice is determined by praxical criteria—fit, relevance, centrality of logic, and so forth—criteria which will be illustrated in this chapter.

EXPLANATION AND ASSESSMENT

Both theory and praxis involve reasoning, but a different reasoning process is employed in each. In *formal theory* the system under consideration is closed at its boundary. That is, it is treated as an independent part system, an independent area of knowledge. The events predicted by the theory are deduced from it if the initial conditions are given. In praxis, attention is shifted from the formal deductive theory to the problems of identifying its relevance to the world, justifying the tools of investigation employed, categorizing the evidence, evaluating alternative concepts, and so forth.

Thus, in its analytical aspects, theory and explanation comprise a closed form of reasoning. In each analytic aspect of praxical assessment, a closed form of reasoning is also employed, but the process of assessment, which is one of relating the theory to the real world, is open. Praxical evaluations necessarily include qualitative elements, including the key element of fit. Closure characterizes the formal aspects of science; yet the real world remains obdurately open. Reason, that is to say, can never exhaust particularity. The difference between theory and praxis will become clearer as these qualitative elements are examined more closely.

Fit

By *fit* I mean consistent with or complementary to. If we say that an object fits an outline, we are using a two-dimensional external measure that is entirely spatial. If we say that a screw fits into a casting, our measure remains spatial but becomes three dimensional and includes the curvature of the threads. If we say that two partners make a good fit because of their complementary abilities, we are using entirely different criteria of fit.

For instance, in a highly competitive small business, in which the products of competing firms are virtually indistinguishable, a good salesperson may make a good fit with a partner who is a good organizer and accountant. On the other hand, high-technology industry would not fit the business climate of Upper Volta because of the absence of skilled workers, of an environment attractive to managerial personnel, and of local facilities. In these instances, we understand the fit or lack thereof in a literal language that refers to a variety of external criteria about which we already have some knowledge. Our knowledge may be of human relationships in general, of the characteristics that make an effective salesperson, of a particular environment, or of the conditions required by a high-technology industry. These are assessments, not proofs; other information or the refinement of existing information may contraindicate our judgments.

Fit: Metaphor or Analogy?

Is the concept of fit a metaphor or an analogy? As a concept, it is a metaphor, for no general external criteria apply to the diverse cases of fit. Fit is like fit only in the sense that an assessment warrants its attribution. A brain operation to remove a tumor and a cool pad for a fevered brow both fit their situations. It is not a metaphor in its applications, however, for, as the examples just used show, there are external criteria for each type of application. Like other praxical criteria, fit is a *sui generis* concept that characterizes a type of assessment.

The concept of fit, except in an actual case, is a metaphor, for the sign "fit" potentially relates widely diverse types of concepts and referents. Fit is like fit only in the sense that an assessment warrants its exemplars. Metaphors, including analogy, familiarize us with the larger realm of knowledge by indicating similarities. The limitation of these similarities evokes their differences, an examination of the significance of these differences, and a comparison.

Metaphors and analogies permit the emergence of new or different literal meaning. They generate scientific thinking by bringing to consciousness a richness of connections between related but non-identical concepts and concept systems and referents. They, thus, assist in producing new ideas or theories by breaking through the constraining barriers of existing intellectual constructs. But the science that is communicated is in literal language.

What seems literal may later become metaphorical when it is contrasted with a new way of making distinctions that discloses new similarities and differences. The meaning of "literal" and "metaphoric" depends upon the relevant realm of knowledge. They are correlatives. The other praxical criteria function similarly, as subsequent discussion will show. Thus it is inappropriate to ask for general literal indicators for application of the praxical criteria. Only when the research problem has been specified and the boundary conditions brought into focus can the relevant indicators be understood. Even then, second-order considerations may be controversial because of the weakness of the orderings of some of these matters. That is why the illustrative materials that follow may be more illuminating than a putative list of criteria. However, there are prescientific elements of judgment involved also, a matter that I will come back to later in the chapter.

Fit and Coherence Theory

Coherence theory requires a universe all of whose elements are interrelated so that they fit together in a strictly univocal and hierarchical whole.

Does fit imply a coherence theory? A *coherence theory* implies that weak orders do not exist anywhere and that the interrelationships of the individual areas of knowledge are strongly ordered. Many theories, however, are weakly ordered. The justification of their truth depends on praxical reasoning whose criteria, although convincing, may possess no simple order. And there is no simple way to order different frames of reference, particularly with respect to problem areas that are under- or over-determined. Furthermore, coherence theory would require that all relations be first-order and internal and I have already shown that second-order reference and external criteria are required to account for important aspects of the world. Thus, coherence theory will not account for knowledge if the contemporary framework of knowledge has any validity.

Objectivity and Subjectivity

By *objectivity*, I mean the state of being a referent. The objective is characterized by an object language. The use of concepts mediated by signs with respect to referents is invariant primarily at a second-order level of reference. Hence, the concepts of strong orders, univocality, and verismilitude are not necessarily invoked, as the subsequent discussion will make clear.

The *subjective* is the knowing of that which is asserted in the object language. There is, however, another common use of "subjective": we often refer to something as subjective when it has no referent outside of consciousness. For instance, if someone hallucinates a snake, the snake is called subjective. On the other hand, the hallucination itself is an objective event, one that can be referred to by others. Even though there is no snake, we can observe that the hallucination is, in fact, occuring and may have good reasons to believe the account of it. It is important to make this distinction, for the implications of the two meanings of "subjective" are quite different.

The preconscious characteristics—the penumbra of concepts—of the minds of scientists that enable them to communicate because their systems are set similarly are objective, and their agreement is intersubjective only in the second sense of "subjective." They are there as actual, objective features of the minds of scientists even though they are not known in detail.

I think that it is appropriate to call these factors objective but idiosyncratic or personal features of the world. They are so dependent on history and on environmental variability that their objectivity becomes a personal matter or is restricted to particular subcultures of a society. The preconscious penumbra of concepts of scientists, for example, is personal but may also be relatively common in this subculture.

The disposition to gain weight may be idiosyncratic but still objective. The referent of a hallucination is idiosyncratic and objective only as idea. The need for honor was common and objective among Japanese samurai, but it was idiosyncratic to the group. In addition, many false beliefs are widely held; that is, their referential status is invalid despite their commonality.

Examples of Fit: The Dinosaur

I may be able to illustrate the praxical mode of argument by reference to the controversy over whether dinosaurs were cold-blooded animals, i.e., *ectotherms*, or warm-blooded animals, i.e., *endotherms*. Several arguments support the recent hypothesis that dinosaurs were endotherms. They were long-limbed. Furthermore, they walked with an erect posture, like that of birds and mammals, holding their limbs nearly vertical beneath the shoulder and hip sockets. This type of limb structure permits greater speed than that of animals whose limbs sprawl to the side. All modern endotherms are erect and all modern ectotherms have limbs that sprawl. Furthermore, dinosaurs existed for 140 million years, and mammals remained very small until the dinosaurs disappeared. Hence, dinosaurs were competitively superior to mammals, indicating a very high rate of activity which is characteristic of endotherms.

On the other hand, some modern lizards, if startled, are as active as rodents. The duration of a reptile's activity is limited not by its ectothermic character, but by the limits placed on its supply of oxygen by its heart and its circulatory system. Although dinosaurs probably had double-pump hearts similar to those of endotherms and although they carried their heads above their hearts, and thus needed high blood pressure, in itself this does not prove that they were endotherms. A four-chambered heart is necessary for such efficiency, but some lizards have such hearts.

It has been hypothesized that some dinosaurs were true endotherms and that others were ectotherms that maintained a constant body temperature by utilizing heat from their environment; in the latter event, their large size may have assisted them in retaining this heat. The evidence does not resolve this ambiguity.

Endotherms must eat far more than ectotherms in order to maintain their internal temperature; it has been estimated that they require at least ten times as much prey as ectotherms. Was there enough prey in the area of the dinosaurs to support them if they were endotherms? This is debatable, but so is the ten-to-one ratio.

Dinosaur bones have a high density of Haversian canals, canals for blood vessels. All modern endotherms are rich in such canals. However, turtles, which are ectotherms, also have such canals.

There is a great similarity between Archaeopteryx, which most specialists believe was the first bird, and certain small dinosaurs called theropods. Archaeopteryx had feathers, which indicates it was a bird. On the other hand, some argue that the feathers of Archaeopteryx may have prevented loss of body heat—an indication that it was not necessarily a bird and therefore not necessarily an endotherm.

No single one of these arguments is sufficient, even if proven, to establish whether dinosaurs were endotherms or ectotherms. Some of the particular arguments are subject to standard inductive tests, although the use of particular tests must itself be justified praxically. This is true, for instance, of the question of the availability of prey.

At the moment, the weight of the evidence tends to favor the proposition that large dinosaurs, at least, were ectotherms. The failure of any dinosaurs to survive the transition from the Cretaceous to the Paleocene age and the hypothesis of thermal inertia tend to support this evaluation.

Eventually, however, the investigation is confronted by a complex web of arguments that will not fit into any simple linear or hierarchical pattern. As the interconnections within the web become more complex, new standards of evidence and new definitions evolve. Praxical assessment, including fit, serves to establish the connections and relatedness necessary to judgment within the realm of experience.

Distant Stars and the Red Shift

Still another example of fit in praxical reasoning is the argument over the significance of the red shift in the spectrum when distant stars are observed. The character of the red shift led astrophysicists to believe that the more distant stars were receding faster than nearer stars. This, plus the discovery in 1965 of a faint radio echo that seemed to be left over from the birth of the cosmos, seemed finally to validate the "big bang" hypothesis as opposed to the steady-state theory of the cosmos.

More recently, anomalies in the red shift have been detected that indicate that it is stronger in one direction than in the opposite direction. This is difficult to reconcile with the standard explanation of the red shift. Work in Israel on relativity has indicated that massive red shifts might be produced by gravitation alone. Other evidence, which indicates that there is a significantly greater red shift in light from the center of the solar disk, is inconsistent with the big bang hypothesis. Moreover, partners in quasar pairs in the galaxy sometimes produce red shifts that imply that one of the sources of light is moving away from the other at up to twice the speed of the other. This seems impossible.

On the one hand, these anomalies in the red shifts may result from the comparative youth of the sources of the anomalies; young sources of light produce great shifts toward the red spectrum. On the other hand, the seeming association of sources of very different red shifts may be caused by their proximity on our two-dimensional photographic film. Is this, however, probable when the association occurs not in one instance, but in a variety of instances?

The evidence is inconclusive, although, on balance, at the present time, it tends to support the significance of the red shift hypothesis. The reasoning and the procedures are objective but, as in the investigation into the nature of dinosaurs, they are based on part-system, praxical considerations of fit.

Cyril Burt and His Twins

Another example of praxical reasoning is given by the debate over whether Cyril Burt falsified his data concerning the intelligence of twins separated at birth, which seemed to show that most of the variance in intelligence was produced by heredity. The attempt by Donald D. Dorfman to show that Burt did falsify the data was challenged by scientists who claimed that they used Dorfman's techniques on data so well documented that the issue of fraud did not arise and that these techniques then led to the incorrect conclusion that the data were fabricated. Dorfman responded by using criteria similar to those of praxical reasoning. He denied that the critics used his techniques and argued,

I would not have concluded that the Scottish tailor had fabricated his data. I would never consider such a hypothesis unless all qualitative and quantitative evidence converged on that conclusion—that is, only if the prior evidence of fraud were extremely strong.[5]

Dorfman then attempted to show how the techniques differed. He stated that there is agreement that Conway, the author of a particular article, had been invented by Burt and that Burt had written the article. Dorfman then inferred the "equation for the relation between Burt's means from Conway's . . . 1959 predictions."[6] In other words, he did not merely fit his curve to Burt's 1961 data, but predicted Burt's regression equation on the basis of the 1959 article. Regardless of whether Dorfman is correct in this particular case, his was a good example of praxical reasoning. His conclusion fit the existing body of evidence much better than did the case in favor of Burt.

The Theory of Relativity

Let us examine, from the standpoint of praxical assessment, why the special theory of relativity became an excellent candidate for testing. Newton's theory had not been falsified. Even the inconsistency between classical relativity and Maxwell's equations did not count as a falsification. However, the Michelson–Morley experiment, non-Euclidean geometries, Lorentz–Fitzgerald contractions, and the non-operational character of Newton's concepts of space and time, and other boundary considerations, produced a bad fit between Newton's theory and the realm of scientific knowledge. After the special theory of relativity had been confirmed by experiments, Einstein offered a general theory of relativity within which the curvature of space produced gravitational effects. This curvature of space could not be directly perceived. And the early tests of general relativity theory were within the range of experimental error. However, the general theory of relativity now fitted the realm of scientific knowledge so well that it tended to be accepted, although its exact specifications are still subject to dispute.

The predisposition to accept Einstein's general theory of relativity even when the early evidence was within the range of experimental error depended upon the concatenation of theoretical and praxical elements. Because there are covering laws in physics—that is, because there are relatively independent measures—strong evidence from tests of theory often becomes available eventually. This, however, only makes it easier to overlook praxical assessment.

Range of Category, Definition, and Relevance of Concepts

I have already referred, and shall again, to the problems of identification and relevance. The ensuing discussion of gene pools, basketball, the J-Curve, and crystals will serve to illustrate these considerations.

Gene Pool and Reproduction

Some sociobiologists argue that the genes are selfish.[7] They deal with con-tradictory evidence by hypothesizing that seemingly altruistic but genetically determined behavior—for instance, behavior that warns neighbors and not merely immediate kin of the approach of predators—increases the likelihood of survival of neighbors whose genes are closely related. This explanation is less convincing than they think. If "nearness" is restricted to the mating pool, it will vary with the characteristics of the ecological niche and even with chance factors. But more members of the pool will survive than if warning were not given. The entire demonstration depends, however, on the ecological constraints on the mating pool. The determination can be made only on the basis of external criteria and, even then, will apply only in specific situations. The issue of identification—in this instance, of the mating pool—is crucial to the conclusion that is reached.

The general concept of fitness being used is metaphoric. It merely means that those parts of the genetic code that increase survivability tend to be reproduced. The moment that we relate the general proposition to concrete cases, it becomes clear how open the proposition is. For instance, consider the situation in which symbiotic or parasitic species contribute to each other's reproduction. If the relevant group is redefined as the symbiotic set, the concept of genetic relatedness is stretched beyond recognition. Even when some genetic relatedness is apparent, it is not independently determined but identified with the circle of closeness within which reproduction is maintained and which in principle—that is, under different environmental or accidental conditions—might have been different; that is, the pool might have been more or less inclusive or might simply have contained different members. There is no absolute reproductive pool, although there may be an outside limit to the mating possibilities of all members of any particularly defined pool: a limit that is determined by biological incompatibility.

If this theory were taken seriously, then it would be simple to turn it on its head. All existing species, with a recently discovered possible exception, have been transformed through mutation; and that methane-producing apparent exception is the source of all others. In their mutated form, all existing species also perpetuate a gene pool, but a gene pool that is different at least in some respects from that from which they evolved. As the history of evolution is the history of such changes, should we then argue for the altruism of a species in the form of donations from gene pools to a transmuted species? This is, after all, a consequence of its biological behavior, that is, of the biological response to the mutation-producing condition. The relative infrequency or even random nature of its occurrence poses no problem: it is consistent with a reasonable likelihood of mutation, both specifically and in more general form, over a properly chosen span of time in a natural environment. That infrequency is also consistent with the lack of viability of at least some of the intermediary species.

Is what survives under duress more fit and, therefore, more real? This concept of fitness underlies much of the argument for selfishness. Actually, however, its proponents hypostatize the worst environment. When applied to humans, the most that is shown by their argument is that some environments bring out the worst in people. They do not show that humans are fundamentally selfish, either as a species or as individuals.

Certain chemical injections will produce schizophrenia in individuals, but schizophrenia does not become more basic to or truer of human nature than mental health because it is the condition that arises under some of the most adverse conditions. Human nature is influenced by environment. It is dispositional. The biological structure and the environment interact to give rise to personal and social patterns. No experiment that is unrelated to this complex process is capable of elucidating the concepts of selfishness and altruism. And the fact that every organism has a breaking point does not make its ensuing behavior definitive or genuine in any fundamental sense. Furthermore, evolution produces gene pools consistent with systems in which choice is prominent and perhaps even dominant.

If one wishes to argue that altruistic behavior is a goal of the evolutionary process, one must proceed with great care, considerable qualification, and avoidance of the misleading use of words such as "goal." Evolutionary altruism is as different from intentional behavior as it is from evolutionary selfishness. It is misleading to say that individual altruism nonetheless is selfish because it preserves a related set of genes. It is merely a truism that behavior that preserves a given gene pool is fitting in an evolutionary sense and that behavior that does not preserve the pool is not fitting in an evolutionary sense. The scope and the variability of the gene pool are praxically undetermined. Moreover, the evolutionary process itself establishes a relationship between the gene pool and the environment that is unrelated to intentional behavior.

Even in its truistic form, the argument that the human species (or even an animal species) is selfish because it perpetuates the gene pool is valid only when a very restricted and reified use of the concept of gene pool is employed. Some tribes and families in earlier societies tried to perpetuate themselves by conflict with neighboring tribes and families even when their gene pools were similar. Conflict, in their civilizations, was based not on differences in the gene pool but upon differences in tribal identification. On the other hand, many tribes have combined, either by conquest or voluntarily, and then preserved their new gene pool. Many times the combined groups had gene pools more similar to their enemies than to their allies. Such alliances, as anthropologists know, depended more upon confluences of interest than upon genetic similarity. Sometimes tribes and their animals combined against other tribes and their animals.

Thus, we can see that no gene pool preserves itself indefinitely. Gene pools are in process. How we draw the boundary of any gene pool depends upon both the purpose of our research and on the accidents of history that create particular ecological niches. Moreover, those portions of the gene pool, or genetic code, that are passed on in the evolutionary process have no clearly defined boundaries. Those portions of the genetic code that are preserved through change depend, like behavioral adaptations, on structural, situational, and ecological factors.

No level of organization—molecular, individual, species, or social—has absolute priority in determining what is preserved or what changes. And no focus of identification or relevance has absolute priority. No theory predetermines this in general although, in context, praxical reasoning determines particular attributions. It identifies, by the use of knowledge of part systems, for certain research purposes, the members of a classification or the relevance of an argument. Thus, a parasite, together with its host, can be a member of a descent group to an ecologist, but not to a geneticist.

To study the behavior of a stable species within a constant environment the standard investigator must ignore mutational transformation. However slow and evolutionary this transforming process may seem, it is radical and revolutionary when an overview is taken. Thus, the customs of experimentation lull us into unwarranted inferences. We take a statement the validity of which is restricted to a particular experimental context, overgeneralize it, and overlook the fact that a variation from one context to another may give rise to a radically different conclusion.

The unintentional mutational transformative process is as real a part of the world as the self-equilibrating processes of particular species. The radical sociobiologist misuses an already ambiguous term, "fitness," as a synonym for "selfishness" in a context that is radically different from its normal use and that carries a meaning that cannot be defended. Literal analyses, such as this one of "selfishness," are relevant to issues that will confront us throughout the book.

For instance, it can be shown that deceptive transvestite behavior among scorpion flies produces a reproductive advantage. If deceptive behavior were of evolutionary advantage, then humans likely would be naturally deceptive. And this would influence the concept of agency that would be applicable.

Basketball

It would probably be easy for us to agree that basketball centers should be comparatively tall, say, at least six feet, eight inches. However, were the population to grow or shrink in size—or were the basket to be raised sufficiently high—we would have to modify our generalization about the players' height.

Thus, it may be true that basketball centers should be tall, that mothers should be good, and that presidents should be intelligent; but we cannot know that someone is tall, or a mother, or intelligent until we have identified a system and associated a relevant generalization or measurement with it. These issues are decided praxically by reference to different part systems in the realm of knowledge and by considerations of fit.

The J-Curve

Contradictory generalizations may be correct. For instance, it may be appropriate to appease aggressors and appropriate to fight aggressors, depending upon the type of system, the characteristics of the aggressor, and the character of the environment. In this respect, a dispute that emerged in the pages of the *American Political Science Review* may be relevant.

James C. Davies attempted to salvage his *J-Curve*—the proposition that "when a long period of rising expectations and gratifications is followed by a short period during which expectations continue to rise while gratifications fall off sharply, the probability of civil violence against government rises rapidly" —by arguing that his opponents were looking at the wrong evidence.[8] His opponents—Abraham H. Miller, Louis H. Bolce, and Mark Halligan—argued that Davies' theory was too vague. They asked:

> How long is a long period? How short is a short period? How sharply must gratifications fall? How large is an intolerable gap? In other words, how will we know a J-Curve when we see it? . . . The theory itself is vague and gives no operational guidance. Consider how an analogous theoretical statement in the natural sciences might appear. The proposition "water solidifies when sufficiently cold" is at about the level of specificity of the J-Curve.[9]

Although I believe that Davies invited attack on other grounds, I wish to analyze this particular—and, in my view, unmerited dispute—because it is a nice illustration of the point I want to make.

Miller, Bolce, and Halligan chose the wrong ground when they treated the J-Curve as if it should have had the form of a covering law. The respected "theory" of evolution would not meet their test, either. We can indeed recognize the role of frustrated expectations in the production of rebellious behavior, particularly if we have related the proposition to qualitative boundary conditions better than Davies did. If, for instance, we state that frustrated expectations will produce less violence in the presence of great repressive force and will even come to awareness less forcefully in the presence of such repressive force; if we are aware that frustrated expectations will be more effective the greater the extent to which horizontal communication, organization, and so forth, produce among the frustrated an awareness of widespread support; and if we attempt, at least qualitatively, to sketch in the role of such relevant factors, we will have begun to develop a basis for assessment that permits a closer evaluation of the relationship between expectations and resort to revolutionary activity.

With this kind of articulation, one might find valid measures for a single system, or for a very closely similar system, if boundary differences are relatively small. But the very idea of a measure that *cuts across* types of systems and boundary differences is fallacious. And the problem of finding rational justification for our measures will be at least as important as their use in testing the hypothesis. Indeed, the failure of a measure to confirm our qualitative understanding may cause us to reject both the measure and its applicability.

We may be far more able to recognize an instance in which frustrated expectations produce violence than we are to find an adequate measure. In short, good reasons based on part-system analysis enable us to identify frustrated expectations, rising periods of expectations, and so forth. Moreover, they may be determined differently and for different research purposes, and these differences in first-order analysis may then be correlated by second-order analysis.

Centrality of Logic

Centrality of logic refers to the relationship between a definition or theorem on the one hand and a theory or method of investigation on the other. How closely does the definition or theorem correspond to the logic of inquiry? The more constrained the definition or theorem is by the remainder of the theory or research schema—that is, the more variance in it would necessitate radical revision elsewhere—the more central it is to its logic.

Is a crystal living or not? What do we mean by living? It would take only seconds to discover that even the unabridged dictionaries are of no help here. May we regard as living any entity that is capable of reproducing itself? If so, a male and a female who are marooned in spacesuits on the moon would not be living, for they could not reproduce themselves. On the other hand, if there were an automated wrench factory the operation of which begins when a wrench is used to start the factory, the wrench would be alive by virtue of its ability to reproduce itself.

These examples seem ridiculous or, at best, contrived. Space is not the normal environment of a human being. Space functions only marginally in a biological account of humans. The wrench, of itself, does not initiate the operation of a wrench factory, nor is a wrench factory the wrench's standard environment. Self-reproduction is at best a vanishingly peripheral function of a wrench. Moreover, the wrench has no metabolism, is not mutable, is not characterized by interactions among its functional elements and such carriers of information as RNA and DNA. In short, the aspects of investigation that characterize studies of life, and indeed that are central to its concept, are not present. Yet obviously these can be varied within some limits without falling outside the domain of what I would call the logic of the investigatory scheme.

Let us consider whether crystals are alive from the standpoint of whether crystals reproduce themselves. Does a crystal reproduce itself? It does participate in the further production of crystalline structures. On the other hand, it does not share in other processes that are common to living systems, such as *ultrastability*, for instance—that is, the ability to change a characteristic mode of behavior when it ceases to be functional—although even this may be ambiguous. Our decision about how to characterize a crystal will depend upon the praxical criteria, of which, in this instance, centrality of logic is most important. It is quite possible that within certain explanatory frameworks—for instance, types of interchange with environment and individual development—we would wish to treat crystals as non-living, and that in a different context—for instance, reproductive processes—we might conceivably treat them as living. At present, their non-template form of reproduction (i.e., they do not produce separate new individuals similar to themselves) leads some biologists, who wish to produce in the laboratory just the form of reproduction they metaphorically call "template," to reject their characterization as living.

Some viruses are crystals even though they contain DNA or RNA, the stuff of heredity. And no virus metabolizes or responds to stimuli. But the virus either may shed its protein outer shell and inject its hereditary material into a cell or be swallowed by the cell. It then uses the cell to make new viruses.

Differences about the characterization of crystals or viruses as live or not, that is, as members of the class of live things or not, should be determined not by disputes over the properties of crystals or by fixed definitions of life, but by the framework of the particular inquiry. This does not make a framework a fiction or a subjective device. Differing characterizations of crystals do not contradict each other when they are relevant to different frameworks of inquiry and different research questions. They are true and objective.

Georg Süssmann, a theoretical physicist, has suggested that the concept of life might be applied to such dynamical things as streams, beams, and flames. This again depends upon the research purpose and whether there is sufficient similarity from this standpoint for the concept to be applied.

This mode of analysis informs my earlier criticism of Kripke and Putnam in chapter 4. The definition of life depends upon the relevant realm of knowledge—a realm that grows more complex, sophisticated, and interrelated as knowledge increases.

Praxical analysis helps us to clarify such determinations as "endotherm," "center," and "life," but the tests used are different. The differences between an endotherm and an ectotherm are so clear that examination of a live dinosaur would settle the issue, at least for an individual species. On the other hand, if the configuration of a basketball court were changed, a center might not be a center or the game might no longer be basketball. Whether a crystal is a live thing is determined in part at least by research purposes that are more sharply circumscribed by internal and external criteria than are decisions about basketball. In this sense, determinations about crystals may be regarded as natural, and about basketball as conventional, although the difference is one of degree that is related to the strength or looseness of the surround. Natural and conventional are also correlatives.

Other Considerations

There are other criteria for the usefulness of a theory—its productivity in generating interesting problems, its success in the past, its ability to account for phenomena that other theories have accounted for, its internal consistency, and so forth. However, these are so well covered in the literature that no additional discussion is necessary.

One last warning may be in order. Powerful theories have more content—and can be more easily falsified—than less powerful theories, as Karl Popper[10] pointed out, and this is ordinarily considered a mark of a good theory. But in those areas in which covering laws do not exist (for reasons given in chapter 3), the search for powerful theories may lead us astray. It is likely that all theories are compromises between power and praxical adequacy. In the social sciences, the successful compromises are likely to have far less range and to be less easily falsifiable.

CONCLUDING OBSERVATIONS ON PRAXIS

Except for relativity, the praxical examples in this chapter have been chosen to emphasize the dependence of scientific judgment on praxical operators such as fit, relevance, or centrality of logic. Most of the examples, as we have seen, do not justify confident assessments. They were selected to emphasize the close dependence between the scientific surround and the assessment of evidence, and also to show that the procedures employed—although metaphors in their general statement—are legitimate examples of literal, scientific justification. Theories and inductive procedures function legitimately only within this praxical framework.

Are these praxical procedures justifiable in the scientific sense? In the concluding discussion, to make the argument for praxis more sharply, I shall turn in part to some more accessible and widely understood examples than those previously discussed in this chapter.

Consider, for example, a geocentric and a heliocentric theory of the planets. Construct a physical model of each. Assess praxically how either theory makes predictions about the real world, how physical models represent them, and how well observations of the real world correspond to the models. A powerful argument for the heliocentric theory was that it alone could be given a physical representation in which the planets had continuous positions. This fit what we then knew about physical objects. The mathematics of the model were less complicated, and this fit what we thought we knew about the relations between theory and reality.

Consider Kuhn's example of a card that can be seen either as a duck or a rabbit. We can show that certain features of design produce this ambiguous picture, and we can match the particular design with pictures of ducks and rabbits to show how it can represent either when the perspective is carefully chosen.

In the discussion of altruism and fitness earlier in this chapter, the conceptual problems of identification and relevance were assessed. The arguments for selfishness and fitness were seen to rest on naive identification and assumptions of relevance that neglected part-system praxical assessments and research purposes. In the controversy about whether dinosaurs were ectotherms or endotherms, similar considerations were applied to inductive procedures.

How and why do we use one standard of relevance rather than another, one standard of identification rather than another? Why, like the forms of logic appropriate to a particular problem, are different inductive statistical procedures employed for different types of problems? A qualitative praxical assessment is made, and only within the framework of this assessment are there good grounds for accepting the conclusions of inductive procedures or for confirming or disproving theories.

We are all very familiar with narrow areas of analysis and with physical theories which rest on an impressive convergence of evidence, stable definitions, and a high degree of relevance. This leads us to focus on the procedures we use and to neglect the qualitative, praxical grounds on which we accept them. But assessments of fit between theory or inductive procedure and surround are also part of scientific reasoning.

The fit between Einsteinian theory and its scientific surround was a valid argument for its acceptance, even though this fit was far more complex than that of heliocentric theory. The strength of praxical evidence of fit justified the expenditure of effort and money to test Einstein's theory further; but the ambiguity of the initial tests of general relativity theory justified a partial suspension of belief in the theory until the necessary investigations were made.

Praxical analysis is more central to the assessment of non-mechanical systems than of mechanical systems. Even strong well-confirmed theories such as relativity theory, however, almost always contain anomalies in their formulation and in their fit with evidence, anomalies that invoke a need for qualitative praxical assessments. This need tends to be obscured by the otherwise tight interconnectedness of the theory with its scientific surround, by the consensus of trained observers, and by the fact that previously implicit and preconscious features of analysis are incorporated into the subsequent analysis of the theory. We fail to see that the periphery and its problems have not been removed but have merely been pushed one stage further back. In the same way, we enrich the axiomatic structure of mathematical theories to prove particular theorems that could not previously have been proved. This does not change the fact that not all theorems that are true within an axiomatic system of mathematics can be proven within that axiom set.

Moreover, a theory that is confirmed by theoretical inner criteria may later be discounted because it fails to fit what we learn of the surround. The correlative relationship between theory and assessment stems from the part-system aspect of analysis that was discussed in chapter 2.

We tend to identify scientific validity with the formal testing of theories or with formal probability analyses. This tendency leads us to underestimate the importance of praxical analysis in helping to determine definitions, relevance, fit, and centrality of logic. It may mislead us badly, especially in the social sciences, where relevance may lie more in diffuse and remote interrelationships and less in inner, more tightly connected parts of a theory.

This does not mean that praxical procedures in the social sciences are not objective or scientific: only that their use is more problematic; the orders they characterize weaker; and second-order analysis more central a feature than in those areas of physics in which theory is strongly ordered. In the social sciences also, implicit and previously preconscious factors become incorporated within explicit and conscious analysis. Here also, relationships among elements are strengthened and clarified and world views are transformed. Here also, at least some aspects of analysis are susceptible to the highly integrated, sharply identified, and clearly relevant identifications with which we are familiar in the physical sciences. However, the mix is different.

The arguments in this chapter show the meaningful character of scientific progress. Einsteinian theory was progressive in a number of senses. It fit the surround of knowledge better. It was confirmed by evidence that disproved the competing Newtonian theory. It was more powerful than competing theories. It is the existence of understandable criteria that makes the concept of scientific progress meaningful, and it is praxical reasoning that distinguishes clear instances of progress from unclear ones.

PRAXIS AND COMMUNICATION

I now propose to integrate the discussion of praxis with the problem of communication raised in the first chapter.

Assessment of fit is not entirely independent of the ability of the transceiver to recognize it. Is Kuhn's ambiguous picture a duck, or is it a rabbit? Does a heliocentric model explain the relationships among the sun and the planets better than a geocentric one?

Relationships can be understood only by those who can perceive them. Some individuals may not be able to switch back and forth, seeing first a duck and then a rabbit, or to see how the trick was devised. To compare the heliocentric and geocentric theories, one must be able to recognize the relationships within each theory as a system of signs and between the theories, physical models, and observations of the real world. Not all can recognize these relationships.

This should not surprise us, for it is true even of simple analytical statements, such as $2 + 2 = 4$ or $a = a$. Countless demonstrations with matchsticks will not demonstrate the first statement to those who cannot perceive the relationship between the numbers or the concept of equality. And, to understand the second statement, one must perceive the a's as identical.

In Irving Langmuir's illuminating essay *Pathological Science*, he cites numerous examples in which scientists, including physicists, mistake the evidence of their senses or misinterpret their instrument readings.[11] The example that is easiest to present briefly and understandably to the reader is that of the mitogenetic ray, which plants were hypothesized to emit. The original experimenter detected such rays. The standard thesis is that replication of the experimental result constitutes proof. Each replication by others produced the same result. Then, a strange thing happened. One experimenter could not produce the result. Subsequent experiments produced results that conformed to an envelope curve, until no experimenter could reproduce the results. This, of course, should give us pause when we consider the results of studies in the social sciences and in the area of morality.

Nevertheless, we can demonstrate objectively that $2 + 2 = 4$. And we make a valid assessment when we assert that relativity theory fits the evidence better than Newtonian theory. Praxical reasoning is not circular, nor is it merely intuitive or confined to the realm of discovery. The confirmation of any logical or statistical procedure also requires recognition and the construction of a web of evidence within which fit can be perceived and valid demonstrations and assessments made.

Indeed, the concept of an error-prone transceiver makes the concept of objectivity meaningful. Think for a moment of a world in which all scientists except one have suffered from brain damage and that this scientist alone knows that water equals H_2O. It remains a truth. Even though science, as a practicable activity, may require community, scientific truth depends upon criteria and not upon consensus or recognition as such. In principle, the failure of a mind to comprehend truth can always be accounted for. Failures may result from brain damage, perceptual or intellectual fallibility, restrictive predispositions, and so forth.

On the other hand, many of these dysfunctions are difficult to detect. And the process of detecting them can never be complete, for, as I argued in chapter 4, concepts always have a preconscious penumbra: there can never be complete communication. Moreover, successful communication depends not merely on the social status of the transceivers but also on their personal predispositions. Unless the latter are also within range, the attempt to communicate will fail. In principle, continued investigation can always bring a particular personal factor into the public arena. In practice, many personal predispositions are so subtle that detection is virtually impossible. Thus, all scientific claims have penumbras that cannot be assessed.

In any event, the fact that preconscious* recognition processes play a role in scientific determination should not occasion surprise. Small children can recognize adults beyond the capabilities of the most sophisticated programmers to replicate in computer recognition programs. And far more sophisticated and complex recognitions are available to the experienced adult. Genius may lie less in the self-conscious capabilities of mind tapped by intelligence tests than in such preconscious processes. It may have been this aspect of mind that Aristotle was aware of when in the *Posterior Analytics* he wrote of the capacity of the mind to recognize true premises, although, according to my analysis, recognition is hypothetical only, no matter how firmly believed. These aspects of judgment are prescientific in the public sense. But they do permit us to specify the literal indicators that are involved in assessments or proofs. These preconscious processes are often stimulated by metaphor. But it is their literal outputs that make them scientific.

I therefore share with intuitionist theorists the position that the knowledge of truth involves the recognition of fit, although my concept of fit is different from theirs. I share with naturalist theorists the view that the character of actual or possible perceptions, whether of facts or of the good, depends upon transactions that involve the transceiver, the transceived, and the environment. I share with verificationist theorists the view that public evidence is crucial to the attribution of truth, although my view of meaning is different from theirs.

---

*Recognition is surely partly pre-self-conscious; but this is a complex subject.

NOTES

1. Charles Sanders Peirce, *Essays in the Philosophy of Science* (New York: Liberal Arts Press, 1957).

2. Carl G. Hempel, *Aspects of Scientific Explanation and Other Essays in the Philosophy of Science* (New York: Free Press of Glencoe, 1965), pp.457 ff.

3. Donald L. Reinken, "Computer Explorations of the 'Balance of Power,' " in *New Approaches to International Relations*, edited by Morton A. Kaplan (New York: St. Martin's Press, 1968), pp. 459 ff.

4. Carl Hempel, *Aspects of Scientific Explanation*.

5. Donald D. Dorfman, Letter to the editor, *Science* 206, no. 4415 (Oct. 12, 1979).

6. Ibid.

7. Richard Dawkins, *The Selfish Gene* (New York: Oxford University Press, 1976).

8. James Chowning Davies, "The J-Curve Theory," *American Political Science Review* 72 (December 1978).

9. Abraham H. Miller, Louis H. Bolce, and Mark Halligan, Letter to the editor, *American Political Science Review* 72 (December 1978).

10. Karl R. Popper, *The Logic of Scientific Discovery* (London: Hutchinson Publishing Group, 1959).

11. I. Langmuir, *Pathological Science*, edited and transcribed by R.N. Hall, *General Electric Technical Information Series*, Report no. 68-C-035 (Schenectady, N.Y.: General Electric Research and Development Center, April 1968).

Chapter 6
Realism and Assessment

Now that I have discussed the roles of theory and of praxis, I intend to examine some alternative positions and to attempt to clarify the meaning of realism. I shall examine Imre Lakatos' position, state my own position on critical experiments, criticize Karl Popper on falsification, argue that confirmation and falsification are intimately related correlative concepts, examine Clark Glymour's position, and relate my position on realism to that of Gerard Radnitzky.

LAKATOS ON THEORY CHOICE

Imre Lakatos distinguished between heuristic or progressive theories and those that are not. For instance, when it was discovered that the orbit of Uranus did not conform to Newton's predictions, scientists either could have rejected Newton's laws or could have projected the existence of a planet beyond Uranus that would account for the discrepancy. They made the latter choice, and Neptune was eventually found. According to Lakatos the resulting theory contained ''a novel auxiliary hypothesis,'' and was ''progressive'' because it predicted something new. Copernican theory, in his view, merely provided a different explanation from that of Ptolemaic theory without predicting any new facts and he rejected its methodology because it merely ''follows in the wake of the facts.''[1]

I believe that the mistake in Lakatos's position lies in his identification of science with theory and in his failure to recognize praxis, or assessment, as a specifiable aspect of scientific procedure. Yet assessment is implicit in his own position in the form of a research program involving a series of theories. It is also implicit in Karl Popper's view that science deals with problems that come to the fore.[2]

Lakatos failed to inquire into the problem that led to the Copernican revolution. Although Copernican theory fit the observed facts no better than the Ptolemaic, it accorded with work in physics that embodied realistic assumptions about the continuous physical movement of the planets and the structure of space, views that are under challenge today, at least at the quantum level. Copernican theory, I believe, was accepted because it fit the entire body of scientific knowledge better on qualitative praxical grounds.

Although Lakatos's concept of progress in theory is a powerful tool, it cannot be used to explain many important shifts in the problems tackled by scientists. Both Lakatos and Popper left virtually untouched the problem of how to identify a problem as a problem. Popper did refer to a form of dogmatism or conservatism—a reluctance to give up beliefs—that is scientifically justified.[3] This, however, makes of assessment a mysterious process. Assessment justifies changed as well as fixed assumptions and is, I believe, a rational and objective technique, even though it is not deductive or inductive in the sense of counting instances for and against.

The assertion that something is a problem that requires resolution depends upon an assessment that refers in some reasoned fashion to other elements of knowledge, even if it cannot be deduced. An atom, for instance, is a mechanical system. We cannot theorize differently about an atomic system and a solar system merely on the basis of *a priori* knowledge. We offer praxical reasons for deciding that differences of scale are essential and that different laws apply, at least in part; and also for praxical reasons, we reject the argument that quantum mechanics constituted a falsification of Newton's theory.

Contrary to what Lakatos argued, assessments of theory *are* made in "the wake of the facts," in this instance, after the discovery that a single set of laws of mechanics does not apply to all physical phenomena (a conclusion that many physicists hope to refute on the basis of new grand unified theories). The distinction had not been required previously. For good reasons, there ensued a praxical assessment, in literal language, that enabled us to understand diverse types of mechanical phenomena and also why they are diverse.

Whether we modify an old theory to take account of new facts, replace it with a new theory, or distinguish different types of phenomena always depends upon a praxical assessment in the literal language: an assessment that is always in the wake of some facts. Although Lakatos, in his concept of progressiveness in theory took some account of this—and although his distinctions of "hard core," "auxiliary hypotheses," and "investigative heuristics" constitute a powerful methodology—I think that they fail to capture all that is involved in the shifting of problems and that he too easily separated research from the general framework of science.

The relevant aspects of the entire framework of science are embedded in praxical assessment. It determines what we accept as evidence, why we insist on some distinctions and not others, why we accept a result as a falsification in one case and not in another, and so forth. Although statistical methods are sometimes used, statistics cannot be used independently to demonstrate an assessment. Every statistical method or procedure rests on assumptions about interpretation and application, including decisions about sampling and classification. The justification of these assumptions and their application to a particular case rest upon praxical procedures, at least some of which are not statistical. Like the rest of science, statistical methods and procedures are qualified by praxical judgments.

There are problems that are so tightly structured, so amenable to quantitative treatment, and so independent of contextual variation that probabilistic reconstructions or calculations of utility may seem obvious. Usually, however, as in the "rat man" case in a subsequent section, the red shift problem discussed earlier, and other difficult problems of praxical assessment, *post hoc* conclusions based on probability obscure much of the important information on which the judgment was based.

ASSESSMENT AND CRITICAL EXPERIMENTS

When that part of the realm of knowledge that forms the immediate environment for a particular experiment is both complete and, according to the current wisdom, known to be true, for all practical purposes there may be a critical experiment in the sense that it both confirms a particular hypothesis and disconfirms its competitors. Although future investigation may eventually cast doubt on the completeness or accuracy of the stated boundary conditions—and therefore on whether or not the experiment was in fact a critical experiment—most scientists, as contrasted with philosophers of science, would argue that some experiments can be considered critical. The argument that there is no such thing as a "narrow hit," that is, an experiment that is virtually critical—the argument that Lakatos tried to defeat with his concept of sophisticated falsification[4]—is misleading, but I come to this conclusion from my own perspective.

POPPER ON FALSIFICATION

Popper argued that the principle of inductive confirmation leads to the conclusion that no law can have greater than zero probability because the actual confirmations are lost in the infinity of possible confirmations. Indeed, if one uses as a standard the proportion of confirmations of a theory to its falsifications, then a hypothesis that has been decisively falsified may be regarded as highly probable. For instance, because all conceivable things can be classified as (1) non-ravens and black ravens and (2) non-black ravens, the instances of the second class must be infinitely smaller than of the first. Thus, a white raven would hardly count against the innumerable confirmations. Hence, Popper's objection.[5]

Rudolf Carnap, who argued for the criterion of confirmation, however, might have argued that Popper confuses probability with degree of confirmation in Carnap's system while elsewhere sharply distinguishing the two concepts. Carnap's concept of inductive confirmation itself seems to imply a quantitative concept of relevance that I find opaque.[6]

In any event, relevance is not a logical property and can be understood only with respect to the larger body of knowledge. Popper's purely logical operation of exhausting the universe of evidence definitionally precluded considerations of relevance and led to his argument that a theory has zero probability on the basis of induction. But if relevant instances and good reasons circumscribe the use of evidence, that conclusion need not follow.

Popper tried to save his position by arguing that a decision to accept evidence as correct is permissible when dealing with observations of facts—for otherwise theories could not be falsified—as if facts were not subject to interpretation also.

But even if one were inclined to accept this evasion—if observations are more reliable than theories, why not prefer them?—the position ultimately is untenable. Theories are not falsified by simple observation in many cases. The correct characterization of an observation often involves complicated and sophisticated reliance on how an experimental apparatus works and on other theories not under immediate test.*

It is true that we cannot know that our range of knowledge is a representative sample of all possible knowledge. We cannot even specify operationally what we mean by the latter concept. Thus, when we estimate the reliability of a particular sample space in our world, we have made assumptions about the representative character of our entire range of experience. It is true that these assumptions cannot be confirmed, for no increments in our range of knowledge can begin to exhaust all possible knowledge. In this limited sense, Popper is right to argue for the criterion of falsification. We accept our range of experience as the equivalent of all possible experience until that assumption is falsified. But that is not how we treat the evidence that supports a theory. We recognize degrees of likelihood, even if not of probability in a frequency sense. To put the matter more precisely and also in the language of chapter 1, the information in the part system not under examination—and this includes external criteria for observations—is accepted until falsified and the information in the part system under examination is evaluated. This includes the consideration, depending on circumstances, of comparative likelihood; and this evidence, in this sense, confirms propositions and theories.

Two kinds of problems need to be distinguished when discussing the confidence with which an assessment can be relied upon. The first is represented by whether an advanced civilization elsewhere in the universe would seek us out and, hence, whether the failure to learn of it establishes that no such civilization exists. We have no good way of assessing whether such a civilization would have discovered a theory of physics that subsumes many of the implications of relativity theory while permitting a faster than light drive or whether it would be motivated to reveal itself if explorers from it did visit us. Assessments of this kind of problem are "subjective" in the terms of some theories of probability but objective, although tenuous and idiosyncratic, in my terms.

Distinguish the former example from that of whether Hitler was going to make a pact with the Soviet Union in 1939. There were good reasons to have confidence in an assessment that he was; and I made such an assessment publicly as a first-year college student. Most of the factors relevant to that assessment were widely known. Assessments in the visitors-from-outer-space example might turn out to be correct and in the Nazi–Soviet example to be wrong. But that does not change the tenuous character of the first type of assessment or reduce warranted confidence in the second. In the example of the visitors from outer

---

*See the example in chapter 1, in which theory does call observation into question.

space, we know that our knowledge, both of the factors relevant to an assessment and of their impact, is dwarfed by our ignorance.*

In the Hitler–Stalin example, praxical reasoning reveals a fit between the assessment and other part systems of the realm of knowledge and compares the factors involved in similar and different cases. This warrants reasonable confidence that we know both what the relevant factors are and how they impact on the issue.

An even better example is that of relativity theory. The fit of relativity theory with other part systems of the realm of knowledge provides a dense web of interconnections that warrants great confidence in applications of the theory. Popper's criterion of falsification does not permit these distinctions between types of examples.

Only confirmation in this latter sense can account for many scientific and practical decisions. When the decision was made to spend billions of dollars on the Manhattan Project to develop nuclear weapons—although it was believed that relativity theory some day would be falsified—reliance was placed on the likelihood that, even after falsification, it would remain at least as adequate as Newtonian theory is for calculations within solar distances. Such reliance may fail, but falsifications also may prove to be faulty after reinterpretation.

Popper's criterion of falsification avoids the issue of relevance: How was the observation made? On what basis do we assert that a white bird is not a raven? On what basis would the colors of birds that are not ravens be relevant to the color of ravens? Only answers to these and other relevant questions permit us to determine that a falsification has been made. But these answers cannot be given by simple description. They depend on the relevant areas of knowledge, including both inner, or theoretical, considerations, and external, or praxical, considerations. Therefore, although it makes good sense to ask an ornithologist, not how many black ravens he has seen but whether he has seen any white ravens, it does not follow that every problem has a form that makes falsification the correct mode of inquiry.

Falsification and confirmation are inherently correlative. I cannot conceive of one in the absence of the other. How can there be a falsification unless some conditions are accepted as confirmed by experience, e.g., that a telescope really permits one to explore the heavens? How can there be a confirmation without at least a potential falsification, e.g., that if I am pinched I will discover that the scene I was seeing was a dream?

An experiment that confirms one hypothesis often falsifies some competitors. Suppose, however, that only one theory permits a particular prediction to be

---

*In examples in which we cannot rely upon assessment but need to make decisions related to alternative possible assessments, we need to evaluate the potential consequences of relying upon the alternative assessments. These are problems of decision making under conditions of uncertainty. Decisions under certainty and uncertainty, of course, are correlatives; and no example is either as such.

made and that is confirmed. Does this not raise our confidence in it over those of competitors, if it is at least as good as them in other respects?

Almost all theories are falsified by some evidence. Shall we reject them? For instance, there is much experimental evidence that is inconsistent with the theory of relativity. It makes more sense, within the contemporary framework of science, to believe that this evidence is in error or that some way will be found to show its consistency with relativity theory than to regard relativity theory as falsified. However, a single replicated experiment that proved that the gravitational constant is weakening would likely result in the rejection of relativity theory because, in the present state of knowledge, it would hit at a central element of the theory's logic.

Whereas Carnap's theory necessitates the procedure of confirmation exclusively and Popper's necessitates that of falsification exclusively, I am arguing against any necessity for the exclusive employment of either. Each case must be considered on its own merits according to praxical criteria. That is why falsifications are sometimes regarded as insignificant and sometimes as critical. That is also why some confirmations, even though they fall within the range of experimental error, may lead to changes in theories.

CLARK GLYMOUR'S BOOTSTRAP THEORY

What Clark Glymour meant by *bootstrap* is that the existing body of science determines both the independent confirmation of individual hypotheses within theories and the relevance of evidence; science, thus, advances by way of its bootstraps.[7] His account accords, in these respects, with the concept of praxical assessment advanced both in this book and in previous works. It seems to differ insofar as confirmation appears to be a yes-or-no procedure and insofar as the concept of fit appears to be irrelevant. In these respects it is a cousin to the Hempelian hypothetico-deductive, or covering-law, model.

Glymour basically asserted a triadic relationship among theories, individual hypotheses, and evidence that is more complex than in the covering-law model. He asserted (more complexly than here stated) that the greater the number of individual theorems or hypotheses within a theory that are confirmed independently, the better the confirmation of the theory. A theory is preferred over another in which fewer individual theorems are independently confirmed. This is very close to Radnitzky's position that a hypothesis added to a theory is not *ad hoc* if it has independently survived attempts at falsification and to his preference for theories that have survived attempted falsifications of more individual hypotheses.[8]

Glymour's reasons for preferring Copernican theory to Ptolemaic included the arguments that Copernican theory permits some determinations of planetary relations that Ptolemaic theory leaves indeterminate and that it explains others that are simply empirical in the Ptolemaic model. The latter is one of Popper's important criteria.[9]

All of Glymour's examples in support of his bootstrap theory, with one exception soon to be noted, dealt with single central theories that are themselves well confirmed by the present state of knowledge. And many of the theorems within the theories are confirmed by independent evidence. Glymour avoided Lakatos's error, for he allowed for the substitution of subsidiary hypotheses within a theory on the basis of independent evidence even in the wake of the facts.

The one example that is not well confirmed is his discussion of Freud's "rat man."[10] The patient was an obsessional neurotic who feared that his father and a woman he loved would be eaten by rats unless he engaged in compulsive rituals. It is an interesting example in that it demonstrates the limitations of Glymour's approach. When there is an important degree of interdependence between a theory and the weighing of evidence, or when various theories bear upon the evidence and its interrelationships, the covering-law model, even in Glymour's sophisticated version, as I shall now argue, founders because it fails to do justice to the complicated relationships among theory, evidence, and hypothesis.

Glymour argued that Freud stated his analysis poorly, and I agree. He also argued that the analysis can be sustained, and with this I do not wholly agree. The question revolves around the rat man's suppressed sexual memories and whether they are the source of the patient's unconscious hatred of his father. Item one in Glymour's case is Freud's proof of infantile masturbation. There is indirect evidence of feelings of guilt about the father's death, direct evidence of the fear of conscious recollection of the father's death, indirect evidence of an unconscious wish for the father's death, and direct evidence of punishment for masturbation and of conflict with the father before the patient was six years old. This is a good bootstrap case. But suppose the unconscious wish for the father's death covered up love for the father and repressed homosexuality. Suppose the punishment for masturbation was experienced as masochistic pleasure. I need not go on. In the end, the hypothesis must rest on simplicity, on interconnections with loosely related but relevant hypotheses, and on the techniques used to assess evidence. The situation is not really different in the physical sciences, as I argued in the last chapter, except that Glymour's scientific examples are so well-confirmed by present evidence that we tend to ignore this limitation when considering them.

What Glymour did—and it is a significant accomplishment—is provide a sophisticated account of theory that hews closely to the confines of covering-law models and that provides criteria for the simplicity of theories and for their confirmation.

However, Glymour's contention that the theory containing more confirmed hypotheses is the better theory fails to account for the fact that much contrary experimental evidence is often dismissed as mistaken. Moreover, the number of confirmed hypotheses is only one of the relevant considerations. He did not address the fact that some contrary evidence, if produced, may be extremely difficult to dismiss or, conversely, the fact that some hypotheses may be more central than others, and their confirmation more crucial. The proportion of confirmed hypotheses, and also the relative absence of anomalies, are merely *ceteris paribus* considerations. Other criteria, and likely more important criteria, are related to other relevant aspects of knowledge in a denser way than Glymour's admittedly partial criterion, in a way that can be understood only praxically.

The less clear the centrality of a single theory, the more subject to dispute the relevance of evidence, and the greater the interdependence of theory and evidence, then the more all hypothetico-deductive accounts of scientific method, even Glymour's version, distort the character of scientific reasoning. And when the centrality of a theory, the strength of the evidence for it, and the lack of satisfactory alternatives characterize the area of inquiry, even less sophisticated versions of the covering-law approach are quite satisfactory.

Glymour argued against what he called *de-occamized theories*. Simply put, a de-occamized theory is one with more numerous hypotheses than an occamized theory but with identical predictions. (The reference is to Occam's razor.) Since more complex theories always have fewer of their hypotheses confirmed than simpler versions, they are better, he said. This seems to me to hypostatize notational systems.

If a hypothesis has a real world reference, if only in terms of a thought experiment,* then most of Glymour's examples are more complex only in terms of their use of signs; and I would deny that they contain more hypotheses. In any event, as I shall argue, it is the relationship between the internal and external criteria for truth, rather than the proportion of confirmed hypotheses of a theory, that is crucial to praxical judgment. Suppose, for instance, that one theory employs the concept of gravity and a second employs $(a + b)$, which functions exactly like gravity in a theory that otherwise differs in no way from the first theory. I see no reason to call one theory better than the other except on aesthetic grounds, unless at least a thought experiment could distinguish gravity from $(a + b)$.

Let us take a second example that does not seem as silly. There could be alternative Newtonian theories in which space is dense or continuous. Mathematically, these geometries are both valid and distinct from each other. When they are applied to the world, no differences in predictions ensue. Although one geometry may be more complex than the other and more difficult to compute, it is not foolish to consider the more complex alternative. It has geometric interest, and it warns us against hypostatizing the continuous concept of space.

Of course, both the difference between $(a + b)$ and gravity, and between continous and dense space, may give rise to assertions about real differences in the world if the state of knowledge changes. Until then, $(a + b)$ seems merely

---

Maxwell's demon is an example of a thought experiment by the famous British physicist, James Clerk Maxwell, that was designed to elucidate what a perpetual motion machine would require. Consider two containers with doors and filled with gas of the same average temperature. If and only if there were a demon with infinite speed of movement and with such precise and immediate perception that he could distinguish between fast and slow particles, could he open and close the doors to particles in a way that would increase the average temperature. Maxwell's thought experiment makes clear that the conditions for a perpetual motion machine cannot be met in the real world.

equivalent to gravity and there is no reason to hypothesize it. On the other hand, there is no reason to assert that real space is dense or continuous though geometric spaces do differ in this respect. Thus, it does make sense to say that real space may be indeterminate in this respect.

Matters are different when we test for simplicity theories that have different real-world implications. Here, the more complex theory or assessment creates progressive disturbances in the part systems from which the external criteria for empirical truth are drawn.

Let us see how simplicity can be determined at the level of concrete processes. With respect to "paranoid" hypotheses, note that we employ reasons that are independent of the paranoid hypothesis: that is, we argue from the surround. So many witnesses could not be lying. A psychiatrist would not behave that way. There is independent evidence that the clerk was really trying to return money and not to trap the paranoid person into a confession. That was not really a gun but only a bulge in the pocket.

We can always reinterpret data to fit paranoid hypotheses. However, the paranoid hypothesis will require so much refitting that it will be in disjunction with external criteria, that is, with our understanding of how the world works, an assessment for which we have much independent evidence.

In this context, occamized and de-occamized theories are not notational equivalents. There are substantive reasons for rejecting one of them. In fact, new evidence is likely to complicate further the de-occamized theory. On the other hand, when new evidence supports the seemingly paranoid hypothesis and resolves the doubts that attended it, the thesis formerly considered paranoid may begin to seem correct. Further evidence will tend to fit it and to force progressive complications of what had earlier appeared to be the simpler theory or hypothesis.

A paranoid hypothesis, although it accounts for the same data as non-paranoid hypotheses, implies real, and not merely notational, differences in the world. The difference between the two is, in general, that new facts will require theoretical convolutions of the paranoid hypothesis. But non-paranoid hypotheses will fit with assessments that are made according to external criteria.

Some have interpreted Quine's proof that alternative theories can always be constructed for the same set of facts to imply that no grounds exist for choosing from among them. I doubt that Quine intended this conclusion, and it is wrong for reasons that the preceding discussion addresses. In principle, one theory is likely to prevail unless the area is weakly ordered or there is insufficient information to support a determination. There is no good reason to believe the radical interpretation of his position: that we will never have sufficiently good reasons to elevate one theory over its rivals. That supposition neglects differences between internal and external criteria.

THE CONVENTIONAL AND NATURAL ASPECTS OF THEORIES

Alternate equivalent notational formulations are conventional with respect to each other but natural in their implications and in those aspects of the theoretical or praxical formulations that do not involve these notational differences. One must distinguish those aspects of theories or assessments that are primarily *conventional*—e.g., number systems based on 2 or 10, a geometry based on continuous or discontinuous space, or rules of the road that differ in different countries—from those in which the *natural* aspects are predominant—true laws of physics or moral rules that meet human requirements. Alternative rules of morality that differ in substance but are of equivalent value are thus not conventional unlike the roles of the road, but natural, even though they have conventional aspects. But then, the rule that there be a rule of the road is not conventional, either, but natural. "Natural" and "conventional" are correlatives; neither concept can be understood apart from the other.

RELATIONSHIP TO RADNITZKY'S POSITION

How does the position expressed in this book differ from the important formulations of Gerard Radnitzky?[11] We both regard the positivistic philosophy, with its emphasis on certainty, as faulty. And to the extent that instrumentalism is correlated with epistemological idealism, we agree in rejecting it. In any event, I regard the idealism-vs.-realism debate as misleading and prefer to think in terms of the correlatives, "potentiality" and "manifest."

Although I am, therefore, in firm disagreement with those instrumentalists who accept an epistemological idealism (or its correlative, materialism), I do agree with them that no sharp boundary can be drawn between the observer and the observed. This follows from the fact that any statement that is made about the manifest world is a statement about a transaction. All statements about properties refer to transactions: e.g., "this sweater is blue" depends upon the physical characteristics of the sweater, the perceiver, and the observational system; "this coin is malleable" depends on the coin, the laboratory, and the instruments of pressure. We cannot make statements about manifest existence that are independent of at least indirect or potential transactions. In this respect, I hark back to Peirce's pragmaticism or to use a more pronounceable noun, pragmatics.[12]

If this transactional process is what Radnitzky means by "a more correct representation of facts" than another statement ("*eine zeitreffendere Darstellung als*"), we are in agreement. If, however, he literally means "a more accurate representation than a sentence competing with it," then we disagree; for this seems to imply that a sentence corresponds to reality, element for element.[13]

I am aware that Radnitzky and some other philosophers believe that the concepts of correspondence and verisimilitude can be divorced from claims that knowledge copies reality. Radnitzky, I assume, would agree that we do not compare the word "green" in a sentence with a green in a color chart, but we may compare a green object with a green in a color chart. Presumably one could compare models of solar systems with physical theories and predictions drawn from those theories with real-world observations. This would involve a second-order relationship in which the model is deemed to represent the real world because the theory generates a realistic model of the real world and gives rise to true predictions about that world. Although the theory would not represent the world directly, in a sense such theories *are* representational. Moreover, when the predictions yielded by a theory are better in some specifiable and literal sense than those of competing theories, these theories may be said to be closer to the truth. However, this last sense of representation and verisimilitude is highly qualified. Moreover, there are important limits beyond which it is misleading.

Consider a portrait and a sketch of a face. The face is often more recognizable in the sketch than in the portrait, unless it is really excellent, although the portrait may be more accurate in its details. Caricatures, to extend the example, gain superior recognizability *because* they are deliberately exaggerated.

The concept "closer to the truth" is not meaningful with respect to choices among theories except when limited to specific ranges of observation, as in measurements of astronomic distances based on either Einsteinian or Newtonian physics. Implicit in the idea of closer to the truth is a limit that can be approached more and more closely, even if never reached in fact, and the corollary idea of a measure or scale. But "closer to the truth" does not mean what the mathematician means by "approaching a limit." What the astrophysicist means is that, for instance, by standards of measurement that are neutral between the two theories, calculations made according to Einsteinian theory would bring an interstellar navigator closer to a target than would calculations made according to Newtonian theory. No concept of an absolute measure is involved, for the concepts are relative and transactional.

As the previous example shows, the concept of verisimilitude functions metaphorically rather than literally. Let us take a related example. We can construct a physical model of a solar system or an analog computer model that employs the laws of physics and that is programmed for initial conditions that correspond to the inferred locations of the planets in the physical model. We can then compare changes in both with astronomical measurements. There is, however, no direct comparison between the models and the solar system. The correspondences have meaning only within a specific second-order frame of reference.

Perhaps the issue can be made even clearer by moving to examples that are not as simple, as determinate, or as strongly ordered as in macromechanics. Bohr's concept of complementarity was that position and momentum cannot be measured simultaneously, for measurements of position require rigid instruments and measurements of momentum require instruments with moving parts. (Note that "moving" and "rigid" are correlatives and, thus, are not such in themselves.) Assertions about either are meaningful only if a choice is made from among alternative modes of measurement.[14] Furthermore, predictions from either framework are probabilistic and can be tested only by classes of events.

When we move to choices from among competing theories, the range of observations of relevant theories, information, and criteria we bring to bear is determined by praxical reasoning at the literal level. This is not a quantitative, statistical, or probabilistic matter even though quantities, statistics, or probability may play a role in praxical reasoning. And it is certainly not a matter of point-by-point correspondence. It is not correct in general, therefore, to say that Einsteinian physics is closer to the truth than Newtonian mechanics. We may, however, say that there are better reasons to believe that it is true or that it is true in more, or more important, respects. Truth is not an absolute attribution; and its meaning changes with context.

Thus, it makes sense to say that a theory is true if, according to the contemporary state of knowledge, we can regard it as true on praxical grounds, even though the history of science leads us to expect that eventually all theories are superseded by others. Of course, some theories may present so many difficulties that we will regard them not as true but as merely useful for some restricted purposes. And they may be better or worse than rival theories in this respect.

Even apart from the fact, noted in my discussion of Kripke in chapter 4, that the references of names, or signs, will depend both on the surround of knowledge and on the purposes of investigations, the available evidence strongly supports the view that the scope of many competing theories cannot be so closely matched that the concept of "closer to the truth" is meaningful.

The concept of "verisimilitude" can often be used as if it had literal meaning, but this is so only within a specific frame of reference and with respect to particular aspects of reference. Taken literally, however, *verisimilitude* is a more and more accurate and internally consistent account that matches coherently and univocally an external world that is independent of transactions with it. In short, the advocates of verisimilitude accept, at least implicitly, the idea of coherence, although on grounds that are opposite to those of Hegel and Marx. Instead of being surprised that they cannot produce an algorithm that will permit a literal account of verisimilitude, they should give up the notion, for it misrepresents how we know things. Whatever is valid in the notion can be better accounted for by praxical reasoning.

POTENTIALITY AND REALISM

Newton's laws were neither observable phenomena nor physical models. With respect to observations, they specified invariant potentialities that determined the values of the properties of certain kinds of phenomena once the initial conditions were given. Praxical criteria determined the definitions, measuring instruments, experiments, and so forth that permitted Newton's theory to be used within the transactional realm.

To gain perspective on inner potentiality as a referent of Newtonian laws, let us turn to society. Think of a financial institution such as a bank. The personnel, e.g., teller, lending officer, and so forth, and their functions, e.g., accepting deposits, making loans, and so forth, are part of a standardized system. Except as a system of signs that has potentialities as its referents, the operations of a bank cannot be understood. The performance of the personnel of a bank is also standardized: we know the functions of each member of its staff, and expect, for example, that a loan officer will inquire into our finances and that a teller will not. These potentialities of roles may be thought of as subroutines in the minds of the role holders, subroutines that are subject to conflicts with other subroutines and that vary with environmental conditions. Also, there are criteria that permit us to identify a bank, a loan officer, a deposit, and so forth, as real entities in a real world and, because it is a bank, as a relatively stable entity.

Newton's laws may be analyzed similarly, except that the laws have as referent a routine not a subroutine, and except that they do not operate through minds. Criteria for the identification of bodies and so forth also exist. Similar criteria apply to waves in the ocean or to the path of a projectile. In effect, we have what might be called a situational or local representation, one that may be perceived alternatively as a structure or thing and as a process.

Now think of the quantum wave equations as a sign system with a routine as its referent. Some experiments give rise to interference patterns like those of a wave, others to patterns that would be made by a particle. But while we may state that ocean waves created the pattern of interference that was observed, we cannot say that photonic waves did, for we have no independent criteria for identifying such waves. The same is true of the particle-like behavior of photons. Thus, although we may take a realistic view of the referents of quantum wave equations as routines, that is, as dispositional potentialities, photonic waves and photonic particles are metaphors, at least in the current state of knowledge. We are observing the smile but not the cat.

Einstein speculate that the quantum wave equations were not completely descriptive. I wish to reach the same conclusion from a somewhat different perspective. The behavior of particles is *dispositional*, as I use that term—that is, it varies with context. Heisenberg's principle of indeterminacy explains the inherent lack of full determination at the quantum level.

Full information is not possible in a world in which all knowledge is qualified by some frame of reference. The concept of full information or complete description implies the existence of a concrete reality that is independent of the information about it. But, instead, ''concrete'' and ''potential'' are correlatives, an axis by means of which we characterize experience.

Some physicists deny that we can speak of the polarization of a photon except at the experimental termini. The reason is that current experiments with quanta provide no possibility of a hypothetical transceiver or even of a thought experiment, except at the termini. Therefore, polarization in the ''path'' between the termini is a metaphor or even a fiction. However, the denial of a photon and path between the termini may be relevant only to a world view that utilizes the concept of verisimilitude. Is it not meaningful to assert the existence of a photon and a path if, for any shortening or lengthening of the path, the photon would be detected? The path and photon then would be conceived of not as reified entities but as transactional potentialities. I must admit, however, that whereas the ocean wave has a definite path the photonic path—which is not a sharp curve but a more or less broad beam or wave—lacks this and is indeterminate as well.

When I speak of a photon as real, I do not imply that it can be observed as it is (whatever that means) but that its existence produces differences in the world that, at least hypothetically, can be distinguished from those of a world in which it does not exist. When scientists speak of conditions in a black hole, even though these cannot be perceived, they are postulating a theory that accounts for some observable effects of the black hole, asserting that this theory is consistent with other relevant physical theory, other relevant aspects of the physical world, and concluding that these non-observable consequences are real inside the hole in a world in which this theory is true.

I believe that one of the reasons that Radnitzky preferred to talk about correspondence was the fear that, in the absence of such a concept, we would deprive the world of meaning that is independent of particular observers. In short, is there thunder in the absence of a being who hears it? Sound requires a transceiver. Is the tree there in the absence of an observer? All its individual and holistic qualitative characteristics—and in their absence no quantitative characteristics can be developed—require some form of transceiver for their meaning.

If I understand the problem correctly, then Charles Sanders Peirce long ago pointed to its solution. What I mean, for instance, when I say that the thunder or the tree exists independently, is that, were a person or any appropriate observer present, he or she would hear the thunder, observe the tree, or engage in transactions such that the process of thunder or the entity of the tree would need to be hypothesized. The potentialities are real and the concrete aspects would be real if appropriate transceivers were present. This is not an idealistic position.

When I say that a person would hear the thunder if he or she were there at the time, the concepts of "person," "there," and "time of thunder" are all transactional. Phenomenologically, there are no transactions in the absence of transceivers, except potentially.

Take the case of the famous murdered quantum cat. Is it dead before someone perceives it? In the absence of a transceiver, the cat, if it were a quantum phenomenon, would be dead with a certain probability and alive with a certain probability.* Is the problem different from the one posed by the quantum photon? A definite position or velocity is meaningful only when a transaction takes place; the quantum equations state only probabilities. The important difference from ordinary quantum problems is that the potential observability of the quantum cat is established by its death. But in both instances the potential and the concrete are correlatives. To ask what the manifest condition of the cat is when it is not perceived or what the position of the photon is when it is not transacted is to ask the wrong question. Eugene Wigner is correct in refusing to make the distinction between the quantum and the observable condition. We can, however, ask what the condition of the cat would be in the presence of a perceiver; because this is a macrophysical event, it is not probabilistic, except peripherally. The

---

*Erwin Schrödinger, whose wave equations heralded a major advance in quantum mechanics, argued that there was no dead cat until there was a macrophysical observation. If this position is pushed farther, it can lead to the multiple worlds hypothesis that John A. Wheeler advanced and then abandoned.

issue is whether all potential transactions about which we speak fit at both the first-order and second-order levels. We must first specify a universe in which these questions are meaningful and then specify the alternative transactions that permit us to speak of fit. When we do so, the problem is not there.

The meaning of something lies in its potentiality to be understood by transceiving systems, a process that, as I argued earlier, includes but is not reducible to perceptual data. In principle, we can construct a second-order language in terms of which first-order differences in perception can be related to a common reality. This is not a matter of convergence to a true picture, but a matter of finding a better and better statement of the nature of reality.

CONSCIOUSNESS, APPEARANCES, AND REALISM

Some modern writers, including some followers of Popper, have argued that we do not know things-in-themselves, but only appearances: that is, only things as they are represented in an evolutionary product, consciousness. But what is a thing-in-itself? The concrete is the correlative of the potential; the thing, of the process; the second-order, of the first-order; and so forth. Hegel pointed to the solution of this problem—and the origin of the pragmaticist test is present in his system—but he had an inadequate account of signs.*

Potentialities that generate processes are real parts of this real world. A negative theory of representation underlies Kant's view that there is a world-in-itself that consciousness merely represents.

However, I believe that consciousness presents the manifest aspects of the real world and that reflexive consciousness—that is, consciousness of consciousness—presents it at a second-order level. At this level, we can assert knowledge of a world of potentialities for which there is evidence. These first- and second-order presentations are relative to the presenting system. Second-order, or neutral, presentations resolve the contradictions between different first-order systems. There is no such thing as an exclusive presenting system and no such thing as a thing-in-itself. Mystical terms such as "the One" reify known and unknown potentialities by implying the existence of an unknowable but complete entity.

Thinghood, process, and potentiality are different phases of an evolving reality and are accounted for by different part systems in the course of analysis. There is no real but transcendent world that is merely represented in these accounts. But there may be radically different presenting systems, the accounts of which would force radical transformations in our second-order accounts if communication of such radically different first-order systems were possible.

---

*Marxists, as I shall argue in Part Four, founder on this early nineteenth-century philosophical error, as well as on the coherence theory and the concept of the concrete universal they took over from Hegel.

NOTES

1. Imre Lakatos, "Falsification and the Methodology of Scientific Research Pro-
   grammes," in *Criticism and the Growth of Knowledge*, edited by Imre Lakatos and
   Alan Musgrave (Cambridge: Cambridge University Press, 1970), pp. 118 ff.

2. Karl Popper, *Unended Quest: An Intellectual Autobiography* (Glasgow: William
   Collins Sons & Co., 1976), pp. 44 ff.

3. Ibid., pp. 170 ff.

4. Lakatos, "Falsification and Methodology," pp. 118 ff.

5. Karl Popper, *The Logic of Scientific Discovery* (London: Hutchinson Publishing
   Group, 1958).

6. Paul Schlipp, *The Library of Living Philosophers*, vol. 2, *The Philosophy of Rudolf
   Carnap* (LaSalle, Ill.: Open Court Publishing Co., 1963).

7. Clark Glymour, *Theory and Evidence* (Princeton: Princeton University Press, 1980),
   pp. 110 ff., 178 ff.

8. Gerard Radnitzky, "Progress and Rationality in Research," in *On Scientific Dis-
   covery*, edited by M. D. Grmek, R. S. Cohen, and G. Cimino (Dordrecht, Holland:
   D. Reidel Publishing Co., 1980), pp. 71 and 61 ff. See also Morton A. Kaplan,
   Macropolitics: Essays on the Philosophy and Science of Politics (Chicago: Aldine
   Publishing Co., 1969), pp. 14–15.

9. See Radnitzky, "Progress and Rationality."

10. Glymour, *Theory and Evidence*, pp. 265 ff.

11. Gerard Radnitzky, "Justifying a Theory vs. Giving Good Reasons for Preferring a
    Theory: On the Big Divide in the Philosophy of Science," in *The Structure and
    Development of Science*, edited by Gerard Radnitzky and G. Anderson, Boston
    Studies in the Philosophy of Science (Dordrecht, Holland: D. Reidel Publishing Co.,
    1981).

12. Charles Sanders Peirce, *Essays in the Philosophy of Science*, (New York: Liberal
    Arts Press, 1957).

13. Radnitzky, "Justifying a Theory."

14. Max Born, *Physics and Politics* (Edinburgh: Oliver & Boyd, 1962), pp. 55 ff.

Chapter 7
Indeterminacy, Intentionality, and Consciousness

INDETERMINACY

The world is neither determinate nor indeterminate as such. What is structure in one framework of analysis is process in another; what is precise in one framework of analysis is imprecise in another; what is determinate in one framework of analysis is indeterminate in another. The determinism of the syllogism or calculation, for instance is bounded by the indeterminism of the assessment that justifies its use; and use of an indeterminate assessment presumes a determinate logic. The idea that the world is either determinate or indeterminate as such stems from a faulty representational theory of signs: that signs match or correspond with reality rather than that they characterize it correlatively.

An element of indeterminacy invests all human activity, even in the physical sciences. But it needs to be stated properly. Even simple measurements in classical physics are never exact, that is, they are never without measurement error. Moreover, the state of the instruments affects the calculations. In principle, any error in measurement can be diminished and any indeterminacy that results from the state of the instruments may be taken account of by a more powerful apparatus. Thus, it may seem that classical physics is determinate in principle.

However, the process is infinite. Because it is, the apparent complete determinism of classical physics is misleading. As Karl Popper has noted, the state of the last set of instruments, at any stage of calculation, is never part of the calculation. Inclusion of it in a further calculation changes the calculation, and so on.[1] Metaphorically, this is the moment of freedom for the experimenter; for the conclusion of a calculation is a factor in a new calculation. Hence, the experimenter's reasoning is at least partly open and, to that extent, not fully determined.

The moment of freedom is also a moment of creativity. Although part of the processing that produces this creative result is preconscious, in the sense that a scanning and assessment process is going on to which the self-reflexively conscious mind has little if any direct access, complete access would not reveal the

83

result prior to the processing. Thus, the result must always, if only in a residual sense, be novel.

Even this mode of analysis understates the character of the moment of freedom. The result is derived from a preexisting mode of analysis. This is the correct form for certain types of retrodiction in mechanics. In other areas, however—even in physics—theoretical and praxical analyses invoke novelty when the framework of analysis has been altered. The new framework itself can be assessed only in the altered light of the new elements in the field of knowledge and vice versa.

This is the limited sense in which the existentialist argument has cogency. However, to the extent that the existentialist position denies an *ex post facto* assessment that relates the novel result to the prior state of the world, including human nature, it makes purely idiosyncratic something that has deep natural roots. These roots are stronger than in chance evolutionary mutations, the advantages of which can be explained *post factum*; for these novelties in human behavior and character are constrained by, although not deductively determined by, preexisting potentialities.

John von Neumann suggested that the preconscious process operates according to a more reliable but less precise code than that of the conscious language,[2] or by some as yet undetermined but analogous procedure. If so, metaphor would likely be the method by which genuinely, and not merely residual, novel rearrangements of the pattern of perceiving events would be produced. By dramatizing for the conscious mind the praxical considerations of consistency, similarity and difference, centrality of logic, and so forth, metaphor would initiate the development of a publicly communicable assessment that could be compared at a second-order level with alternative ways of ordering, accounting for, and assessing experience. Metaphor would ignite the creative spark in an environment that is at least partly ambiguous. Science, whether theoretical or praxical, involves the articulation of the metaphorical pattern into the kind of explicit literal language that permits the objective procedures of science to be employed.

There is another way of viewing indeterminism in history—an indeterminism that provides the medium for freedom, creative novelty, and scientific progress—that may be even more revealing and that has been explored by Robert G. Sachs.[3] The laws of physics are generally regarded as invariant with respect to time or space. For instance, if one photographs the mirror image of the path of a moving object, then, by duplicating all the initial conditions of the photograph, the result will replicate what was seen in the mirror.

The same invariance will not be observed if one constructs a permanent magnet with a uniform magnetic field and shoots an electrically charged particle from the side into the field. In this instance, one may conclude that time-reversal invariance is violated. Or one may conclude that the magnetic field of the permanent magnet is produced "by motion of particles within the iron rather than by stationary particles of a particular magnetic pole strength," in which case the lack of symmetry results from a failure to make the appropriate changes in the initial conditions of the motion of the particles. The second explanation is confirmed praxically by evidence that magnetic fields are generated by the motion of electric charges and that they are reversed when the motions of the charges are reversed.[4] Consider, however, more complex systems such as a motion picture in which four blocks of wood are placed in a stack, knocked over, and then each caught by one of four individuals. As Robert Sachs points out, if this picture is played back from the end to the beginning, the viewers will know immediately that they are watching a photographic trick because

> . . . there are such a vast number of ways in which the actors can throw four bricks [that] the probability of their finding just that one precise way needed for the stunt is extremely small. Thus, the incredibility may be equated to improbability.

When dealing with more complex systems, "there is much greater incredibility attached to the probability for reversal of a motion from an ordered to a disordered arrangement." In such systems, one can no longer perceive enough detailed information to know how the initial conditions should be fixed in order to reverse the motion. Such systems can be described only in terms of averages, such as thermodynamic variables, rather than as detailed molecular motions. "Thus, from the coarse-grained or thermodynamic point of view the motion is irreversible, although the detailed motion . . . is governed by reversible laws."[5]

Although Sachs is dealing with the differences between molecules and liquids, the problem arises in an even more acute form when we deal with human reality. Therefore, there are not and cannot be any time-reversible laws of history. Thus, from a point of view different from that presented in chapter 3, a similar conclusion is reached. Human history, being a fundamentally and not merely residually open system, is therefore time-irreversible. This fact limits all evolutionary "theories," Darwinian as well as Marxian.

SUBJECTIVITY, INTENTIONALITY, AND INTENTIONS

It may be useful to distinguish the position I shall take with respect to intentionality from that of phenomenology, and, in particular, from that of Husserl, who meant by the intentionality of consciousness that consciousness was directed toward objects, not that objects existed in consciousness. Only those psychological phenomena that resulted in acts had intentionality, he said, but the same object of intention may be referred to from a variety of intentional frames of reference. So far our positions may seem not to be in conflict. However, according to Husserl, scientific intuition presents such intentional objects in their most adequate and self-evident form. This occurs, he said, when they are presented in univocal general or universal form as essences. The reasons why I reject any type of essentialism and also the consequent belief in scientific certainty that Husserl held have been made clear in the three previous chapters. I will now attempt to show why the techniques of theory and assessment apply generally to both the physical and social sciences, a showing that I hope will make irrelevant such techniques as the phenomenal or eidetic reductions that Husserl proposed or those of subsequent phenomenologists.

The failure to understand problems of determinism and strong and weak orders in science leads many social philosophers to believe that the methodology of the social sciences is fundamentally different from that of the physical sciences. Whether their reasoning is based on the belief that the intentions of individuals are responsible for this difference or that individuals interrogate each other whereas they merely account for nature, I shall show that the intentional aspects of human behavior do not require a methodology different from that of the physical sciences.

Many of the problems of social science—even those in which intentions play a role—may be solved by either theoretical or praxical analysis, although the weakness of the order may produce alternative solutions rather than a unique solution. For reasons stated earlier, including the absence of independent measures, these solutions will require context-dependent praxical assessments.

Let me examine, briefly, the role of intentions in theory and also in praxical assessment to illustrate the prior contentions. Consider a large country of small farmers. All intend to earn enough money to support a family. The farmers raise wheat. The price of wheat goes down. Therefore, they each seek some way to increase the size of the crop to earn more money; perhaps by planting idle land, perhaps by using more fertilizer, and so forth. Each succeeds. The wheat crop of the country increases and the price drops further. Economic theory explains this result in the context of independent decision making. Intentions function only at the boundary of the problem.*

When the farmers notice the unintended drop in price, they organize and lobby for price supports or some other collective solution to the problem. They do this for praxical reasons. Earlier, they were dealing rationally with the problem as independent decision makers. Now they have expanded their analysis, assessed a collective solution, and found good reasons for choosing it.

Have I overlooked the fact that humans communicate with each other and that this changes the social reality about which they talk, whereas the physical realities we study remain unaffected by our study? But physical realities are changed by our transactions with them; and, in the quantum case, such concepts as position and momentum have meaning only in terms of incompatible experimental frameworks.

On the other hand, the laws of physics, we believe, are not changed by our study of them whereas the norms of society may be so changed. But this is responsive only to the fact that covering laws do not account for homeostatic behavior. Even a homeostatic system composed only of physical elements, if reworked, will require a new account of its behavior, although the physical system that constitutes its boundary will obey unchanged covering laws.

---

*In chapter 11, I examine some specific problems in which the knowledge and intentions of some players do affect the knowledge and intentions of others and show that analysis based on game theory does constrain the solutions.

Social systems are homeostatic systems, although their feedback processes are far more complex than is the case in homeostatic systems in which all the elements are physical. Although some transactions among humans may approach the indeterminism of the quantum case, that is not the usual case, particularly when we are dealing with large-scale events. Although often we cannot make projections, or sometimes even retrodictions, with great confidence, fairly reliable knowledge is often possible, particularly if information is comparative.

Our communications with each other are responsive to our learning within much wider frameworks of investigation. This should surprise no one. We sometimes learn that we misunderstood our own motivation as we examine critically our behavior under a wide variety of circumstances. We may use game theoretical models as heuristic devices rather than the calculus. But, as in physics, we use theory and assessment in investigating an objective world to which our language and our conversations are adapted.

ALL KNOWLEDGE IS INTENSIONAL

All knowledge is, in some respects, intentional or, more properly, intensional,* for all experience consists of meaningful transactions with aspects of the world. By *intensional*, I mean that the structure and coding of the system provide a framework for experiencing and understanding the world in a relevant way.

Directed awareness—the phenomenological concern—rather than internal meaning is the key concept in the argument that the human and the physical sciences must differ fundamentally in their methodologies, for internal meanings in principle are consistent with the methods of physical science. But we have already seen that the concepts of physical science are transactional and involve directed awareness, that is, that they are directed toward referents and mediated by signs. They do not merely copy or correspond with a first-order external reality.

We sometimes overlook this fact because we ordinarily think of physics, for instance, in terms of the bodies accounted for by macrophysics. Even there, however, that apparent first-order reality is a reification, although it does not mislead us in practical situations. In the realm of quantum physics, however, the transaction between the experimenter and the physical world is intimate and the theory accounts for alternative experiments.

In any event, the meaning of our experience will vary with our conditions of life and our understanding, whether in physics or society. These contextual aspects of meaning are consistent with objectivity, as I have already shown. They are taken account of in the spiral, neutral web of understanding at both first-order and second-order levels of understanding.

I hope that you, the reader, will by now agree that all knowledge is intensional

---

*If we define intentionality as directed awareness, it is a self-conscious activity. Intensionality, on the other hand, requires only awareness and can be non-conscious, e.g., a brain-damaged person, who walks around an obstacle and who denies that he saw it.

in some respects and that the physical and social sciences do not differ in this regard. Nonetheless, you may also have found plausible the arguments of sociologists, or of philosophers who argue that language is constitutive of reality or that dialogue requires a radically different methodology. I do not deny that we need language and dialogue to investigate reality. This is true also in the physical sciences, where the dialogue admittedly is among scientists in the investigation of nature. But then the scientific investigation of the human and the social sciences also involves dialogue among scientists in the investigation of human and social nature. And if social scientists sometimes engage in intimate transactions with their subject matter, this is the case in quantum physics also. I shall now briefly sketch how such investigations are conducted.

Consider a classroom that society regards as part of an educational process but that a particular student regards as imprisonment. If the focus of reference is kept in account, both attributions may be correct, particularly if the student's claim is regarded as metaphoric. A part-system analysis that employs literal language will distinguish, in general, between schools and prisons. Then a neutral second-order analysis can show that the school operates as an educational institution for most students and as a prison in many respects for particular students.

Consider a somewhat tougher case such as an inmate in an asylum. Michel Foucault has shown how society produces "mad" behavior by its definitions and sometimes defines as mad, behavior that is otherwise rational.[6] Part-system analysis will be of help here also, for presumably symptoms distinguished potential inmates from other people. And in other cases, it can be shown that these inmates differed from others only in filling social roles that, with a different set of social definitions, would be considered mere eccentricity or even legitimate protest.

Foucault's own analysis would have solved the problem if he had carried it one step farther. Second-order analysis could have been used to compare various categories of people with the same symptoms who are given different types of institutional treatment, different types of non-institutional treatment, or placed in different types of societies. They can also be compared with people who do not exhibit symptoms but who are placed in similar environments. Comparative analysis would show how other societies process the demands of those defined as mad because of protests, and how this society thrusts some people into situations that elicit "mad" protests.

One would then have a set of dispositional transactions that does not depend on fixed or universal definitions. Although the analysis of a social transaction is more complexly related to its environment and involves different kinds of values than a physical analysis, the procedure is essentially the same. Thus, although Foucault could have been correct in believing that madness was not a phenomenon that could have appeared before a certain epoch—I believe him to have been incorrect but that is not relevant to my present argument—because of its dependence upon a systemic range of understanding and belief, I think that I have sketched a procedure that encompasses the phenomenon within a wider and relatively neutral realm of understanding.

Second-order part-system analysis thus reveals social reality, even though that reality is loosely ordered. Whether great differences in the characteristics of humans would be consistent with at least a common second-order moral universe is a subject that will be discussed in Part Three. In any event, although analysis is not independent of linguistic usage, it is not determined by it.

CONSCIOUSNESS

Consciousness, or subjectivity, is the process or state of knowing. *Self-consciousness* involves the knowledge of consciousness: the informational processing of experience which is, in turn, informationally processed. Self-consciousness is subjectivity which is reflexive, or self-referring.

Thus far, it might be possible to infer that a computer that could process information in this way would be conscious or even self-conscious. Some computers can mimic conversation or even the analyst's role in counseling. Although I cannot prove that a computer cannot achieve consciousness, I do not believe that this is possible, even in principle, of the type of computers we are now able to build.

I suspect that there are other necessary aspects of consciousness and that these include some lack of discreteness in the elements of knowledge and in their retention, some holistic functioning of the brain. Perhaps it is also necessary that the store of information be widely distributed, that vast amounts of information be capable of producing a display that is not coextensive with the store, and that there be an inherent process of association.[7]

The model of mind proposed by Hume and Kant would be consistent with consciousness in computers as we know them because it assumes discrete moments of consciousness. This is not a correct account of the physiology of perception, but it does suggest moving pictures in which the rapid flashing of discrete pictures produces the perception of movement. I should like to suggest that this illusion of movement occurs precisely because the span of attention is wider than the interval between the frames of a movie and that a system of which this is not so would not have awareness or consciousness. The perception of change and associated memory are likely necessary to awareness. The reflexive processing of this information would then produce self-consciousness by directing attention to an ego, that is, to a focus of reference for the process.

Can there be subjectivity in non-living matter? Most would deny this possibility. In any event, one cannot be reduced to the other. Although knowledge of the correlative pair "subjective" and "objective" may have resulted from an evolutionary process, it is universal of actual and potential experience. Neither aspect of this pair "subjective" and "objective" can be reduced to the other.

Perhaps the former question would be less opaque if we recognized concrete, qualitative reality and information, in the terminology of Niels Bohr, as products of techniques of assessment that are in a state of complementarity. Every physical transaction, for instance, can be analyzed in terms of states of information and vice versa. These processes are not causal, parallel, or reducible. Thus, even so-called inert matter has informational aspects, although if its elements share this information, we would not assert awareness of them. Awareness likely arose with certain types of complex organization permitting non-serial and non-digital information flows. Self-awareness or self-consciousness then likely is associated with even more complex organizational forms constituted by hierarchically organized neural structures within which a system can recognize its own states and thereby organize its succeeding states. If this is so, then there is a kind of continuity in the development of consciousness, although certain transitions would involve qualitative steps, a process that is now believed also to characterize the evolution of species. If this assessment is correct, materialism and idealism are false opposites, that is, they are not opposites as such. And this conclusion, which nicely fits my earlier approaches to language and ontology, would remove much of the mystery from the question of the origin of consciousness in a previously material universe.

NOTES

1. Karl Popper, *The Open Universe: An Argument for Indeterminism*, edited by W.W. Bartley III (Totowa, N.J.: Rowman & Littlefield, 1982).

2. John von Neumann, *The Computer and the Brain* (New Haven: Yale University Press, 1958), pp. 70 ff.

3. Robert G. Sachs, "Time Reversal," *Science* 176 (May 12, 1972), pp. 589 ff.

4. Ibid., p. 589.

5. Ibid., pp. 589, 590.

6. Michel Foucault, *Madness and Civilization: A History of Insanity in the Age of Reason*, translated by Richard Howard (New York: Vintage Books, 1973).

7. Karl Pribram discussed identical factors in "Non-Locality and Localization: A Review of the Place of the Holographic Hypothesis of Brain Function in Perception and Memory," ms.

PART TWO
ANTITHETICAL VIEWS OF
LANGUAGE

IN PART ONE, basic problems in the philosophy of science were examined and I suggested a resolution of these problems that invoked theory and praxis as correlative techniques. My analysis is unlike many other approaches to the philosophy of science in that meaning and language, including sign theory, are intrinsic to it. All knowledge involves interpretation.

In Part Two, philosophical positions to which investigations of language are central will be examined. In chapter 8, I investigate problems of communication and relate my analysis to the general conclusions of Part One. This discussion leads to chapter 9, on Ludwig Wittgenstein, who developed the idea of language games into the core of an analytic philosophy that stands in sharp contrast to philosophies of science, such as those of Karl Popper, Rudolf Carnap, Thomas Kuhn, and many others, that assume a world that is independent of linguistic structure.

This book was already in draft when one of my colleagues suggested that large sections of Part One read like the Wittgenstein of *On Certainty*.[1] Until then, I had known Ludwig Wittgenstein's writings only through followers such as Gilbert Ryle and Stephen Toulmin.[2] In *Justice, Human Nature, and Political Obligation*,[3] I showed how and why Toulmin's use of the concept of language games flawed his theory of morals. I was, therefore, disinclined to explore the concept of language games further, but I take suggestions of colleagues seriously. My investigation of Wittgenstein also prompted chapter 10, an analysis of Jacques Derrida's deconstructionist approach.[4]

Now that I have read both *On Certainty and Philosophical Investigations*,[5] I can appreciate why Wittgenstein deserved his enormous influence. Moreover, I found his treatment of meaning, which is reminiscent of Charles Sanders Peirce's pragmaticism, congenial. Nonetheless, Wittgenstein's emphasis on language games, in my opinion, undervalues the role of science in the analysis even of language. And his treatment of what he calls "private knowledge" both mystifies it and divorces it from science in a way I regard as misleading. I agree that there are tacit or private aspects of knowledge that cannot be communicated publicly, but I believe that Wittgenstein constructs the line incorrectly.

Therefore, I attempt, in chapter 9, to state those aspects of Wittgenstein's position with which I feel comfortable and to indicate where my disquiet arises. Whether or not the reader agrees with my interpretation of Wittgenstein, the discussion will make my own position clearer.

The continental phenomenological and existential tradition contrasts sharply with Wittgenstein's. Jacques Derrida, its leading contemporary exponent, attempts to show that the mode of literal analysis that is intrinsic to both philosophy of science and linguistic analysis conceals absences and gaps and that it obscures more than it reveals. His method of deconstruction poses an alternative to all philosophies of science.

Unless I relate my argument in Part One for the literal methods of science to the strongest contemporary challenge to science and the literal use of language, that of Jacques Derrida, it may appear that I have attempted to win my point by default. In chapter 10, therefore, I examine one of Derrida's most important books, *Writing and Difference*, to see whether its position can withstand scientific analysis.

What is Derrida's position? Is Derrida a phenomenologist or an anti-phenomenologist? Surely he confutes both Edmund Husserl and Martin Heidegger. He turns Husserl's quest for certainty into a demonstration of the limitation of all existence.

His philosophic style builds on, or at least from, Heidegger's mode of analysis and swarms with metaphors. And yet he shows Heidegger's antimetaphysical stance to be a continuation of the metaphysical method of Greek philosophy. In Derrida's hands, reason is turned against itself and made the focus of difference and the antithesis of presence. "Force" becomes the antithesis of an ethical attitude based upon an orientation to "the other."

What, however, do his statements mean? This is hard to say. Derrida's style is so discursive, so allusive, so poetic and glittering, so steeped in paradox and preciosity that he is difficult to understand. If I interpret him correctly, however, I believe that he does note genuine difficulties in the use of language. Yet I believe that these difficulties are better handled by the literal language of science and by an appropriate philosophy of science than by Derrida's method of deconstruction.

How shall I attempt to show this? If the views I express in Part One are correct, I must disregard his stricture that a position can be denied only in its own language and with its own weapons. This is internal examination only, and my canvas is larger. I am able to use non-allusive terms and literal language. Moreover, as I argued in chapter 4, metaphor itself becomes comprehensible only in the presence of literal understanding.

In the three chapters that follow, I shall examine the writings of Wittgenstein and Derrida in an attempt to show how and why the language philosophers and the continental hermeneutical philosophers go wrong. In brief, Wittgenstein believes that philosophy has no subject matter other than the investigation of the language games of scientists. This might have been the case if science consisted merely of the confirmation or falsification of theories or propositions. But science also involves a process of assessment in which the surround of a particular subject matter is relevant to its interpretation. An assessment of the entire realm of science takes us to the traditional problems of philosophy and, in turn, influences the interpretation of particular subject matters.

Derrida (and also Heidegger) believe that meaning can be assessed independently of the findings of science and, thus, represent an even more radical break with the Western philosophical tradition than does Wittgenstein. Although they incorporate useful insights from Eastern philosophy, as did Hegel, their failure to reflect upon the findings of the individual sciences undermines their efforts.

This assessment of language and meaning will prepare the way for an inquiry into values in Part Three and into social science, including Marxism, in Part Four.

NOTES

1. Ludwig Wittgenstein, *On Certainty*, edited by G. E. M. Anscombe and G. H. von Wright, translated by Denis Paul and G. E. M. Anscombe (New York: Harper & Row, Publishers, 1969).

2. Gilbert Ryle, *Concept of Mind* (London: Hutchinson University Library, 1949); Stephen Toulmin, *Reason in Ethics* (Cambridge: Cambridge University Press, 1950).

3. Morton A. Kaplan, *Justice, Human Nature, and Political Obligation* (New York: Free Press, 1976), pp. 69 ff.

4. Jacques Derrida, *Writing and Difference*, translated by Alan Bass (Chicago: University of Chicago Press, 1978).

5. Ludwig Wittgenstein, *Philosophical Investigations*, translated by G. E. M. Anscombe (Oxford: Basil Blackwell & Mott, 1958).

Chapter 8
Language, Reality, and Communication

Distinctions, linguistic or real, are not absolute. They are related to use and they change with both the instruments and purposes of use. Newton's system was conceived as if it were independent of instrumental means of measurement. Einstein's theory, on the other hand, made c, the constant for light, the medium of measurement, a major element in the relativity of his system. Nonetheless, his equations are determinate with respect to relations among objects within inertial systems, and they produce similar but transposed predictions from independent inertial systems. In quantum theory, the relationship between instrument and system of reference is more intimate; position and momentum can be measured only by incompatible experimental designs.

A theory is about a subject matter: large bodies, atoms, electrons, nations, personalities, and so forth. The instruments and operations ancillary to the inquiry are among the conditions governing the statement or application of the theory and are taken into account only insofar as necessary.

Both boundary conditions and instrumentation are, of course, essential to the scientific process. In qualitative investigations—for instance, investigation involving colors—the optic and other related physiological systems become essential boundary conditions of the validity of any statement that ensues. In quantitative investigations, the choice of instrumentation is important, e.g., whether time is measured by a sundial, a clock, a quartz crystal, a cesium atom, or so forth. At a second-order level of discussion, differences in statements about properties, whether qualitative or quantitative, can be related to differences in boundary conditions. Investigations into the perception of color include not only physiological systems—an object that looks blue to a human looks gray to a dog—but also lighting systems, and so forth. These aspects of the inquiry are praxical rather than theoretical. Such second-order discussion also produces statements that may be subjected to the canons of science.

LANGUAGE AS INSTRUMENT

Language, also, is an instrument of inquiry. Language helps to determine the kinds of statements that can be called true or false. One can also engage in comparative analysis at this level, and therefore one can develop a second-order discussion that relates the characteristics of statements to the characteristics of the language of inquiry—a scientific activity of a praxical order.

The concept of a second-order level of analysis is essential to my argument, in chapter 5, that science is objective, and to the argument that values are objective, advanced in Part Three of this book. Although it is true that the language of inquiry constrains the kinds of statements that can be made, translations are possible that distill from each framework those claims that are common to each. Even when the claims are not common, we can use second-order discourse to begin to work out the boundary conditions to which the differences are related. For example, in some societies the word we translate as "mother" refers to all females of a given age group with respect to all children of a given age group. This is not the meaning of "mother" in our society, but they have no more specific term. However, the difference in usage can be related to the organization of the two societies and the conditions that support that organization. The different consequences of the two usages can then be understood at a second-order level that can have common, though perhaps not identical, meanings in both languages even though the definitions and contexts of the signs used in the two languages are different.

In these respects, the analysis of language, including the use of concepts, is essential to inquiry. However, to make the analysis of language the focus of inquiry would be as serious a mistake as to make the theoretical discussion of telescope construction the focus of astrophysical inquiry. The sterility of most discussions that make the common language the central focus of inquiry arises from the fact that attention is directed away from the subject matter of the inquiry.

LANGUAGE: ABSTRACT AND FAMILY GROUPING

In abstract conceptual analysis concepts are treated as if their meaning can be detached from their context. In one form of analysis, this is a search for the true and universal meaning of a concept. In other forms, as in analysis of common language, meaning bears a relationship to context and it is embedded in problems of usage. However, even the idea that concepts may apply to diverse activities that have only family relationships does not do full justice to the object of the inquiry. "Human being" once meant a member of the tribe. In time, tribal membership came to mean civilized humans, as contrasted to barbarians, while all *homo sapiens* were regarded as human. Were we someday to meet biologically quite different reasoning beings from another solar system, the concept of humanity might be expanded to include all biological beings capable of scientific and moral thought. Suppose further that one day we develop robots that think as we do and that are also capable of moral behavior. The concept of humanity might then be altered to exclude the biological component.

In the course of the development of language, family relationships among the classes to which a term is applied have stretched the meaning of terms and concepts. In Platonic philosophy the "real" was the Idea of a chair, for instance, not the chair itself, which was only an exemplar. Today "real" means manifest, an almost complete reversal of meaning. "Sincere" originally meant without wax, as in a sincere wood table. Is there even a family resemblance here? Yet each use of these terms was legitimate within its own context.

Thus, attempts to compare meanings that are centered on language can rise to a level of abstraction that is sterile precisely because the analysis is unrelated to the considerations that govern praxical inquiries into the subject matter.

SECOND-ORDER COMMUNICATION REVISITED

In chapter 2, I mentioned a second-order set of statements (i.e., translation) that permits a common and objective order of discourse between speakers of different languages. Let me now apply the same analysis to different realms of knowledge. As I have discussed the concept of praxis, our choices between different axioms, theorems, and theories derive their relevance from the larger realm of knowledge even though local aspects of that realm are especially relevant to certain types of assertions.

Suppose we were confronted with visitors from outer space whose knowledge had developed out of a different historical pattern and whose sciences, theories, and axioms were different from ours. The instruments of their science might also be different from ours, as well as their criteria for identification.

In an effort to establish discourse, teams of scientists from both cultures would attempt to communicate the status of their science. They would attempt to construct a second-order level of concepts, definitions, theorems, instruments, and so forth. They would face the complex task of finding similarities and of accounting for differences by relating them to differences in concepts, in observational factors, in instrumentation, and so forth. It is perhaps no accident that scientists who attempt to communicate with extraterrestrial civilizations broadcast such things as the formula for π. They need to find neutral areas which could serve as a basis for investigating disagreement.

By means of these endeavors, the teams of scientists would, if successful, construct a new realm of knowledge encompassing those aspects of the two previous realms of knowledge that survived their mutual exchange and analysis. Presumably this would lead to a deeper understanding of both realms of science. Although the process described would be sociological in the sense that a new society of scientists would be created, historical in the sense that their knowledge would be determined by the history of the two systems, and discontinuous with respect to the past realms of knowledge of both groups, what would emerge would be objective and common.

Let me restate this thesis in more traditional terms and relate it to the earlier discussion of language as an instrument. Reality is partly a function of the instrument employed, whether the instrument be a telescope or a word. In this limited sense only, instruments help to produce reality. For instance, a telescope produces circular orbs and a spectroscope produces colored vertical areas. The gamma ray meets a porous reality that the fist meets as solid.

Yet the realities they produce do not contradict each other, and they can be encompassed within a second-order framework. For instance, the solid atomic pile is a reality for which there is a subatomic explanation, within the terms of which nothing is solid. On the other hand, solidity is produced by the assemblage of non-solid phenomena. Moreover, we can specify the experimental frameworks within which the transformations can be produced.

Quite often, a second-order level of discussion between the speakers of two languages is a transitional arrangement needed only until a first-order reference to the scientific information is found. When the Israelis resurrected Hebrew, they had to invent, borrow, or adapt words for many scientific concepts. Ultimately, these foreign terms were incorporated into Hebrew, making it a first-order language adequate for many scientific purposes.

Because there are covering laws and independent measures for scientific terms, the translation of scientific concepts from language to language at a first-order level is far easier and more exact than translations of social or moral concepts, the meanings of which depend so much on cultural contexts which differ in important ways from culture to culture.

The problem of translation from one language to another is usually solved by part-system comparisons, not by a lexicon that offers a one-to-one correspondence of words in the two languages. A variety of part-system analyses, both first-order and second-order, is used to approach different aspects of translation that simple word correspondences miss. This should not surprise us; we know that concepts in one language are not identical to those in another. And we know that we can show in one language how another language handles similar concepts differently and how the differences function as part of a system of concepts. That this project can never be carried through completely or precisely is not of great significance, for we can almost invariably carry it through well enough to deal with the particular problems that concern us. It is more important to realize that no language complex enough to deal with the problems of everyday life can be complete, for we always have to adapt it to changing ideas and information. Thus, the problem of translation between languages merely replicates the problem of handling similar concepts in different part systems of the same language. Difficulties in reconstructing the meaning of concepts in past civilizations arise mainly from our inability to explore these issues in transactions with their participants. We are able to solve similar problems, at least in part, when we analyze strange contemporary cultures that likely are even more different from us than was classical Greece, for instance.

The meeting with alien scientists, thus, is merely an extreme version of a more common problem. The transformative second-order language and the set of experiments that would be required to produce a common language of science is an objective process. It is inconsistent only with the concept of a world theory that specifies reality in terms of a strong order and of a set of one-to-one relationships between a string of sentences and an external world whose characteristics are entirely independent of transactions between perceiver and perceived.

I am not arguing that a second-order level of discourse will solve all praxical disagreements. But it will solve some of them by providing an expanded and more systematic articulation of theoretical assumptions and boundaries. If the world is not strongly ordered, these praxical disagreements may turn out to be complementary ways of understanding aspects of it. It does not follow, however, that the results of these different approaches are merely additional elements in a univocal puzzle and, therefore, that together they permit a representation of an external world of which they are a copy. Instead, they provide a richer and more complex understanding of reality from a variety of viewpoints.

Before proceeding with the analysis of Wittgenstein and Derrida in the following chapters, I shall now link the discussion in this chapter to their positions, as well as to the discussion of Kripke and Putnam on the one hand and of Foucault on the other in Part One. The key to this is the discussion just concluded, which needs only to be linked to the correlative character of language.

In my discussion of Kripke and Putnam I noted that intension and extension are internally related correlatives: if we do not comprehend the meaning of something, we cannot know what we are pointing at; and if we do not know where we are pointing, we cannot determine the referent of the meaning. It was their failure to assess this adequately that led Kripke and Putnam to identify the empirical concept of truth with the analytical concept of truth and, thus, to assert that if an empirical assertion is true, it is necessarily true.

It is now easy to understand why partial and only partial translatability is possible. Although the correlatives "intension" and "extension" are internally related, their application—like the application of quantum theory to position and momentum, in which incompatible experimental instruments are required—utilizes different part-system frameworks and external criteria. This is the bridge that in more complex forms accounts for partial and only partial translatability, and in the absence of which Quine's thesis would hold.

Translatability cannot be total because second-order neutral analysis selects those elements from the first-order schemas that permit coordination and ignores those elements of the first-order schemas that are irrelevant to the second order analysis but that nonetheless remain part of the first-order understanding of the elements. Thus, empirical knowledge is not in principle perfectible.

The failure of Kripke and Putnam to understand this led them to assert metaphysical necessity. The same failure drove Wittgenstein to the disjunctive literalism of "language games." As we saw in chapter 7, Foucault attempted to solve this problem by asserting the insularity of the world views of an epoch much as Wittgenstein treated a language game, while retreating to metaphor in bridging these architectonic wholes. It is but a short march to Derrida, who refused to see any kind of valid second-order meaning in a text and who, therefore, asserted an infinity of potential meanings that are approached through metaphor.

However, were my account not correct, we could not communicate with others or even with ourselves, for there would be no method by means of which we could assert a sameness between our thought at one time and at another, the frameworks having changed in the interim. Indeed, our "thought" then would be incoherent and we would be in that aboriginal state of "madness" of which Derrida writes and the written discussion of which we can understand, at least in part, in a second-order neutral manner *only* because his thesis is false.

There is a sense in which there can be no claim advanced for the communication of a single true meaning of any text. Even in the case of an author's reading of his own text, he will do so from at least a partly new perspective within which he understands his own intentions at least somewhat differently. Moreover, even his memory of what he intended is invoked in a partly new context that is likely to influence it in some way. On the other hand, it is nonsense to argue that the text, and the environment in which it was written, do not place limitations on how we can interpret it. If the deconstruction of a text is intended to do more than raise questions to be addressed by literal analysis, it is an invitation to manic behavior.

Biblical scholars sometimes argue that Abraham could not have intended to sacrifice Isaac because sacrifice was not part of the culture at that time. Yet child sacrifice is not part of the culture of contemporary India and still it occurs. Thus, the question must remain partly open, although it is better to regard the story as metaphoric. That is, we would require additional evidence before we would read the text literally with confidence.

There are such things as warranted beliefs and canons of evidence. The recent trends among some legal scholars to allow their own values to determine—rather than merely to influence within the range of indetermination—the legal conclusions they reach turn a partial looseness of constraint into an absence of constraint and judicial interpretation into judicial tyranny. No responsible person would urge this course.

Chapter 9
Language Games*

I agree with Ludwig Wittgenstein's statement that language is an instrument and that meaning requires language. I agree with his attempt to avoid the fallacy of essentialism, i.e., the belief in essences that lie behind appearances of classical philosophy and of phenomenology. By the end of this chapter, however, I shall have shown that a serious error affects Wittgenstein's analysis. In chapter 4, we showed that meaning involves a triadic relationship between a referent, a sign, and a concept. In the discussion of Kripke in that chapter, it was noted that ostensive and intensive definitions were correlatives, that we could not work with one concept without invoking the other. For this reason, we cannot know whether we are using language in the same way as another person ostensively if we do not know what his language use refers to intensively. In short, how do we know the liquid called "red" is the ostensive characterization of "liquid" unless we know intensively what a liquid is or vice versa? It is but a short step from this to showing that a language game cannot be self-encapsulated, that external criteria can be used to critique it, and that we can move from this result to a validation of a synoptic approach to philosophy. How minds reform languages will be considered when I discuss Gilbert Ryle's concept of category error.

In any event, what is a language game? Wittgenstein asked:

> But how many kinds of sentence are there? Say assertion, question, and command: —There are *countless* kinds: countless different kinds of use of what we call "symbols," "words," "sentences." And this multiplicity is not something fixed, given once for all; but new types of language, new language-games, as we may say, come into existence, and others become obsolete and get forgotten.[1]

Let us grant that these so-called language games use terms that have different meanings, sometimes even when the signs are similar, and that the rules for using these terms differ from game to game. Are these differences philosophically

---

*The quotations from Ludwig Wittgenstein used throughout this chapter are from his *On Certainty*, copyright © 1969, Harper & Row, Publishers, and *Philosophical Investigations*, copyright © 1956, Basil Blackwell & Mott, by courtesy of Basil Blackwell Publisher.

important? Are the theories of physics and biology determined by language games or by aspects of the world that the theories are designed to explain? Are not at least some of the problems that theories of biology and physics respond to formulated according to criteria from other subsystems of knowledge? To what extent do the more technical moves in the games depend upon conventions of statement, and to what extent are different conventions translatable into a common second-order language? Does not the acceptability of notational and semantic conventions depend upon their capacity to produce information that is relevant?

What, Wittgenstein asked, is the difference between two pictures? The degree to which a sharp picture can resemble a vague one depends on the latter's degree of vagueness, he said. Consider a blurred red triangle. If the colors merge without outline, will it not, he asks

> . . . become a hopeless task to draw a sharp picture corresponding to the blurred one? . . . And this is the position you are in if you look for definitions corresponding to our concepts in aesthetics or ethics.
>
> In such a difficulty always ask yourself: How did we *learn* the meaning of the word ("good" for instance)? From what sort of examples? In what language-games? Then it will be easier for you to see that the word must have a family of meanings.[2]

I agree that the meaning of the word "good" depends upon how it is used and that its uses in different contexts will be different. In this sense, there will be a family of uses. But do I use "good" in certain ways because of a language game? Or does the language game exist to permit public communication with respect to things that are good? Is it not true that evolutionary advantage required at least a primitive coding for goodness and badness? Does not a more sophisticated language game for morals require a notational system and rules that enable us to move more effectively with respect to good and bad things? In brief, cannot we distinguish between good and bad uses of "good"? What is conventional and what not in the formulation of rules for moral systems? Cannot we avoid essentialism if we ask these questions seriously?

Wittgenstein illustrated his point as follows:

> Now—judged by the usual criteria—the pupil has mastered the series of natural numbers. Next we teach him to write down other series of cardinal numbers and get him to the point of writing down series of the form.
>
> $$O, n, 2n, 3n, \text{etc.}$$
>
> at an order of the form " $+n$ "; so at the order " $+1$ " he writes down the series of natural numbers.—Let us suppose we have done exercises and given tests up to 1000.
>
> Now we get the pupil to continue a series (say $+2$) beyond 1000—and he writes 1000, 1004, 1008, 1012.
>
> We say to him: "Look what you've done!"—He doesn't understand. We say: "You

were meant to add *two*: look how you began the series!'' He answers: ''Yes, isn't it right? I thought that was how I was *meant* to do it.''[3]

Here Wittgenstein showed that a notation for transformation may be interpreted in more than one way and that the correct conventional way depends upon use. One interpretation, or rule, is as good as another if we understand when and where to use it. The different uses of interpretations, or rules, was presented well by Wittgenstein and can be easily understood. But does it follow that all rules for using numbers are equally good? Might not some be more powerful than others? Might some not give rise to contradictions? One of the reasons for the development of modern logic was that we knew that Aristotle knew that ''If horses are animals, the heads of horses are the head of animals'' and that this truth could not be expressed in Aristotelian logic.

Can we not show that Einstein's theory of relativity permits an actual falsification of Newtonian theory by external and neutral criteria? If so, it is not a matter of convention which language games we employ in physics, although conventional alternatives within the Einsteinian framework may be acceptable.

How did Wittgenstein deal with this question?

> Is it wrong for me to be guided in my actions by the propositions of physics? Am I to say I have no good ground for doing so? Isn't precisely this what we call a ''good ground''?

> Supposing we met people who did not regard that as a telling reason. Now, how do we imagine this? Instead of the physicist, they consult an oracle. (And for that we consider them primitive.) Is it wrong for them to consult an oracle and be guided by it?—If we call this ''wrong'' aren't we using our language-game as a base from which to *combat* theirs?[4]

Was Wittgenstein really saying that we can engage only in combat with the oracle and that we cannot reason with him? Is this not simply a variant of the danda problem that misleads Stephen Pepper (a subject discussed in chapter 1)?

Wittgenstein made a further point:

> Grammar does not tell us how language must be constructed in order to fulfill its purpose, in order to have such-and-such an effect on human beings. It only describes and in no way explains the use of signs.

> The rules of grammar may be called ''arbitrary,'' if that is to mean that the *aim* of grammar is nothing but that of the language.

> If someone says ''If our language had not this grammar, it could not express these facts''—it should be asked what ''*could*'' means here.[5]

Shall we interpret Wittgenstein as casting doubt on the suggestion itself, which seems likely? If our language did not have this grammar, could we not reconstruct language as we did with the proposition, ''If horses are animals . . .''? Could we not then learn this new language and use whichever is more appropriate in a given situation? We learn of a need for a new grammar because exterior criteria, that is, criteria from other part systems, alert us to the need.

BELIEF AND KNOWLEDGE

How do language games determine truth? What do we mean by evidence?

> It would be nonsense to say that we regard something as sure evidence because it is certainly true.
>
> Rather, we must first determine the role of deciding for or against a proposition. . . .
>
> Really "The proposition is either true or false" only means that it must be possible to decide for or against it. But this does not say what the ground for such a decision is like. . . .
>
> [. . . If everything speaks *for* an hypothesis and nothing against it, is it objectively *certain*? One can *call* it that. But does it *necessarily* agree with the world of facts? At the very best it shows us what "agreement" means. We find it difficult to imagine it to be false, but also difficult to make use of it.]
>
> What does this agreement consist in, if not in the fact that what is evidence in these language games speaks for our proposition? (*Tractatus Logico-Philosophicus*)[6]

Our knowledge is often superior to the reasons we can offer. Although a physicist might offer excellent reasons for the hypothesis that the earth is more than five billion years old, the reasons most of us can offer for believing that it is even five thousand years old are very shaky. This is even more true of the proposition that the earth is not flat. And yet we know these things in a way that is firmer than the reasons we can offer. Almost all that we know would fall into doubt if the world were not even one hundred years old. We have information from a variety of part systems. In this sense, we cannot doubt the proposition.

It would be wrong, however, to argue that our beliefs do not require reasons even when they are seriously challenged. Wittgenstein is correct in seeing that there would be an endless regress if we insisted on a single chain of reasoning, but he finds the wrong solution. I shall return to this problem later in the chapter, in the section on part systems and global systems.

Let me first present Gilbert Ryle's attempt to show the existence of a regress, because it is somewhat easier to understand than Wittgenstein's exposition. According to Ryle:

> The crucial objection to the intellectualist legend is this. The consideration of propositions is itself an operation the execution of which can be more or less intelligent, less or more stupid. But if, for any operation to be intelligently executed, a prior theoretical operation had first to be performed and performed intelligently, it would be a logical impossibility for anyone ever to break into the circle.
>
> Let us consider some salient points at which this regress would arise. According to the legend, whenever an agent does anything intelligently, his act is preceded and steered by another internal act of considering a regulative proposition appropriate to his practical problem. But what makes him consider the one maxim which is appropriate rather than any of the thousands which are not? . . . Must we then say that for the hero's reflections how to be intelligent he must first reflect how best to reflect how to act? The endlessness of this implied regress shows that the application of the

criterion of appropriateness does not entail the occurrence of a process of considering this criterion.[7]

But this regress exists only in the form in which Ryle presented it, from the standpoint of a single global theory. If, however, we consider things from the standpoint of the appropriateness of the result, given the rest of the relevant information in the realm of knowledge, then there are criteria according to which an isolated process may be judged. It fits not merely its own internal criteria but also external criteria, i.e., neighboring realms of knowledge; otherwise, we might reconsider our judgment.

Let us now turn to Wittgenstein's objection.

"But then how does an explanation help me to understand, if after all it is not the final one? In that case the explanation is never completed; so I still don't understand what he means and never shall!"—As though an explanation as it were hung in the air unless supported by another one. Whereas an explanation may indeed rest on another one that has been given, but none stands in need of another—unless *we* require it to prevent a misunderstanding. . . .

It may easily look as if every doubt merely *revealed* an existing gap in the foundations; so that secure understanding is only possible if we first doubt everything that *can* be doubted and then remove all these doubts.

The sign-post is in order—if, under normal circumstances, it fulfills its purpose.[8]

Here Wittgenstein seemed to understand the role of part systems in the scientific argument.

A few pages later, Wittgenstein seemed to be saying something else:

It was true to say that our considerations could not be scientific ones. It was not of any possible interest to us to find out empirically "that, contrary to our preconceived ideas, it is possible to think such-and-such"—whatever that may mean. (The conception of thought as a gaseous medium.) And we may not advance any kind of theory. There must not be anything hypothetical in our considerations. We must do away with all *explanation*, and description alone must take its place. And this description gets its light, that is to say its purpose, from the philosophical problems; they are solved, rather, by looking into the workings of our language, and that in such a way as to make us recognize those workings: *in despite of* an urge to misunderstand them. The problems are solved, not by giving new information, but by arranging what we have always known. Philosophy is a battle against the bewitchment of our intelligence by means of language.[9]

Let us now begin to disentangle the problems involved in this thesis.

HYPOTHESES AND DESCRIPTIONS

How can we do away with all hypotheses? Can we really distinguish between language and science in this way? What is it that we know that is not in the end hypothetical? When Captain Cook saw the Hawaiians steal items from his boat, they did not think that they were stealing. They were merely taking from what belonged to all in their culture.

And what, descriptively, made the Hawaiians Hawaiians and Cook a captain? Do we really mean that Lyndon Johnson, an individual, ordered troops, a collection of men, into the Dominican Republic in 1965? Can we understand his move sufficiently well to describe it if we do not know what a "United States," a "president," and men organized in a military unit are? Try to describe this event otherwise.

Could Wittgenstein have saved his case by arguing that he was talking about language and not the referents of language? Can we simply describe how we use language without entertaining any hypotheses? Let us see how Wittgenstein handled the same duck or rabbit problem I discussed in chapter 6, in describing Thomas Kuhn's position.

> I am shewn a picture-rabbit and asked what it is; I say "It's a rabbit." Not "Now it's a rabbit." I am reporting my perception.—I am shewn the duck-rabbit and asked what it is; I *may* say "It's a duck-rabbit." But I may also react to the question quite differently.—The answer that it is a duck-rabbit is again the report of a perception; the answer "Now it's a rabbit" is not. Had I replied "It's a rabbit," the ambiguity would have escaped me, and I should have been reporting my perception.[10]

Is this a simply descriptive use of language? Are there no hypotheses here? If our language did not permit us to report changes and ambiguities, would we not modify it to do so? Is it really wrong to say, "I see a picture that now looks like a rabbit and now looks like a duck"? Do we not use external criteria to fit our description to what we discover in reality?

Is it correct to state that this is not an empirical problem, that it can be solved "by looking into the workings of our language," not by "giving new information, but by arranging what we have all always known." Is there such a thing as a description in the absence of at least tacit hypotheses? Do not our descriptions change as we consider them? Does not the language we use to investigate them change as we confront particular types of problems?

There are choices of hypotheses, both within and among language games, in the absence of which description is not possible. They may be made without conscious thought; and in this sense only can description be said to precede hypothesis. Descriptions are only tentative, selective, and subject to praxical revision. Description and selection are analytically, but not concretely, distinct procedures.

Would Wittgenstein have argued that if a caveman lived long enough, by a constant rearranging of what he knew, he would become aware of electrons, quasars, quarks, cloud chambers, electron microscopes, microbes, and modern philosophy?

I know what it is to rearrange coins in a pile or cards in a pack. But is there even a family relationship between these acts and those above? Have not things been transformed so radically that the underlying concepts are unrelated?

In a trivial sense, Wittgenstein was correct. We can know only in ways that are naturally accessible to us. Thus, descriptive terms like colors, shapes, and so forth can be rearranged and a lion become a griffin. But even this is difficult to specify.

Is learning the distinction between crimson and maroon merely a rearrangement of red? Is our learning about colors in the ultraviolet range merely descriptive rearrangement of what we know? In any non-trivial sense, Wittgenstein was wrong. How is a quark or a black hole a descriptive rearrangement of what we know? By rearranging some elements of the range of knowledge, we learn how to construct strange descriptions and strange concepts. We metaphorize them and then create new literal accounts.

Unless this account is substantially correct, how could Wittgenstein have accounted for new languages: for instance, set theory, Einsteinian mechanics, quantum theory? Where did these new language games come from? Although they are surely not entirely *de novo*, they are just as surely not merely descriptive rearrangements. These, as well as novel social situations, are what Jacques Derrida referred to as discontinuities.[11] We certainly can learn novel descriptions from comparisons with other languages. What of the aardvark? The quark? If these are only recombinations, is there anything that is not a recombination? If so, then an existing language would not have significant limits, and the argument would collapse from a different perspective.

The error in Wittgenstein's position becomes even clearer if we consider the photon. We have all seen waves and particles, numbers and letters. But the photon is neither a wave nor a particle; and the photonic quantum equations are signs, not the signed. The idea of the photon is pointed to by the prior elements but not exhausted by them. The idea of the photon includes new elements that are not merely rearrangements of what had been known. This statement seems obvious when we apply it to quarks, quantum colors, and so forth, but a little analysis will show it to be true of strange creatures or social institutions, such as Portuguese men-of-war or trusts. There are aspects of novel things and concepts which are not exhausted by the rearrangement of descriptive elements that were known previously.

WHAT IS A PROPOSITION? A THEORY? A CONVENTION?

Let us see if we can pursue Wittgenstein's argument further:

And to say that a proposition is whatever can be true or false amounts to saying: we call something a proposition when *in our language* we apply the calculus of truth functions to it.

Now it looks as if the definition—a proposition is whatever can be true or false— determined what a proposition was, by saying: what fits the concept "true," or what the concept "true" fits, is a proposition. . . .

But this is a bad picture. It is as if one were to say "The king in chess is *the* piece that one can check." But this can mean no more than that in our game of chess we only check the king. Just as the proposition that only a *proposition* can be true or false can say no more than that we only predicate "true" and "false" of what we call a proposition. And what a proposition is is in one sense determined by the rules of sentence formation (in English for example), and in another sense by the use of the sign in the language-game. . . .[12]

But is this correct? It is true that to say that the king is the only piece that can be checked is to say that in the game of chess only the king can be checked. But that is not all that we are saying. Suppose you were watching a chess game in which all the pieces were structured differently from the way they are structured in the normal game of chess. Yet you observe that some pieces are placed where pawns are placed at the beginning of the game and are of the required number, and so forth. Furthermore, you note that the piece which is placed where the king is normally placed is eventually checked and that in a series of games it is the only piece that is checked.

Now suppose, in the game we are watching, that the positions are similar except that the piece that is checked is placed where we normally place the queen. Might we not say that this is a game of chess in which the queen is checked or, possibly, that the positions of the king and queen are reversed at the beginning of the game? If the game were modified even more, we might say that it is a game resembling chess, but not chess.

But now we see that something more is involved, as Wittgenstein notices when he states that we can judge not single propositions but "nests of propositions." The meaning of the assertion that the king and only the king can be checked implies a nest of propositions concerning the nature of the board, the types of and numbers of players, and the moves they can make. In the game of chess, these are predetermined. It is a conventional game, just as the standard meter is a conventional measure.

On the other hand, consider the sentence, "He swung his net and captured a thought." When the brain scans this proposition, there is a peculiar pattern of brain wave that is produced at the time that the sentence ends, and that can be distinguished from normal brain waves and from simple surprises. It is a brain wave that signifies recognition of nonsense.

A sentence that is nonsense is different from one that is merely false. It has the form but not the content that permits a meaningful judgment of its truth. Thus, what a proposition is, although determined "in one sense . . . by the rules of sentence formation . . ., and in another sense by the use of the sign in the language-game," is also determined by the character of the world: that is, by the use of a sign with respect to its referent. But this is not a language game, except in a sense that begs every issue and that makes the concept useless. That the sentence is nonsense is not because English grammar supposedly forbids it. Surely it is not a rule of English grammar that a thought cannot be captured in a net.

Wittgenstein knew that a baby's exclamation "Car!" may mean "A car hit a woman." The meaning in this case is given not by the utterance, but by its context. This is factual.

It is a matter of fact, determined by external criteria, and not of grammar or semantics that the idea of capturing a thought in a net is nonsense in our world. In a world in which thoughts took on solid form and flew from the heads of their authors, it might very well be possible to scoop them up in a net, and in that world the sentence would not be nonsense, even if otherwise the concepts of thought bear a family relationship. We know that nets and thoughts are unconnected. This information supports the proposition that the sentence is nonsense in this world. The sentence even may be true in a fictional world in which the terms are connected. This boundary information also permits us to say that the child's "Car!" is a proposition rather than a word. These things are not determined by usage—for we adapt our language to what we learn about the character of the world. Even truth tables are adapted, as the example of "the heads of horses" made clear.

In chapter 8, I discussed the fact that the term translated as "mother" may have a meaning that only partly corresponds with it. In the latter half of the nineteenth century, Lewis Morgan reported in *Systems of Consanguinity* that the term "mother" in some native American tribes referred to any woman of a particular age group with respect to children of certain age groups.[13] On the surface, this would seem to support Wittgenstein's position that these tribes were playing a different language game from that of standard American or European society. Let us investigate this proposition. In the first place, Morgan and members of these tribes could have agreed upon the biological fact that particular women had in fact borne particular children. They then could have understood, by means of second-order language discussions, that the English term "mother" united this biological fact with a complex of social activities and that, in certain tribes, the distinction between biological descent and certain constellations of rights and duties with respect to children was not observed. This use of a second-order language would have enabled them to compare the two systems with respect to activities and use of names. They would have been able to note similarities and differences.

Whatever the differences in the first-order languages, translation would have permitted common direct comparisons. They might disagree on what was acceptable food and yet be able to understand the relationship between food, nourishment, and survival; and that providing food, whatever its form, was an aspect of the social activity of parenthood. There would be no absence of hypotheses in these descriptive accounts, for reasons I offered earlier in this chapter. Furthermore, they would have been playing the normal "science game," for they would have to be able to agree that providing food was a necessary function for the upbringing of children; that is, they would have to be able to recognize, according to neutral external criteria, the relationship between the activities of the women and their function as mothers.

This is what speaks against Wittgenstein's distinction between the "science game" and the "oracle game." There is an Indonesian cult whose members still go daily to the beach to wait for God to send ships that will unload merchandise, as the U.S. Army did in World War II—an event they could explain only as an act of the deity. Their belief, however, is not valid. To the contrary, if the members of the cult were taken to the United States, if they saw huge factories, if they saw these factories produce merchandise, and if they saw the merchandise put on the ships by human beings, the experience would probably alter their theological beliefs. At least, nothing in their oracle game precludes their adjusting that game to take account of real cause-and-effect relationships to the extent that, over a significant period of time, it would be transformed into our normal science game. This is why there are scientific revolutions: because at some point the necessary readjustments of beliefs require a reorganization that produces a qualitatively different framework of interpretation.

As I argued in chapter 5, that is how praxis operates. It is the interrelationship between praxis and theory that provides transformation. In fact, we could not even describe the oracle game unless we could translate it into a second-order language that revealed its similarities to and differences from our science game. It is the slipping forward and back between these different coding systems that permits such comparisons and that paves the way for the transformations. This is how we build a common world. This is the science game at its best, and it is the master game.

Perhaps the most interesting analysis of the way in which language and rules for its interpretation govern thought was presented by Michel Foucault in *The Order of Things: The Archaeology of Human Sciences*.[14] Foucault's investigation was deeper than Wittgenstein's because he dealt directly with a more concrete, specific, and coherent framework of interpretation. He demonstrated convincingly that "magicians" such as Paracelsus were in fact empirical scientists who applied the rules of interpretation of their age. In the sixteenth century, the key concept was that of resemblance. Heavy things are attracted to the heaviness of earth, in this view. The guarantee of resemblance was given by "signature," a visible sign in things; thus, e.g., a short line in a hand shows a short life. The search for names in their relationships to things was part of an empirical process in which evidence was used and accumulated according to neutral external criteria.

The classical age of the seventeenth century, in which the key figure was Descartes, juxtaposed with this view of reality one that broke the relationships between names and things. Descartes' view of reality was not strictly mathematical. He identified things on the basis of ordering principles that were either quantitative or qualitative. In his view, the science of the sixteenth century was metaphor, largely in the form of analogy. And he was able to point out differences, in his new literal language, between the statements of sixteenth-century science and the character of things as determined by neutral external criteria.

Foucault superbly delineated and compared these contrasting developments in thought. However, he paid little attention to why Descartes broke with the sixteenth-century view and broke ground for the perspective that led, after successive adaptations and even revolutions, to the modern usage. I believe that one would discover that a series of praxical inconsistencies had been building up in the period preceding Descartes. Foucault himself gave a number of examples, including Bodin's proof that gold as money was not merely a mark of value but also a commodity.[15]

Inconsistencies could be ignored or submerged—as seemingly disconfirming experiments are in modern science—until their accumulation produced disturbances that could no longer be ignored. Before Descartes there must have been numerous thinkers who were searching for and who found partial solutions to these disturbing problems that were based upon concepts that differed from resemblance. Beneath the surface of the philosophical equilibrium, things would have been approaching a "step function" (to use a key concept in systems analysis).

In short, Europe must have been ripe for a revolutionary philosophy when Descartes propounded his new ideas. With them, he could produce a new literal language within the terms of which the language of the sixteenth century could be perceived as metaphor.

Descartes' new literal language permitted new understandings of relationships. Moreover, these understandings would fit together: they would be understandable both in their own terms and in terms of the immediate surround in the realm of knowledge. And here I must disagree with Foucault, who asserted that all language is metaphor. Language is potentially both metaphoric and literal: metaphor is such only in contrast to language that is literal and vice versa.

In theories of physical science, on the whole, quantitative signs are used, while qualitative signs are used in the social and moral sciences. These signs have meanings that are given by their use and, like definitions, are representational only within their framework of use. Signs, however, are not representational as such, that is, apart from the framework of use that permits their interpretation in this fashion. Thus I see unity in the physical and social sciences, whereas Foucault saw disjunction.

The language game is always subordinate to the science game. It is surely possible to show, in terms of our own understanding of science, how the science game of the oracular priest or of the magician of the sixteenth century became transformed into the science game of the seventeenth century. This showing, I am confident, would demonstrate the presence of theory and praxis even in the simple society of the oracle or in the sixteenth century. Our own science game will no doubt be shown by subsequent generations of scientists to contain the core of their science game. It is within this framework that scientific theories and languages develop. There has been progress in science.

I am aware that Wittgenstein was not a complete relativist. But he placed as constraints on linguistic conventions only those objective facts that are rooted in the pre-linguistic world: the primitive, pre-linguistic behavior of beings who react and judge in the same way in similar situations, as, for instance, in the presence of pain. However, our ability to refer to such facts presupposes signs and language and, thus, linguistic means for referring to them. A person's ability to act depends upon perceptual coding and, hence, on at least implicit language.

Furthermore, unless these coding systems are divisible into part systems, they could not be transformed and learning could not occur. We would have an even more inelastic structure than Noam Chomsky's, and one inconsistent with both evolutionary advantage and survival.* Finally, because transactions between part coding systems permit transformations both within the systems and in transactions with the external world, a universal identity of the starting states of the systems is not required for the achievement of similar contemporary states, although it is conceivable that sufficiently great discrepancies in transactional capabilities could debar communication. Wittgenstein's only attempt to escape the circularity of language games is, thus, neither sufficient nor even necessary.

Finally, the categories Wittgenstein uses, such as pain, misrepresent aboriginal coding or implicit language. When an infant reaches for a nipple, it is responding to some variant in the "nourishment" or "non-nourishment" correlative realm and perhaps some identification of a locator, or source, as well. In no case does a person respond to sensation alone, for even pain is a coded event. Sensation is inferred in order to explain the event. The resulting perception—and experience consists of perceptions—is a product of a transaction. We see trees. We do not see sense representations of a tree. We cannot even make that concept meaningful in the absence of transactions, for the very existence of a tree—indeed, of any object or process that belongs to an established category—depends not merely upon the character of the transmitter but also on the character of the transceiver and its previous experience. Even in *Philosophical Investigations*, Wittgenstein did not really cut loose from his positivistic metaphysics or the somewhat similar metaphysics of English empiricism.

PRIVACY AND CONSCIOUSNESS

Consider Wittgenstein's use of ostensive or extensional definition, that is, definition by pointing or by extension: " 'Red' means the color that occurs to me when I hear the word 'red'—would be a *definition*. Not an explanation of *what it is* to use a word as a name."[16]

Wittgenstein then went on:

> If language is to be a means of communication there must be agreement not only in definitions but also (queer as this may sound) in judgements. This seems to abolish logic, but does not do so.—It is one thing to describe methods of measurement, and another to obtain and state results of measurement. But what we call "measuring" is partly determined by a certain constancy in results of measurement.[17]

So far there is nothing to quarrel over. What I mean when I say "red" is the color I (and other people) think of when they use the word. If our judgments

---

*Extensive linguistic analysis by other scientists has led Chomsky finally to admit, as some of us had argued on evolutionary grounds, that there is no deep structure from which the grammar of all languages can be derived. He now argues for a deep structure that can be transformed in certain ways under a variety of conditions. That is not unreasonable and within limits is almost certainly correct. However, his statement runs the serious risk either of being excessively deterministic or of being ad hoc.

are highly variable, there can be no communication, either from myself at one time to myself at another time or among different people. In this sense, communication means building a common world, and it does include grammar and language games.

Is it true, however, as Wittgenstein argued, that "If a lion could talk, we could not understand him"?[18] Lion tamers and lions understand each other without talking. The example is poor, although perhaps the point Wittgenstein wanted to make is that a constancy of results, a common world, is what is required. A creature with a span of attention of ten thousand years could not communicate with us nor we with it.

Wittgenstein asked hard questions:

> What is the criterion for the sameness of two images?—What is the criterion for the redness of an image? For me, when it is someone else's image: what he says and does. For myself, when it is my image: nothing. And what goes for "red" also goes for "same." . . .

> How do I know that this colour is red?—It would be an answer to say: "I have learnt English."[19]

What did Wittgenstein mean when he said that red is what red is in English? That that is how we use English? That it is a name? We can hardly take exception to this: the meaning that a sign conveys depends upon how we use it. But what is use?

Someone says he sees a red screen. We know that seeing a red screen is a product of a perceiver, an object, and an environment. It is not a copy of something either inside or outside our heads.

But what does it mean to ask whether what we see is the same? Both redness and sameness are products. Their warrants are public. We know that others see what we see; and that this is not merely a matter of language and of ostensive definition. Real-world meaning is invoked; and language and definition are merely tools that help us to invoke meaning.

How do we compare the red we saw ten minutes ago with the red we see now? Has the lighting changed? Are filters present? Have I been introduced to distinctions of which I was not previously aware that have altered my internal recognition signalling system so that now I no longer see merely red but crimson or maroon? If none of these, or any other relevant elements, have been altered, that lack of alteration is our warrant. And that is also our warrant for asserting that others see what we see. That which is perceived is a transactional, and hence public, although hypothetical, fact. The element of privacy or tacit knowledge is not relevant in the context in which Wittgenstein raises it. "They see what we see" means that in this environment, under these conditions, they participate in producing what we participate in producing. My statement is an assessment, not a proof, but there are praxical grounds for my judgements, including, but not restricted to, knowledge of the physiology of others.

Now we see that naming, description, and science are not independent systems or games. They do not occur in discrete form. They are part systems interrelated in analysis. Now we vary one aspect while tentatively keeping the others constant (otherwise our minds would be overloaded). Now we vary another. Some aspects involve theory. Others praxis. The so-called games are transformed in the process. Sometimes they are merely modified. Sometimes they are radically changed. But then the analysis of games *qua* games is an irrelevance. It is not the game that is afoot but the scientific problem. The game is not conventional, like chess. These are games in which the referees, the scientists, evaluate alternative rules according to neutral criteria.

Let us see how naming and science are interrelated. Whether a game that resembles chess is called chess is a conventional matter. Einsteinian and Newtonian mechanics are both theories of mechanics. The name "mechanics" is partly conventional and partly determined by similarities in the central logic of the theories. However, a preference for one of the theories over the other is not conventional. Neutral criteria determine which is to be preferred. This is a theoretical decision if the relevant boundary conditions are known and permit a so-called critical experiment to be performed. It is a praxical decision if the relevant boundary conditions are uncertain and require assessment. In neither case is the decision conventional.

CONSCIOUSNESS AND PRIVACY

Now let us return to problems of consciousness and privacy; for, as in his discussion of naming and redness, Wittgenstein got it wrong. Is it really true, as Wittgenstein said, that when one says something to oneself, ". . . I do *not* say it from observation of my behaviour. But it only makes sense because I do behave in this way.—Then it is not because I *mean* it that it makes sense"?[20] It is not true that I do not say it from observation of my behavior. Sometimes a complete thought pops into our minds, and then we say we must have been thinking it even though we were not conscious of it. And do we not think about thinking, and does this not involve observation of our thinking? What is it that we are talking about? If we are talking about subjectivity, which is the ultimate reflexive element of thought and consciousness, then we surely cannot observe it, for it is the field within which reference occurs. If, however, we refer to prior stages of the process, then we either do observe it directly—that is, we talk to ourselves about talking to ourselves—or we infer it from other observations; and so it enters the field of objectivity.

Earlier, discussing privacy, Wittgenstein wrote:

In what sense are my sensations *private*? Well, only I can know whether I am really in pain; another person can only surmise it.—In one way this is wrong, and in another nonsense. . . .

Other people cannot be said to learn of my sensations *only* from my behavior,—for I cannot be said to learn of them. I *have* them.

The truth is: it makes sense to say about other people that they doubt whether I am in pain; but not to say it about myself.

"Only you can know if you had that intention." One might tell someone this when one was explaining the meaning of the word "intention" to him. For then it means: *that* is how we use it.

(And here "know" means that the expression of uncertainty is senseless.)[21]

It is true that if we experience something we call pain, we have experienced it. That is tautological. Even here, however, as the reader will remember from chapter 4, the empirical is the correlate of the analytical, and there is room for doubt. I may have dreamt the pain. We use empirical cues in judging whether we have dreamt something or, alternatively, whether we have a false memory of something that occurred in the past.

Wittgenstein, who was still in the grip of a positivistic metaphysics, obscured more than he illuminated by his tautology. Is it really senseless to assert that I only think I am in pain? Is pain a simple phenomenon? Can I not distinguish between pain that is physically produced and pain that is imaginatively produced?

The amputee feels pain in the foot that is no longer there. Is that nonsense because the foot is no longer there? Is this pain any different from the pain felt when the foot was there? Yet it is surely false that the foot is causing pain or that the pain is in the foot, although the amputee undoubtedly feels pain in "his" foot.

Perhaps Wittgenstein would have argued that I have to distinguish between the pain that is actually felt and the lack of pain that occurs after we have sorted out our own psychic state. Even so, this is a difference.

But would this distinction have saved Wittgenstein with respect to intentions? Suppose that a gambler bets and loses. He says, "I intended to win but failed." His opponent says, "No; you are a compulsive gambler and intended to lose." He responds, "Gee, you're right." Is that necessarily nonsense? Perhaps the meaning of intention is more complex than Wittgenstein granted.

The essential thing about private experience is really not that each person possesses his own exemplar, but that nobody knows whether other people also have *this* or something else. The assumption would thus be possible—though unverifiable—that one section of mankind had one sensation of red and another section another.[22]

But we don't know sensations directly, not even privately. Sensations are public but not known, except as inferences. One's own experiences and feelings are known directly and are private, but can become public. The preconscious internal signalling system that recognizes sameness may be private in the sense that we do not know—at least in detail—what produces sameness; and possibly, in complex situations, an experience may differ from person to person. In computers, the matching or signalling system is known and may, or may not, be "private" in the sense that it may differ from computer to computer.

In any other sense, what Wittgenstein wrote is false. A computer that learned to recognize colors would code a given angstrom pattern as "yellow," for instance, not as yellow. That is, it would associate an angstrom pattern with a sign, not a concept or qualitative experience with a sign. We know that it "sees" differently from us. We may not be sure what red-green color-blind people see when they report seeing red or green, but we know that what they see is different from what we see. We also know that their eyes are structured differently. And we know, even though dogs cannot report to us, that dogs do not see the colors that we see. We know, too, that what we see as red under one lighting system we will not see as red under a different lighting system. We also know that filters of various types will transform colors for us. This is what permits us to say, "This color appears to be green but is really blue." We mean that we know that under standard conditions it would look blue.

Suppose we see a green bush. Our neighbor sees the same bush and reports that it is green. Do we believe that we do not know that he sees a green bush? Or does "green bush" mean that what we see as a green bush is what he is referring to when he calls *x* a green bush? Do we really rely upon ostensive or extensional definitions: that he uses the word "green" whenever he points to what we see as green and that he uses the word "bush" whenever he observes things having certain spatial forms and biological characteristics? Or do we assert that he sees what we see: a green bush? And do we not have substantial evidence to "justify" this belief even though his seeing is not our seeing? If intensional meaning were not also part of the real world, how could we know what are the referents of ostensive naming?

Suppose that our brains had been built like modern amplifiers with plug-in parts? Then suppose we took the optic apparatus out of one person's brain and put it into another's so that he now is using the other person's optic apparatus. What he formerly saw as green he still sees as green. Now let us substitute an optic apparatus that produces different types of color tones. He now tells us that perceiving green is an experience he no longer has. Is this different in kind from our former evidence? Or does it merely increase our confidence in a judgment about which we were already confident? Is it not really so that his experience is a public fact and not merely a private one? How, after all, do we know that the red we see now is the red we saw before?

Suppose we possessed one optic apparatus between us and that it communicated to both of us? Our optic processes would be identical (except for differences introduced by the respective casings) but our self-consciousness would be different—that is, our knowing of our common vision would be different. My argument here is not dependent on the practicality of such an experiment but on the meaning of meaning and on what provides confidence in a public judgment.

Elsewhere, Wittgenstein wrote something similar:

> What am I to say about the word "red"?—that it means something "confronting us all" and that everyone should really have another word, besides this one, to mean his *own* sensation of red? Or is it like this: the word "red" means something known to everyone; and in addition, for each person, it means something known only to him? (Or perhaps rather: it *refers* to something known only to him.)[23]

This is less than clear. Was Wittgenstein saying that people share the same public experience when they use the sign "red" but that there is a tacit cueing that accomplishes this? Or did he mean that they share merely a public language that is constitutive of meaning, while experiences are merely private? Or did he mean that experience is partly private? There are tacit and preconscious elements in experience, and these no doubt are private. But they are not communicated even to ourselves.

Consider Wittgenstein's treatment of the "misleading parallel" between psychology and physics:

> Misleading parallel: psychology treats of processes in the psychical sphere, as does physics in the physical.

> Seeing, hearing, thinking, feeling, willing, are not the subject of psychology *in the same sense* as that in which the movements of bodies, the phenomena of electricity, etc., are the subject of physics. You can see this from the fact that the physicist sees, hears, thinks about, and informs us of these phenomena, and the psychologist observes the *external reactions* (the behavior) of the subject.[24]

But what is electric current and how do we know it? Do we ever observe the current or only its manifestations? Do we not infer the presence of the current from shock? From a flash of light? According to Rudolf Carnap, we cannot define it. It must be treated in terms of what he calls a reduction sentence or, in my terms, as a dispositional concept. But then how does this differ from psychology? Are the criteria so different from those of physics that they do not fit into at least a family?

How do we know that a quark exists? What is an atom if not a disposition to behave in certain ways? Even defined terms, as Wittgenstein elsewhere recognized, begin to lose their sharpness at the edges and to merge into other concepts as their dispositional behavior unfolds. Is this not a consequence of the fact that meaning is expressed in terms of correlatives?

But Wittgenstein went on to play his little tricks on us and again appeared to be in agreement:

> "When I say 'I am in pain' I am at any rate justified *before myself*."—What does that mean? Does it mean: "If someone else could know what I am calling 'pain,' he would admit that I was using the word correctly"?

> To use a word without a justification does not mean to use it without right.[25]

Now, if what Wittgenstein intended to say was that language is an instrument and that it does not require a corresponding image, as he appeared to state in aphorisms 293 and 300 on pages 100e and 101e, respectively, of *Philosophical Investigations*, this is possibly acceptable. If he was asserting that meaning is private—"Suppose everyone had a box with something in it: we call it a beetle. No one can look into anyone else's box, and everyone says he knows what a beetle is only by looking at *his* beetle—Here it would be quite possible for

everyone to have something different in his box.''[26]—he may have been referring
only to the tacit elements of experience.

If, however, Wittgenstein was saying that the fact of someone else feeling
pain is unknowable, I disagree. Pain itself is a public phenomenon even though
the experience of it is not. We may feel pain in the entire arm. However, after
the doctor tells us that the pain is really localized in the elbow, that may be
where we feel it.

Could we imagine an automaton that would give all the right responses and
yet not feel pain? Suppose we prick it when it is asleep. Suppose it always
groans desperately when the pain is supposed to be grave? Perhaps. But then
perhaps the world is a dream and we only dream our own pain. We can never
be certain. But that does not mean that we cannot have remarkable grounds for
confidence, even about knowing what others feel and see.

Consider what Wittgenstein said about dreaming:

> The argument ''I may be dreaming'' is senseless for this reason: if I am dreaming,
> this remark is being dreamed as well—and indeed it is also being dreamed that these
> words have any meaning.[27]

But this is not true. A dream is part of a complex event. I may be asleep
and dreaming and yet have some awareness that I am dreaming. In fact, this
has happened to me on a number of occasions, as it has happened to a great
many other people. If we interpret Wittgenstein's comment in this fashion, then
it is factually incorrect in an almost trivial way.

Suppose, however, that Wittgenstein was arguing against the position that
all of our experience is a dream. Is this, philosophically speaking, better guarded
against the previous objection? Of course, we do not believe that our experience
is a dream; we have experienced the differences between dreams and reality.
Undoubtedly, it is some cue of this type that alerts us to the dream-like nature
of a dream during some near-waking states of dream experience. Suppose,
however, that in some ''brave new world'' we were hooked up to instruments
that provided us with quite coherent daily experiences. Suppose that someone
asks whether this is reality or merely a dream. Perhaps there was some slip-up
in the program. Perhaps that person caught some clue or cue that triggered the
notion that we were being systematically fooled.

In this imagined situation also, the thought that one is dreaming need not be
part of the dream in the sense that Wittgenstein suggested. It occurs in the dream
but is not merely part of it. Thus, whether Wittgenstein's position is proof even
against the suggestion that this experience is nothing but a dream depends upon
what one means by ''nothing but a dream.''

Perhaps the reader thinks that I have not paid sufficient attention to the fact
that Wittgenstein is not talking about the cause of pain but about knowledge of
it. This does not invalidate the prior critique but instead reinforces it. The concept
of knowing is more complex than Wittgenstein's language-games methodology
recognizes. Wittgenstein's analysis is insufficient with respect to both the part
system–whole system problem and with respect to the specification of the knower.

Consider, for instance, an individual whose *corpus callosum* has been severed. Such individuals have been known to deny that they see a chair in the room but also have been observed to walk around it. The severed halves of the brain perform different functions. This individual "knows" in the sense of consciousness or awareness that the chair is present but the self-conscious reflexive function of the brain does not possess this information. He "knows" but does not know of the presence of the chair.

Suppose that the same thing were to occur with pain. The principle is identical even if the factual situation should be different. In this case the individual would "know" but not know his pain. If the external observer sees bodily indications of pain, he knows of the pain whereas the individual in pain does not. A sufficiently empathetic observer may even feel pain. Does he know the pain of the other individual?

To argue that the observer may know of the pain but not know it is to argue that there cannot be in principle a transient connection between the two individuals. I have already argued that knowing applies to a part system and not to the entire individual. When I say I know my own pain, I have adopted a useful ellipsis of expression. For my pain to be known by me in terms of self-consciousness, there must be a transmission of information from one part system to another. This is what happens when the empathetic observer feels pain when pain is produced in another body. The two loci of self-consciousness are different. Two different neurological systems are involved in producing the pain. It involves a more complex ellipsis when I say I know someone else's pain than when I say I know my pain. But it is not entirely incorrect to say that I may know someone else's pain.

Could not Wittgenstein respond that the quality of the pain may be different, that I know someone else's pain differently? This is so because the physiological and neurological systems are different. This, however, is true also with respect to my own pain, which retrospectively I know only self-reflexively and through memory. There are weakly-ordered means of assessing these qualitiative differences—whether between the pain felt by different individuals or of the pain felt by the same individual at different times—comparatively.

Nothing is left of Wittgenstein's account except the fact that two different self-consciousnesses are related to two different neurological subsystems. This, however, is a real-world fact, not a product of a language game. Some science fiction writers have speculated about shared consciousnesses. Nothing in language prevents this. We reject it only because there is no evidence for it.

Wittgenstein's error is similar to that of the continental hermeneutic philosophers, who fail to fully take into account the fact that meaning involves a triadic relationship between concept, sign, and referent. Meaning requires real-world reference and attention to frameworks of reference. A complex process of assessment is required for this task. At the conceptual level, the meaning of concepts is influenced by the realm of concepts. At the scientific level, the interpretation of theories and propositions is dependent upon an assessment process that takes into account the scientific surround. Relations between the realms are mediated by signs. There is a rich process of reassessment and reinterpretation. As this is extended to the entire realm of knowledge synoptically, the traditional problems of philosophy reemerge, although their statement and the conclusions that are reached change. This is a spiral process that, when sufficiently radicalized, rejects previous statements of questions and the answers to them. When Wittgenstein rejected as metaphysical not merely previous ways of formulating the traditional questions of philosophy but the entire body of questions, he also threw out the entire scientific and conceptual surround in the absence of which we cannot properly assess the current state of knowledge. The task of philosophy is to develop a synoptic world view that interpenetrates the findings of the individual sciences and that reformulates the perennial problems of philosophy rather than dismisses them as meaningless.

GLOBAL AND PART PROCESSES

Wittgenstein seemed to treat the process of thought as if it were a unified global process. For instance, he wrote:

> Now if it were asked: "Do you have the thought before finding the expression?" what would one have to reply? And what, to the question: "What did the thought consist in, as it existed before its expression?"[28]

However, what is it that we mean when, after uttering a thought, we state: "That's what we had in mind"? Although we can communicate to others the knowledge that we have this belief, and even sometimes the foundations on which it rests, to some extent at least this is tacit, private, or personal knowledge. But it is not simply like Wittgenstein's beetle in a box. There may be processes going on in the mind, perhaps even using a different kind of language, to which we have partial access and some aspects of which we implicitly recognize. It seems rather difficult even to imagine how mental processes might operate if this were not so. One may admit cheerfully that this process employs signs and rules, that the verbal and symbolic system it uses operates only with respect to referents, and that thought would be impossible in its absence. But language is merely one of the producers of thought. Language itself can be divided into part systems and, as a whole, it is a part system within a larger system.

To give Wittgenstein his due, however, the correlatives "subjective" and "objective" are themselves terms that are essential to meaning. Knowledge can deal only with those things that are possible objects of knowledge. On the other hand, no object of knowledge can exist apart from its potentiality as a referent in the field of knowledge. If this is all that Wittgenstein meant when he asserted that there is no need for a ghost in the system, there is no cause to object.

Thus when Wittgenstein asked—"But then how is it with man: where does *he* say things to himself?"[29]—we can agree with him, if he was referring to the subjective aspect. If he was talking about the objective aspect, then this internal talk occurs within the cerebral cortex. Objectively, we can discuss the preconditions of a process of thinking or imagination and even some elements of its progress.

Consider how Ryle treated this problem:

> But it does not matter for my general argument whether this excursus into philology is correct or not. It will serve to draw attention to the sorts of things which we say are "in our heads," namely, such things as imagined words, tunes, and perhaps, vistas. When people employ the idiom "in the mind," they are usually expressing over-sophisticatedly what we ordinarily express by the less misleading metaphorical use of "in the head."[30]

But whether the thought is in the head depends upon whether we are referring to the correlative "knowing" or the correlative "known." The process that produces the thought as an item of knowledge is in the head. Consciously, we know only those things to which the categories of space and time apply, but space and time are not relevant to the knowing of them.

Ryle was correct in stating that there is such a thing as a category mistake, for instance, putting a school in the same category as classrooms, teachers, students, and lessons. "School" and "classroom" are system and element, respectively. A system does equal its elements in their organized relationships; and it is a category mistake to regard it as something additional, except from the standpoint of its corporate relation to the world, other foci of reference, and whatever potentialities of its elements may be obscured by this formulation. But Ryle's example of "mind" and "imagined words, tunes, and perhaps vistas" was not a category mistake. "Mind" is not to "word" as "school" is to "classroom." The mind-word pair invokes a correlative relationship: the subjective and objective aspects of the world. Ryle in effect mistakenly dismisses consciousness as a correlative of the objective. With this illicit move, Ryle has made an unfathomable mystery of how we know the world.

Furthermore, although Ryle uses the term "concept" in his title *Concept of Mind*, he fails to take it seriously. The "imagined" word is not the concept. The concept—which is part of a system of concepts and which has a preconscious penumbra—is merely represented by the "imagined" word. The "imagined" word is the private aspect of a public sign which, with the concept, has an intensional directness toward a referent. Language develops as adjustments are made among concepts, among signs, among referents, and in the interrelationships among the three elements. Mind cannot be reduced to the neurological system. It includes information also, the investigation of which employs methods that are in a condition of complementarity to those with which neurological systems are investigated.* Mind in relating to the world produces languages and changes them. Although languages do help to shape our knowledge of the world, they do so in ways that are constrained by a wide variety of part systems that are both internal and external.

---

*The relationship of consciousness to information is discussed in Chapter 7.

REFERENCE: THE "I" IN LANGUAGE GAMES

"I" is not the name of a person, nor "here" of a place, and "this" is not a name. But they are connected with names. Names are explained by means of them. It is also true that it is characteristic of physics not to use these words.[31]

Was Wittgenstein correct or did he misunderstand physics? Doesn't relativity theory have its equivalent to "I" in the concept of an observer on an inertial system? Place is a necessary reference for motion. Location is a necessary reference for pain. Some of the differences between physics and psychology involve differences in the range of propositions in which reference to loci is important. Furthermore, the transactions between experiments and experimenters in quantum mechanics also exemplify an "I" type of phenomenon.

The seeming monolithic unity of the "I" is an artifact of hemispheric dominance in the brain. In the normal personality, the "I" is integrated into a complex self. In certain neuroses, the "I" dominates and distorts other aspects of the self; it produces ontological dysfunctions. In extreme cases, multiple personalities may be produced. Furthermore, the non-dominant half of the brain may also be conscious. The "I" of the dominant half at best will have only indirect access to the processes of this consciousness through the *corpus callosum*; and it may be entirely unaware of it.

"I" is a referential locus that is part of the meaning of experiences. It is not a self-subsisting entity, beyond knowledge, or utterly different in its function from other systems the accounts of which require loci of reference.

Consider the following example in this respect. Wittgenstein said:

One can say "I will, but my body does not obey me"—but not: "My will does not obey me." (Augustine.)

But in the sense in which I cannot fail to will, I cannot try to will either.[32]

But are there not part systems here also? Can I not will to will to stop smoking? And if I fail, cannot I say that my will has failed me even though I tried to will? In this sense, is there that significant a difference between the body failing to obey the willed impulse and the will failing to obey it? Wittgenstein treated this matter not only as if there are not part systems but as if there is not a reflexive process. We do not will or not will. Willing is a complex and reflexive process within a complex decentralized system.

Consider another example. Wittgenstein said:

So one might say: voluntary movement is marked by the absence of surprise. And now I do not mean you to ask "But *why* isn't one surprised here?"[33]

Cannot someone say, truthfully: "When I saw him, I got so angry that I punched him. I surprised myself"? The bully threatens me. Instead of running, as I used to do, I stand up to him; and this surprises me. Is my own act involuntary because it surprises me? Does even a language game require this conclusion?

It is only the thought or the willed act that we think about that can fail to surprise us, for it is a datum, an objective fact. Then the surprise is gone, except perhaps in a residual sense. Neither thought nor will as act is a datum, unless it is subsumed reflexively to another act of will or thought; therefore our thought, our will, and our act can surprise us. This is not a matter of language games but of the adaptation of language to a reality that is more complex than Wittgenstein suggested.

What did Wittgenstein mean when he wrote:

> Why do I want to tell him about an intention too, as well as telling him what I did?—Not because the intention was also something which was going on at that time. But because I want to tell him something about *myself*, which goes beyond what happened at that time.

> I reveal to him something of myself when I tell him what I was going to do.—Not, however, on grounds of self-observation, but by way of a response (it might also be called an intuition).[34]

What did Wittgenstein mean by saying that this is merely a response or an intuition but not self-observation? If he meant that we do not taste, see, or feel the intention, then of course he was correct. But is not the statement made on the basis of a body of experience? Part of the experience deals with thinking about thoughts. Another part of the experience deals with the relationship between intentional thought and behavior and the conditions under which these intentions tend to become manifest in action or to be repressed. That is how I know I had an intention that was not expressed. Then I made an observation and communicated it. If Wittgenstein wished to use his language differently, I have good grounds for preferring my usage.

Consider further Wittgenstein's statement, "One can mistrust one's own senses, but not one's own belief."[35] He added:

> I say of someone else "He seems to believe. . . ." and other people say it of me. Now, why do I never say it of myself, not even when others *rightly* say it of me? —Do I myself not see and hear myself, then?—That can be said.[36]

Cannot I say that I believe that the sun is shining but suspect that the LSD that I took is producing this belief? Is it possible to observe that I believe that John is honest, notice, however, that I never engage in business dealings with him, and begin to wonder whether I really believe my belief? How does my argument differ from Wittgenstein's later argument: " 'I know . . .' may mean 'I do not doubt . . .' but does not mean that the words 'I doubt . . .' are *senseless*, that doubt is logically excluded."[37] Belief is also a very complex concept. It may be true that I do not doubt that I have a belief and also true that I do not believe that it is correct. Therefore, there is also a sense in which I can doubt I have it.

Consider another of Wittgenstein's statements:

> Two points, however, are important: one, that in many cases someone else cannot predict my actions, whereas I foresee them in my intentions; the other, that my

prediction (in my expression of intention) has not the same foundation as his prediction of what I shall do, and the conclusions to be drawn from these predictions are quite different.[38]

But perhaps the psychiatrist can foresee the intentions of the doer better than the doer himself. Yes, it is perfectly true that predictions based on different information may produce different conclusions. The compulsive gambler may not know that he intends to lose. A professional gambler who plays this "fish" may know of his intention to lose. Again, this merely tells us that there are different funds of information. Not even with respect to intentions can the doer's fund be said to be necessarily better than the observer's.

This is true even of dreams. Wittgenstein tells us:

> The question whether the dreamer's memory deceives him when he reports the dream after waking cannot arise, unless indeed we introduce a completely new criterion for the report's "agreeing" with the dream, a criterion which gives us a concept of "truth" as distinct from "truthfulness" here.[39]

The psychoanalyist, however, may be able to reconstruct the actual dream better from the dreamer's report than the dreamer himself. Wittgenstein is correct that the concepts of "truth" and "truthfulness" are relevant here. However, even apart from the problem that the dreamer may remember the dream poorly, his implication that the truth of the dream can be known only through the dreamer's report is not necessarily accurate. The analyst may be able to reconstruct it despite the dreamer's inaccurate report. And he may have a huge comparative data base on which to base his hypotheses—admittedly fallible, but so are the dreamer's memories and reconstructions.

Wittgenstein elsewhere seems to be aware of this: "I can be as *certain* of someone else's sensations [sic] as of any fact."[40] Yet, he states so many seemingly contradictory things that we cannot be sure.

CONCLUSION

Wittgenstein's demonstration of the interpretation of a rule for the formulation of a mathematical series is a striking example of the pragmaticist position that an analytical system does not have meaning purely in its own terms. The linguistic interpretation of the rule is conventional, and a second-order language can be used to translate the conventions of one language into those of another. Science is itself conventional in this sense.

However, the more important aspect of rules is not their conventional use but their use in the pragmaticist sense, that is, in the sense of their ability to convey useful information about the world. In this sense, conventions are bounded by their usefulness. And in this sense, they are natural.

It is misleading to talk of a physics language game as distinguished from a biology language game. The difference is not in language but in subject matter. Language is merely an instrument designed to elicit meaning, to place meaning within a framework that shapes it.

No language adjudicates statements about the world. To the contrary, reality that is, external criteria, determines the usefulness of a language. Wittgenstein's language-games concept was useful primarily to combat the essentialist metaphysics of classical philosophy and of phenomenology. Although Wittgenstein never fully falls into the traps that plague some of his followers, his emphasis is distracting. If, perhaps, those followers took him seriously—that is, that his intention was to use this mode of philosophical analysis merely to get rid of metaphysical traps or puzzles—no harm would have been done. However; in many cases, the method became a substitute for science. And this produced language games in the pejorative sense. Adequate recognition of the correlative tasks of theory and praxis is all that is required to combat the fallacy of essentialism and to permit a consistent pragmaticist interpretation of the world.

NOTES

1. Ludwig Wittgenstein, *Philosophical Investigations*, translated by G.E.M. Anscomb (Oxford: Basil Blackwell & Mott, 1958), pp. 11e.–12e.

2. Ibid., p. 36e.

3. Ibid., pp. 74e–75e.

4. Ludwig Wittgenstein, *On Certainty*, edited by G.E.M. Anscombe, translated by Denis Paul and G.E.M. Anscombe, (New York: Harper & Row, Publishers, 1969), p. 80e.

5. Wittgenstein, *Philosophical Investigations*, p. 138e.

6. Wittgenstein, *On Certainty*, pp. 27e.–28e. (Part in brackets, crossed out in ms.) Wording of English text corrected at request of executors of Wittgenstein's estate.

7. Gilbert Ryle, *Concept of Mind* (London: Hutchinson Publishing Group, 1949), pp. 30–31.

8. Wittgenstein, *Philosophical Investigations*, pp.40–41e.

9. Ibid., p. 47e

10. Ibid., p. 195e.

11. Jacques Derrida, *Writing and Difference*, translated by Alan Bass (Chicago: University of Chicago Press, 1978).

12. Wittgenstein, *Philosophical Investigations*, pp. 52e–53e.

13. Lewis Morgan, *Systems of Consanguinity*, (Washington, D.C.: Smithsonian Institute, 1980).

14. Michel Foucault, *The Order of Things: The Archaeology of Human Sciences* (New York: Pantheon Books, 1970).

15. Ibid., p. 171.

16. Wittgenstein, *Philosophical Investigations*, p. 88e.

17. Ibid.

18. Ibid., p. 223e.

19. Ibid., p. 117e.

20. Ibid., p. 113e.

21. Ibid., p. 89e.

22. Ibid., pp. 94e–95e.

23. Ibid., p.95e.

24. Ibid., p. 151e.

25. Ibid., p. 99e.

26. Ibid., p. 100e.

27. Wittgenstein, *On Certainty*, p. 49e.

28. Wittgenstein, *Philosophical Investigations*, p. 116.

29. Ibid., p. 114e.

30. Ryle, *Concept of Mind*, pp. 39–40.

31. Wittgenstein, *Philosophical Investigations*, p. 116.

32. Ibid., p. 161e.

33. Ibid., p. 162e.

34. Ibid., p. 167e.

35. Ibid., p. 190e.

36. Ibid., p.191e.

37. Ibid., p. 221e.

38. Ibid., p. 224e.

39. Ibid., pp. 222e–223e.

40. Ibid., p. 224e.

Chapter 10
Deconstruction: An Alternative
To Science

In Derrida's opinion, all of Western thought stemmed from Greek philosophy or metaphysics, from the attempt to know, to structure, to systematize, to differentiate and separate. Science, in its Greek sense, is the philosophical source of differentiation or separation. But, Derrida said, all language (écriture), and not merely Greek philosophy, ends up in incoherence, in an infinite sequence of signifiers, each of which leaves gaps in dealing with presences: that which philosophy and literal language hide and which is the source of meaning and truth. In the search for presence, he wrote, we move from gap to gap or from absence to absence.*

To understand the Greek program and its limitations, Derrida said, one must understand that the program emerged from the *pre-logos*. Before reason, there was hubris or madness. This pre-logos phase constitutes the *other*: that which transcends reason and logic. It is the necessary counterpart to writing and difference: the counterpart that is denied by science. The other is the true infinity, not a determinate totality that is a false infinity, a not-finity.

All determination, as expressed in writing, according to Derrida, is finite; and this finitude is the source of metaphysics. It is also the foundation of the historicity of ideas, for all writing deals only with limited truths that rest upon the truth of the limited ideas from which they emerge. They can be understood only in relation to each other. Therefore, there is one book, which is always being rewritten, and deconstruction tears apart finite books in the search for that truly infinite one book that finite books hide.

My summary undoubtedly does less than justice to the complexity of Derrida's claims. However, I think that I can show, for reasons explicated in Part One, that the analyst's task is not to deconstruct a text in search of the one true book but to elucidate its first-order referential character, to contrast it with other relevant first-order references, and to relate these at a second-order level.

---

*The quotations from Jacques Derrida, *Writing and Difference*, translated by Alan Bass, copyright © 1978, The University of Chicago Press, are used by permission of the publisher.

To begin with, in the phase before logos, I do not agree that there was the other. There was only the different and the same. The ape that sees or hears does not experience the other. Perception cannot be understood apart from information. Apes perceive, they recognize, they react. Information requires selection and determination. Receptors receive within a range; they determine the form and content of perceiving and reasoning.

Just as perception was ordered in what Derrida called the pre-logos, so was behavior. Although it is true that, to communicate this order to the reader, I must use writing and language, what we show with writing and language is the existence of order that does not depend upon them and that is prerequisite to both. The order of spheres is part of nature. That the heart pumps the blood is part of the order of the body. The dysfunctioning of the heart is to its ordered relationship within the body as the dysfunctioning of thought, or madness, is to reason. Madness is a dysfunction of order, a finite negation of order that is recognized by contrast.

Under many conditions, we have an intuitive awareness of order and disorder. It is true that verbalizing order differentiates and refines it, in the process sacrificing some information to gain still more information—almost, in Derrida's sense, destroying similarities, as by distinguishing and naming shades of red. If this process creates or produces finite properties, they are among the potentialities of the referents. It is a process that refines knowledge and experience. It increases our freedom by increasing our power. And, contrary to Derrida, it reduces our intrusion upon others by permitting greater independence and greater comprehension of differences in them. It is the mad person who does not apprehend the irreducible reality of others as autonomous human beings with value in their own right and persons of reason who can both appreciate and control their passions, and who alone are capable of seeing others as autonomous beings, as ethical others. It is the limitation and the mortality of others—the shocks and injuries that are part of life—that produce pathos and arouse empathy in persons of reason, who know how so many dreams and hopes must end.[1]

To continue: Can ideas be understood only historically? Must we deconstruct ideas according to their history? True, Hegel's contributions to philosophy, for instance, can best be understood by understanding the problems which philosophers confronted as the Kantian system broke down. However, the Hegelian system was not the only possible response to the failure of the Kantian. Such interrelationships are weakly ordered. The longer the sequence takes, the weaker the order and the more indirect the relationships; then the more a theory can be understood in its own terms and independently of its history. Although we cannot understand Einstein's development of the theory of relativity except in terms of the problems confronting Newtonian theorists after the Michelson–Morley experiment, the discovery of neo-Euclidean geometries, and Lorentz contractions, the validity of his theory does not depend on those relationships. A different civilization might have arrived at a similar theory by a different route. Furthermore, the theory of relativity can be communicated without recapitulating the history of physics.

Derrida's claim that the other is the negation of the specifically determined was mistaken reasoning. One "other" of a specifically determined thing, event, or process is the "not this specifically determined thing or event or process." Another other of a specifically determined thing is the potentiality of this specifically determined thing. But this is also determinate. A third other of a determinate thing or process is its indeterminate correlative, e.g., the indeterminateness of location when the momentum of an electron is known. This is not an as such indeterminateness, but is of a specific or determinate kind. Things that are determinate are not determinate as such, but as specific things. Hence they are not negated by the other. Suppose we assert the existence of an infinite set or of an infinite summation of infinite sets. Such summations do not add up to a totality in any meaningful sense, for that would imply a very strong order in the universe (and the very structuralism Derrida detests), and yet the correlative (the other) of the set of odd numbers is the set of even numbers. The correlative of the set of solid objects is the set of non-solid objects. And so forth. What, then, is the correlative, the other, of the set of all possible sets? That other consists of all the sets that are not members of the set of all sets; and its membership is zero. It is a null set, an empty negation.

If, however, Derrida was saying that all things that are members of a set are also members of an infinity of sets—that is, that their center is in a finite set and yet in the other—he has characterized an infinite set. True, all things are members of an infinite set. Moreover, there is an infinity of infinite sets. If this is what Derrida means by "true infinity," he means that an infinite set is a member of the class of infinite sets and that for any actual summation of infinite sets, there is always another infinite set. The correlative, the other, would be the appropriate class of finite sets. There is no contradiction here, for, as we saw in chapter 4, correlative concepts do not imply that there are dichotomies in their referents.

To be an object of knowledge—even non-lingual or tacit knowledge—is to be determinatively meaningful. Properly employed, determination and language are ways of producing meaning. They can be used compulsively or obsessively.[2] Other dysfunctions may detach people from their moorings; they may produce a loss of identity. But no set of determinations can exhaust reality. What pushes us beyond the particular determinations is not the other, but a potential meaning or determination that has not yet been produced or even anticipated but that is present as a possibility.

Scientific theory, when stated dogmatically, tends to totalize and restrict its subject matter. Praxis, as a correlative to theory, does not permit this result; praxically, all theories are partial and tentative. Their justification can be assessed but never "proved," i.e., deduced. Theories provide information about reality, and perhaps truly so, but they do not exhaust reality or provide certainty. The categorizations of reality employed are neither exclusive nor exhaustive.

Derrida wished to avoid totalitarian systematizing. However, his philosophical method of inquiry was not necessary to his purpose. Is his a successful method? I think not. Let me be more specific.

What does *logos* mean to Derrida?

> In its most impoverished syntax, logos is reason and, indeed, a historical reason. And if madness in general, beyond any factitious and determined historical structure is the absence of a work, then madness is indeed, essentially and generally silence, stifled speech, within a caesura and a wound that *open up* life as *historicity in general.*[3]

Here, Derrida claims more than he can deliver. Speech, with the exception of gibberish, always includes determinate elements. Since determination is always selective, all speech is partly open. And is it meaningful to speak of silences in gibberish? Perhaps the significant difference is between ordered and disordered speech. This could be true of action as well. If this is so, it is reason and not madness that "opens up life as historicity in general," because silences, gaps, and inderterminations, as we shall see later, can be clarified only in literal language.

> Even if I do not *in fact* grasp the totality, if I neither understand nor embrace it, I still formulate the project of doing so, and this project is meaningful in such a way that it can be defined only in relation to a precomprehension of the infinite and undetermined totality.[4]

I can understand what an indeterminate meaning is. Indeterminate meaning always involves a relationship to determinate meaning. If the momentum of an electron can be determined, its location cannot, for instance. Alternatively, as Rudolf Carnap implies when he states that a complete description is infinitely long, the argument that reason never exhausts the universe means, among other things, that no set of determinations includes all the determinations that can be made. We can attempt to take this into account, but always only with reference to the known. The concept of "indeterminacy" invokes that of "determinacy." The terms are correlatives and they permit, and even require, surprises. Our project is never to know the totality, but to widen our sphere of interest in yet unknown aspects of the world.

Derrida's philosophy of metaphor is the antithesis of a metaphysics based on a strongly ordered, hierarchical universe. If, however, one recognizes the role of correlatives, complementarities, weak orders, and part systems, his solution ceases to be necessary. Derrida was not wrong in recognizing a problem in the views he opposed or in recognizing that any system of signs creates "gaps." Where he was wrong is in misunderstanding how literal, scientific approaches can cope with this problem. He also drew the wrong conclusion: that there is only one book that is constantly being rewritten. In his own way, he was asserting as strong a coherence in the world as the metaphysicians he attacked, but a coherence that literal language, he believed, cannot express.

> . . . this project is mad, and acknowledges madness as its liberty and its very possibility. This is why it is not human, in the sense of anthropological factuality, but is rather metaphysical and demonic: it first awakens to itself in its war with the demon, the evil genius of nonmeaning, by pitting itself against the strength of the evil genius, and by resisting him through reduction of the natural man within itself.[5]

But this "project" did not arise out of an undifferentiated totality. It arose out of a relationship to a historical problem. Although not fully determined by its historical moorings, what one knows, the realm of knowledge, is neither infinite nor completely undetermined. Its potential usefulness stems not from thought alone, not even from self-conscious thought alone, but from the existence of order within a realm of knowledge. An entirely disordered Cartesian ego could not raise the problem of its reason or madness. Indeed, it would not have memory and hence could not be conscious, for memory presupposes order and a "trace," as Derrida himself asserted in his discussion of Freud's wax tablet.[6] It is knowledge, and not thinking, that gives assurance. We know that we think because we know things about which we think. Thinking about thinking is reflexive and hence involves a secondary phase of thinking in which it becomes an object of knowledge. The relationships of the items of knowledge may be questionable; even their individual characterizations may be questionable. But in the absence of all order, there would be neither ego nor knowledge. Compulsive thought may shackle the natural in us. But this is not a necessary consequence of literal and therefore finite language.

> One could do for Husserl what Foucault has done for Descartes: demonstrate how the neutralization of the factual world is a neutralization (in the sense in which to neutralize is also to master, to reduce, to leave free in a straitjacket) of nonmeaning, the most subtle form of an act of force. And in truth, Husserl increasingly associated the theme of normality with the theme of the transcendental reduction. . . .

> The historicity proper to philosophy is located and constituted in the transition, the dialogue between hyperbole and the finite structure, between that which exceeds the totality and the closed totality, in the difference between history and historicity; that is, in the place where, or rather at the moment when, the Cogito and all that it symbolizes here (madness, derangement, hyperbole, etc.) pronounce and reassure themselves then to fall, necessarily forgetting themselves until their reactivation, their reawakening in another statement of the excess which also later will become another decline and another crisis.[7]

There are two senses in which we can speak of "acts of force," as Derrida used that concept. Any mode of categorizing excludes an alternative mode. However, this exclusion may be of two kinds: tentative and partial or total. Edmund Husserl's bracketing, the setting aside of one or another consideration during analysis, was a tentative bracketing of a more complex reality. Husserl's concept of "transcendental reduction," was an attempt to find the essences that lie behind experience, a search for certitude that indeed may be viewed as a straitjacket.

Husserl was undoubtedly correct when he said that meaning involves an intentional—or at least an intensional—relationship to the world. His concept of transcendental reduction, however, is neither necessary nor desirable. The dialogue, not between meaning and the world (for knowledge of the world does not exist in the absence of meaning), but between particular structures of meaning generates problems, thus producing the disintegration of particular modes of interpretation and new reconstructions.

This assistance given to God by man's writing does not contradict writing's inability to "help itself" (Phaedrus). Is not the divine—the disappearance of man—announced in this distress of writing? . . . There is an essential *lapse* between significations which is not the simple and positive fraudulence of a word, nor even the nocturnal memory of all language. To allege that one reduces this lapse through narration, philosophical discourse, or the order of reasons or deduction, is to misconstrue language, to misconstrue that language is the *rupture* with totality itself.[8]

But language is not a rupture with totality. No one ever knew a totality, unless we define totality as all that we know at a particular time. Even here, "know" is inadequate, for it implies not awareness but its potentiality; we do not consciously know, in the sense of immediate awareness, all that we know. If, as I have argued, realms of knowledge are always realms of determination, or even of indeterminations the meanings of which are given by a determinate correlative, it may be true that there are lapses or at least gaps. This is the necessary concomitant of the fact that perception is selective, that all theories are partial, that most orders are weak, that much discourse is second-order, and that language is not a picture or a reconstruction but a "talking about." However, this is true of all information processes. The difference between man and the amoeba is that the amoeba is not aware that its perception is selective.

From the discussion thus far, I might appear to be denying a distinction between linguistic and prelinguistic, or perceptual, coding. There is an important distinction between them, however. In terms of neurology, perception is a continuous, non-serial, analogical process, whether in humans or in animals. Language, however, is serial, discrete, and digital. That is why reflexive discourse tends to reify difference.

Moreover, with respect to a perceptual frame of reference, language is metaphoric, for its discrete code never exhausts continuous, non-serial perception. On the other hand, perceptions are sometimes metaphoric from the frame of reference of language; otherwise, language could never assist in refining perceptions. Yet we do refine perceptions both on the basis of experience and on the basis of language.

Note that I have made these distinctions in the literal language of science; and it is precisely this literal language that enables me, as the reader will soon see, to avoid Derrida's metaphysics: the assertion of a mystical other or totality—the really real—that he shares with Buddhists, Hegelians, and Marxists, although he supports the position in his own way.

Discourse and perception are different, but interacting, processes of characterizing reals that, in the absence of particular transactions, can be characterized only as potentialities. There is no exclusive frame of reference for characterizing reality.

The concepts of totality, the other, and Being, on the one hand, and of verisimilitude, on the other hand, represent antithetical metaphysical systems that result from the reflexive misuse of language.

Only the other, the totally other, can be manifested as what it is before the shared truth, within a certain nonmanifestation and a certain absence. It can be said only of the other that its phenomenon is a certain nonphenomenon, its presence (*is*) a certain absence. Not pure and simple absence, for there logic could make its claim, but a *certain* absence. Such a formulation shows clearly that within this experience of the other the logic of noncontradiction, that is, everything which Levinas designates as "formal logic," is contested in its root. This root would be not only the root of our language, but the root of all western philosophy, particularly phenomenology and ontology.[9]

It is true that what is absent is not itself determinate, except in a very weak sense; but its meaning is given by its relationship to the determinate. When we say that specific categories of information do not exhaust what we could say about something, the range of what is open is indeterminate except to the extent that what is excluded from the indeterminate has been determined. This claim is made meaningful by two conditions: the determinate statement of what is excluded and a programmatic claim that whatever further determination we make, there is always another that can be made.

The absolute alterity of each instant, without which there would be no time, cannot be produced—constituted—within the identity of the subject or the existent. It comes into time through the other. . . . More seriously, to renounce the other (not by being weaned from it, but by detaching oneself from it, which is actually to be in relation to it, to respect it while nevertheless overlooking it, that is, while knowing it, identifying it, assimilating it), to renounce the other is to enclose oneself within solitude (the bad solitude of solidity and self-identity) and to repress ethical transcendence. . . .

Incapable of respecting the Being and meaning of the other, phenomenology and ontology would be philosophies of violence. Through them, the entire philosophical tradition, in its meaning and at bottom, would make common cause with oppression and with the totalitarianism of the same.[10]

But we have already seen that the "totally other" was misjudged by Derrida. Furthermore, there are no "instants." Therefore, each instant is not, as Derrida argued, "an absolute alterity of each other instant." An instant is a construct. A world of instants would be a world without time, without memory, and without consciousness.

Derrida informed us of Emmanuel Levinas' distinction between need and desire and of the inexhaustibility of desire:

Neither theoretical intentionality nor the affectivity of need exhaust the movement of desire: they have as their meaning and end their own accomplishment, their own fulfillment and satisfaction within the totality and identity of the same. Desire, on the contrary, permits itself to be appealed to by the absolutely irreducible exteriority of the other to which it must remain infinitely inadequate. Desire is equal only to excess. No totality will ever encompass it. Thus, the metaphysics of desire is a metaphysics of infinite separation.[11]

According to Levinas, need and intentionality are satisfied by their fulfillment whereas desire is not. Therefore, desire alone recognizes its essential incompletion and hence the "essential exteriority" of the other.[12] If we are being told that humankind never ceases to be motivated short of death, that is certainly correct, but Levinas's distinction between need and desire seems merely precious. "Exteriority" here means incompletion only in the sense that however many desires are fulfilled, there are still others that confront one as external conditions.

Even though Levinas was anti-Hegelian, he repeated Hegel's distinction in a different form. In Hegel's system, for instance, completion could occur only in the Absolute; never in time. Exteriority in a different sense, that of being different and separate from someone else in a phenomenal sense, is implied by the same Hegelian framework. The concrete identity of self and other occurs only within the Absolute. But that is an infinite set of infinite sets. Even Alfred North Whitehead's concept of God as the primordial unconscious has more concrete meaning. Levinas' distinction between need and desire falters as badly as Hegel's. One whose desires had been entirely satisfied, if not dead, would be entirely passive. This would be true of needs also.

> If one is to believe Levinas, Husserl and Heidegger, at bottom, accepted the classical subordination of language to thought, and body to language. On the contrary, Merleau-Ponty, "better than others," would have shown "that disincarnated thought, thinking of speech before speaking it, thought as constitutive of the world of speech, was a myth."[13]

There is certainly a germ of truth here. If we can think a thought before we speak it—and in a limited sense we can, or sometimes we can rehearse mentally what we are going to say—thought and speech nonetheless are so intimately related that in effect this claim would mean that we could think something before we thought it. But all this means is that thinking is a reflexive process, that it can be contemporaneous with speech or writing, and that it can draw on knowledge stored in other part systems. This process occurs within a structure, the biological structure of a person, and in particular the cortex of the brain. However, although it is false, as I have argued in Part One, to think of language as constitutive of reality in the sense in which some philosophers argue, there is no doubt that the categories of language and of perception are part of a structure of information in the absence of which nothing is determined. Language and thought, however, are surely neither autonomous nor determinately fixed. Moreover, there can be tacit thought, that is, thought that cannot be expressed in language. Perhaps there can even be thoughts that do not occur within the categories of language. This may be true of the nonlinguistic hemisphere of the brain. In much of our life, however, just as Derrida argued, thought and language are inseparable and part of a common endeavor.

> Now, the infinite(-ly) other cannot be an object because it is speech, the origin of meaning and the world. Therefore, no phenomenology can account for ethics, speech, and justice.

But if all justice begins with speech, all speech is not just. Rhetoric may amount to the violence of theory, which *reduces* the other when it *leads* the other, whether through psychology, demagogy, or even pedagogy which is not instruction.[14]

But can the infinitely other truly be speech? Or is it merely a sound? I have argued the latter earlier in this chapter and will argue it more explicitly again before I conclude. In any event, was Derrida not here saying that justice does not reside in the logos but in that which transcends the logos? According to this interpretation, he was again merely arguing against reduction of the human to theories and closed categories.

In other words, in a world where the face would be fully respected (as that which is not of this world), there no longer would be war. In a world where the face no longer would be absolutely respected, where there no longer would be a face, there would be no more cause for war. God, therefore, is implicated in war. . . . We can have a relation to God only within such a system. Therefore war—*for war there is*—is the difference between the face and the finite world without a face.[15]

Certainly there can be no war in the absence of thought. But also there can be no peace in the absence of thought. Moreover, there is no system of war, only systems in which war occurs. But in these same systems peace occurs. If we are being told that in the absence of animal life, war, peace, and respect would not exist, that is quite true. But if we are being told that "totalitarian" systematizing creates false antitheses, or unnecessary wars, it is an obscure method of doing so.

And, if you will, the attempt to achieve an opening toward the beyond of philosophical discourse, by means of philosophical discourse, which can never be shaken off completely, cannot possibly succeed *within language*—and Levinas recognizes that there is no thought before language and outside of it—except by *formally* and *thematically* posing *the question of the relation between belonging and the opening, the question of closure*. Formally—that is by posing it in the most effective and most formal, the most formalized, way possible: not in a *logic*, in other words a philosophy, but in an inscribed description, in an inscription of the relations between the philosophical and the nonphilosophical, in a kind of unheard of *graphics*, within which philosophical conceptuality would be no more than a *function*.[16]

My dog, which refuses to eat until my other dogs have eaten, so that it can tease them, has a thought that it has never thought in language. We do not need an unheard of graphics to refer to the indeterminate. Indeed, modern physics deals with the concept rather neatly.

As soon as one attempts to think Infinity as a positive plenitude (one pole of Levinas's nonnegative transcendence), the other becomes unthinkable, impossible, unutterable. Perhaps Levinas calls us toward this unthinkable-impossible-unutterable beyond (tradition's) Being and Logos. But it must not be possible either to think or state this call. In any event, that the positive plenitude of classical infinity is translated into language only by betraying itself in a negative word (in-finite) perhaps situates, in the most profound way, the point where thought breaks with language. A break which afterward will but resonate throughout all language.[17]

I agree that there can be thought without explicit language, but I deny that there is a thought that is not a determinate thought unless the indetermination itself is limited by a determinate relationship.

> . . . the transcendental syntax of the expression *alter ego* tolerates no relationship of substantive to adjective, of absolute to epithet, in one sense or the other. This is its strangeness. A necessity due to the finitude of meaning: the other is absolutely other only if he is an ego, that is, in a certain way, if he is the same as I. Inversely, the other as *res* is simultaneously less other (not absolutely other) and less "the same" than I. Simultaneously more and less other, which means, once more, that the absolute of alterity is the same.[18]

But this is really no better than what Derrida rejected in Levinas. Is Derrida saying that things are more transparent than other egos or that we have more in common with them? In either case, the position is strange. The alter ego is the same as I in the sense of being an ego. It is different from me in the sense of whose ego it is. Words are being reified. I shall come back to some of these points when I discuss Derrida's concept of the transcategorical.

BEING AND THE OTHER

> If every "philosophy," every "metaphysics," has always sought to determine the first existent, the excellent and truly existent existent, then the thought of the Being of the existent is not this metaphysics or first philosophy. It is not even ontology (cf. above), if ontology is another name for first philosophy. Since it is not first philosophy concerned with the archi-existent, that is, the first thing or first cause which governs, then the thought of Being is neither concerned with, nor exercises, any power. For power is a relationship between existents.[19]

Perhaps the thought of Being is not concerned with power because it is not a thought of any real thing, event, or process but only of a word, a sign detached from any real referent, or even any potentiality of a real referent. And what is "power"? Ideas can truly be power, as Derrida suggests. But can there be a humanistic philosophy that is unrelated to ideas in a determinate sense, for instance, the idea of a specific other as worthy of dignity?

> If it belongs to the essence of the other first and foremost to be an "interlocutor" and to be "interpellated," then the "letting-be" will let the other be what it is, will respect it as interpellated-interlocutor. . . .
>
> That Being is not *above* the existent does not imply that it is *beside* it. For then it would be another existent. Therefore, it is difficult to speak of "the ontological significance of the existent in the general economy of Being"—which Heidegger simply places *beside* Being through a distinction. . . .[20]

Even Derrida's mode of stating the problem implied a relationship and, hence, finitude. Moreover, it implied discourse, for each must be an interlocutor and each must be interpellated. This implies a process in which each changes. He knew this and tried to sidestep this conclusion by evasion—by speaking of an unheard-of graphics, of going beyond thought and speech. The design has failed and we shall soon see why.

> Now the Idea or the project which animates and unifies every *determined* historical structure, every *Weltanschauung*, is *finite*: on the basis of the structural description of a vision of the world one can account for everything except the infinite opening to truth, that is, philosophy. Moreover, it is always something like an opening which will frustrate the structuralist project. What I can never understand, in a structure, is that by means of which it is not closed.[21]

Only if one wishes to reduce the world to theory does Derrida's objection hold.

> . . . a pure idiom is not language; it becomes so only through repetition; repetition always already divides the point of departure of the first time.[22].

In the absence of repetition, there can be no memory. In the absence of memory, there cannot be language. What beyond this does Derrida mean?

> This movement then makes philosophy appear as a form of natural or naive consciousness (which in Hegel also means cultural consciousness). For as long as the *Aufhebung* remains within restricted economy, it is a prisoner of this natural consciousness. The "we" of the *Phenomenology of the Mind* presents itself in vain as the knowledge of what the naive consciousness, embedded in its history and in the determinations of its figures, does not yet know. . . . To this extent, philosophy, Hegelian speculation, absolute knowledge and everything that they govern, and will govern endlessly in their closure, remain determinations of natural, servile, and vulgar consciousness. Self-consciousness is servile.[23]

But as we saw, in my discussion of the so-called circularity of knowledge and even the the extreme circumstance of a meeting with aliens, it is possible to develop a second-order set of statements that is neutral with respect to first-order statements.

Derrida's "the other" was a misuse of language. It obscured the process by which all others come to appreciate their similarities and differences, their independence and dependence. Here, I will comment on his belief that "Being" and "pure Being" are transcategorical and infinite terms that apply to all things, for it is at the heart of Derrida's circumlocutions.

Derrida told us that the logos, including the principle of identity, does not hold for the other. Can this be so? At first, Derrida's transcategorical use of Being may seem to violate the first principle of information theory. If it is true of everything, it is true of nothing. There is not one "bit" of information.

It may also be read as a disguised axiom of identity: that is, $b = b$, or $b \supset b$, or $(x)\, (a = b)\, \pi\, (a) \supset \pi\, (b)$, (for every x, if $a = b$, then, if π of a, π of b follows). If so, however, an assertion of its being is an assertion only that it is identical with itself. That is why we can assert that a number or any other non-sensible concept can function as a referent of a sign. It has being in the sense that it is what it is. This does not go beyond logos.

Of course, Derrida might argue that I have confounded Being and existence. Yet, none of the above formulations of identity contains the slightest statement about existence.

Derrida fell victim to the obverse of Martin Heidegger's difficulty in relating Being and existence, which he attempted ineffectively to solve by circumlocutions such as neither "above nor beside." However, if we recognize that logic, rather than determining existence, is a tool for investigating it, we do not need a transcategorical category of Being and we do not create a "straitjacket." Statements about sameness, or identity, and difference then become hypothetical, weakly ordered, and capable of transformation, even in a surprising way.

The existential quantifier ($\exists x$), which asserts that there exists an x, then serves not to assert existence as such, but the meaningful use, in one realm, of a category from another. Most often, it relates a category in a formal system to one in a non-formal system.[24] This is the "other" that obviates the "straitjacket" of reason.

If we assert existence—($\exists b$), $b \supset b$, or ($\exists b$) $(a = b) \pi (a) \supset \pi (b)$—the assertion may be either true or false and, hence, informative. This does take us beyond logos. It does not deny logos, but transcends it and attests to the incompleteness of tautology (logical or theoretical). Praxis, assessment, links logos to the world or to what we in the pragmatistic tradition call the "surd": that which can be reasoned about but which cannot be reduced to reason; that which can be known but about which information can never be exhaustive.

In short, Being is either non informative or else what it asserts it asserts only of itself. Thus, what beings have in common is their identity with themselves and their differences from each other. In other language, they are members of the class of things that are identical to themselves and different from other things. This is the class of all things, for the class is a member of itself. In other senses (except for specified characteristics), things are not the same nor different. Thus, in neither interpretation can pure being or the other be employed as Derrida employed the terms. Even indeterminate negativity is expressed with respect to its determinate corollary; this relationship alone gives it meaning in use.

> The center is at the center of the totality, and yet, since the center does not belong to the totality (is not a part of the totality), the totality *has its center elsewhere*. The center is not the center.[25]

This statement is very difficult to interpret. Obviously most systems or structures do not have centers in any meaningful sense. Derrida did not believe in essence. But if not, why should there be only one way of identifying things? Could not something be warm and at the same time register so many degrees of heat? Must the term "mother" mean the same thing in different societies? I argued, in chapter 9, that even Wittgenstein's concept of family relationships may be insufficient. Perhaps Derrida's statement is an argument that a center from one perspective is not such from another and that there is no center, as such, to the world. I would take no exception to his conclusion if this is what he meant. But I do object to what he did with it.

If Derrida is trying to awaken our sense of wonder in the face of the "surdity" of the world—that is, its reality, which resists our efforts to comprehend it—I admire his purpose. No one has achieved this better than Dostoyevski, in whose work that which creates the greatest surprise or shock is seen retrospectively as almost preordained; or Mann, in the *Magic Mountain*, when the abundant vitality of Peeperkorn turns the contending rationalists, Naptha and Settembrini, into shadows. But this sense of wonder is conveyed better in literature than by Derrida. And the philosopher, including the ethical philosopher, pays an excessive price for making the effort.

> For the signification "sign" has always been understood and determined, in its meaning, as a sign-of, a signifier referring to a signified, a signifier different from its signified. If one erases the radical difference between signifier and signified, it is the word "signifier" itself which must be abandoned as a metaphysical concept.[26]

But "sign" and "signed" are correlatives; in the absence of one, their meaning is absent. Of course, signs are meaningless merely as signs. Such semantic concepts belong on the ash heap. It is the use of the sign as a mediator of a concept with respect to the signed, whether sensible or intelligible, that produces meaning, and its limitations in use that produces openness and surprise.

> Obviously there is no scandal except within a system of concepts which accredits the difference between nature and culture. By commencing his work on the *factum* of the incest prohibition, Levi-Strauss thus places himself at the point at which this difference, which has always been assumed to be self-evident, finds itself erased or questioned.[27]

But perhaps Derrida, who mistakenly identified the problems of Levi-Strauss with the problems of modern social science and philosophy, found Levi-Strauss a scandal for the wrong reasons. Why does the fact that something is universal make it natural? Suppose we said that what is biologically determined is natural and that what is socially determined is cultural. In that case, sex would be natural and the mode of its manifestations cultural. If a rule against incest were merely one aspect of the regulation of sex, its universality would not necessarily be surprising even though its expression is cultural. Moreover, if the terms "nature" and "culture" are understood as correlative rather than dichotomous, and as contextually determined to some extent, the scandal is absent; for then there is no culture without nature or nature without culture.

> This field is in effect that of *play*, that is to say, a field of infinite substitutions only because it is finite, that is to say because instead of being an inexhaustible field, as in the classical hypothesis, instead of being too large, there is something missing from it: a center which arrests and grounds the play of substitutions.[28]

But these are false alternatives. Praxical criteria determine the choices. Not play, but problems in a real world determine outcomes. Because most orders are weak rather than strong, some variations, even playful ones, are possible, but real-world possibilities bound substitution.

> For example, the appearance of a new structure, or an original system, always comes about—and this is the very condition of its structural specificity—by a rupture with its past, its origin, and its cause. Therefore one can describe what is peculiar to the structural organization only by not taking into account, in the very moment of this description, its past conditions: by omitting to posit the problem of the transition from one structure to another, by putting history between brackets. In this "structuralist" moment, the concepts of chance and discontinuity are indispensable.[29]

Of course, a theory of the capitalistic economy does not explain why a socialist economy was adopted in the Soviet Union by the Communists. This is contingency, from the standpoint of economic theory. However, when one employs the appropriate theory—even though the appropriate theory may often be impossible to formulate until the discontinuity occurs—and states the appropriate initial conditions, it is possible to understand the development and, sometimes, to show the probability.

> But what disposes it in this way, we now know, is not the origin, but that which takes its place; which is not, moreover, the opposite of an origin. It is not absence instead of presence, but a trace which replaces a presence which has never been present, an origin by means of which nothing has begun.[30]

Here Derrida recognized that we cannot know the primordial past. We cannot know the origin. However, it leaves its trace. As in memory, we recapture the past through traces. Derrida also rejected the antithesis of presence and absence and, thus, contradicted Heidegger. In this sense, perhaps, what is—and what is is always novel to some extent—contains the past only as a trace. The present, viewed as future, is potentially a trace, and not simply either a presence or absence.*

There is a type of discontinuity in the assessment of which the concept of "trace" may be useful: that in which the praxical criterion of centrality of logic does not link the new to the old. However, "potentiality" is sometimes the correct concept. We can see how Einsteinian mechanics was potential in Newtonian mechanics, i.e., we can see important similarities in their central logic. It would take a theoretical physicist, however, to see a trace of prior theories of mechanics in quantum mechanics. Consider the discontinuity between primates and their distant evolutionary precursors, lizards. The potentiality is present in the gene structure, but it is very weakly ordered. Modern science retains just a trace of shamanistic "science." In this and other instances, the concept of

---

*In Chapter 13, I explain why I prefer the concept of "potentiality," although not in its Aristotelian first-order sense, to Derrida's concept of "trace."

"trace" is useful as a correlative for "potentiality" to indicate differences in distance.

In Derrida, phenomenology has been turned on its head. Science has been turned into poetry and into "glance." Despite certain striking insights, vast philosophical knowledge, and great intelligence, Derrida's work constitutes a detour in the history of Western thought. Rather than simply removing the remaining essentialism from the Greco-modern tradition of philosophy—and this would have been of enormous service—Derrida, like the early Hindu and Buddhist thinkers, replaced it with poetic metaphor.

GRAMMATOLOGY

Derrida advocated a linguistics, or "grammatology," that is formalized and mathematical in notation. Although he recognized that "it will always be impossible to reduce absolutely the natural languages and nonmathematical notation," he pursued a formal grammatology that *"inscribes* and *delimits* science."[31]

I agree with Derrida's reformulation of the pragmaticist dictum that life cannot be reduced to logic and with his cogent argument that voice and language are intimately linked, even though neither can be reduced to the other. However, I cannot accept the concept of a theory of language that *"inscribes* and *delimits* science."

Some aspects of Derrida's method of deconstruction—that a text needs to be interpreted in terms of the evolution of the concepts employed and of the light that is shed by world conditions external to the text—seem acceptable. But I would qualify the first criterion much more strongly than he. And I would add that the framework of the text also needs to be taken into account.

It is true that every choice of theory limits what can be known by that means—for every theory circumscribes a subject matter—but it is the choice of subject matter that governs the choice of signs and of the limits of discourse; it is not grammatology that does so. Language and signs are used in making these choices, but the language and signs are those of other part systems of the realm of knowledge. The new theory and its associated signs have the function, among others, of freeing knowledge not from all circumscriptions but from those of previous theories and part systems.

Although much of the interest in linguistic theory may stem from the hope that it will produce a philosopher's stone that will reveal the external secrets of the universe and the internal secrets of the mind, this hope springs from a basic misunderstanding of the function of language in discourse. Language is a tool we use to unlock the secrets of nature by shaping it to particular tasks, not a code that when broken reveals them. Its success in these tasks is determined by using other tools, including other forms of language. The literal language of science in its different types and forms is a key tool, but only when used to develop theories and propositions. Because these literal uses differ in different contexts and part systems, the phenomena that Derrida referred to as *différence* arise. They can be accounted for in literal language without the metaphors that Derrida employed. The recognition of correlatives in language possibly responds to other aspects of his use of *différence*, and certainly to his critique of the Hegelian dialectic.

NOTES

1. For an analysis of finitude and distortion that is different from that of Derrida, see Morton A. Kaplan, *Alienation and Identification*, (New York: Free Press, 1976), pp. 118 ff. For a discussion that shows how extrapolations from finite analysis produce ontological dysfunctions of the mind, dysfunctions that need to be avoided, see pp. 131 ff. For the further specification and resolution of the problem, see the remainder of the book. For an analysis of mental dysfunctions from a cybernetic point of view, see Morton A. Kaplan, *Macropolitics: Essays on the Philosophy and Science of Politics* (Chicago: Aldine Publishing Co., 1969), pp. 137 ff., revised and reprinted from Morton A. Kaplan, *System and Process in International Politics* (New York: John Wiley & Sons, 1957), pp. 253 ff.

2. See Morton A. Kaplan, *Alienation and Identification* (Chicago: University of Chicago Press, 1969).

3. Jacques Derrida, *Writing and Difference*, translated by Alan Bass (Chicago: University of Chicago Press, 1978), p. 54.

4. Ibid., p. 56.

5. Ibid.

6. Ibid., pp. 193 ff.

7. Ibid., p. 60.

8. Ibid., p. 71.

9. Ibid., p. 90.

10. Ibid., p. 91.

11. Ibid., p. 93.

12. Emmanuel Levinas, *Totalité et infini: Essai sur l'exteriorité* (The Hague: Martinus Nijhoff Publishers, 1961); Derrida, *Writing and Difference*, p. 83.

13. Jacques Derrida, *Writing and Difference*, pp. 103–104.

14. Ibid., p. 106.

15. Ibid., p. 107.

16. Ibid., pp. 110–111.

17. Ibid., p. 114.

18. Ibid., p. 127.

19. Ibid., p. 137.

20. Ibid., p. 138.

21. Ibid., p. 160.

22. Ibid., p. 213.

23. Ibid., pp. 275–276.

24. For a discussion of the stipulative character of the existential quantifier, see Leonard Linsky, *Names and Descriptions* (Chicago: University of Chicago Press, 1977), pp. 115 ff. From my standpoint, of course, praxis determines the character of stipulation.

25. Jacques Derrida, *Writing and Difference*, p. 279.

26. Ibid., p. 281.

27. Ibid., p. 283.

28. Ibid., p. 289.

29. Ibid., p. 291.

30. Ibid., p. 295.

31. Jacques Derrida, *Positions*, translated by Alan Bass (Chicago: University of Chicago Press, 1981), pp. 35, 36.

PART THREE
THE OBJECTIVITY OF THE
REALM OF VALUES

IN THE PAST many philosophers argued that values are objective, that they are part of the natural universe. According to the arguments of positivists, however, values are preferences, not facts. No ought statement, they said, can be deduced from a descriptive premise.

Many contemporary philosophers disagree with the positivistic argument that values are merely preferences. They may find their basis in a language of morality, in reasons that support moral preferences, or in formal theories of ethics.

Despite the decline of positivism, and despite disagreement with the contention of positivists that values are merely preferences, there is a substantial consensus behind the argument of the positivists that the good is not a factual aspect of nature. This consensus, I believe, results in part from a failure to distinguish between the definitional and the dispositional aspects of the world.

We tend to think that if something is good, it is good in a sense that can be defined independently of conditions. Yet moral and ethical behavior, like all human behavior, is dispositional. It is complexly interdependent with other values and with our environment. To attempt to define right or justice, or what is good, abstractly is to mistake the use of signs or, even worse, to employ an earlier view of the universe in which everything has a sign, every sign a definition, and every definition a place in the world order.

I shall show that goods cannot be arranged in a universal hierarchy. Statements about them, although objective, are weakly ordered, particularly when we consider the more important values. Although a concept of justice can be developed within this framework and both moral and political obligation can be accounted for by it, the values of different individuals and of different societies are not necessarily the same or even compatible.

In chapter 11, I investigate some similarities and some differences in goal-oriented behavior between contemporary automatons and humans. A major difference is that we can change and even transform our goals. I shall then show that the valuable is not necessarily identical with the valued; and that dysfunctional assessments occur in moral analysis as well as in ordinary scientific analysis. I shall then use examples based upon game theoretical principles to show that context is an element in determining what is good. Subsequently, I shall attempt to show that John von Neumann's treatment of the utility function is not sufficiently dispositional and that adopting a more fully dispositional view of the utility function permits interpersonal comparisons.

Max Weber's classical distinction between instrumental and intrinsic rationality,[1] as I shall show, is of only limited value. If enough questions are asked and answered, an analysis of instrumental means necessarily raises issues concerning intrinsic goals. The two are inextricably linked in a web and are correlatives. Finally I distinguish the good and the just.

The search for moral theory, let alone a general one, results from a failure to recognize the dispositional and context-dominated character of valuational behavior. This subject is pursued in chapter 12, where I shall show the defects in several such theories. In particular, I shall argue that exclusively consequence-oriented and exclusively rule-oriented moral theories fail to deal adequately with moral analysis.

We do need a method for ordering moral judgements, but it will be far more complex than that provided by theories, whether general or not. My method is discussed in chapter 13. There I suggest a method for the second-order analysis of moral problems. This permits, in principle at least, a weak but still objective ordering of good and bad, even though the procedures for determining the order are low-confidence procedures. The ordering depends in part on the state of the perceiving system, in our case, the human, and on its information. These establish a partial ordering we can use to assess our own values, for both our situations and our beliefs are relevant to our good and are subject to reconsideration only within the limits of our own plasticity. The possession of extensive comparative information and the ability to use it are likely only in relatively advanced societies. Thus, good in the form of justice is potentially developmental, because the range of information that can be brought to bear upon it is potentially progressive.

The test-in-principle and other comparative modes of analysis, which are discussed in Chapter 13, point to the possibility of a common universe of good: one in which all human beings would share compatible second-order preferences. Although this is a hypothesis, I give reasons for believing in it. In principle we could use these forms of analysis to discover criteria for judging better and worse within and among social systems.

I shall show what first-order valuations of morality are relative to and why moral conflicts and dilemmas arise. This will lead to a brief discussion of moral obligation and of conflicting frames of obligation, subjects treated at greater length in an earlier book.[2] In this briefer analysis, I shall extend that discussion to obligations to past and future generations and to animals.

NOTES

1. Max Weber, *The Theory of Social and Economic Organization*, translated and edited by A.M. Henderson and Talcott Parsons (Glencoe, Ill.: Free Press, 1957), Introduction.

2. Morton A. Kaplan, *Justice, Human Nature, and Political Obligation* (New York: Free Press, 1976).

Chapter 11
The Good

In chapter 4, the concept of the dispositional was discussed. Let us begin the discussion of the dispositional character of valuational behavior via a metaphor: an automatic pilot in an airplane. The automatic pilot adjusts the flight pattern of the plane when it deviates from the programmed pattern. If an automatic pilot possessed consciousness, it might perceive its purpose in life, that is, its good, as the maintenance of the stability of the plane. It would achieve the perceived good simply by invoking a set of rules. The automatic pilot would be subject to no uncertainty, even with respect to means. There would be an exact and direct relationship between the good and the instrumental goal, the adjustment of the plane.

If we now turn to a slightly more complex illustration—for instance, a self-moving machine that refills its own gas tank and recharges its own battery—it might, on an occasion in which they ran down simultaneously, have to choose between recharging its battery and refilling its tank. In principle, however, we could specify a complete set of rules to govern decisions of this type.

If we turn to a transfinitely stable system, the human being, for instance, the situation becomes far more complex. A transfinitely stable system has a complex coding system that depends on its context and that can transform itself as the internal criteria of its subsystems are reshaped by assessments that include external criteria. This kind of system is capable of self-reference, i.e., reflexive procedures, and of second-order language. In pursuing its purposes, it may err in its knowledge of the world. It may err in its logic. It may err in estimating the consequences of its action. It may err in reporting its own desires. In principle, each one of these possible sources of error is subject to some form of objective test, although in practice the confidence we can place in these tests may not be great.

Let us return to the self-moving machine to illustrate dysfunctional behavior. This machine is programmed to fill its tank only when the tank is nearly empty. If its internal reporting system becomes inaccurate, it might seek to fill the tank when it is already full or to refrain from filling it when it is nearly empty. Such behavior would seem to contradict our statement of its coding, but it would be subject to analysis and we might be able to demonstrate the source of the malfunction. In principle, we can always analyze its behavior, including its aberrant behavior. We infer its code—that is, its engineering specifications—from its goals; and its errors can be recognized as such.[1] However, because it has been unambiguously programmed, it cannot pursue, even in an unfavorable environment, a secondary set of goals—or what Freud calls secondary gains—that constitutes a costly adjustment or mistakenly "perceive" these as preferable to the initially coded goals. The transfinitely stable system, however, is capable of such dysfunctional behavior. Its analysis, therefore, is correspondingly more complex, requiring a distinction between the valuable and the valued, a distinction that does not have to be made with the simpler system.

Furthermore, the simple self-moving machine operates in an environment it cannot change. It cannot evaluate a good differently in different environments; it cannot compare the benefits of changing its behavior with the benefits of changing the environment; and it cannot reflexively reconsider its own system of valuation in the process. The transfinitely stable system is capable of all these activities, and its set of values is correspondingly more complex and difficult to analyze.

THE VALUABLE AND THE VALUED

If we characterize the "valuable" as that which would be judged good in the presence of correct information and on the basis of supportive reasoning of a praxical type, we can distinguish between the valued and valuable. What is valuable, thus, depends on both the system and the environment. And this assessment will make use of both internal and external criteria.

Our own statement of what we value is evidence of what is valuable for us, but it is rebuttable evidence. A being, who is transfinitely stable, can behave in a way that is pathological. Suppose we are in a harmful environment, one that prevents us from satisfying an important need. Since this is unpleasant, the psychological mechanism of denial may come into play. We may even reinforce the denial by overvaluing inferior substitute goals. We may then pursue these secondary goals and support them by ancillary arrangements and beliefs to the point where we are unable to recognize favorable changes in the environment, changes that would permit us to pursue, if not our original goal, goals that we would otherwise have pursued.

These distinctions between functional and dysfunctional evaluations are difficult to make in practice, although there is substantial evidence, from psychiatry and systems analysis, of their validity. They make objectively meaningful the distinction between the valuable and the valued, even if, in complex situations, judgments are problematic.

The proposition I am arguing here is that, with sufficient information, one will value what is valuable. Of course these values are not necessarily the same in all environments, for all persons, or even for the same person or system at a different time. What is valued depends on the dispositions of a complex transfinite system. What is good depends on the relationship between environmental possibility and the system's needs. What is valued depends upon perception of these relationships, and perception can be distorted.

Certain conditions may alter preferences. For instance, no one would choose to be a paraplegic, except in preference to something worse. But the paraplegic must, in order to find life livable, elevate values that under better conditions would be secondary, and some paraplegics use the psychological mechanism of denial to alter their values in order to maintain their sanity.

I chose such an extreme example to demonstrate the difficulty of a praxical assessment of what is good. The scientist is often portrayed as disinterested, but self-interest sometimes corrupts scientific results. Toward the end of chapter 5, I referred to Langmuir's essay *Pathological Science*, in which he cites many examples of scientists who misinterpret their observations of instrument readings.[2] The problem is much more acute in the moral realm.

The transfinite system we are talking about is a complex and sophisticated example of a non-mechanical system. This means that there are no covering laws, so useful in mechanics, to help us to explain its behavior. From the viewpoint of the investigator, information is merely an element within a larger system; and although the logical forms used in reasoning are an essential part of reasoning, no analysis of moral behavior limited to logical reasoning can explain it. If these considerations are kept in mind, moral reasoning can be seen as similar to reasoning about other partly dispositional processes. Consider two contrasting objective statements: "This is yellow" and "This is a dove." Both are statements of fact. However, both are also elliptical and dispositional accounts. "This is yellow" stands for "this is seen as yellow by this observational system through this filter." That is, a human is disposed to see something as yellow under specified conditions of bodily state, object, and environment. Even the more specific statement is only comparatively non-elliptical; an absolutely non-elliptical statement would contain an exhaustive, and potentially infinite, set of conditions.

Each statement of the type "this is yellow" or "this is a dove" implies something about transactions between an observer, an external object or event, and the context of observation. In ordinary language, common-sense distinctions are made between "is" and "appears." If we are incautious, these can lead to reifications that produce false conclusions.

There is an important distinction between "dove" and "yellow" with respect to the disjunction between "is" and "appears." Although a piece of floating paper may appear to be a dove at a distance, whether or not the object is a bird can be determined within a wide range of contexts and by a wide range of perceptual systems and objective tests. The distinction between "is" and "appears" with respect to color, however, depends upon conventional stipulations that are much more limited.

As I have noted earlier, even the same type of observational system might report differently when in different states, as it does with respect to taste for foods. These reported differences are not merely linguistic, for there is a difference in experiences. Moreover, differently evolved creatures might report different experiences with respect to the same second-order referent. In principle, these differences in experience could be confirmed by operations on the physiologies of the two species that transform one into the other and that then reverse the process. Even so, the report that "*x* is yellow" could not be used to achieve second-order agreement about the referent *x* without specifying the observational system used and the context of the report. Attributions of color are, in any event, closer to the dispositional correlative than determination of whether something is a dove, which is closer to the definitional, for instance, whether it is biological. So far, I have argued only that dispositional aspects of human behavior can, at least in principle, be examined objectively. The argument will be continued through this and the succeeding two chapters. Now let us consider the problem of context.

THE ROLE OF CONTEXT

Because moral judgments are dispositional, the specification of context, as well as of the participants in the transaction, is essential to their analysis. Let us ask just a few relevant questions before we analyze this problem in terms of game theory.

Should Attila the Hun have viewed pity as important? How could his values be divorced from his society and the problems faced by that type of society? Should we tell American parents that they are not training their sons in the manly virtues that would have enabled them to survive in Attila's society? How relevant would this be? How can values be detached from the nexus that makes them meaningful? I am not arguing a relativistic position that societies and their values are above criticism, and shall return in chapter 13 to that issue. I am arguing only against using an abstract universalism to treat values and relations among values as if they are entirely independent of the context of choice.

Let me try to show more simply that values are dependent upon the context of choices. Consider a simple game against nature, an opponent that cannot deliberately attempt to get the better of us. I will now show that even if the numbers in the payoff boxes are fixed, preference for a rule will vary with need and context.

The minimax principle, the first criterion of choice that will be considered, specifies that a player should choose that strategy which, even if it known to the opponent, would guarantee him the largest of his minimal payoffs for any of his strategies. The alternative minimax regret principle specifies that a player should choose that strategy that guarantees the least of the maximal differences between the actual payoff and that which would have been received had he correctly judged how nature (or his opponent) would choose. Consider how these alternative principles of choice apply to figure 1.

If one applies the minimax principle to figure 1, the solution is the d_3 decision, for this guarantees that the player will not do worse than 5, which is the maximum of the minimum outcomes.

Circumstances

	c_1	c_2	c_3
d_1	−7	8	12
d_2	−8	7	14
d_3	5	6	8

(Decisions)

Figure 1

Now let us change the matrix to figure 2.

Circumstances

	c_1	c_2	c_3
d_1	−7	8	12
d_2	−8	7	300
d_3	5	6	8

(Decisions)

Figure 2

The minimax solution would still be d_3 although the reader might begin to entertain doubts about the principle. (In chapter 4, I pointed out that the concept of rationality is itself context-dependent and that it varies in strength as the relevant criteria change.) These doubts likely would increase with the size of the *utile number* (the assigned value) in the d_2, c_3 payoff box. Let us therefore consider an alternative principle.

The minimax *regret principle* is that a player should compare the payoff in any row with the payoff of correctly guessing nature's strategy. For instance, if one knows that nature will choose c_3, d_2 is clearly called for. Thus, if you choose d_3, and nature is in the c_3 position, you lose 6 points in the matrix in figure 1 and 292 in the matrix in figure 2. The minimax regret matrix derived from figure 2 is presented as figure 3; the minimax regret matrix for figure 1 is presented in figure 4. The minimax regret solution for figure 3 is d_2, whereas the minimax solution for figure 2 is d_3.

Circumstances

	c_1	c_2	c_3
d_1	−12	0	−288
d_2	−13	−1	0
d_3	0	−2	−292

(Decisions)

Figure 3

Circumstances

	c_1	c_2	c_3
d_1	-12	0	-2
d_2	-13	-1	0
d_3	0	-2	-6

Decisions

Figure 4

Different types of matrices generate different sets of solutions. Let us consider the well-known *prisoners' dilemma* in which individual rationality produces collective irrationality. Consider figure 5, in which each player must choose a strategy without knowing the other player's choice.

	A	B
A	1,1	10,0
B	0,10	9,9

Figure 5

Because of the dominance of the A strategies—and dominance is the strongest criterion of rationality known to decision theory because it produces a better outcome regardless of what the other player does—a jointly undesirable outcome (1,1) is achieved.[3] If the players could choose between mutual use of the B strategies or mutual use of the A strategies, they would clearly prefer the former. If the players were offered the freedom to choose their A or B strategies independently of each other, they would find that freedom unattractive, for that extension of their freedom of choice would condemn them to the jointly undesirable outcome.

The choice between a mutual promise to follow either A or B in figure 5 is counterfactual in the prisoners' dilemma. However, the players might wish that they were able to bind themselves to the B strategies; that is, they might wish they were part of a moral or, alternatively, a disciplined community. This wish is worthless under the actual conditions of the game, as John Harsanyi has shown,[4] and therefore they prefer the A strategies.

	A	B
A	5,5	9,3
B	3,9	6,6

Figure 6

The particular prisoners' dilemma represented by figure 5 was chosen to emphasize a situation in which individual rationality produces an extremely undesirable joint outcome. Other numbers can be placed in the boxes without changing the game from that of a prisoners' dilemma, and such changes may require a discussion different from that of figure 5 even though the game remains a prisoners' dilemma.[5] In figure 6, for instance, the players may not prefer the cooperative solution; each player might prefer to avoid a joint decision. A player might prefer to rely upon sentiment or lack of intelligence on the part of the other players, In short, he may prefer a situation in which he can choose *A* and hope that the other player will choose *B*. If so, he forecloses a sure (6,6) outcome, risks only that the outcome will be (5,5), and hopes that it will be (9,3). In a society characterized by such a matrix, some might be opposed in principle to moral rules, although not necessarily opposed to others' believing in them. Whether we predict that the others will be opposed to moral rules depends upon our hypotheses about human nature and the particular situation. For instance, one might believe that people would be trustworthy in a good society but, in self defense, would choose deceitful behavior in a society in which there is massive deceit that one cannot hope to change. And vice versa. Thus, to consider the context is essential even in this limited framework. Context affects the meanings of outcomes.

W. Ross Ashby, who so often developed illuminating examples, graphically illustrated that choices from among alternatives can be isolated from their context only in special instances and that changes in context may change the meanings of outcomes.[6] He pointed out that mathematicians argue that irrelevant alternatives should not affect choice. If you go to a butcher shop and order chicken after the butcher states that he has only beef and chicken, you should not change your order to beef after the butcher suddenly remembers that there is pork in the freezer. Pork is the irrelevant alternative that does not affect your previous preference for chicken.

Ashby, however, pointed out that an irrelevant alternative can change the order of preferences. In England, certain standard telegrams can be sent cheaply by code. Thus, a vacationing husband might be able to send either of two inexpensive telegrams to his wife: (*a*) having a wonderful time or (*b*) wish you were here. An Englishman on vacation decides to send telegram (*b*). The telegrapher tells him that there is a new third choice: (*c*) please join me at once. The husband changes his mind and sends telegram (*a*). The seemingly irrelevant alternative has, in fact, affected the meaning of the first two alternatives and, therefore, his preference. One might argue correctly that the new third choice is no longer irrelevant, but it is irrelevant in mathematical usage. Mathematicians mean, by irrelevance, that the addition of a choice that ranks lower than existing choices should not affect the rankings of the higher choices, as the addition of pork should not affect your preference for chicken.

If a mother asks you whether her son died in an accident, the decision to tell her the truth changes its meaning depending upon whether she is well or is being wheeled into the operating room for a serious operation necessitated by the accident. The meaning of a blow to the jaw differs, depending upon whether it is intended to injure the other person or to prevent a drowning swimmer from interfering with a rescuer. The meaning of telling a woman that she looks pretty differs depending upon whether she is going to a party or whether her husband has just died. The meaning of "pretty" is different still if the comment is made to a youth who is unsure of his manhood. Giving directions has a different meaning if one is giving them to a motorist seeking help for an injured person or to a rapist chasing his victim. The virtue of trying to disarm a gunman depends on how dangerous he is, whether others are around who may be injured by the attempt, and on what the gunman may do with his weapon if he is not stopped.

Who is innocent? At certain times and under certain circumstances, no member of a tribe at war with another tribe was considered innocent. During certain periods of war in Europe, everyone except the soldiers in the field was considered innocent. During other periods, those near military installations were not considered fully innocent.

There is considerable evidence that members of the syndicate do not consider themselves bad persons. They go to church. They do not inform on their friends. They remain loyal to the group unless somebody breaks some other element of the ethical code, such as encroaching on someone else's territory or calling too much attention to the group's activities. Again, the Japanese ethical code of Bushido is considerably different from our own. Much of the confusion in ethical and in historical discourse is caused by employing terms that have relatively clear meanings in limited contexts and discussing them as if those meanings stay fixed even though times and contexts change. This blurs distinctions and creates the illusion of an almost theoretical framework of analysis in which conclusions can be derived from premises with little attention to differentiating circumstances. Even in physics, however, theories are this simple only in some textbooks.

Confusion also arises from the fact that meanings are treated almost deductively. This misstates their praxical character. The central concept of rationality is a metaphor that we can understand only because we understand its literal exemplars.

THE UTILITY FUNCTION

The relationship between decisions and context becomes even clearer if we examine the way in which John von Neumann derives utility numbers. Von Neumann's axioms constitute a theory of utility formation that is independent of all contexts but one: paired lotteries. According to von Neumann's axioms, utile numbers are derived from an infinite set of lotteries in which all choices are paired and assessed. However, we can easily find an example in which we will reject what logically follows from those axioms. Consider the following example:

1,2	3,1
0,−200	2,−300

Figure 7

Luce and Raiffa argued that the solution to figure 7 is (3,1).[7] Thomas Schelling, however, said that if the player choosing between the columns commits himself to his first strategy, the outcome will be (1,2).[8] This will happen because, if the player controlling the rows were to choose his second strategy, he would receive zero utiles, and one is better than zero. Many of us would resist allowing ourselves to be coerced by a commitment in this fashion, and for good reasons, as we shall soon see. First, let us consider a related case.

Consider an example in which two players can divide one hundred dollars if and only if they can agree on a division. One player phones the other and says, "I get ninety-nine dollars, you get one." He then breaks the connection, which cannot be restored until the second player submits the offer to a referee. Now, one dollar has more utility for a person than zero dollars, because the paired lotteries have already established these values. But most people would prefer to have zero dollars, while the coercer gets zero, than one dollar if the coercer gets ninety-nine dollars. And this is partly independent of considerations of precedent or repeated play. Thus, there can be no final setting of the utile numbers that is entirely independent of further contextual constraints. Thus far, we can see that von Neumann's axioms generate utility numbers only for items that can be considered in a paired lottery and, even then, only in situations in which the context does not change the meaning of the lottery.

Our attitude toward risk, which von Neumann did take into account, may often affect our choices. Still, risk may very often be a peripheral factor. If individuals are asked how their choices affect their identity, their society, their families' future, their children's conduct—aspects of life that are richly interconnected and widely influenced by a variety of conditions—they will see that the notion of sets of paired lotteries is too artificial to be useful except for limited types of problems. It is as if a biologist were to chop a human body into segments and then attempt to reconstruct a functioning organism from the segments. I am not arguing that the whole is different from or greater than the parts or that analysis of complex problems is impossible, but that the wrong mode of analysis distorts the character of the problem. I shall now suggest how both interpersonal and intrapersonal comparisons can be made.

INTERPERSONAL COMPARISONS

The standard view of mathematicians is that von Neumann's axioms provide a general ordinal measure for intrapersonal comparisons of utilities but that no method exists for interpersonal comparisons. If you turn back to figure 7, you will quickly see that Luce and Raiffa's solution for figure 7 depends upon an interpersonal comparison: the player controlling the rows can force the (3,1) solution because then the other player can be hurt more than the first player can be hurt in return. There can be no doubt that, in practice, people recognize this type of comparison.

The virtue of the von Neumann axioms was that they provided a method for determining an ordinal utility scale that could be used to develop the theory of games. The mistake made by a number of social scientists who did not understand the limitations of theory in context-influenced spheres was to identify the limitations of a particular set of axioms, designed for a particular purpose, with the character of the world. In fact, the von Neumann procedures cannot fully be carried out. We cannot know that we have exhausted the universe of possible lotteries. And, as I have shown, any actual utility ordering may change in a different context. In this sense, the von Neumann axioms function as an asymptote, as do the standards for theory in the physical sciences. However, whereas the "as if" elements in physical science rarely limit the applications of theory, thus permitting great power, the "as if" elements in social science are much more limiting.

There are many circumstances in which the type of precise orderings permitted by the von Neumann axioms cannot be obtained. However, where this is the case, the ranking of utilities will owe more to praxical assessment than to theoretical models, such as the von Neumann axioms.

Let us see how treating utility rankings as dispositional can help us to understand actual comparisons that are both intrapersonal and interpersonal. Take punishment, for example. Suppose we ask how intensely children desire to avoid a beating from a parent. Will they run away from home? Will they hide for several hours? Will they cry in advance in order to blunt the parent's anger? Or, take reward. How hard will we work for a specified reward? How many hours will we work? Under what conditions of danger will we work? Under what conditions of discomfort will we work?

An idiosyncratic basis for utility is implicit in von Neumann's set of axioms. In the previous section, I asserted that our reasons for preferring one rule over another—for instance, minimax to minimax regret—rest on actual circumstances. In the previous paragraph, I adumbrated a method for charting or graphing the individual's disposition both to seek certain ends and to avoid others. This was the method used earlier in the chapter to make meaningful the concept of good. By comparing the intensity of our disposition to attain different goods, under different conditions, we can compare intrapersonal utilities, or values. By comparing the efforts of different individuals to obtain a good or to avoid an evil under given conditions, we can begin to develop an interpersonal chart.

These charts may be of negative as well as of positive dispositions. The conclusion that the failure to get a promotion hurt Sue more than Jim might be reinforced by evidence that, after the failure, Sue no longer performed as diligently, while Jim was his same old ambitious self. Psychological change may also enter into such assessments. The conclusion that their failure to receive their college degrees hurt Bill more than Jane may be reinforced by evidence that Jane continued to function efficiently while Bob declined into melancholia. The testimony of individuals about the importance of a good or evil cannot be ignored but, like all other evidence, its reliability must be assessed.

That interpersonal comparisons are so difficult—the ordering system is extremely weak—does not mean that such comparisons cannot be made. It means only that large differences are more likely to be discerned with some reasonable degree of confidence than are small differences. Moreover, no one criterion can be used except in the simplest situations. But if we keep in mind the dispositional aspect of comparisons, it becomes clear how and why we can make interpersonal comparisons.

If interpersonal comparisons rested only on graphs or charts of dispositions, they would have the same status as the measurement of electric current, a subject discussed in chapter 4. However, it is possible to infer from their behavior what is important to individuals *in situ*; that is, what is good becomes situationally manifest, if fallibly perceived, and different with different situations, some of which may be quite stable (one reason that utility curves turn out to be kinky when plotted as concrete outcomes). That is, for instance, a person while poor may place a high value on being invited to certain social affairs and place a low value on such invitations after becoming rich. In the discussion below of the distinction between intrinsic and instrumental values, I shall try to show that valuations of outcomes and means depend in part on a web of reasons and of interrelationships between outcomes and means, and not merely upon paired comparisons like von Neumann's.

Very important goods constitute needs. It should follow that the ability of society to satisfy needs is central to a judgment about its justness. Yet we would not wish to accommodate all needs: for instance, those of the compulsive gambler, the murderer, the thief, or the psychopath. These needs are injurious to society. Most people have some distorted needs, and, for the most part, these needs are not injurious to society. Likely we would wish to accommodate these needs to some extent, for otherwise we would damage these individuals.

GOOD AND EVIL

Modern utility theory is conceptually as different from the analysis of "good" and "bad" as the scientific concept of temperature or heat is from the qualitative "hot" and "cold." Utility theory presents us with a scale for ordering preference. Although we may place pluses and minuses before the utile numbers we use, it would make no difference were we to set the lowest value on the scale at zero. Von Neumann did take risk into account in establishing a scale, but he ignored all the other factors that affect preferences. Because valuational behavior is not mechanical, this attempt to establish a consistent scale of values seriously distorted the situation.

If, however, we think in terms of social or individual systems, "good," at least for preliminary purposes, may be conceived of as those outcomes that improve the system and "bad" as those that worsen it.* Moral goods would be more central to the web of good things and, with respect to social systems, would include justice. Evils would be those bad things that injure the more central features of a system, including its moral values. For instance, if humans are not merely featherless bipeds but rational beings, then it would be evil to keep them in a drugged state. If people need to express love and dependence, then a sanitized social system that outlawed sentiment would be evil. If people are happier, more productive, and better citizens when they are free to reach their own conclusions, a social system that hypnotized them into an euphoric stupor would be evil. The central values of a society would include what it means to be a human being, to have a sense of identity, to be a member of a group, and so forth.

Such illustrative values, and others also, place constraints on what can be good for humans. They are constraints because one cannot derive moral conclusions from them as one can derive conclusions from scientific theories. But praxical assessments can be made.

THE MORE CENTRAL FEATURES OF VALUE SYSTEMS

Understanding the importance of context is essential to understanding some interesting differences between analysis in the realms of physical science and morality. Whereas the more central aspects of the scientific realm tend to be highly confirmed and theoretical, the central aspects of the moral realm tend to occupy that position because of their complex interdependence with other values and with alternative states of the world—that is, their dependence on context. This dependence means that statements about central values are likely to be problematic.

On the other hand, unlike peripheral features, the central features of the realm of values are likely to be stable because change in the center has so many ramifications that it tends to shake the entire system of values. Unlike changes in minor values, such as a preference for chocolate rather than vanilla ice cream, changes in important values usually entail changes in other important values and the personality. They produce oscillation in the system and hence are strongly resisted. Individuals perceive them as facts of existence that must be taken into account and about which they have little or no choice. Even in the realm of science, this is true of world views; the whole tends to be stronger than its parts and to allow for easy variation only at the periphery.

A one-to-one relationship between states of the world and a transitive moral scale in which each possible state of the world has a unique position, as each degree of temperature has its unique place on a thermometer, is a strong condition that is unnecessary for asserting the objectivity of the good. Because of the

---

*Many of the qualitative and preliminary statements made in this chapter are treated more systematically in chapter 13, where the test-in-principle and other assessments are discussed.

complexity of the subject matter and the interdependence of its elements, there are almost surely alternative patternings of values that are within some range of equivalence. Nevertheless, a weaker ordering, in which some external states of the world are judged as better or worse than others, is compatible with objectivity.

ENDS AND MEANS

Perhaps we can better understand the complexity of the moral realm by examining the distinction that has been made between intrinsic and instrumental values. This distinction, which Max Weber argued is a dichotomous one,[9] accords with the beliefs of some psychiatrists that even psychotic behavior is not irrational in instrumental terms: it is merely a response to goals and beliefs that are highly idiosyncratic.

Initially, at least, Weber's distinction seems to be a common-sense one. If you wish to drive an automobile and the gas tank is empty, common sense would dictate that the rational act is to fill the tank with gasoline and that to fill it with water is irrational. In this simple and concrete situation, there are clear criteria for distinguishing means from ends and, hence, for establishing the concept of a means-end rationality. The goal is given and the means of achieving it are clear. But are our problems really divided into means and ends, so that we can treat the latter as given and examine the former in terms of efficiency? This will not work.

Suppose I ask why you wish to drive the car? The answer might be that this is instrumental to still some other activity, such as meeting your employer. If this kind of examination produces a chain of ends, then whether we are talking about means or about ends will depend not so much on the existence of a hierarchy of values as upon the phase of the problem under consideration. Although there is no absolute distinction between means and ends in this analysis, an analytic distinction nonetheless might seem to permit each phase of the problem to be considered independently, thereby permitting us to treat every problem in instrumental terms without raising seemingly insoluble questions about intrinsic rationality.

Let us examine our example further. Perhaps you want to drive your car to meet your employer. We can now ask whether driving is instrumentally rational. It might be only a short walk, or hailing a taxi instead might avoid a parking problem. Suppose we ask why you wish to see your employer. Perhaps you wish to ingratiate yourself and gain a promotion. The same time might be spent looking for a better job. Suppose we ask why you want a promotion. You may want to have more money for cultural activities. However, there is often a tradeoff between money and leisure. If we ask why you want to engage in more cultural activities, you might say that you want to be more proud of the way you live. But then, what of your pride in your occupation? The business you are engaged in may require ruthless competition. It might be worthwhile to take a job that pays less and provides you with even less money for books and theatre tickets, if the ethics of the work situation is more consistent with your image of what you want to be. On the other hand, if you have a family to support, there may be a trade-off here as well.

We may be able to show a rational relationship between means and ends in the context of a particular problem, a class of problems, or a type of society. Other relationships, however, may emerge as problems or circumstances change, and the prior ordering of values may become more or less appropriate or rational. New alternatives may create new empirical relationships among values.

What is a means and what is an end depends on the problem that requires decision. The links among the elements of the problem are determined by its conditions, and not by a prior system of classification. There are many ways of arranging means and ends, depending on what questions are asked and how they are analyzed. Because of the multiplicity of questions that can be asked and because the questions branch out rather than narrow—as we saw in analyzing the problem that began with an empty gas tank—when we attempt to trace the chain of ends, the distinction between means and ends becomes less clear as the question asked becomes more important. This is not a simple matter of the means transforming the end; the end simply cannot be analyzed or evaluated in isolation from its context, except for very limited purposes. It is impossible to make a purely instrumental analysis except when the problem is severely circumscribed—gas or water, for example. The more significant and broadly ranging the questions asked, the more the analyst is forced to investigate broad problems involving values, and the dichotomous distinction between the instrinsic and instrumental breaks down. In its broadest sense, this leads to an investigation of the nature of humanity and the character of society.

Moral rules are not merely conventional, although their particular form has conventional aspects. Moral rules are not merely instrumental conveniences, for conceptions of what is a good person or a good society, at least in part, determine those rules. It is not only the interrelatedness of consequences that matters, but also the interrelatedness of moral ends.

The notion of instrumental rationality rests on the belief that objectives can be placed in a linear hierarchy such that lower-ranking objectives are always validated by higher-ranking ones. We have seen that this does not work.

Neither does a hierarchical approach to values work, even if they are considered abstractly, let alone in terms of specific ends. Any attempt to order values in a hierarchy—that is, in an order in which each level of values will contain fewer values than the next lower one until at the top of the hierarchy there is a single value—will produce a supreme value so abstract that nothing can be derived from it. Thus, happiness, freedom, or some other value may be regarded as supreme.

This fallacy underlies all formal attempts to make the world fall into a strongly ordered logical schema, whether of law, of ethics, or of science. Whether formal theories refer back to rules or to values, there is a basic failure to understand signs: an attempt to retain the defined values of signs through various transformations without either error or loss of information.

Clyde Kluckhohn, for example, argued that values were universal because all societies have rules against murder and incest.[10] But this shows only that all societies are organized. The important difference lies in what constitutes murder or incest in different societies. Concepts such as happiness and freedom do not always have the same meaning, either. When Hans Kelsen tried to construct a formal theory of law, he had to make legality the supreme value.[11] In the end, his formal theory was consistent with any system of law and with any mix of legal values within any system of laws. It was a mere definition masquerading as a theory.

Valid choices are made in the realm of praxis. They are not derivable from the deductive, covering-law type of theory that treats other aspects of the larger realm of knowledge as if they were given.

THE SELF AND ITS ENDS

The relationship between the self and its ends is as interdependent as the means-ends correlative. For instance, we sometimes hear an argument that a woman who wants an abortion and cannot get it is a prisoner of the fetus until delivery. I shall discuss abortion in chapter 13. I note here only that whether that woman regards herself as a prisoner depends on how she views herself. If she sees herself as a person who freely engaged in the activities that produced the fetus and who has duties as well as responsibilities, she will see her situation not as something to be escaped but as a duty to be accepted. I am aware that perceptions in fact are not as dichotomous as I have indicated, but I stress the contrast in order to emphasize the conclusion I intend to reach.

The kind of society that is produced by the kind of people who live in it and vice versa depend on how we respond to situations of the former type. These serve as control devices that shape our conceptions of ourselves and of moral ends and moral means. There may be circumstances in which the bar justifiably may turn down candidates of poor moral standing. However, if a law professor fails a student for the same reason although he turned in a brilliant examination, the student's moral failings will find an echo in the institutional setting. If many professors accept that standard, the moral rot will have hit the institution and the perception by other students of what they are and consequently of how it is appropriate to behave.

In short, we can avoid degenerate societies only if a significant number of individuals are virtuous. (My readers will have noted from previous discussion that which virtues are relevant to particular societies, and their concrete character, is dispositional and depends to a great extent upon boundary conditions.)

There is a tendency in our society to speak of individual choice independently of boundary conditions. But surely the freedom of choice that is worth defending and preserving is that of a moral human being. To elevate abstract choice into an appropriate criterion is to overlook the interdependence between the choices we legitimate and the kinds of people and society fostered by such choices. There is a world of difference, for instance, between the individual who steals a loaf of bread to feed a starving child and one who pockets $50 that the money machine incorrectly feeds out. To exculpate the former is to show humanity while to exculpate the latter is to foster a destructive attitude. An abortion for a family that is raising four brain-damaged children when amniocentesis shows the fetus is similarly damaged sends a quite different signal than does abortion on demand. I recognize that damage to real individuals occurs when abortions are difficult to get in a society in which the concern for personal responsibility is subordinated to the values of a transient self, but I believe much greater damage both to society and to individuals results from overt legitimation and the consequent amplification of such values.

Perhaps my judgments are incorrect in the examples I have employed. These matters are weakly ordered. There may be good counter-arguments I have not anticipated. But the interdependence I assert is difficult to deny. Surely we should be wary of imposing our preconceptions on an entire society. But just as surely we cannot safely ignore this interdependency. Hegel called absolute freedom absolute death, a death as meaningless as quaffing a glass of water or clefting a head of cabbage. To elevate an abstract concept of freedom into an absolute social standard is dangerous indeed.

It is the conception of self and of society that lies at the heart of moral behavior. A moral self is not merely a bundle of transient desires and needs. It has an integrity that endures through development and boundary-influenced changes. It is encased in a web that looks backward and that projects forward in time and that respects the achievements of those who helped to build the world in which we live and the rights of those who will succeed us. Society can ignore this interdependency only at great cost. It is the argument of this section of the book that we can make objective even though weak judgments about these matters.

IS THE ARGUMENT CIRCULAR?

Despite advances in philosophy, most of us, except in technical discussions, assume that objectivity involves a correspondence between an internal or subjective representation and an external or objective reality. The valid procedures of science appear to reinforce this conception: we measure with rulers, weigh with scales, and solve equations according to rules that others can follow. Such procedures establish what John Dewey called publicly communicable information.[12] But the appearance is deceptive, for we really compare test conditions and results in one experiment with those in another, not with ideas. Yet if we cannot recognize a scale, or a color, that is, if we do not know how to apply ideas to referents, we cannot communicate our procedures to others or report results they can compare with theirs. The same is true of logical and mathematical operations; they cannot be conveyed to those who are incapable of recognizing them.

We necessarily begin with a field of knowledge for otherwise we could not receive information, but we adjust parts of that field as new information indicates inconsistencies or lack of fit in the field. Thus we can develop non-Aristotelian forms of logic, we can refine our ability to perceive properties, and we can learn that an indicator shows something quite different from what it seemed to show. In the same way, organisms could not act—even by instinct or tropism—in the absence of coding.

In theoretical science, the terms and axioms of a theory, the apparatus and test conditions, and the set of definitions constitute the givens of a scientific experiment. But the entire mélange, as well as all other knowledge, floats, so to speak, in a constantly readjusting equilibrium of scientific knowledge. The status of our knowledge of values is similar. Because the positivistic theorists of knowledge mistake this process, the distinction they make between knowledge of values and other types of knowledge is also wrong.

There is no external color or size to which an internal representation of color or size corresponds. Neither is there such a thing as an atom or a planet entirely independent of the framework of investigation and of transactions within which the names we have given them have meaning. Values have a similar transactional and dispositional actuality, for which tensile strength might serve as metaphor.

It is not true that values are subjective because they do not refer to corresponding external objects. Values, like other transactional and dispositional concepts, are concepts in a differentiated field of knowledge in which some events are internal to a self and others are external. Every hypothesis that serves as a potential assessment of either category, internal or external, presumes a transaction between a self and its environment, a transaction that produces the categories in terms of which an assessment is offered and that is confirmed or disconfirmed by contemporaneous or subsequent knowledge.

If assertions about what is valuable refer at least in part to processes internal to the person, so do psychological and physiological assessments. Even if the latter made no reference to external factors, and of course they do, they would differ from valuations only in terms of the categories of assessment and not in terms of location. Location inside the self does not make an assessment subjective, even to those who still believe in a dichotomy between an external and objective world of reality and an internal subjective world of representations.

Is our knowledge circular because it is located inside the self? Only in the universal sense that we cannot account for any information or knowledge except by assuming that we begin with some information or knowledge. And this statement applies to information about physical facts as well as about values.

Learning involves negative feedback; and this necessitates only that the initial organization of our field of information be capable of correction as well as reinforcement. Thus, beliefs about the valuable will be altered as more is learned about man and his environment.

CODING AND MORAL DEVELOPMENT

The coding apparatus of the infant is relatively crude, and attuned to the immediate satisfaction of wants or needs. What is good, in this phase, is what satisfies the organism's needs. In time, the infant's wants or needs become more complex, the objects that can satisfy them more diverse, and connections between them are perceived. A conception of the self as a unity develops, and a character and personality.

Fit now begins to involve not merely a relationship between a want and its source of satisfaction (as in propositional knowledge) or even between a complex of wants and their immediate environment (as in theoretical knowledge). There develops an even more complex and indirect relationship between a system of wants and the surround which is intellectual and somewhat removed from immediate needs. The concepts of good that emerge during this process are transformed by it, both in their original meaning and in their relative order of importance in actual and imagined environments. This complex process permits considerable variability in development.

The question is not whether the process is objective, for surely it is, but whether there is any second-order objective system of valuation that permits some degree of common or public discourse among members of the same society whose development has been different, and even between members of different societies. I believe there is, that this type of second-order discourse is meaningful and that it has impact upon the first-order system of valuations. It is an extension or generalization of the same process of intellectual adjustment that occurs in individual development, and it is thus potential in human nature.

GOOD AND JUSTICE

Ordinary goods are goods that are valuable to the individual without reference to their availability to others or their worth to society. It may be a good, in the ordinary sense, for John Jones to go to the movies or to buy a newspaper.

Suppose that John's moviegoing means that his wife stays home with their child that night. If so, his going out involves a question of justice. We can ask whether it is just that he go if this forces his wife to stay home. This raises questions about the distribution of goods and efforts within the family. And also about what constitutes a good family member and a good family.

The newspaper purchase also raises the question of justice. Is it just that newspapers be available? This depends upon what is considered a social good. Is a variety of newspapers, with a variety of viewpoints, available to him? This questions entails social values. Such questions are usually central to a social system, and they go to the foundation of the concept of justice. And so an exploration of John Jones's ordinary goods raises issues about a good person, a just society, and the relationships between the concepts under a variety of conditions.

Is justice a good? Only by praxical investigation can we attempt to answer this question.

JUSTICE: SUBSTANCE OR PROCEDURE

The concept of "justice" invokes a distinction between substantive outcomes and the procedures that generate them. An outcome is just if all receive what they should receive or if it produces a social good as, for example, an excellent educational system. A rule is just if it specifies a procedure that will produce a just outcome.* Just procedures are those that individuals can rely upon to produce decisions that are the same for all people in similar circumstances and in the absence of which they would be subject to the arbitrary will of others.

A just procedure will not, however, necessarily produce a just outcome. The rules of baseball, for instance, are designed to allow the better team to win. Each team plays an equal number of games against every other team, using standard procedures, and according to a predetermined schedule. Particular games, however, are sometimes determined by accident. A ball may strike a pebble and produce a winning run. A worried pitcher may play poorly. Rains may cause postponements that create advantages or disadvantages for particular teams. The assumption is that such accidents will cancel each other out, but we know that this is often not true. Sportswriters might even agree that the team that won the pennant was not the best team.

Substantive justice might mean replacing the pennant winner with the best team, but procedural justice means abiding by the consequences of fair procedures. The procedures determine an objective verdict—that is, they are procedurally objective and can be seen by all to be such—whereas evaluations of a team's excellence, although in principle objective, are so weakly ordered that it is easy for bias to enter judgment. We usually stay with the procedurally determined results. If the procedures consistently produce results judged to be substantively unjust, we change the procedures rather than the particular results. Yet, on occasion, a procedural result may be so substantively unjust that we ignore the procedure. During the Great Depression of the 1930s, legal farm foreclosures were prevented by popular action. We may argue about particular examples, but each of us will be able to find some limiting situation in which we can justify a substantive good even if procedures must be damaged.

LANGUAGE GAMES AND ETHICS

In chapter 9, I argued against the claim that language games determine the limits of the questions that can be raised within them. An interesting example is Stephen Toulmin's argument that it is not possible to evaluate an ethical system except from outside its framework.[13]

The recognition of limiting questions is legitimate and its application to ethical discussion is appealing. No answer to the question of why the speed of light is a limiting constant in all physical systems can be given within the framework of relativity theory. Either the theory provides a valid account of reality or it does not. If some new theory provides a better account, then we will accept that one. Toulmin adopts a deceptively similar position when he argues that the test of an ethical theory is whether it correctly states existing social practices. Muslim

---

*Although I shall not consider this case specifically, the reader will be able to see by the end of this chapter why even Plato's just ruler would need to take rules into account.

ethics apply to a Muslim society and Christian ethics to a Christian society. Any choice between them is purely personal.

Toulmin, thus, has no genuine argument to offer someone who chooses to believe in an entirely different system, except to say that the other system may possibly increase distress. He does not even have grounds for arguing against moral systems that exclude reasoned argument, except to exclude them by definition.

It does absolutely no good to say that one's behavior is wrong when it violates an ethical precept of a society if there is no argument against one's personal rejection of the ethical premises of the system, other than the practical one, that punishment will follow. It is possible to test the conflicting predictions of Newtonian and Einsteinian theories within the contemporary framework of physics, but Toulmin's theory permits no way in which such tests of ethics can be made.

Physicists are aware that physical theories require testing. They know it is nonsense to argue that Newtonian and Einsteinian theory cannot be tested comparatively. Although the concepts of "mass" employed in the two theories are incommensurable, their adequacy is adjudicated within the frame of reference of modern physics; and within that framework a sufficiency of theoretical terms, other theories, measurements, test procedures, and so forth, are not at issue. When such a sufficiency of criteria does not exist, as it does not when judging competing theories of astrophysics, the matter remains unresolved. In moral theory also, the question is not merely one of acceptance, of whether a given society accepts a set of social norms, but of whether these norms are good for the society. The issue is not how ethical philosophers use words, but the truth of what they assert, i.e., whether both external and internal criteria apply to the question.

Geometers, for example, are in a quite different position. They are concerned primarily with the consistency and elegance of a purely mathematical system. As a formal system of signs, it can be criticized only by internal criteria. Unless ethical theories are to be considered as systems of pure logic—and their lack of elegance as well as logical interest disqualifies them for such treatment—the most interesting questions concern their application. It does not justify a system of ethics to show that some people or some societies adhere to it. That is a mere description of behavior. It states that moral behavior is consistent with the premises of the system. It does not explain moral behavior except in the almost vacuous sense in which a group of modern Euclidian geometers could defend themselves by saying that the postulates of Euclid explain their behavior. It does not explain why they chose Euclidian geometry and it tells us nothing about the validity of Euclidian geometry except that it is logical. If two members of a society of Euclidian geometers developed a non-Euclidian geometry, their associates could hardly argue that the new choice of assumptions was false or even inappropriate. Even the argument that they should found a new society would be weak, for they might argue back that the whole group should become a society of geometers without further restriction, i.e., that the central logics of the two systems are similar and the subject matters common ones. They might be outvoted or excluded by force, but this result would have no relevance to mathematics. It is difficult to imagine great passion in this example. But that is not true when we change some moral rules of a society, e.g., abortion.

To argue that we ought to follow a rule is convincing to those who accept the rule. It explains their behavior to say that they personally accept the rule and therefore follow it. However, the intermediate step of accepting the rule as valid is essential to the moral enterprise. When we challenge the goodness of the code of our society, we think that this is meaningful action in other than a purely personal sense. This belief may be true or false, but we cannot escape a belief that ethics is either merely a matter of preference or of morally arbitrary commands—the subjective and imperative positions of ethics, respectively— unless it contains some element of truth.

Let us return to Toulmin. He says that a particular promise ought to be kept because of a rule that promises should be kept.[14] However, what most of us mean when we say that a particular promise should be kept is that we should conform with the rule because the rule ought to be followed in this instance. We may hold this view either because we regard the rule as good in itself, or because it is part of a good set of rules which would be injured in its absence, or because we regard the particular instance as an appropriate one in which to apply the rule.

Note how this situation differs from Toulmin's example of the rules of the road. It is quite clear that we need rules of the road to avoid accidents. We really don't care if the rule requires driving on the left or driving on the right, as long as we do it consistently. We will not change whatever rule we have in the absence of strong reasons, for this would create considerable uncertainty during the period of change. No one would think that the rule involves moral behavior, although not following it would be immoral if it is immoral to risk the life of other people. But it is the latter rule that is a moral rule, not the rule of the road.

When we deal with rules regarded as moral rules—for example, not risking the lives of other people—we do not regard them as easily changeable or simple matters of convenience. Our resistance to change is based not upon expediency, but upon a sense of morality that does not attend discussions of changing the rules of the road. This is the fundamental subject matter of ethical discussion and Toulmin's analysis fundamentally avoids it by terming it a "limiting question";[15] in other words, a non-question.

The collapse of Toulmin's whole system of analysis would be more evident except for the fact that much of what he is saying accords with our ethical beliefs. Since it is quite true that we do reason about right actions, his statements about ethical reasons are deceptively appealing. Our willingness to accept his argument is evidence that moral reasoning is part of moral behavior, just as our ordinary language contains evidence of a strong relationship between factual and moral elements. However, the evidence is no better than the framework within which assessment occurs, and this framework is fundamentally faulty in Toulmin's theory.

We are not interested in ethical problems either out of curiosity, which

Aristotle cites as the motivation for science, or because of the elegance of their presentation, which motivates some mathematicians. Physics and mathematics appeal to those whose motivation is curiosity or elegance. But we are interested in ethical behavior because we wish to know what it is. If all we can be told is that acceptance of an ethical system is a matter of personal choice, the "ought" in moral statements would mean even less than the statement that we ought to add one to three if we wish to obtain four. At least that advice is a formal truth. Using Toulmin's ethical theory, we can only tell people to obey a rule when they prefer to do otherwise, because contrary behavior is unethical by definition, by arbitrary convention.

If our choice of moral systems were personal, there would be no reason not to change our ethics daily, as we change our linen, except for the purely expedient reason of avoiding failures of communication or of being reprimanded by Toulmin for behaving unconventionally and therefore unethically. Such reasons would hardly induce anyone to run a personal risk in order to uphold a moral rule. Honor, decency, and integrity would become valueless as soon as they entailed personal risk.

Surely a mathematician, if confronted by a crazed gunman, would be willing to state that two plus three equal six if that were demanded. But the mathematician would at least have the counter-incentive of intellectual integrity: two plus three do not equal six. In situations of risk, however, why should an individual live up to a conventional moral code if all that is involved is playing a game according to the rules? Why not play a different game? Why should not the cheat in life cheat in the moral game also? Language games turn science upside down and make the tool, rather than reality, the arbiter.

NOTES

1. See Morton A. Kaplan, *System and Process in International Politics* (New York: John Wiley & Sons, 1957), reprinted in Morton A. Kaplan, *Macropolitics: Essays on the Philosophy and Science of Politics* (Chicago: Aldine Publishing Co., 1969). The only similar position I have come across is Alan Gewirth's in his "The Normative Structure of Action," *Review of Metaphysics* 25, no. 2 (December 1971).

2. Irving Langmuir, *Pathological Science*, edited and transcribed by R.N. Hall, *General Electric Technical Information Series*, Report no. 68-c-035C (Schenectady, N.Y.: General Electric Research and Development Corporation, 1968).

3. John von Neumann and Oskar Morgenstern, *Theory of Games and Economic Behavior* (Princeton: Princeton University Press, 1944).

4. The attempts to avoid this outcome by resort to metastrategies are theoretically unsound. See John C. Harsanyi, Review of *Paradoxes of Rationality* by Nigel Howard, in *American Political Science Review* 67 (June 1973) and Nigel Howard's and John Harsanyi's letters in ibid. 68 (June 1974). See also Morton A. Kaplan, "Strategy and Morality," in *Strategic Thinking and Its Moral Implications* (Chicago: Center for Policy Study, 1973).

5. Morton A. Kaplan, *Justice, Human Nature and Political Obligation* (New York: Free Press, 1976). p. 122.

6. Conversation with W. Ross Ashby, 1954.

7. R. Duncan Luce and Howard Raiffa, *Games and Decisions* (New York: John Wiley & Sons, 1957), pp. 110–11, 119–20, 143–44.

8. Thomas C. Schelling, *The Stategy of Conflict* (Cambridge: Harvard University Press, 1960) pp. 125 ff. See also Morton A. Kaplan, "Strategy and International Politics," in *World Politics*, July 1961.

9. Max Weber, *The Theory of Social and Economic Organization*, translated and edited by A.M. Henderson and Talcott Parsons (Glencoe, Ill.: Free Press, 1957), Introduction.

10. Clyde Kluckhohn and Others, "Values and Value Orientation in the Theory of Action;" in *Toward a General Theory of Action*, edited by Talcott Parsons and Edward Shils (Cambridge: Harvard University Press, 1951).

11. Hans Kelsen, *General Theory of the State and Law* (Cambridge: Harvard University Press, 1946).

12. John Dewey, *Experience and Nature* (Chicago: Open Court Press, 1965).

13. Stephen Toulmin, *Reason in Ethics* (Cambridge: Cambridge University Press, 1950), pp. 145 ff.

14. Toulmin, ibid.

15. Toulmin, ibid.

Chapter 12
General Theories of Ethics

All general and all formal theories of ethics are defective. I shall refer to one such theory, that of John Rawls, discuss briefly another, that of Alan Gewirth, and then consider at greater length those of Jonathan Glover and Alan Donagan as part of my argument that consequences and rules are correlatives, neither of which can be given absolute priority in moral discourse.

In *Justice, Human Nature, and Political Obligation*, I argued that John Rawl's *Theory of Justice* necessarily fails on formal grounds and, in detail, that its flaws were irreparable.[1]

Alan Gewirth has argued elegantly that he can derive a theory of ethics from the concept of rational agency.[2] In brief, his argument is that agents regard their purposes as good and, therefore, their freedom as good. The agent consequently assumes a right to freedom and, to be logically consistent, must then concede this freedom to others. Gewirth's conclusions followed from his undefended concept of rational agency. If, instead, one accepts my argument that external, as well as internal, criteria govern the use of concepts, a number of difficulties attend his position.

Even apart from the fact that some people do perceive their purposes as bad or evil, and apart from the fact that even good purposes may be such only in context, the rest of Gewirth's argument does not follow. One may have a motive to pursue what one regards as good, but it does not follow that others have a duty to recognize this as a right. Even when one argues that one should be free to pursue x because x is good for society, it does not follow that the good of society in general, or of a particular society, is either an overriding good or a good for other individuals. It does not follow that one person's right to freedom to pursue the good entails any duty of others. Their frames of reference may be different.

But what if independent frames of reference are not at issue? What is agency? Consider the agency of the long-term jailbird who cannot live outside prison and who commits a crime to be sent back to a safe environment. Or of stupid persons who are sufficiently aware of their stupidity to recognize that they are unfit to make their own decisions. Or of the judge who commits retarded persons for their "own protection." I have chosen simple examples to make it clear that, even when independent frames of reference are not at issue, the moral relevance of freedom is highly dependent on its context.

By definition, one cannot be an agent unless one acts intentionally to produce a result. However, the character of the agency is only loosely constrained by this definition. Agency is always a particular kind of agency. It may be selfish or altruistic, rational or irrational, honest or deceitful, and may be so in general or in particular. The meaning of agency, in any concrete situation, depends upon the actors who are agents.

Think of a world in which food is so scarce that most must starve. Assume, further, that force is self-destructive and that deceit is necessary to survival. In such a world, only the deceitful survive. What does the concept of symmetry require of such deceitful actors? Respect for the freedom of others to obtain food or recognition of their freedom to deceive? Gewirth seemed to imply that only the dictionary definition of agency is relevant, and not the characters of the agents and of the world—as if the sign or concept of agency determine its use rather than the character of the agents.

Visualize a less harsh world. If individuals are deceitful and selfish by nature, then they will still be agents, but deceitful or selfish agents. Symmetry would require only a reciprocal right to deceive. This is not inconsistent with enslaving others if one can get away with it. Slaves would retain the right to deceive the masters or even to usurp them.

To produce more restricted conclusions, stronger assumptions than symmetry and purposeful behavior are required. If one is part of a moral community, then one has an interest in the good of others and, if they are agents also, in their moral freedom and in the conditions conducive to its exercise. Now, agency is relevant to moral community, but it is still, in the abstract sense of agency, neither a necessary nor a sufficient condition for it.

Even when there is a moral community, practical conditions may modify the freedom that considerations of agency and symmetry might otherwise require. Agency is modified by social role and circumstance. Symmetry is also modified by role and circumstance. That is, even if freedom is required, it is limited by the agent's appropriate role. The right of a pilot to control the path of a plane takes priority over that of a passenger who disagrees with him.

The only symmetrical freedom that the abstract concept of agency requires is moral freedom. The prisoner, though confined, is morally free: he is not compelled to act immorally within his prison. The moron and the sociopath, however, are unconfined, but not morally free: the moron does not understand moral behavior and the sociopath is incapable of it.

The relationship between moral freedom and other freedoms, i.e., the rules governing society, is dominated by context. Moral and other freedoms are not identical. Their relationship is assessed by praxical and not by theoretical reasoning. In some situations, moral freedom can lose its priority; for instance, in circumstances in which survival of some important social values requires the presence of authoritarian control.

Consideration of the frame of reference permits assessment of situations in which there is either no moral community or only a limited one.

Gewirth's criterion of freedom is too abstract. We are not free, even in the absence of others, simply to pursue what is good. Some goods are incompatible with others. In my hypothesized deceitful world, the freedom to deceive is incompatible with the freedom to act openly and honestly. But, it has priority because it is a necessary condition for the getting of food. Does symmetry in this world require conceding more to others than their right to deceive us? If it does, we cannot derive this conclusion from symmetry arguments alone.

The same considerations that attend a discussion of agency reemerge in similar form when we analyze the nature of the good. Suppose that the good can be achieved only by limiting the freedom of some people to achieve it. For instance, suppose that good government requires restricting the freedom of citizens and that elections corrupt governments. Then, hereditary authoritarian rule may be superior even when the rulers are not superior. It is possible that most individuals, including the ruler, should not be free to pursue the good, except within the limits that government permits. Nothing about agency or symmetry rules out such conclusions in this or other possible situations.

The most that can be legitimately inferred from the argument for agency is that each agent wants the freedom to act for the good insofar as that freedom does not injure more important values. Symmetry then may extend the appropriately limited freedoms to others. Appropriateness, however, may differ with real-world conditions or with differences in position or role.

If humans are agents, no conclusion about freedom can be drawn from that fact by merely formal argument. The nature of humanity, including agency, is certainly relevant to ethical arguments, and that nature qualifies the character of agency. Symmetry, if appropriately specified, also has a role to play. However, Gewirth's argument is flawed.

THE ETHICS OF CONSEQUENCES

A different attempt to achieve generality fails for similar reasons. Many students of ethics think they have said something substantive when they argue that the best decision should be made. That is a rationalistic fallacy. Although there will always be some sense of "best" in which that recommendation is correct, that sense is tautological. The real problem is to determine what is best.

Let us examine a recent approach to ethics by a rationalist to show that consequences are the correlatives of rules and that an ethical system cannot be based on consequences alone.

In *Causing Death and Saving Lives*, Jonathan Glover has raised a number of profound moral questions.[3] Glover pointed out that people talk about the sanctity of human life but make a large number of exceptions such as killing during war, capital punishment, abortion, self-defense, and "pulling the plug" of life-support systems. Therefore, in his view, the essential question was whether there is a sufficient justification for killing. He believed that killing may be justified in many situations: for example, young children with birth defects and adults whose lives are either no longer worth living or are damaging to others, particularly if they are willing to die. Moreover, he wondered why we spare no expense to rescue a trapped miner while refusing to spend money to improve safety within the mines.

Glover made his point by finding circumstances in which ordinary moral precepts break down, a procedure that made his task deceptively easy. It is one thing to argue that any rule, precept, or generalization is inadequate or wrong in a particular instance. It is entirely different to argue that rules, precepts, or generalizations are irrelevant.

There are various psychological mechanisms, including projection. To call someone bad may be a projection of one's own badness on another. Yet when Winston Churchill called Hitler a bad man, this was not necessarily a projection. Much of the skill of the social scientist involves the ability to determine when a generalization or rule is applicable. Thus, even though Glover found circumstances in which he could reject a precept, this does not invalidate it in other situations. He merely showed that it lacks universal validity. A brief exploration of some of the relevant issues will show that some of the precepts to which Glover took exception are valid provided that they are not treated as universally true; this finding, in turn, will invalidate some of his specific conclusions.

Let me take two simple examples; first, a married couple who are experiencing difficulties. Should they calculate the advantages of divorce? It is obvious, from the frequency of divorce in present-day society, that sufficiently difficult marriages are ruptured. It is also clear that the existence of procedures for divorce is a social good. However, if during the course of every marriage the husband and wife constantly examined the equity of their situation and investigated whether their present partner could be replaced to advantage, the number of marriages that would survive would be few indeed, and the functions that they perform, either for married individuals or for society at large, would be jeopardized. In marriage, diffuse relationships are involved; therefore, calculations of its value are inappropriate until a threshold at which the marriage becomes seriously damaging to the parties has been approached.

My second example is a worker on a skyscraper. It is common knowledge that few, if any, skyscrapers are constructed without some workers being killed. The scale of pay reflects this risk somewhat and serves as an incentive to the worker to engage in this hazardous occupation. Yet, if such a worker catches a foot in rope and dangles precariously from a girder, large sums will be spent, and other lives risked, for a problematic rescue. Glover would regard this as the illogic of common sense.

In the skyscraper example, the situation is instrumental rather than diffuse as in marriage. The price paid for the labor takes into account the risk to life. We cannot justify the social or economic costs of eliminating hazardous occupations, and the normality as well as the usefulness of such work minimize its symbolic cost. All societies thrust some individuals into hazardous occupations by means of various incentives, whether dollars or medals and marching bands.

Why, then, risk so much money, as well as other human lives, to rescue a dangling worker who understood the risks of the job before accepting it? Why send a platoon to rescue a few encircled soldiers when the probability is that more lives will be lost than if they were left to their fate?

We do it because circumstances create a dramatic focus that lifts such situations from the instrumental context to what I would call a sacred context, one in which the identification of particular individuals as members of society is at issue. Glover rejects the drama as a form of manipulative sleight-of-hand by an élite or as collective self-deception.[4] He wants to save the greater number. However, I shall argue that the dramatic event is structured differently from ordinary events, and that this difference is essential to our holding onto our humanity.

Whereas the normal context of dangerous work is akin to a force of nature over which we lack power, the dramatic event challenges our capacity to influence it and produces an entirely different set of considerations. These dramatic situations symbolize the obligations that bind all people to each other within a moral community, and they emphasize the features that define us as human beings with a claim upon one another that transcends the instrumental. The dramatic juncture calls forth a process of social reinforcement, in the absence of which our immediate conflicts of interest would isolate us from each other. At this symbolic level, damage to an individual bleeds out into the larger symbolic patterns of society. These patterns constitute webs rather than deductive chains; and the meanings of the elements depend on their place in the web. Thus, a death in one context is not the same as a death in a different context.

True, there is a level at which the disproportion in deaths may overwhelm obligations to specific individuals. Clearly, we will not start a nuclear war to rescue one person. Such a solution is perceived as beyond our power; it entails the sacrifice of incomprehensibly many lives for one and, in addition, the sacrifice of values that would not survive the solution. There is, thus, a higher threshold at which the claims of individuals cease to be decisive, just as there is a lower threshold—e.g., the dangling building worker—at which they become decisive. Events that occur in the gray areas—those not clearly above or below one or the other threshold—are a source of human tragedy and often become the subject of great drama, for their resolution, ambiguous at best, evokes the most serious contemplation and understanding of human self-definition and collective obligation.

Let us inquire further into the adequacy of Glover's rational approach. In principle, it is possible that even extremely large disproportions in casualties could be below the threshold at which rescue is barred by rational considerations. Suppose that our pleasure-seeking and self-centered society leads to a situation in which 90 percent of us are permanently hooked up to computer-run entertainment systems so that we have lost our access to any other experiences and, with it, our ability to make either rational or moral decisions. Suppose that the remainder of humanity can escape forcible subjection to this system only by destroying the computer network and that its destruction will be fatal for the 90 percent that is already connected to it. Suppose one concluded that happiness as such is not an overwhelming good and that the only way to save human beings as thinking and moral beings would be to destroy 90 percent of the society. Such an act would not be the greatest good for the greatest number, unless one takes hypothetical future generations into account. Yet I believe that it would be the correct thing to do, even if future generations are left out of account.

Contrariwise, suppose that these were not entertainment centers that individuals were hooked up to, but computers and science factories and that their bodies, except for the brains, would atrophy. But the brains would be immortal, and the people would still exist as thinking creatures. Would they be human? And would those who wished to escape this fate be justified in destroying the computers? See how the change of circumstances can affect the hierarchy of values.

Anyone who thinks that real circumstances offer alternatives and consequences as clear-cut as my imaginary examples is suffering from hubris. Real situations are much murkier. My imaginary examples nevertheless show that qualitative assessments, assessments related to concepts of human nature, decent societies, appropriate social relationships, and so forth are at the core of appropriate analysis. Rationalistic solutions are overgeneralized abstractions that confuse and distort the character of moral decisions.

My examples also inform, although they do not solve, a more basic problem. Suppose, in the early stages of our imaginary computerized society, there is strong evidence that the society was slowly moving to one of these horrible states. To what extent would forcible intervention be justified? One could not be sure. Still, what forcible measures are warranted to prevent what? High thresholds, a sense of humility, and a recognition that many fearsome transitions develop into changes that are welcome to new and morally intelligent generations must inform our decisions. There is a range of uncertainty that supports nonintervention or cautious and modest intervention. But such problems exist, and moral people have a legitimate interest in coping with them.

The primary reason such great disproportion is acceptable in our imaginary example is that the condition of *homo sapiens* in the hypothecated world would require the sacrifice of the vital aspects of humanity and substitute mere biological survival. Many would be willing to sacrifice the great bulk of the human race, not merely because we would have broken the bonds of identification with it but because its survival would be inconsistent with the survival of what is vital to humanity and society.

To return to the skyscraper worker, the common-sense response to life-and-death situations to which Glover takes exception is appropriate and rational for a related reason. In the absence of this common-sense response, we would tear apart the bonds of identification and solidarity that alone permit community to function and in the absence of which we would be at each other's throats.

That this is so will surprise no one who has followed the argument in Part One that applications of generalizations fall into the arena of praxis and that, the more complex and interrelated the social elements, the less we can deduce from general principles and the more the context differentiates cases from each other. If the real world were like my imaginary computer example, an extremely radical disproportion in casualties could be justified. The example thus establishes a principle but permits us to explore its relevance to real situations.

I can now examine a range of problems that illustrate many of the considerations that are involved in moral judgments. These illustrations will establish the fact that whether a disproportion is relevant cannot be determined in the absence of its context. This does not mean that generalizations are useless. It does mean that the core of a problem is to identify their relevant aspects. The failure to do so will defeat the effort to find the relevant generalizations and will result in a highly abstract approach to ethics that fails to account for most moral behavior and for its causes.

Consider a situation in which terrorists hold hostage both persons and valuable works of art. The hostages are in an inner redoubt; the terrorists, however, can be fought in an outer redoubt. The outer redoubt may be either flimsy or extremely difficult to take. Depending upon circumstances, the estimated casualties are 5, 25, 50 and 5,000. The hostages may be 15 children, 20 adults, the pope, or the president; the art may be a collection of Rembrandts that had been on a world tour or a "pop" painting.

Because these problems are in the area of praxis, our reasoning lacks necessity—that is, conclusions do not follow as in a mathematical derivation— and one cannot demonstrate how many casualties one should be willing to incur in each case. However, we can make some general comparisons, indicate the reasons for them, and make distinctions that are both real and relevant. For example, we are more likely to risk more casualties to save the children, particularly if they might be tortured. Our reason might be that children have their whole lives ahead of them, that society has a special responsibility for young people, and perhaps even that crimes against children are more heinous that crimes against adults. Perhaps we also believe that adults are more able to help themselves, more responsible for the situations in which they find themselves, or that they have some special social responsibilities, including a willingness to accept risks. Wherever one would draw the line, few would disagree that more lives would be risked to save children than adults. Some individuals, when weighing the reasons and the risks, would be unwilling to risk substantially more adults than children; others might agree that substantially more adults could justifiably be risked. I doubt, however, that any could advance a compelling reason to risk as many as 5,000 adults to save 15 children.

The number risked would also depend upon the assaulting force. One would more likely risk more casualties if the force were composed of volunteers. One would more likely risk more casualties if the force were composed of professional soldiers or police than if the force were composed of civilians, perhaps on the ground that the occupations themselves are risky. Who the children are would also enter into the calculation. We would likely risk more for normal children than for mental defectives. We might argue that the lives of normal children are worth more or even that mental defectives are less than fully human.

Let us consider the Rembrandts. We might disagree on how many people should be risked to save these works of art, but many people would agree that some lives should be risked. A number of reasons would probably be offered, including that great works of art are part of our heritage and that their destruction diminishes all of us. Many would be willing to risk their own lives to save a Rembrandt. But I doubt that anyone would be willing to risk life and limb to save a painting by a "pop" artist.

Some individuals might even be willing to risk 5,000 to 10,000 casualties to save the pope, the president, and the collection of Rembrandts. One reason would be that holding such hostages is an assault on the core of modern civilization. It would be such a nihilistic attack that large numbers of casualties would be justified, even if the hostages could not be saved, in order to reinforce the society's commitment to its central values.

Conflicts between rules can also be analyzed by praxical reasoning. The rule of law may be surrendered during war to protect one's country. The principle of punishing a morally corrupt president may be suspended if he is the only person who can save the country. Injury to one's country may be permitted in order to preserve the human values of its citizens.

The objective order in situations of this sort is extremely weak. It is far, far weaker than in conflicting astrophysical theories. Nonetheless, just as astrophysical evidence permits the coexistence of several theories about the red shift in distant stars while excluding others—at least as of the time of this writing— the objective evidence in the realm of moral inquiry also permits both inclusion and exclusion. Furthermore, new information may lead to changes in conclusions. For instance, if it could be shown that mental deficiency is a physiological state that can be completely corrected, the calculation with respect to such children would be changed. If we had historical evidence that the assassination of leaders and the destruction of works of art leads to a rebirth of morality and art, the number of casualties we would risk to save them would be greatly reduced. Our decisions, thus, are affected by the weight of the relevant evidence. Even though we can never be sure that we know all the relevant facts, we should often be able to weigh them comparatively, giving great weight to some and less to others. Although we may not be able to demonstrate clear and direct relationships between the relevant considerations, the risks run, and the actions chosen, we often have reasonable grounds for the claims that we make.

The illusion that this kind of reasoning is not objective harks back to a discredited conception of science—namely, that science always ultimately permits a truly critical experiment. That view of science is supported by neither reason nor evidence. It is an outmoded, nineteenth-century concept, but it still bedevils the discussion of values.

No Single Focus of Analysis

The reader will have noted by now that some of my examples require a consideration of costs and benefits to society, while others require the consideration of rule-oriented behavior. This should not surprise a reader who has followed the arguments about the area of praxis. Even in the physical sciences, problems at the periphery of knowledge require a shifting of the frame of reference: from theory to evidence, from evidence to theory, from theory to theory, and from evidence to evidence.

In figure 7, and in the example of the division of $100, both in chapter 11, von Neumann's solution failed for two reasons: considerations of repeated play in subsequent situations and resentment of what was regarded as an unfair commitment. In the skyscraper example, the decisive factor was the obligation that binds people within a community. In the society in which most people were hooked up to computers, the moral issue of human identity was the decisive factor. Calculations could virtually be ignored.

It would be simple, of course, to find real-life situations that emphasize the harmony between rule-oriented behavior and consequences as well as the conflict between them. Examples in which rules and outcomes are of equal importance would also be easy to find, but they would only obscure the relevance of each. The value of a contrived example that emphasizes one consideration over the other lies in its relative clarity.

The Limits of the Moral Rule Approach

The symbolic "conventional moral views"[5] which Glover found so unreasonable are part of the warp and woof of our system of values. In their absence, we would have only a minimal and destructive order of the Hobbesian variety in which life would be nasty, brutish, and short. Symbols are the currency of thought and consciousness. And their meaning depends deeply upon context and metaphor. An additional argument for this position is that game theory can be used to prove that moral rules are required in some social situations.[6] Moral rules express an important aspect of moral life that is lost in the abstractions of a rationalistic approach.

Consider, for example, the shortage of water in New York City in the 1960s. The mayor asked all citizens to take baths rather than showers, which waste water. A citizen who preferred showers, and who took them in the privacy of home, would on any such occasion deprive the other citizens of New York of less than a drop of water each. Moreover, no one else would be influenced by this behavior because no one would know about it. Therefore, even if the individual were altruistic, it would be rational to take a shower. However, if a large number of citizens preferred to shower rather than bathe, a much more serious shortage would be produced by individually rational behavior. Only a moral rule would prevent it.

The Rationality of Rules

There are many social situations in which moral rules are important, situations in which the absence of the rule would produce a worse society. This consideration has led even some of the less rigid rule-oriented but rationalistic philosophers to a conclusion that is the opposite of Glover's. Alan Donagan, for instance, argued that one must always follow a moral rule, except in situations for which it was not intended. He says, for example, that one may use violence against a prisoner only if the prisoner fails to satisfy "the conditions for immunity to violence."[7] The terrorist fails to satisfy these conditions, according to Donagan, for the terrorist is participating "in an attempt on the lives or the bodily security of other persons." If, therefore, the terrorist knows where other terrorists are, torture may, in the last resort, become permissible although it may be absolutely impermissible to torture innocent parties.

Donagan's argument that the rule is to be followed in all situations in which it is intended to apply is fair enough as far as it goes, for rules always require interpretation within a context. Moreover, if moral rules did not take priority over costs in most situations—if, on the contrary, they fitted only the exceptional situation—they would not be compelling. But this creates the illusion that rules are the core of all moral analysis and that following a rule is always more important than the consequences of doing so.

In the earlier sections of this chapter, I have taken the position that rules, outcomes, and virtues depend for their meaning upon context, including social conditions. Part of the illusory quality of Donagan's argument results from his using terms like "innocent" as if their meaning does not vary. But his major mistake was to fail to understand that the context of the problem may shift the focus of analysis away from rules and to outcomes. How, after all, do we determine when to obey a rule? What are the criteria? For instance, if a terrorist is about to gain control of a jet plane which is carrying a nuclear weapon and intends to use it to destroy a nearby metropolis, it may be necessary to shoot through innocent hostages to stop him. Would Donagan accept this result by likening the problem to that of the fetus that threatens the life of a woman? He says that, in that situation, a different rule—duty to the woman—takes precedence over the innocence of the fetus. But suppose that the terrorist threatened only one, two, or three persons? Would he still make this argument?

Or would he retreat to a concept of proportionality? If Donagan cannot accept the concept of proportionality in this instance, few will follow him. But if he does, then he accepts an argument based on consequences, not on rules. Or will he construct a new rule?

Donagan's qualification of moral rules by their intended scope of application is rigged. Although it is certainly true that one would always attempt to avoid killing innocent victims—rules, after all, are not irrelevant—we must also take consequences into account.

We can reach this same conclusion by a slightly different route. Donagan will accept an abortion or a hysterectomy to save a pregnant woman's life, and argues that the method used does not affect the principle. However, he rejects the double-effect argument that the fetus's life may be taken, even though it is innocent, but only as a byproduct of saving the mother's life. Whereas the double-effect moralist, according to Donagan would reject decerebration which kills the fetus directly (single-effect), he would accept a hysterectomy that does this indirectly (double-effect). Donagan argues that the fetus is killed regardless of how one makes this distinction and that the mother's life should be saved in both cases and not merely the second.

Let us vary the context. Would we reach this same narrow conclusion if society had a serious problem of underpopulation? Or suppose this fetus were the last possible legitimate ruler and its existence necessary to prevent a contest over the throne?

Moreover, do we wish to rule out all double-effect arguments or just some? Do we wish to argue that we can never bomb military targets in war because some innocent civilians—perhaps babes in arms—may be killed? If we agree to the bombing, will we argue that it does not matter whether civilians are aimed at or whether they are hit because they happen to be close to a military target? If we reach either of these conclusions as a matter of principle, we will find ourselves in an absurd position in some real situations. Moreover, we remove an important constraint on violence. Does not the relationship between economic production and the war effort affect the position we take? Suppose the destruction of German weapons plants had been the only way to prevent Hitler from winning?

It should be clear that no single focus of argument will suffice and that a complex of reasons and justifications is required. From the viewpoint of the rules, we judge the value of the consequences. From the viewpoint of the consequences, we evaluate either the rules or their particular application. From the viewpoint of values, we evaluate both rules and consequences; and vice versa. These are part-system problems. There is no single foundation for analysis.

To take into account that one act may have a double effect—the woman's life-saving hysterectomy necessarily kills the fetus as surely as an abortion—is sometimes to make an irrelevant distinction. But this does not mean that there is *never* an important and relevant distinction in the absence of which the moral universe would be poorer and more perverse. Even the predominance of one emphasis—whether on rules, outcomes, or virtues—depends upon a persisting concatenation of situational constraints. Each perspective, in its dogmatic form, has a theoretical basis, and Donagan saves his theory only by using restricted examples and *ad hoc* principles.

Let us use still another example to show that whether particular moral rules or particular outcomes determine the moral analysis of particular situations depends upon the context. Assume that five million Cambodians are left alive and that we could not evade the moral responsibility either for killing all of them or, alternatively, for killing ten million Chinese, who are attacking Cambodia. Which choice should be made? Should the choice be governed by a rule against genocide or by the total of deaths? I suspect that many people would judge it better to kill twice the number of Chinese. Even if some balk at this disproportion, I am confident that we can find some number of Chinese at which the moral rule against genocide outweighs the consequences: five million, one hundred thousand Chinese?

The particular horror with which the crime of genocide is invested affects this judgement. The identity of a defined group has an important value, partly because of our respect for pluralism. Quantitative considerations do not have universal priority.

We can also hypothesize a world in which the rule against genocide can lose its value. For instance, consider a world of forty billion souls in which no defined group has a membership of more than fifty. I suspect that, in this world, the rule against genocide would seem inconsequential and that, if any rule applied, it would simply be one against killing at all. On the other hand, if, in a world of one hundred billion, starvation and the fight for food killed seven billion yearly, I suspect that the taking of life would be regarded as trivial.

Whether priority should be given to rules or to consequences depends upon which emphasis best fits the problem. Like all praxical decisions, this can be made only at the literal level. Still, comparative analysis at the literal level will reveal indicators that can help us to make choices.

RULES, VIOLATIONS, AND COSTS

Donagan denies the "tragic view" that politics often necessitates violations of ordinary morality. He says that

> . . . it is not seriously defensible . . . that the political goods that matter can be procured only by courses of action which involve grave violations of common morality, if not in the use of power, then in its acquisition.[8]

Still, this is precisely what happens in all societies about which I possess significant information. The acquisition of political office, or even the successful holding of it, almost always requires the violation of moral rules and the pursuit of ends that violate the public good. The extent of these violations varies in different political systems, and the moral person attempts to minimize them. Still, they are inescapable: different goals cannot be maximized simultaneously and all institutions require motives and means that are at least partly inconsistent with their stated objectives.

Any complex social structure requires compromises that corrupt some members of that society. And every social equilibrium depends upon the existence of at least some social rules which inhibit virtue or produce side effects that corrupt. We may believe that a city's vice squad could carry out its function without corrupting its members. What of the narcotics squad? Or internal security forces? Many political and business functions necessary to a society's well-being may similarly corrupt those who carry them out. And every effort to restructure society, even though some efforts will improve it, will have some residual corruptive consequences. Every society tends to produce its own type of criminal because the compromises necessary to sustain the society place unequal burdens on its members, particularly on those whose weakness of character exposes them to temptation. This is true in the university also, and one wonders in what compartmentalized universe those live who believe differently.

Although it is certainly true that a second-order moral inquiry into the conditions of a society would uncover ways to diminish corruption, there will never be a complex society in which it is entirely absent. All complex social choices have social and moral costs. Society as a whole places upon some of its members heavy burdens that are the price of the benefits and the virtues that the society enjoys.

In many complex cases, moral rules, moral goods, and personal virtue must by weighed in a praxical balance in which none of these considerations has clear priority. Was President Franklin Roosevelt justified in his illegal assistance to Great Britian in World War II in an effort to prevent a Nazi victory, or in his consistent lying about it? A host of questions is raised here. One has to examine the constraints of time, the practical consequences of telling the truth or even allowing it to become known, the legal requirements of constitutional behavior, the implied obligation to protect the institutions of the nation, and so on. There are also procedural considerations.[9] Was there a relatively direct relationship between Roosevelt's breaking of the rules and the end to be achieved? Was the end to be achieved—the defeat of the Nazis—sufficiently valuable to justify breaking the rules? Which type of consideration takes priority, or whether we must balance a complex of considerations, depends upon the context. No single *a priori* criterion can be successfully used.

Tragic questions of this kind—or even minor versions of them, for the breaking of rules can be justified at all levels of society—are extremely complex, not easily answerable, and involve shifting frames of reference. Contrary to what Kant asserted, moral rules do not apply within all frames of reference. Lying to one's enemies during war is not always perceived as breaking a moral code. On the other hand, it is not clear that wardens have a right to lie to inmates to break an insurgency. Nor is it always acceptable to lie to the enemy in war.

Consider whether a teacher should fail a student who is an evil person who might do much harm after receiving a degree. The refusal of a moral teacher to fail the student will depend not upon its direct consequences but upon self-conceptualization, the ethics of the profession, and a conception of how a university should be organized and run. The teacher of good character would probably refuse to fail the student even if the teacher's dishonesty could be successfully hidden and, therefore, would not affect the teacher's career or the behavior of other teachers. Here, the teacher's *non*-utilitarian decision is essential to the survival of good social contexts. The judgment about the student's success at evil is highly fallible, the relationship between failing him and his success is remote. I do not see how a teacher who would fail the student could escape moral corruption. Or how an institution that would expect such behavior could escape corruption.

The more easily frames of reference shade into each other—for instance, in situations in which the public good may be served by lying to the public as distinguished from those in which lying cannot be justified—the more difficult it is for us to make the appropriate distinctions. But if the rules are broken too often at the highest reaches of social and political life, then the corruption, rather than being minor, will begin to pervade institutions and transform personalities. Perhaps strong persons can limit their own corruption, but most individuals undergo personality changes and identity problems as they try to explain their behavior to themselves when such compromises become integral to their life style.[10]

Donagan is wrong in denying that life sometimes offers us only tragic choices. It does, but they can still be analyzed morally. The correct type of analysis, however, will involve not only moral rules, but also moral ends and personal and social virtues. Such moral analysis helps to contain moral corruption and rot. Whether it succeeds in doing so depends upon the benignity of circumstances.

SOME TENTATIVE APPLICATIONS

Before I attempt to apply the foregoing analysis, some further comments may be useful. If the reader harks back to my discussion of weak orders and neighborhood effects in the physical sciences, it will be clear that moral analysis is extremely complex, that it responds to many foci of analysis and identification, and that it depends on what facts we perceive. We saw that the interpretation of data and the use of instruments may be open to serious question even in analyzing the red shift. In moral analysis, even apart from factual interpretation and general frameworks of identification, particular problems involve overlapping centers of interest: the self, the family, the group, society at large, the world situation. Each of these frameworks may be relevant, although each may lead to a somewhat different conclusion. Thus, no deductive procedure can serve as the single focus of analysis and alternative assessments are possible.

Objective procedures and assessments permit rational discourse and exclude some proposed answers. They do not assure or even make probable an identity of answers. If different winning coalitions—and who is in a winning coalition is of vital importance to the actors—satisfy von Neumann's solution, different responses to moral problems, even within a single society, may be objectively neutral in second order terms even though the differences in outcome are crucial to particular moral actors. Thus, in the examples I use below, the reader should pay less attention to the particular answers I reach—for other answers may be praxically defensible—than to the method of analysis, particularly as it is seen to mitigate against the exclusively consequence-oriented approach of Glover and the exclusively rule-oriented approach of Donagan.

Some Current Controversies

How does the foregoing analysis fit into some current moral controversies? Whereas rationalists like Donagan try to determine positions according to rule, rationalists such as Glover argue for consequences: if it can be shown that capital punishment does not deter crime, it is merely retributive and unjustifiably cruel. But there is one clear virtue of capital punishment that is not directly related to consequences. In Biblical times, sinners were stoned, and I think we can understand the significance of such types of punishment. They reinforced moral solidarity by excluding the sinner from the community. One argument for capital punishment, for at least certain types of murders, would be to signify society's horror and outrage over the taking of life: such horror that the criminal must be cast out, regarded as non-human in the figurative sense of identification. (Presumably exile to a patrolled distant island would also work.) However, it must be admitted that the legal delays, haphazard sentencing, and the modes of execution in our society, may even make capital punishment counter-productive in terms of its symbolic meaning. On the other hand, one suspects that the inability of contemporary society to find some way of expressing its horror of murder is one of the factors that cheapens life and that even may create more sympathy for the killer than for the victim.

Time may change circumstances. If we merely jail killers and if they are genuinely rehabilitated, they should be set free. Continued punishment serves no purpose, even a symbolic one. The tie between the deed and the punishment has been broken by the temporal gap. Even so, the horror of the crime can overwhelm the effect of a temporal gap. The public reaction to Herbert Kappler's escape in Italy in 1977 resulted from the effect of this higher threshold. Mass murder was part of the Nazi practice for which Kappler shared guilt. Thus, even at a late date, the escape of this poor, old, and terminally ill criminal, whose release would normally be granted in any humane penal system, was a serious blow to the moral solidarity of the relatives of the victims. It threatened their identification as human beings who counted to society. Of course, Glover might consider this a side effect.

For Glover, a side effect is a consideration that enables him to escape an absurd result, just as a restricted area of application serves a similar function for Donagan. But it is no accident, I think, that Glover and Donagan ignore the concept of thresholds. If Glover were to treat any sufficient reason as a side effect, his position would become absolutely open, except for his opposition to universal rules. And Donagan's position would become absolutely open if any acceptable criterion were to permit the evasion of a rule or the formulation of a new rule.

What Glover fails to recognize is that, in his discussion of moral issues, he arbitrarily—arbitrarily because he provides no independent justification—selects the same moral consequences that we would consider relevant. Donagan selects rules arbitrarily. Neither rules nor consequences, nor particular rights or duties, have absolute status.

Let me offer a few examples. In at least one society, aged parents were eaten. In some past societies, children were abandoned and left to die. Such practices helped to preserve those societies in conditions of great scarcity, and the practices were reinforced by other values and a consonant conception of humanity. However, consider a large contemporary family with three-month-old triplets, lost in the wilderness without food. The family members wait until they are at the point of death and then kill and eat one of the triplets, and so on until all three are eaten. Then they are rescued. They admit that the triplets did not die naturally but were killed. They state that they chose only those members of the family without developed personalities, who were therefore not fully human. Even so, it was done only as a last resort. Clearly, lives were saved. Furthermore, they argue, there could be no appreciable side effects because such situations are so rare and, therefore, clearly distinguished from normal ones.

I do not think that this would wash. If they were not found insane, I believe there would be appropriate criminal penalties. The reason is that their behavior would challenge the web of identifications of values, rights, duties, and moral precepts that sustain our conceptions of human worth. The duties of a parent to a child—even though not absolute and even though there are exceptions—are too central to our web of values for such cannibalism to be tolerated. We would feel that parents who ate their children would not have lives worth saving. On the other hand, if a baby were sitting near a button that would blow up a city, were clearly about to press it, and if there were no other way to stop it, we might well justify the parent's shooting the child. This somehow does not challenge so gravely our central set of values because here the baby has become almost a force of nature. Moreover, duty to the city takes precedence. But what to do if only the family is involved? Alas, here we have a twilight zone and a tragic dilemma.

These structural aspects are lost in Glover's approach, which treats outcomes abstractly, as if they had values independent of their neighborhood; in Donagan's approach, outcomes are lost in an abstract set of rules with exceptions. This is hidden by Glover's acceptance of contemporary values, just as Donagan's sleight-of-hand is hidden by his use only of applications approved by contemporary morality.

The most central questions of the moral enterprise concern the identification of moral rules and moral consequences, and of the circumstances in which they are appropriate. Many of the most important aspects of this moral web can be understood only situationally.

Thresholds are important to a situational determination. The force of the distinction (not dichotomy) between nature and human control is only one of many thresholds. There may be more than one threshold in any real situation, and their force may be inconsistent. Whether a threshold exists depends on the entire situation; it can no more be determined abstractly than can be the value of particular outcomes.

The meaning of moral questions depends on types of situation and on specific circumstances in particular types of society. Even whether something should be considered an act or part of a situation cannot be determined abstractly, but only within a context.

Our abstract vocabulary—a life worth living, honor, and so forth—only points to but cannot define moral values in the absence of the unspoken understandings that flesh out and particularize a civilization. A rupture in this web of meanings affects a neighborhood of values—often containably if the rest of the web is uninjured. A moral approach in which values are treated abstractly and apart from their situational meanings threatens to dissolve the web of meanings that permits structured individual character and civilized moral social structure.

The advice to "do what is best" is a sleight-of-hand because it diverts our attention from the fact that "what is best" depends upon parts of the web for its force.

What is a cost and what is a gain? These general questions were discussed in the previous chapter in my critique of von Neumann's utility axioms. They become concrete here. Promotion is a cost to an individual who does not desire responsibility. A duelling scar was a badge of honor for a German university student before World War I. Is Glover willing to accept the concrete values of an individual? If so, how then can he argue for counting lives, or anything else, in a diverse population in which lives have different values? How can he argue against individuals assigning their own values to rules? And if rules do affect values, how can he deny the moral relevance of rules?

If we push Glover's position to an extreme, we shall see that his procedures dissolve his criteria. Suppose we evaluate every individual on each fifth or tenth year of life and decide whether each is of net benefit or of net cost to society. And if the net cost is sufficiently great, suppose we eliminate that person. Does Glover reply that he has included in his calculations whether the individual wishes to go on living? Why should this impress us if that person's life has a sufficiently adverse effect upon others, another element of Glover's reasoning? However, let us include Glover's criterion of willingness to die as an absolute requirement, despite its arbitrary character. Would not the periodic review undermine both our sense of social solidarity and our sense of our own humanity even if such eliminations were not carried out? And in these circumstances, if we proved sufficiently costly, would not our wish to live, our conception of our worth, and our ability to withstand the mores of our society all diminish? Even if this were done less formally, the results would be the same. That costly soul is a symbol to us—of what we might have become under other circumstances —and our own sense of worth and the conditions under which we are willing to live are changed as we engage in this type of analysis. Our sense of human worth requires a barrier against precisely this type of abstract analysis.

It is quite true that medical triage sometimes reduces our humanity in this fashion. Normally, however, triage is used when the scarcity of resources allows for no alternative. However, to turn such a necessity into a principle would be destructive of the moral foundations of society. To be sure, many of the functions of society require instrumental analysis. These functions, however, are carried out within the framework of the sacred glue that holds societies together through the symbols that identify us with that society and its concept of humanity. Our moral bonds require rule-oriented behavior in a variety of situations, and an absence of calculation although not of judgment, when we decide which rule to follow. A moral analysis that fails to respond to the moral aspect of the nature of rules will either be irrelevant or, by affecting the behavior of people, destructive.

Glover dislikes taboos and equates such precepts as the sanctity of life or the double-effect argument with taboos. Perhaps he should not so easily dismiss the value of taboos in primitive societies, as well as in modern societies—provided that they are used with judgment and with sensitivity to real differences. He may find that they have a rational function that is important or even essential.

The sense of the worth and identity of the self is the rudder that steers the human ship. In its absence, character dissolves and behavior atomizes and disintegrates. Goals and values do not exist independently of this process; their reification in calculations or rules, however useful in limited analysis, corrupts when it is generalized.

Some Further Distinctions

Brand Blanshard has taken a position on moral issues that resembles mine in some important respects. I agree with his striking devastation of subjectivistic and linguistic approaches to the good, and also with his assertion that moral choices require a naturalistic ground.[11] I differ with his detailed argument, however. I do not agree that anything is good in itself:[12] the inability to deceive oneself may be bad for a paraplegic and good health may be bad for someone whose moral collapse has eroded the meaning of life. This, however, is not a fatal defect, for Blanshard could and would argue that goods are what the individual would choose under more benign circumstances. However, he attempts even a stronger argument. Love, for instance, would still be good even if humans were by nature amoral beasts.[13] Blanshard argues that the inability of a beast to know love is not proof that it is not good; the beast would desire love were it capable of knowing love.

But love is not good, as Blanshard admits, except in relationship to human nature. It may not be good for the human-beast or for the human-angel. It is not merely lack of knowledge that produces the difference, but a difference in nature. It is as if Blanshard had argued that cows would desire to eat meat if they could experience food as humans do. Would he argue for a test-in-principle according to which cows would choose to be human if given the opportunity? In the following chapter, I shall argue for a test-in-principle, but this type of application would stretch the concept beyond meaning. Alternatively, such an argument could be sustained if we could show that there is a telos in evolution. This may be so, but we do not have contemporary grounds for asserting it.

Blanshard has not entirely avoided the problem of utilitarian theory. By stressing the most comprehensive possible fulfillment of satisfaction or desire[14] he is at best truistic; he is left with the equivalent of utilitarianism's ultimate maxim: do what is best. No one chooses a good on the ground that it is the most comprehensive fulfillment of satisfaction or desire. We choose what is good for good reasons, because, for instance, it is in keeping with our character or is good for nation or family. Moral choices are made in a rich context and are understandable only in that surround. Satisfaction is a product, not the grounds for choice. Blanshard's argument that choice of the good is a rational procedure that depends upon knowledge of what is good requires his conclusion. And he seems driven to this expedient by the need to find simple naturalistic grounds, which he calls desire, for rational choice. My concept of moral coding meets the naturalistic requirement and avoids this *non sequitur*.

Despite much agreement, I must reject his position because it fails adequately to carry through the relational aspect that he himself admits is necessary to the concept of good. In both his moral theory and his ontology, Blanshard seems to accept the classical modern concept of an ultimate, unique, first-order set of criteria that has universal applicability. I have argued that this is not possible. Now I turn to the test-in-principle to show how to cope with the problem without this disabling assumption.

NOTES

1. Morton A. Kaplan, *Justice, Human Nature, and Political Obligation* (New York: Free Press, 1976), pp. 107ff.; John Rawls, *A Theory of Justice* (Cambridge: Belknap Press of Harvard University, 1971).

2. Alan Gewirth, *Reason and Morality* (Chicago: University of Chicago Press, 1978).

3. Jonathan Glover, *Causing Deaths and Saving Lives* (New York: Penguin Books, 1977).

4. Ibid., pp. 210–211.

5. Ibid.

6 . See Morton A. Kaplan, "Some Problems of the Extreme Utilitarian Position," *Ethics* 70, no. 3 (April 1960) and "Restricted Utilitarianism," *Ethics* 71, no. 4 (July 1961).

7. Alan Donagan, *The Theory of Morality* (Chicago: University of Chicago Press, 1977), p. 184.

8. Ibid., p. 188.

9. See Morton A. Kaplan, *Dissent and the State in Peace and War: An Essay on the Grounds of Public Morality* (New York: Dunellen, 1970), pp. 46–48.

10. For a discussion of these issues see Morton A. Kaplan, *Alienation and Identification* (New York: Free Press, 1976), all of part 2, but especially pp. 166–168.

11. Brand Blanshard, *Reason and Goodness* (London: George Allen & Unwin Publishers, 1961).

12. Ibid., pp. 281–282.

13. Ibid., p. 299.

14. Ibid., p. 311.

Chapter 13
An Approach to Ethics

Despite the earlier arguments for objectivity, is not the position taken in this book relativistic? This depends on whether we mean relative to local conditions, which is the way anthropologists tend to use the concept, or relative to a frame of reference, e.g., an inertial system in relativity physics.

The argument for the anthropologist's usage, which I reject, is strong. Although it is true, as Clyde Kluckhohn argued, that all societies have rules against murder, stealing, incest, and so forth,[1] it does not follow that the same moral virtues are cherished in all societies. Moral issues arise when we ask what the rules should be and what the acceptable moral values are. Unless these questions can be answered, the entire moral agenda remains open.

If we look only at the practices of mankind, we can discover every extreme. The ovens of Buchenwald and the spires of Chartres are both manifestations of human nature. The competitiveness of the Kwakiutl and the cooperativeness of the Hopi are also manifestations of human nature. Consideration for others and barbarism coexist as potentialities in human nature.

The concept of virtue is susceptible to the same sort of analysis as that of values. One will find similar virtues—honor and generosity, for example—stressed in many different civilizations. But the content of the concepts and the mix among them has differed.

Take the concept of honor, for instance. In some societies it is not honorable to respond to insults. In others one loses honor if one does not respond. And in some societies honor is not recognized as a virtue. The range within which honor as a virtue may apply even within the same general society may vary with conditions. Take, for instance, the problem of whether a failure to report on a cheater during an examination is also a violation of the honor code. Might it not make sense to distinguish between the case of West Point cadets where a rigid code may be related to the requirements of war and that of students in an ordinary college where the conflict between an austere code and local values may be too severe? Because it is very difficult to evaluate all the components of a situation and because it is very easy to interpret them in a self-serving way, we can become confused in situations in which rule-violating behavior is a good.

We must always reason from within the framework of our own circumstances, whether social or personal. Attila could not have aspired to work for universal peace. We are no more able to build value systems from an abstract framework than we are able to reconstruct language without assessing one or more real languages. Our understanding of our own possibilities is grounded, at least in part, in our transactions with others. Our understanding of right and wrong is grounded in our socialization. Our acceptance or rejection of social standards, regardless of our reasons, is precisely that: an acceptance, rejection, or modification of a particular code. We can learn about ourselves only from experience.

Am I then asserting a relativistic position: that values can be related only to particular societies and situations? Not in the anthropologist's sense, if we rely upon the concept of objectivity and the praxical criteria—particularly second-order neutral reasoning—developed in Part One of this book.

Reason, abstraction, and generalization require a clay which, despite its manipulability, has definite characteristics. We are not merely prisoners of our individual experience. We are inherently autonomous and self-regulating.* Our knowledge of ethnology and physiology may cause us to reflect upon certain emotional and social characteristics of human nature, however speculatively. Our knowledge of history shows us that there are alternative arrangements of human affairs. As in scientific inquiry, some aspects of the current state of knowledge are tentatively held constant and others are varied. The relevance of values changes as these procedures are employed.

A systematic study of these different areas may succeed in relating them to specific environmental conditions, the state of human knowledge, and the alternatives that members of a society are able to consider. Our exercise of empathic imagination can illuminate the situations of other individuals in other roles in other social systems. In principle—provided we keep its heuristic function in mind—this entire sequence of potential choice can be elucidated by the test-in-principle I formulated in an earlier book:

> Consider a situation in which a man would be able to relive his past in thought. He could be confronted with each of the branching points of his major life decisions and allowed subjectively to live the alternative lives. If individual choices could be tested in this fashion, social and political and moral choices could be tested in analogous fashion by confrontations with different patterns of social, political, and moral organization under different environmental constraints.

> Presumably this would confront men with choices that are meaningful. Thus, where the material environments of the social and political systems were presented as "givens," the individual would observe the consequences of different positionings and different circumstances within the systems. He could observe which roles he would prefer if he could choose his roles and how much he would like or dislike the system if roles were chosen for him. Within his own life patterning, he could compare choices over those things where he in fact had the freedom to choose differently. Within these constraints, his conceptions of the good depend upon the limitations of institutional life and material environment, again in two ways. He could compare

---

*The concept of "transfinite stability" used in chapter 11 is relevant here, as are the concepts in Appendix 2.

systems as to which he would prefer if he could choose his role and which he would prefer if his role were assigned to him. On the basis of a more limited freedom, he could compare differences in the existing institutional structures with respect to his past decision points, where he had had some freedom to effect changes in them.

After experiencing these alternatives, the individual would return to his actual situation. He would then have to choose in the present on the basis of the limited alternatives available to him. He now has a standard against which to judge his practicable choices; if he has interdependent utilities, it will be too uncomfortable for him not to make some effort to move the system closer to alternatives that are practicable, not too deprivational for him, and better for others as well. Presumably he will not confuse himself about the harm he does to others because of his needs under existing constraints.[2]

These experiments cannot be carried out in fact. However, just as the praxical procedures of science specify valid methods of investigating problems—methods that we understand better by contrasting them with the discarded view that scientific knowledge is entirely theoretical—the praxical procedures for examining moral problems are illuminated by an examination of their similarities and differences from thought experiments such as the test-in-principle.

PRAXICAL ASSESSMENT OR DISCOVERY

Although the test-in-principle is a tool of discovery, it alerts the moral reasoner to the praxical considerations that affect moral discourse. It thus becomes part of the information on which we base that discourse, because the conditions in which individuals produce certain values are essential elements of truth in moral discourse.

That people's values are affected by situations is a problem because the relative independence from the environment that characterizes theoretical problems in macrophysics is absent. The problem, although real, is not insuperable. We infer values from behavior under varying conditions.

Some simple "purposive" systems are easily analyzed; e.g., Grey Walter's machine, which plugged itself into an electric socket when the battery for its light began to run down and which refilled its tank from a gas pump when its fuel was low.[3] The analysis of organisms that can modify their behavior is much more problematic. But a comparative analysis of behavior, including verbal statements, under a variety of conditions permits us to make reasonable inferences about the purposes and nature even of humans.

Two actions may be identical but their moral meanings may be different. For instance, an individual lied to protect a brother from being fired. However, the same information—that a brother was in danger of being fired—may sustain different inferences about the character of the liar because of the way it fits with other information. The person may have lied because it was the easy way out, or only because the brother's children were in the hospital.

The use of the test-in-principle for discovery is not analytically identical with its praxical use. In discovery, we investigate the circumstances that produce different outcomes or interpretations. In praxical analysis, there is also a reasoned argument to sustain the conclusions, including the reasons behavior differs in different circumstances. Praxical reasoning is used to assess the extent to which information—about moral alternatives, psychological needs, biological needs, social conditions, individual and social needs, relationships between choices and consequences, and so forth—has been taken into account.

How shall we proceed with the praxical assessment of moral matters? We cannot make a complete set of comparisons, but we can approach a second-order set of evaluations by making those comparisons about which we have reasonable confidence because we have sufficient information. We will gain this degree of confidence by examining the efforts that people make in a variety of situations to obtain certain ends and to avoid others. As I explained a bit earlier, behavior, in itself, is not sufficient for its interpretation. Individuals may make mistakes about circumstances or confuse primary and secondary goals.

Nonetheless, by a sufficiently enriched set of comparisons of behavior in a variety of circumstances, we gain a degree of confidence in specific comparisons. Our procedures are objective, we take evidence into account, and we can communicate our procedures to others. Moreover, our ability to relate our evaluations to life and social experience itself dissolves narrow evaluations. At least some of the instances in which some individuals justly turn against their own society, e.g., Germans under the Nazis, can be understood in terms of such comparisons. Our conception of the human being as an evaluating system is meaningful; the idea that there are limits to plasticity and that there is a cost for incorrect choices is meaningful; and, therefore, at minimum the notion that we can make specific comparisons is meaningful. We can also seek empathic insights into those with different psychological propensities, and enter this insight into our judgments.

The process of imaginatively switching roles within a society and of comparing societies has a profound effect on our conception of humanity and of good societies. One learns how some roles corrupt or cripple human potentiality and how some permit that potentiality to flourish; how some societies force even good people into bad actions and how others predispose even potentially bad people toward the best; what humans have in common with each other and perhaps even with animals and nature; how some environments rupture identification and sociability and how others foster it. The procedures that support bad behavior and bad societies are revealed as such. Learning of this type changes our character, our understanding of the world, our evaluations of outcomes, our definitions, our identifications, and everything else that is central to moral analysis, in ways that are consistent with a better and more systematic understanding of the moral universe.

There is one other form of empirical testing that in principle sheds light on our problem. Individuals confronted by evidence that personally beneficial conditions are harmful to others could be forced to employ pathological reasoning because of their need to avoid empathic knowledge of the harm they are doing, for instance, if the tax collector assessing an account became aware he was driving the subject to suicide. We are rarely confronted with desperate choices of this kind because the process of socialization produces both the expectation that certain rewards are justified and an inattention to the deprivations they entail. In consequence, individuals do not have to divert their attention from the deprivations of others; they are on the whole not confronted by them. When information is presented to the individual, however, it would presumably generate pathological information processing, and this might be ascertainable.

The suggestion is offered hesitantly, for I fully recognize the immense difficulty of attempting to validate a particular explanation of an informational disturbance of this kind. Moreover, in social systems that are sufficiently pathological, it would be the empathic individuals, who recognized injustice, who might manifest the most disturbance. However, although these individuals would suffer in most actual situations because of their greater sensitivity to information, in principle we could show that it is their recognition of, or at least their beliefs about, the ways in which current conditions deprive other individuals that produces the pathology. Presumably by confronting others with data of this kind, we could produce similar pathologies in them.

Full information, of course, is not available. We cannot have full information even about the physical world. Some day we may learn that our theories are wrong. Comparative knowledge, however, at least widens our perception of the range of human possibility. Our ability to perceive this range broadly depends upon the range of comparative experience available to us. The primitive people of 5000 B.C. could not have conceived of modern technological society. If we were able to go back in a time machine, to teach such primitive people English, and to present them with books about the modern age, we would merely bewilder them. They would not understand our science or our customs.

Let me be more specific about how a comparative evaluation might proceed and what it has in common with scientific method. My examples will be the most obvious I can find, for the complexity of human beings and of society, as well as their complex linkages, make it very difficult to acquire even problematic information about the values of human beings in different circumstances.

If we examine any society and its norms, we discover complex links between any feature of a society and its environment. In a society in which children were abandoned or aged parents eaten, for instance, such customs were supported by institutions and other norms. Suppose we discover that such customs existed only in societies whose supply of food was insufficient. We might then hypothesize that this factor produced this particular value and, therefore, that it is only a secondary gain. In principle, a member of such a society who became familiar with social anthropology might have come to the same conclusion and become an advocate of increased food production to ameliorate conditions and, eventually, to produce a better society with changed values.

A few simple illustrations may clarify how conclusions can be drawn concerning the relative desirability of different personality or social systems. For instance, consider a masochistic person. We may disagree with the accounts of particular theories of psychology, whether Freudian or other, of the genesis, etiology, or specific functioning of masochism. But we can recognize the costs of this type of secondary gain for the personality. Again, consider a system in which almost everyone lies and cheats. It may be difficult to reform this system, but its inadequacies are evident to all, except perhaps those who would argue, incorrectly, as it would be easy to show, that this is how things really are in their nature and that one would be a fool to think that a better system is possible even in principle. In short, no matter how much difficulty there may be in making some comparative evaluations—and I do not believe that a completely univocal and transitive ordering is possible—others not only are possible but we make them often on the basis of adequate evidence.

Information, therefore, and not merely the existing norms, is used in arriving at these conclusions. In a similar way, a series of comparative judgments might completely change the normative and institutional structure of a society. Usually, however, societies change in response to environmental changes, without regard to the comparative experience of humanity and, therefore, without an enlightened evaluation of the factors involved.

The information we bring to bear upon this praxical process is not restricted to comparative knowledge of social institutions. Comparative knowledge of economics, increased knowledge of human physiology and psychology, and indeed all of human knowledge, have a bearing on judgments about what rules and outcomes are good.

The larger judgments we reach, those that take all these factors into account, are analogous to science as a corporate body rather than to any particular theory. In this respect, knowledge, whether of science or of the valuable, can be likened to a field that is constantly readjusted rather than to a deductive system. Thus, judgments of value are not deduced from rules, facts, or assessments of good outcomes; rather, these coexist in a loose balance as we arrive at a value judgment.

One consequence is that the normative rules of a particular social system coalesce in a way that is meaningful in that system, rather than deducible from some over-arching normative system. The relationship is not deductive or hierarchially systematic. And, because our judgments about values are often low-confidence judgments, they resemble what the ancients incorrectly called opinion more than they resemble what physicists, for instance, call science. The ability to use something like the test-in-principle in specifying these weakly ordered normative systems is a potentiality of the transfinitely stable character of the human system.

The transfinite process is one of investigation and discovery—including the discovery of what it is to be human—and also of the justification of evaluations by means of evidence and argument. If being human involves being moral, as I believe it does, then transstability is the process by which people, in learning of their humanity, become human and learn how to build a society fit for humans. My hypothesis would be that those who thought through moral questions globally, whether directed by religious attitudes or by deep insights into humans and society, would be among those who, for instance, were more likely than others to run risks to protect Jews during World War II.

Because this transsstable process takes place in the realm of praxis, our concepts develop through comparative understanding of how human behavior, social institutions, culture, science, and so forth, are linked in alternative possible or real worlds, each of which is characterized by a world view that is textured and enriched by the entire web of social existence and deepened by comparative understanding of alternative possibilities.

This method does not differ from that of hard science, which also requires discovery. Many scientific discoveries have arisen from a consideration of why other hypotheses have failed to account for aspects of what we know. Galileo, for instance, knew that a feather would not fall as fast as a rock. He thought of objects that would not be affected by barometric pressure and then of a formula that would be valid in a vacuum. After discovery, the elements that justify the attribute "true" are brought together in a praxical account. Discovery and justification are different phases of science. Both are also phases of inquiry into values. "Discovery" and "justification" are correlatives.

THE MORAL ORDER AND OBJECTIVITY

I can now tie up some loose ends in the discussion of objectivity. If you are partly color-blind, you cannot distinguish some colors. That does not mean that you can distinguish none. And the distinctions you do make are objective. To the extent that your optic system functions properly, your perceptions will coincide with those of a visually normal person. In turn, the normal person cannot make some distinctions made by laboratory equipment.

Think of an indifference curve resulting from different mixes of different social goods. Some of these mixes would be morally equivalent to others. Presumably, we could find some second-order criteria in terms of which we would argue that the values of some societies are, in principle, substitutable for the values of other societies. These societies, then, would occupy a similar place in a scale of values that is weakly ordered. Other societies might be higher or lower in this qualitative ordering. This process would establish a weak ordering of societies that would be consistent with objectivity and presumably general.

Individuals, in any system, have a weakly ordered preference for roles in that system. The order of preference depends upon information and circumstances. Within any system, individuals have a weakly ordered preference for the values of that system. These preferences also depend upon information and conditions. Individuals have a weakly ordered set of preferences for alterations to the system. These also depend on information and conditions. Individuals have a weakly ordered set of preferences for other types of systems. These preferences also depend on information and conditions. Individuals have a weakly ordered set of preferences for alternative environmental conditions. These also depend on roles, systems, and information. The complete set of weak orderings will establish a weakly ordered hierarchy of preferences. It is *invariant*, that is, it is determined within specified limits for specified conditions.

We can carry this weak ordering one step further and it will still be invariant.

Let us assume that all agree that some societies are among the worst and that some are among the best, but that they disagree about other comparative evaluations. I call the former judgments second-order and objective. I call the latter evaluations objective but idiosyncratic first-order judgments. If some aspects of moral orderings are not subject to second-order evaluation, that would not invalidate the neutrality of those aspects that are subject to a second-order ranking.

Second-order criteria could be used to determine a possible invariant order of changes within systems or for transitions between them. The second-order criteria would be determined by step functions, that is, any significant alteration of conditions or systems would result in a new constellation or ordering of values. The possibility of such change would make it possible to consider a new ordering in making decisions. Because the order is weak, some alternatives might not be morally distinguishable; still, the relationships of values in each would be different. Because first-order choices are related to real conditions, the potentially best values would play only a marginal role in moral choices—that is, although most people would not wish to foreclose the possibility of the best, they might not choose it now.

Transitional orderings, except for some zones of relative indifference, would place all possibilities, except the best and worst, below some and above others. Although reasons could be offered for transitional values—for example, as there is no longer a shortage of resources, the values associated with shortages are inappropriate—the method of inquiry is that of praxis. Hence, no unique theory would permit the derivation of uniquely appropriate reasons. Finally, unlike a hierarchy of abstract values, this hierarchy of societies would already have taken differences of context into account.

OBJECTIVITY AND HUMAN NATURE

The ordering of preferences represents the dispositions of humans under different conditions. Human nature means, to me, the kind of dispositional ordering established by the ordered hierarchy outlined in the previous section.

Hereditary physiological differences may produce temperamental differences that, in turn, affect decisions about what is valuable. If so, each physiological type would have its own moral hierarchy.

Even if we assume such physiological variation, it need not follow that individuals identify only with their own physiological type. Their parents, spouses, siblings, and offspring may be different in type. This wider set of identifications may produce internal conflict. Whether the conflict could be resolved would depend upon conditions. It might even result in a preference for a pluralistic society that provides adequate opportunities for each type. This ultimate preference might have little relevance, for instance, in tribal societies that must constantly war with others to preserve themselves, but it could still play an evolutionary role.

Even if this latter consideration is not operative—although I strongly suspect that it is—one variant of the test-in-principle still may be applicable: a variant in which individuals compare the preferences for moral rules that they would have, depending upon their hereditary physiologies and upon their preferences for physiological types. This might permit recognition of a "best" type or, at least, of "better" types. Almost surely this judgment could be made of those who are obviously crippled, such as persons who have undeveloped physical parts or brain damage. Although such identifications would not resolve conflict over moral principles, a common recognition of "best" or "better" would serve as a modifying agent that restores some common moral ground.

NOVELTY AND FRAME OF REFERENCE

Let me attempt to relate the idea of a moral universe to the idea that the future is discontinuous with the past, that novelty exists, and that freedom produces it. Many existentialists who take this position thereby sunder ethical understanding from human history and from human nature by relativizing it.

As we saw in chapter 10, Jacques Derrida also argued for historical discontinuity, but he recognized a trace of the past in the present. My position is somewhat different. I agree that the world is a product and that discontinuities or novelties are not predictable from theories in the sense that they can be derived from axioms, although they may be intuitively foreshadowed.

What I argue for—and this does distinguish my position from that of the existentialists—is that, although chance may give novelty an opening, chance is only a boundary condition for the novel production. It is a product that can be accounted for praxically after the event. Different courses, both of people and societies, can be understood and related to a common basis praxically in second-order discourse. In principle, a common reality can be produced that is objective and that is in the nature of things, but not in the first-order Aristotelian sense that posits a strong order in the world and, hence, in its development. Although praxical reasoning lacks necessity in the logical sense, a common framework of understanding can nonetheless be produced through second-order discourse.

Discourse about ethics becomes invalid if it is not extended to the second-order level. The production of the future carries more than a trace of the past. It expresses the potentialities of the present, and, under the best conditions, the best potentialities of the present. Because "freedom" and "necessity" are correlatives and not a dichotomy, freedom of production does not exclude the strong dependence of the future upon present conditions.

OBJECTIVITY AND THE FRAME OF REFERENCE

I have noted that statements about colors, for instance, always imply a system of reference, even though the usual elliptical statements do not specify one. Statements about the good are also elliptical.

Josiah Royce pointed out that we perceive the stars as stationary and the planets as moving.[4] A creature with a span of perception of ten thousand years would perceive the stars as moving and the planets as stationary circles of lights.

We think of our bodies as solid. Yet, our bodies are porous to an incoming gamma particle.

Although such statements as "our bodies are solid" and "our bodies are porous" seem contradictory, the contradiction disappears as soon as the appropriate context is provided. Second-order statements, in which the first-order statements are related to their frame of reference, are just as objective as our first-order statements. There are, of course, limits. Creatures with a span of perception of ten thousand years would have difficulty understanding human beings, and vice versa. Their dissimilarities would overwhelm the likelihood of communication by some second-order language.

Such pragmaticistic use of concepts helps to distinguish my own usage from the old debate about relativism vs. absolutism. Change and permanence are no more characteristics or properties of "things-in-themselves" than are colors. Just as color requires a perceiving system to become meaningful, change requires a stable point of reference. The atoms of a ruler are in constant motion, but the ruler is stable for ordinary measurements. Change is always relative to something that is unchanged, although that unchanging something may itself be changing in relation to something else. There is no external standard by which everything else is measured.

JUSTICE AND RELATIVITY

Both second-order and first-order objectivity are relevant to a conception of justice. To illustrate the difference between the two concepts, let us employ the "clock paradox" of Einstein's relativity theory. Two observers, on each of two independent inertial systems moving with respect to the other, will observe that time on the other system is elapsing more slowly. Now, it seems contradictory to say that time in each system is moving more slowly than time in the other. Yet, because motion is relative to independent inertial systems, each observer makes just such a calculation. The observer who is familiar with relativity theory will recognize that the calculation of the other observer, on the other system, is a mirror image that is produced from a different frame of reference. The equations of relativity theory provide a second-order system within which the contradictory calculations are objective and non-contradictory. If the observers are not familiar with relativity theory, they will indeed arrive at different truths because they lack a neutral frame of reference.

If, on the other hand, one of a pair of twins enters a spaceship, flies out into space, and returns, biological measurements will establish that the space traveler is younger than the twin who remained on earth. We know, however, that the twin who went into space needed to accelerate to leave the gravitational pull of the earth and to return to it. This acceleration was observable and measurable. Since a system that accelerates is known to move with respect to another system, the first-order calculations of the twins are identical. The twin who goes into space expects to be younger than the one who remains on earth. The first-order calculations of each predict and confirm the fact. Observers who share a common universe also share a common framework of first-order objective truth; the apparent paradox arises only with respect to systems that are on independent inertial paths.

Values result from the transactions of real people in real environments, but judgments concerning them are, at least partly, analogous to judgments concerning time on different inertial systems. First-order space-time coordinates, in Einsteinian theory, are calculated from the inertial frame of reference of observers. This produces the disjunction between the conclusions of observers on different inertial systems, although each conclusion is objectively given by each observer's frame of reference and each observer will know what conclusions the other will reach. Placement in different inertial systems precludes common first-order objective statements, but is consistent with common and neutral second-order objective statements.

According to my hypothesis, all individuals with similar information about social systems and related norms, like observers on different inertial systems, will understand how both will attempt to optimize their individual or their society's values. Many, however, differ in the foci with which they are identified. Their different frameworks of identification will produce different first-order objective assessments about which person's success is preferable or about which principle should be used in a particular circumstance. There may be common second-order evaluations, but there are different first-order evaluations.

If two independent inertial systems could somehow coalesce into a single inertial system, the people on them would arrive at common first-order as well as second-order evaluations of many features of their common social life. This is what happens as individuals extend their sense of identification and create a wider common frame of reference. Circumstances may break or attenuate this bond. Still, it is the common, second-order framework of morality that not only permits but mandates, at least in benign circumstances, the extension of the moral frame of reference and forces recognition of others as moral others.

We have a multiplicity of moral frames of reference. Although each individual's circumstances are different, and this undermines the possibility of one all-inclusive, first-order morality, overlapping is possible and its extent may be increased by working on the environment. Thus, the concept of justice is contextual, transactional, and developmental. Although it may always seem necessary to compromise the good or even to do evil to some, a common second-order framework of reference establishes a pull toward the avoidance of evil.

Even a strong second-order moral order would only modify the potential conflict between different groups. Weaker orders—and all real moral orders are necessarily weak—would exclude conflicts over some means and ends while admitting conflict about some others and divergent opinions about still others.

THE RELATIVE AND THE ABSOLUTE

The moral absolutist argues that what is good does not depend upon the features of a particular society or of its environment. Thus, what is morally required will depend either on an absolute hierarchy of goods or, as John Rawls argued, on an absolute hierarchy of rules.[5] It is this artificial hierarchy, as I have already shown, that makes moral absolutism irrelevant to real life.

Relativists, as that term is usually employed, believe that different rules apply to different societies, but may argue that those who live in a society should accept its rules. Although many reforms can be carried out within a society's rules—and practically none will be possible that ignores them—this position ignores the leavening of the judgment that some societies and some environments are better than others.

Thus, the absolutist reifies moral and social orders—as mechanists once reified time and space—and relativists who accept anthropological relativism identify them with social and cultural boundary conditions. This type of relativism is as intellectually inadequate as arguing that observers on independent inertial systems cannot possess a neutral second-order frame of reference. Both the absolutist and the relativist detach values from their pragmaticistic significance.

Let us clarify the question of whether moral rules are absolute or relative. I have claimed only that the moral ordering of societies is a weak one: that is, some are clearly better than others and some are worse. Even within societies, some moral rules are of indifferent general value, although particular rules may be costly to particular individuals in particular cases. Why then should a moral rule be observed by those who find it costly?

To the extent that humans are of moral character, the very existence of a particular rule establishes its priority over alternative rules of potentially equivalent worth. This priority is important to the sense of identity and the character of moral people. To denigrate the accidental or relative qualities of moral rules is to attack the moral cement of society and to injure gravely the interest the moral person has in the welfare of society. This is why a philosopher will recognize the imperative force of actual moral rules, whereas a sophist will recognize only their relativity. And that is why moral rules that are not related to a particular society will be irrelevant in the formulation of moral judgments within that society.

Even in a society that is not the best, a philosopher will recognize that it may not be possible to substitute the best, or even to work toward it. Depending upon conditions, one may regard even the norms of an unenlightened society as binding, particularly as they affect public performance.

But there will often come a point at which the moral individual will have to reject the welfare of his more immediate identification in favor of some wider or different circle of identification. Whereas this would have been extremely unlikely, and perhaps impossible, in a tribal society in a tribal environment, complex modern society presents us with alternative frames of reference that permit a more sophisticated moral judgment, one that can make use of the distinction between first-order and second-order moral judgments. Moral individuals capable of judgment at this level of sophistication will make reasoned choices from among alternative rules of behavior by giving due weight to time, circumstances, and consequences.

OBLIGATION

A theory of obligation depends on the nature of people and society. Obligations exist if people are disposed, by their nature, toward community. If humans were like the transvestite fly, this likely would not be so. But if it is so, informed individuals will recognize that at least some conflicts between narrow self-interest and the wider good should be decided in favor of the wider good. Their sense of identity, the integrity of their personality, their understanding of the good and of moral life help them to understand obligation. How to balance self-interest and wider goods, however, depends on our nature, the character of the social system, the environment, and the particular situation. It follows that our obligations will sometimes be very broad and sometimes very narrow.

An attempt to establish the proper balance in contemporary society is beyond the scope of this book. However, if the evolution of the human system, the generalizing aspects of the mind, our need for a sense of identity, our empathic insight into others, the limited plasticity of our personalities, as well as other relevant factors, operate the way I believe they do, then the problems of people as revealed by pragmaticistic tests will establish a substantial realm of obligation in which wider interests will often take precedence over narrow self-interest.

Political obligation is subject to the same analysis. It is not consent, but our natural interest in good social norms, that obliges us to obey laws, to tell the truth, and to serve our society. If the good and justice are objective, then obligation is also objective.[6]

OBLIGATION AND FRAME OF REFERENCE

The discussion of second-order objectivity in which Einsteinian relativity was used as a metaphor makes meaningful the problem of the frame of reference of obligations or, more generally, of rights and duties. Even if our membership in a nation does not create an exclusive framework of obligation, it is relevant to the determination of obligations. Moreover, individuals who are citizens of different nations may have conflicting obligations.

Conflicting frameworks of legitimate obligation may not be merely geographic or organizational. They may be functional as well. There may, for example, be circumstances in which individuals have a moral obligation to evade service in a war they regard as unjust, while the government has not only the legal right but also the moral obligation to prosecute them for violating the law. One can distinguish, thus, between the moral duty of an individual and the obligation of the citizen. Moreover, the legal right of the state to prosecute does not contradict the moral duty to disobey.

Most human activity is complex and ambiguous. Few wars are fought for simple objectives that are easy to understand. Even if there is agreement that it is wrong to wage war against the liberties of others, it does not follow that citizens have the right to make this judgment independently and that the state has a duty to accept such a judgment. We have established procedures for making these determinations and have elected officials whose duty it is to make them.

It is misleading, and it can be self-serving, to state that citizens have a right (although they may have a moral duty and perhaps even a duty as good citizens) to refuse military service and that the political system has a correlative obligation to recognize this right. If anything, the contrary is the case; citizens have an obligation to give serious consideration to their country's political decisions, even though they may disagree with them or doubt their justice. If a war still seems particularly outrageous after giving due weight to every appropriate consideration, one may refuse to serve, but one has no right to do so that must be recognized by the political system. Public recognition of such a right would encourage others to make self-serving interpretations of the issue and would create invidious distinctions between those who serve and those who evade service. Such a situation would threaten the moral sentiments that hold a nation together.

Still, many philosophers argue that where there is a right there is also a corollary duty. Rawls, for instance, argued that the state has a duty to allow the conscientious objector to a particular war not to serve.[7] In a brilliant attack upon this position that relies in part upon H.L.A. Hart, Roslyn Weiss argues that there are duties which do not invoke correlative rights.[8] That seems close to my position, but she neglects to consider the frame of reference. The concept of frame of reference permits us to disentangle issues from their murky context, to show that various failures of analysis are related, at least implicitly, to the misuse of the concepts of theory and covering law discussed in Part One, and to discuss some interesting moral issues in passing.

In "The Perils of Personhood" and especially her third thesis, Weiss argues: "Rights alone can therefore not form a solid basis for the moral issue of abortion; the importance of duties emerges."[9] I note with interest that there is a threshold above which a woman's duty to the fetus is abridged, e.g., rape, for it makes of duty a concept that depends upon the context rather than a purely abstract one. Thus we are forced to ask not only to whom or what the duty is owed, but also under what conditions it is owed and under what conditions it is relaxed or abrogated. However, there is no reason why the rights of the person to which Weiss seems to take exception also cannot be subsumed in a contextual analysis.

In effect, she has been too kind to her opponents, for it is not merely their neglect of the concept of duties but their handling of the concepts of rights and person as well that requires reformulation. Weiss's modest willingness to argue within the framework of her opponents' logic has to some extent obscured the merit of her own position, which is free of a dichotomous view of the world, is related to contextual analysis and, unlike her opponents' views, is open to genuine moral inquiry. Even the untutored must be aware that there can be no simple and logical relationship between entity and right. Otherwise, if we argue that persons have a right to life, how can we justify demanding that they sacrifice that right so that a battle may be won? If we have a simple duty not to injure others, how could we justify knocking down a pedestrian while chasing a murderer? The entity argument is only slightly more complex, and I will come to it quickly.

The position that Weiss is refuting is wrong on a fundamental basis that she seems clear enough about in her own analysis but that she obscures somewhat in her presentation. In essence, her opponents attempt to treat moral theory syllogistically. If an entity can be defined and the concept of rights limited to it, then those entities that fail to meet the definition are entitled to none of the rights. If they meet the definition, they possess all the specified rights. Thus, the argument over abortion becomes primarily a problem of definition and logic.

This syllogistic procedure becomes clearer if we refer it to the philosophy of science. It is our old friend, theory and covering law: identify certain objects, apply the appropriate law, and derive the conclusion, which is then confirmed by an observation. In science, where this type of theory works within limits, it is an acceptable procedure. However, it works only on the basis of tentatively fixed assumptions. Are quasars really very distant? That depends on how we interpret the red shift. The concept of a critical experiment turns out to be ambiguous, and what is axiomatic or what derived depends upon particular frameworks of experimentation. It also involves a misuse of signs; it treats them as if their meanings do not change in different contexts.

At the frontiers of science, neither deductive nor inductive procedures work simply, and we must apply a more complex form of reasoning, namely, praxis. In the social sciences, theory is virtually non-existent. The employment of categories is crucially dependent on context and background information. This is true also of the allied area of moral inquiry. Dichotomous *a priori* procedures are virtually certain to obscure moral analysis which, like all analysis in the social sciences, must be at least as concerned with context, applicability, and comparison as with rules or attributions of value.

The failure to distinguish adequately between theory and praxis carries with it two closely allied mistakes: the treatment of a correlative pair, such as "person" and "non-person," as if the distinction were a dichotomy, and a definition of "person" that ignores the dispositional character of the referent. The adult human, and certainly the infant, is dispositionally present in the fetus. Although one may wish to protect this dispositional element only, or perhaps particularly, after it has recognizably human features, including a brain, definitions will not help us to reach a decision but will themselves be adapted to the requirements of praxical inquiry.

We ordinarily discuss these problems as if they were segmented and encapsulated. We do not ask, among other questions, how they affect human self-images. Perhaps the problem of abortion lies less in abortion than in our procedures for permitting it and the conditions under which it is permitted. Perhaps if a woman seeking an abortion had to go through procedures of justification before a board, perhaps if a solemn funeral were held for the fetus, perhaps, perhaps, and so forth, the effect on our self-image and, thus on our moral concepts, would be far less injurious, even if only a small percentage of abortions were forbidden.

Weiss's own analysis of the concept of duty is fully consistent with this approach. If she had rejected her opponents' position as radically as her own approach would suggest, a similar treatment of rights would have been possible and she would not have been forced into her awkward restriction of the range of the corollary character of rights and duties.

Although I agree that there are duties for which there are no correlative rights, because the frames of reference are different, I would argue that in virtually every case Weiss discusses, rights and duties are related because the frame of reference is the same. For instance, in arguing for a duty in the absence of a right, she takes over from H.L.A. Hart the argument that "If X promises Y to look after Y's mother, then it is surely wrong for X not to look after Y's mother. But there is more than one wrong here. X has wronged both Y and Y's mother; he has broken a promise to Y and has neglected Y's mother (who, I suppose, needs looking after and stands to suffer by not being looked after)." However, Y's mother, according to Hart, has no corollary right. There is only one duty: to the person to whom the promise was made. And that person is the only rightful claimant. The mother has not been injured; she is as much a passive recipient of the promise as a wall that there is a promise to paint. Even if there is a real injury, she is no worse off than she would have been in the absence of a promise to which she had no claim.

There are a number of ways, however, in which agreements can create duties and also rights in third parties. One, for instance, is by creating expectations that are injured in the absence of the keeping of the agreement. Suppose the mother learns of the agreement. We could argue that there is now some degree of duty to the mother, but we would also have introduced some form of claim or right as well. It arises from a legitimating expectation within a moral community, and it has nothing to do with inanimate objects such as walls. The promise now becomes transitive in form, particularly if it is the promisor who has told the mother. This may not be a strong enough claim under contract law, but that does not determine the moral issue. Under some conditions, it may be appropriate to argue that even a mistaken expectation may establish a claim.

A second way of creating a web of moral rights and duties is by extending the realm of obligation. For instance, the political incorporation of a territory by an agreement between two sovereigns may create rights and duties among the subjects and between them and the new sovereign even if the subjects are unaware of the agreement.

One possible interpretation of the previously discussed promise is that the grantor has extended his moral web to include the mother of the second individual, in which case both rights and duties develop, although perhaps not in as full a panoply as within his own family. Such a state of affairs may develop even in the absence of a promise, if the relationship between two individuals develops to the point where it is almost familial. Circumstances are as relevant to moral webs as rules and principles, which in the absence of context are too abstract to permit either a choice among rules or a cogent analysis of their morality.

To illustrate the matter more clearly, let us consider Weiss's argument that there is a duty not to torture animals. Is this a duty to the animal, or to a society that may object to torture? How does it differ from an injunction not to play a radio too loud or not to damage a valuable painting even if one owns it? The duty is to the rest of society, or to the artist, i.e., to the repository of a correlative right, or we are close to the argument that the animal has a right not to be tortured.

Is it really true that "Justice may demand that we refrain from harming or mistreating even those who have no claims upon us," as Weiss argues?[10] She says that simple justice requires that we not torture kittens and that we distribute food equally among pups. However, some raisers of animals cull the animals. Is this unjust? Is there also a duty not to douse wasps with gasoline and burn them to death? Does justice demand that in tilling our fields we do not injure the moles?

One gets the impression from Weiss's discussion that she would in fact be sympathetic to animals' claims. Yet these questions cannot be answered without raising questions about persons, humanity, life, nature, and so forth. Several thousand years ago, enemy tribesmen were not regarded as human. In some ages, lower classes were viewed as not genuinely human and therefore as not possessing rights. The issue revolves around the moral nature of the universe and our ability to conceive of that moral nature. To the extent that we are capable of identifying with other creatures, even those not human or intelligent, we have extended a moral web that involves rights as well as duties, even though the two may not be symmetrical: that is, we cannot claim our rights from animals that are incapable of recognizing them, although their failure to act in certain ways may limit our duties to them. Moreover, just as the right of a mature, sentient human being to life, and the duty of others to help preserve it, may be eroded under a number of conditions, the simple absence of one or more of the elements of identification need not mean a total absence of either rights or duties. One might argue that moles are not without a claim but that the claim is so weak that we should not sacrifice our tilling to it. We might regard the wasp as without any claim at all. One who paid more attention to the requirements of other beings than these standards would warrant would do it neither out of duty nor in response to their rights, but out of a feeling of benevolence.

If we drop the dichotomous view of rights and duties, we ask our questions in terms of distinctions and thresholds. Is it worse to destroy a partly completed statue than to scatter the sculptor's tools before work has begun? A fetus is potentially a human being. To the extent that its conception is voluntary, that its development is no threat to the mother's life, and that some degree of recognizably human development has begun, its claim and the corresponding duty may be very strong. It is not morally irrelevant that it is on a natural path to being a person. It may have a claim to life in which the rest of society, and not merely the prospective mother, has an interest. However, even the claim of a raped woman to an abortion might be weakened if, in the absence of any impediments, she failed to ask for an abortion within, say, the first three months. Even this fetus is not totally without rights. It is only that the threshold at which its claims gain substance is higher.

I see no great difficulty in recognizing claims either of past or of future generations. A more sensitive legal system might prevent the heirs of a great family from dissipating recklessly what it built. The present generation has no right simply to squander resources that have been bequeathed to it or entirely to neglect the rights of succeeding generations. The mere fact that neither past nor future generations can actually lay a claim against us does create asymmetry. However, our ability to represent them in imagination is one of the great assets of the mind. Moreover, the capacity of past or future generations to assist themselves may not be substantially weaker than that of the victim of an assault who is dependent upon the willingness of passersby to come to his or her assistance. That victim could, in principle, formulate a claim upon our assistance, but in practice cannot. Future generations or the environment cannot, even in principle, formulate a claim upon us, but that does not prevent us from acting in part as an agent for them, much as we may appoint guardians for children or for incapacitated adults.

It is important to distinguish the existence of a claim, or right, from the capability to formulate a claim, particularly through language. Animals may, in fact, press claims without language. No doubt the arena of linguistically expressed claims represents an important and highly special class of rights, for it encompasses the special area of contract. Even precise contractual claims, however, may be attenuated by circumstances and by other claims and duties that are not symmetrical. And generalization from contractual claims reduces the moral whole to the special part.

I suspect that at the basis of the abstract view of the rights argument, which Weiss rightly opposes, there lies an implicit theory of contract. In this view, rights stem from voluntary contracts and can be entered into only by thinking beings. These contracts are thus an expression of the individual's freedom. I reject this framework as essentially immoral, and I have argued elsewhere that contract theories are intellectually untenable.[11] I object to them on moral grounds because they imply that personal decisions or agreements form the foundation of ethics, whereas I believe that ethics must be related to the character of the world. Although ethical theorizing is impossible in the absence of creatures that can think, it does not follow that ethical claims can be made only on behalf of creatures that can think. Ethical thinking is an inquiry into the requirements of morality which raises it to the level of self-consciousness. It is a condition of a moral life and it can infuse the world.

The real horror in the pro-abortion solution is not that abortions occur—for many of these can be justified—but that, by granting abortion merely on demand, the moral lives of its beneficiaries are trivialized by exaggerating the importance of their feelings. It drives them to ask not who or what they are and how they are related to others and the world, but what they want; and they begin to define themselves as a rootless system of wants. That is destructive of their moral being.

Those who believe that a fetus does not have a substantially greater claim against surgical removal than a wart are as morally deaf as some are tone deaf. Yet, if a significant difference is recognized, then one can no longer argue that society has no interest in whether or not abortions are performed. The issue becomes which abortions should be permitted and under what conditions they should be permitted. No answer to these questions will be without its moral costs, but this is the moral way to handle the problem of abortion.

The abortion issue is not unrelated to other medical issues, and these help us to understand it. We do not recognize the right of an individual to order a surgeon to cut out his eyes or the right of a surgeon to obey such an order. Indeed, we would agree that he has a duty to refuse that order. Suppose a pregnant woman wanted a surgeon to place a substance in the fetus that would stifle the development of the cortex but that otherwise would not injure it. In that case, it would be born but would never be a person and could be given the status of a pet or even a slave. Would we permit this? Obviously not. Whether one finds the justification for forbidding this in the right of the fetus, of the future decerebated creature, or of society, there is a right to forbid and a duty not to do something of this kind.

Where the line is drawn depends upon the level of community understanding. In some societies it was not a crime to kill children, for they were not considered human. The argument that the courts cannot forbid abortion must rest either on the claim that there is no community standard, or that it is not based on a preponderance of evidence, or on a *non sequitur*. For, even if there is a great disagreement on when human life begins, there may be a preponderance of evidence that it begins at some particular stage of pregnancy, and there may be a standard definition of human life and potential human life. The stage at which rights are acquired and at which there are associated duties is subject to praxical analysis.

One can always distinguish among situations. The question, really, is: which distinctions are appropriate? Whatever uncertainty may exist, it is very likely that dichotomous distinctions according to which rights are fully possessed on one side of a line and fully lacking on the other, are wrong.

SOME POSSIBLE OBJECTIONS

There may be some readers who still have doubts concerning the relevance of a weak order to an objective moral analysis. One possible comparison that may help to illuminate this issue is between the ordering of lengths of pieces of wood and the ordering of preferences for flavors of ice cream. Suppose that observers disagree about the lengths of the pieces of wood or about the desirability of the flavors of ice cream. The problems are formally similar, but their implications are very different. The differences about the lengths of wood stem from limited powers of sensory discrimination and can be resolved by using a micrometer. But there is no way of converting the ranking of ice-cream flavors, which is weakly ordered, into a strong order.

Even this distinction is misleading, because we have failed to distinguish between a strong order and a common order. There are stong orders that are not common, e.g., a rigid hierarchy in a particular nation that does not exist elsewhere. We can also have common orders that are not strong, e.g., the preference of all members of a family for locating their house near a lake, a preference that could be satisfied by a number of houses near many lakes.

The insistence upon a strong order as a prerequisite for objectivity, with its metaphor of a moral micrometer, resembles Stephen Toulmin's "language games" approach to what makes something a given color, for instance, red or green.[12] I have already shown how this reifies qualitative concepts. More, it means treating metaphors as if they were literal language, and dispositional concepts as if they were definitional.

This position also implies that complex realities cannot be spoken of objectively. But this is not correct. For instance, there are different ways of building high-fidelity amplifiers that are about equally good. These can be distinguished from less good amplifiers. There may be particular reasons for choosing among the best, but there may be no neutral basis for ranking them.

Air raid systems, for instance, are designed to satisfy two criteria: to give warning of attack and not to give false alarms. With respect to state-of-the-art, or optimal systems, any improvement in one of these characteristics will affect the others adversely. There may be first-order or even idiosyncratic reasons for preferring one optimal design to another, but they may not be susceptible to neutral arbitration. Still, the fact that not all choices can be ranked in a discrete ordinal form does not mean that no ground for selection exists. All the best designs are preferable to all the inferior designs, and this is an objective and neutral judgment.

In any society, there may be a number of good social arrangements in which costs and benefits are distributed differently. Each one of these good designs could be supported by good reasons. Very likely, one's social position will determine one's preference. This may be what the sociology of knowledge, which related beliefs to social position, was about, although in a confused manner. The preference for one solution within a good set may be regarded metaphorically as equivalent to the measurement of relative motion by an observer on an inertial system. But observers on different inertial systems can understand what observations their opposite numbers will make, and why. And those in different social positions can make second-order judgments about what others will prefer, and why. Nor will our choices depend merely on class. Class will be merely one element in determining "motion," that is, preference for social order. Some social solutions will be considered less than good because the deprivations they impose on others are inconsistent with a moral person's sense of human identity. This is one of the factors that tend to produce evolutionary progress in moral orders.

Let me now distinguish this from taste. Preferences for varieties of ice cream are partly communicable to others. But to a considerable extent, these preferences have tacit aspects that cannot be communicated to others, except perhaps after a very long period of acculturation; even then the communication does not occur in a genuinely public fashion.

The argument I am making for the objectivity of social values, however, involves public features for which there are good reasons and good evidence. Moreover, they tend to be more central to the structure of preferences, more interdependent, and more stable. This is what makes them neutral and objective despite their weak order. For example, our horror over the mass suicide at Jonestown in Guyana in 1978 is not merely a matter of taste. It is based on publicly communicable criteria. Other situations may be less clear to us. But this should not occlude recognition that many moral distinctions can be made objectively and often neutrally as well.

Doctors, to take another example, do not always agree on a diagnosis. Particular symptoms do not invariably point to specific diseases. Yet, it is possible for doctors to offer different, and fallible, diagnoses, each of which has its foundation in objective evidence.

Although some academics have argued that morality is a matter of taste, or at least very much like matters of taste, few ordinary people would concede that it is merely a matter of taste whether or not one approves of the ovens of Buchenwald. Impressive reasons can be offered against such practices, reasons that are based on the nature of humans and of societies. Even in less stark situations, the reasoning remains objective and neutral.

Nonetheless, the concept of good taste is an illuminating one in the moral realm. Many people may have good moral taste in the sense that they will do the good or right thing even without being able to say why it is right or good. Conversely, many people who are facile with words may think so abstractly, whether with regard to rule-oriented or consequence-oriented moral behavior, that they believe wrong or bad things to be good: that is, they have poor moral taste.

There are aspects of moral behavior which involve the social structuring of relations of respect, the avoidance of shock, and so forth. Consider the circumstances in which nudity is appropriate. There are so many alternative modes of viewing this question that the existence of a particular way of doing things often becomes its own justification. Such social rules can be reasoned about objectively, but they are idiosyncratic. One becomes so acculturated to them that tacit understanding of what is considered good taste is its own justification.

This does not mean, however, that the more important elements of the moral realm are not objectively and neutrally constrained. The type of critical inquiry which variants of the test-in-principle alone can produce—the important knowledge that stems from comparative analysis—can be conducted only by objective and neutral methods. And these are dependent on good reasons, the goodness of which is determined by their praxical assessment with respect to other aspects of the realm of knowledge. They are grounded in, although not derived from, other aspects of the natural world: for example, excessive deference may be inconsistent with a natural desire for autonomy. Furthermore, praxical reasoning about what makes deference excessive will take into account roles, real-world conditions, and so forth. That is, it will move from the abstract to the literal and concrete. Praxical criteria ground these constraints, although they are understood in each case in the literal language to which the praxical criteria point. Perhaps a critic may think that the test-in-principle or its equivalents merely eliminate the effect of personal interest and restriction of information. Some critics may think that dedicated and well-informed egalitarians, for instance, who rank systems solely on the basis of their effect on equality, will not change their preferences after a test-in-principle.

Will not users of the test-in-principle, however, reflect upon the character of human nature and of moral virtues as they make these tests? Will they not examine the effect of different types of both non-egalitarian and egalitarian systems on the relationships among the members of society? To say no is to say that the egalitarians' dedicated and well-informed position is merely an *idée fixe*.

I am quite willing to admit the possibility, although not the likelihood, that such preconceptions will remain unshaken by a variety of experiences. After all, there are still individuals who believe that the world is flat. But one should consider the possibility, and indeed the likelihood, that there will be considerable changes in the judgments of properly trained and motivated individuals as these tests are carried out.

Let me offer an example to illustrate this point. Consider individuals who are narrowly self-interested and who take advantage of others. I hypothesize that two types of influence will be at work: (1) a belief that human nature and society really work that way and (2) an inability to empathize with others and to distance themselves from their impulsive needs. Secondary gains, or even arrested development, may make many of these people incorrigible. Even here, however, the test-in-principle could stand as a metaphor for the moral development of those capable of moral education. I believe that this conjecture is more plausible than the objections to it.

Let me now summarize my conclusions. That moral systems are weakly ordered is only peripherally due to a deficiency in the procedures that determine such orders. The weakness of the moral order is inherent in the moral world. In the moral realm, no single criterion determines goodness in the way that a physical instrument measures length. Goodness involves indirect and complex relationships that affect the meanings of the concepts we employ. Therefore, recognition that some states of affairs will be relatively equivalent is a recognition of the character of the moral realm: a realm in which the basic elements and the boundaries are interdependent. Why should we try to order strongly something that is inherently weakly ordered? And why should we argue that only strongly ordered concepts are objective or neutral?

The concept of objectivity in moral inquiry focuses attention on those facets of the evidence and the standards for applying it that permit us to discriminate among good, less good, and evil at any particular stage of civilization. We do not need—and could not use—moral micrometers for this purpose. Complete and strong orders are inappropriate criteria for the moral realm. The correct objective and neutral procedures are those that are appropriate to the character of the moral realm.

Perhaps, a critic may argue, this all sounds good, but you cannot prove your point. One can argue, they may say, that, the schools cripple children and that this is unacceptable. However, people will disagree about the extent of the damage, the capacity of the educational system to change, and the financial and social cost of the effort to change it. What good is it to talk of objectivity and neutrality if all the important issues are undecidable objectively and neutrally?

The objection is plausible but misleading. If these issues were not highly uncertain, the schools would already be changing. The issues arise, in large part, from a new understanding of human nature and of satisfactory social conditions, an understanding produced both by new problems and by the solution of old ones. The issues are important because they are controversial. They are controversial partly because our understanding has sensitized us to them and directed our energies toward their solution. Once they are solved, it will be difficult for us to understand the issue—much as we wonder that it was only after World War I that British courts were willing to hold that rat-infested houses were unfit for manual workers. But even if some problems remain unsolvable, that does not mean that none can be solved.

NOTES

1. Clyde Kluckhohn and Others, "Values and Value Orientation in the Theory of Action," in *Toward a General Theory of Action*, edited by Talcott Parsons and Edward Shils (Cambridge: Harvard University Press, 1951).

2. Morton A. Kaplan, *Macropolitics: Essays on the Philosophy and Science of Politics* (Chicago: Aldine Publishing Co., 1969), pp. 42–43.

3. Conversation with W. Ross Ashby, 1954.

4. Josiah Royce, *Studies in Good and Evil: A Series of Essays Upon Problems of Philosophy and of Life* (New York: D. Appleton & Company, 1915).

5. John Rawls, *A Theory of Justice* (Cambridge: Harvard University Press, 1971).

6. For a fuller discussion of this subject, see chapter 4 of Morton A. Kaplan, *Justice, Human Nature, and Political Obligation* (New York: Free Press. 1976).

7. Rawls, *A Theory of Justice*, p. 381.

8. Roslyn Weiss, "The Perils of Personhood," *Ethics* 89, no. 1 (October 1978); H. L. A. Hart, *The Concept of Law* (Oxford: Clarendon Press, 1961).

9. Ibid.

10. Ibid.

11. Kaplan, *Justice, Human Nature, and Political Obligation* (New York: Free Press, 1976), pp. 193–194.

12. Stephen Toulmin, *Reason in Ethics* (Cambridge: At the University Press, 1950).

PART FOUR
THE SOCIAL SCIENCES

IN THIS PART of the book, Marxism, neo-classical economic theory, and my own theory of international relations are examined in an effort to show the intimate relationship between theory and praxis in the social sciences and thereby to show that the position I developed in Part One applies here also. Although, in my opinion, neo-classical economic theory has much more to say of the world that is valid than Marxian theory, both mistake the role of theory and the conditions under which its conclusions have validity.

In chapter 14, I examine Marx's view of science, the evolutionary elements in his theory, and his theory of surplus value. I argue that his sociological account of production is insufficiently sociological because it mistakes the correlative roles of theory and praxis. And contemporary attempts to avoid Marx's mistake through reformulations do not solve the problems in his positions.

The metaphysical elements in Marx's philosophy, such as his reified definition of class, which are intimately linked to his classical conception of truth, and his failure to understand the correlative character of the definitional and dispositional combine to defeat contemporary efforts to reinterpret him in a non-deterministic way. These reinterpretations emphasize the indeterministic elements in Marx that characterize his phenomenology but not his understanding of essence. (There is a close parallel in this respect with Hegel, for whom history was the realm of accident in which necessity nevertheless worked itself out.) These contemporary writers, however, retain Marx's essentialist assumptions and thus reintroduce into their new interpretations the very determinism they thought they had excluded.

In chapter 15, I examine what I call the spirit of Marx's writing. In my opinion, Marx's nineteenth century philosophical outlook, based on Hegelian metaphysics, distorted his understanding of both people and society. Even that most liberated Marxist, Antonio Gramsci, fell into similar difficulties.

Marxian theory involves many problems both in philosophy and in social science theory. With respect to social science theories that are stated with relative independence from philosophy, the main point to be kept in mind is that no theory applies to the real world directly or without the specification of initial conditions. In pure physics, as contrasted with engineering applications of phys-

215

ics, the presence of independent measures and covering laws permits us to treat the subject matter relatively independently of variations in boundary conditions.

In the social sciences there is a complex interdependency between the subject matters of propositions and theory sketches and their environments and an absence of independent measures. Therefore the application of propositions and theory sketches to the real world is not general. And the belief that theories or theory sketches of elements of the real world eventually can be combined into some form of supratheory is based on a misunderstanding of the role of theory. The most general laws of macrophysics apply directly only to two-body problems and can be applied to multi-body problems only iteratively. But this is precisely what cannot be done in the social sciences because of the complex interdependencies between the elements of which the theory sketches are composed and boundary elements. Moreover, even if counterfactually one could know how to put together such a theory, it would be so complex that no one would know how to understand or analyze it. In the last two chapters, I shall attempt to show how the interdependencies between theory sketches and real-world boundary conditions affect the application and interpretation of two types of social science theories, a showing that, I believe, has general applicability.

In chapter 16, I use my colleague Milton Friedman's approach to show that neo-classical economists misuse the concept of theory and fail to respond properly to the correlative concept of praxis.

Chapter 17 contains a brief examination of my own theory of international politics, in an attempt to show how properly qualified theory can be supplemented by praxical discourse to arrive at valid interpretations of international systems.

Chapter 14
The Marxian Heritage

I have chosen to focus on Karl Marx's work for a number of reasons. Marx asked many of the right questions. An analysis of his errors will therefore be revealing.

Moreover, even the most sophisticated contemporary Marxists make mistakes that parallel his. These residues harden the resistance of social scientists not merely to the findings of contemporary Marxists, but also to the methods and the problems posed by the Marxian tradition that are central to an understanding of the most important problems of modern society.

Despite the valiant efforts of both Hegel and Marx to move away from the errors of past metaphysics, their philosophical assumptions led them to believe in a systematic inevitability of outcome, regardless of indeterminacies and accidents during the process of history. Present-day Marxists, as I shall attempt to show, reproduce these errors in one form or another because they accept either explicitly or implicitly the metaphysical assumptions that produced them.

BASE AND SUPERSTRUCTURE

Many contemporary Marxists argue that Marx recognized that human transactions with other humans and with nature produce both the economic forces and relations of production and the cultural superstructure of society. That position is correct in part. Base and superstructure, however, cannot be produced by humans in transactions with nature unless, in a prior phase, both of them and nature are present to consciousness, the content of which is also a product of a transactional process. What humans are, and how they are distinguished from nature, cannot be understood except in relation to a material world and culture. None of these distinctions can be understood except by mind.

There is no paradox here, for the concepts—"human," "nature," "base," and "superstructure"—are part systems; and "mind" is their correlative. One is not, and cannot be, an ultimate ground from which the others are derived. Instead, some are held constant in analysis while others are varied. Which focus of analysis is most fruitful depends on the problem and on the phase of analysis.

Marx recognized this in his phenomenological analyses, as did Hegel. Each, however, thought that he had discovered the essences, the true foundation, that drove the process: Hegel in his idealistic dialectic and Marx in his materialist dialectic and the labor theory of value. These were the scientific truths, in their view, that determined the phenomenological, accidental world, much as the concept "heat" underlay the phenomenon "hot" or as the law of gravity determined the movement of bodies (although, as we know, phenomenologically most bodies do not seem to obey it, as when leaves drift in the air.)

The transactional reading of Marx's phenomenology by present-day Marxists also implies that social relations and forces—not merely economic ones, although they do have considerable power that at times seems independent—produce social outcomes, including economic outcomes. After making this point, most contemporary Marxists then proceed to argue as if the economic base produces the cultural superstructure: that is, they revert to Marx's essentialism.

THE GENERAL PROBLEM OF EVOLUTIONARY THEORY

Lewis S. Feuer has written about the influence of Darwinian evolutionary theory on Marx and Engels.[1] Although the extent of this influence on each man varied, the important point is that Marx had a theory of social evolution and that it is subject to the problems of any evolutionary theory.

From Darwinian theory, which is surely better confirmed and subject to far better critieria for confirmation than Marxian theory, we cannot predict any particular evolution, whether in form or substance. The most we can say of most mutations is that, if they fitted their ecological niches, they survived, or that they survived by adaptation, selection and so forth.

Darwinian theory is really a praxical assessment, and not a theory, as I use these terms. It accounts for evolution as a natural process on the basis of criteria such as advantage and selection. Analysis of continuities and changes in DNA supports the belief that changes in hereditary material produce changes in the organism. Analysis of the environment supports the contention, not that changes in species occurred because they were advantageous, but that the survival of a species is usually related to advantage. Whether mutational change is gradual or sudden is argued on the basis of how either view fits a variety of evidence and criteria.

Marx's view of evolution, stated in simplified form, rests on the assumption that a system changes if, and only if, it exhausts its ability to advance society's productive forces. Stagnation is also a possibility. However, the thesis is not true in this form; and that is why Louis Althusser adopted the "weak link" hypothesis—that the socialist revolution would occur in the weakest link of the system of capitalist states rather than in the most advanced—of Parvus* and Leon Trotsky to explain the 1917 revolution in Russia.[2] Russia certainly had not exhausted its ability to grow as a capitalist society, as comparison with Japan, which moved toward capitalism at the same time shows.

---

*A pseudonym for Alexander Helphand.

I have shown elsewhere[3] that Althusser's formulation is completely open-ended, both theoretically and praxically. Neither Marx's nor Althusser's version of the hypothesis is scientifically valid because no boundary conditions were stated. And, in the particular instance of Russia, it was the combination of a Leninist party, defeat in war, and the intransigence of right-wing generals, rather than weakness alone, that created the conditions in which a Communist revolution could succeed. Not all, or even many, weak links succumb to Communism. One cannot predict that a particular type of revolution will occur although, with sufficient comparative evidence, one may be able to make not implausible conjectures.

It may be possible, in the social sciences, to predict some forms of social change, although with considerable fallibility. Even so, both the analysis and the projection must be closely linked to actual conditions, not to some global hypothesis. As long as boundary conditions are unspecified, an almost unlimited variety of predictions is possible. In any event, there are no laws of history and the indeterminism inherent in historical predictions make them especially risky in very complex matters.

Marx's evolutionary theory of society, even when it permits some variation, is flawed. It is such a simple and dichotomous model of the evolution of capitalism that it is not even heuristic. In a far weaker form—namely, that life in societies produces conditions that in turn lead to their transformation—the theory is correct. In this form, however, almost all the important questions are left open; the only exclusions are an unchanging society and supernatural intervention.

MARX'S EVOLUTIONARY ACCOUNT OF CAPITALISM

Although the socialist doctrine of *The Communist Manifesto* does not mention the labor theory of value, that theory is the "scientific kernel" that, together with Marx's essentialism and dialectics, drives the Marxian evolutionary theory of the transition from capitalism to socialism.[4]

Marx adapted the concept of the *labor theory of value* from earlier philosophers and political economists; like Hegel he placed it in an enormously richer context than they provided. Originally, the concept was essentially that nothing in nature had value until people appropriated or modified it. In this broad sense, all the labor theory of value meant was that things in nature had value in society only because people used or worked on them. As yet, the theory had neither sociological nor economic content, for the distinctions that would permit either a sociological or an economic analysis had not yet been made.

One of Marx's contributions to the discussion was to argue that the entire value of the product was produced either by present labor or by congealed, or past, labor in the form of machinery. The capitalist, by virtue of his control of the means of production, seized from the worker surplus value, i.e., profit, the difference between what was paid the worker and what was received from sale of the product. As more and more machinery was introduced, and as the surplus that could be captured from living labor declined, the rate of profit would decline and competition among capitalists would increase intensely. And because the workers are reduced to the status of a commodity in this process, their labor is not merely alienated—that is, their work results in a product that is separated from them—but is estranged from them. This, along with the increasing centralization of ownership of industry, was considered part of the process that would produce a revolutionary consciousness that would lead to a socialist revolution as capitalism exhausted its ability to satisfy social needs.

However many facets of the thesis are discarded by contemporary Marxists, and however much they may modify their conception of socialism (which Marx in any event did not specify in any detail), this remains the core of their complaint against capitalism.

Even so precise and careful a writer as Gerald A. Cohen is so captured by the "inner logic" of Marx's writing that, in defense of Marx's evolutionary theory, he refuses to recognize what we all know and looks only at the evidence that fits his thesis. Cohen says that capitalism is subject to the basic contradiction Marx states and that socialism under a command system, that is, a centrally and politically managed economy, is the only alternative to stagnation because

> . . . despite the responsibility of capitalism for technical power on an unprecedented scale, . . . [it] *inherently tends to promote just one of the options, output expansion, since the other, toil reduction, threatens a sacrifice of the profit associated with increased output and sales.*[5]

The empirical evidence is inconsistent with this conclusion. Furthermore, Cohen does not show why a command economy will reduce toil or why it should do even as well as a market economy in satisfying wants, including leisure. Cohen claims that the predominant tendency of market capitalism is to prevent reduction in the toil of workers. If Cohen's thesis is accepted, how do we explain the reduction in the number of working days from six to five; of hours of work per day from twelve, to ten, to eight or less, often in the absence of legislation or even of collective bargaining? Indeed the decline in income from property from about three-quarters of total national income in the late nineteenth century to less than one-quarter today can be attributed largely to the increase in human capital.

In evaluating any theory, we can often obtain some insight by comparing an abstract model of a process with a particular example of the actual process. But there are limits beyond which this type of comparison loses its heuristic value. If, for instance, one were to construct a computer model of the American economy, even in virtual isolation from other elements of the social system, one would find that the model would produce radically different answers, depending upon the designated feedback routes or even small changes in the flows of economic transactions along the routes. This would not surprise anyone who is familiar with, for example, a computer program for the analysis of a high-fidelity amplifier, a comparatively uncomplicated system.

Serious questions arise the moment one attempts to identify the details of the structure of a model of the economy with the detailed structure of the real world. This is why many economists prefer heuristic models: they are simpler to understand and their analysis is focussed less on the result a model produces than its superiority to another model. But a society is enormously more complex and even less subject to quantitative analysis than its economy alone.

If one wishes to justify Marxian evolutionary theory as a heuristic device rather than as a scientific theory, in the broader sense, which Marx often intended, of *Wissenschaft*, or systematic knowledge, the discussion must be based on precisely those areas that Marxists fail to subject to extensive analysis: the justification of Marx's use of the concepts of classes, forces, and relations of production. The reader will quickly see that this is exactly the area of discussion on which my own attack on Marx's conclusions is focussed. The attempts of contemporary Marxists to defend Marx's theory by referring to his intensive studies of concrete historical changes do not really touch these crucial issues.

THE LABOR THEORY OF VALUE

As Marx pointed out, the founder of modern political economy, William Petty, used the labor theory of value. According to Petty, it was the labor time that went into the production of a product that determined its value or "true price."[6] He also developed the notion that the value of labor is determined by the cost of the means necessary for subsistence. Surplus value also exists in Petty's analysis: in rent of land and rent of money. Therefore, according to Petty, the value of land is nothing but the capitalized rent. Adam Smith also employed a labor theory of value although it differed from that of Marx. John Locke, as Marx pointed out, picked up Petty's notion and argued that persons have a right only to themselves and therefore that (with some minor qualifications) those things only are ours that we produce with our labor. According to Locke, labor bestows on objects virtually their whole value. The remainder, which does not come from labor, is, according to Locke, a gift of nature.

Hegel's concept of work, on the other hand, is transactional: the process by which reality is made consists of the transactions between people and the world. Meaning and value are intrinsic products of this transactional process. Philosophically, Marx was in the Hegelian tradition. His economic analysis, however, reached almost entirely back to the English tradition. Moreover, he treated wage labor as the only source of value (apart from the gifts of nature) in society. He argued that wage laborers receive for their work only what their labor power— that is, their labor as a commodity—can command, and not the value of what they have produced.

According to Marx:

> The lowest and the only necessary wage rate is that providing for the subsistence of the worker for the duration of his work and as much more as is necessary for him to support a family and for the race of laborers not to die out. . . . [It is compatible only] with cattle-like existence. . . . *The demand for men necessarily governs the*

production of men, as of every commodity. . . . . Whilst the division of labor raises
the productive power of labor and increases the wealth and refinement of society, it
impoverishes the worker and reduces him to a machine.[7]

Actual wages, the value of the "average wage or the value of labor" is
determined "by the labor time which it costs for its production—by the quantity
of labor materialized in the laborer's means of subsistence."[8]

Marx wrote that value itself is determined in the following way:

. . . that which determines the magnitude of the value of any article is the amount
of labor socially necessary or the labor-time socially necessary, for its production.
Each individual commodity in this connection is to be considered as average sample
of its class. . . . As values, all commodities are only definite masses of congealed
labor time.[9]

Marx then compares the two ways of creating value:

If we now compare the two processes of producing value and of creating surplus
value, we see that the latter is nothing but a continuation of the former beyond a
definite point. If, on the one hand, the process be not carried beyond the point where
the value paid by the capitalist for the labor-power is replaced by an exact equivalent,
it is simply a process of producing value; if, on the other hand, it be continued
beyond that point, it becomes a process of creating surplus-value.[10]

According to Marx, use value does not create a surplus if it is not productive
of capital. Thus, even if a man hires his own tailor as a household servant to
make his clothes, and even if he pays him less than the going rate in industry,
the labor is not productive (or exploited) because nothing is left over that can
be used for further production.[11] Thus, by definition, Marx was saying that even
if the worker and society are both enriched by capitalist activity, they are nonetheless exploited because capital is formed in the process and because the laborer
is not paid for it and does not own it.

How did Marx actually calculate the production of surplus? In his discussion
of David Ricardo's theory of profit in his unfinished fourth volume of *Capital*,
Marx compared a farmer and a cotton manufacturer, each of whom invests $8,000
the first year. The farmer grows $10,000 worth of corn and pays $8,000 for
labor, from which he has a profit of $2,000. The cotton producer builds a machine
worth $10,000 and pays $8,000 for labor. Each entrepreneur thus has made a
profit of 25 percent, the surplus value of the labor.

Marx then went on to consider what might happen in the next year. Suppose,
he says, that in the subsequent year the farmer doubles his production to $20,000
and thus also doubles his profit to $4,000. He now has a surplus of $6,000 in
the two years, or 25 percent of his investment over that period. The manufacturer,
however, will gain only $2,000 in the second year since he gains no surplus
value from the $10,000 of the machinery, but only from the $8,000 paid in
wages. His profit is therefore only 11⅑ percent in the second year, or 15⁵⁄₁₃
percent in the two years. The only way, according to Marx, in which an average

profit can be obtained is if the manufacturer adds on 5 percent and the farmer subtracts the same amount. This results, according to Marx, from the fact that:

> If the rate of profit is to be the same in both cases, then the commodity of the one must be sold above, and that of the other below, its value. Since competition strives to level off values into prices of production, this is what happens. . . . [This] is due rather to the acceptance of a general rate of profit, which in spite of the different values gives rise to prices of production which are equal and different from these values determined only by labor time.[12]

Let us now attempt to see what is wrong in Marx's use of the labor theory of value. Obviously the simple number of labor hours cannot determine the value of a product. If it could, then the hours of a ditch digger and a watchsmith would be equal in value as would the hours of a Stradivari or a Guarnari and those of an ordinary violin maker. If the number of hours of labor going into a product determines its value, then it makes little difference whether the product is one that is greatly desired by customers or one that no one wants.

Classical economic theory, or political economy, was designed to account for the production by standardized workers of standardized products for which there was a ready market. It was trying to explain ordinary farming or ordinary manufacture. Thus, calculations were based on the concept of the average worker and the average product.

Marx, however, was trying to achieve a far more general and powerful result than that sought by the classical economists. He therefore expanded their simplification into rigid definitions, axioms, and theorems. And he immediately produced a paradox. Marx argued that the value of a commodity is determined by the average amount of socially necessary labor that goes into its production. Regardless of whether he was talking about use value or exchange value—and I believe it is the latter he was talking about—his problem cannot be solved by his theory.

What makes something socially necessary? The only thing that can make production socially necessary in a sense that accounts for purchases is that people want those products. Does Marx then mean use value? If so, his definition is circular. It is not possible to avoid circularity if there is a common element in the definition and in the defined term and if it cannot be replaced in a finite sequence as in recursive definitions. But Marx cannot have meant use value for another reason: If he had meant use value, he could not have used the difference between the exchange value of the product and the worker's pay as the measure of surplus value.

However, it will not help to say that Marx meant exchange value, for use value or utility is one of the determinants of exchange value. In short, Marx used an implicitly invalid circular definition. Let us see why it is essential to turn to neoclassical marginal analysis to cope with these problems.

Marx chose an inadequate way of explaining how the rate of profit is equalized: the owner without machinery reduces his profit and the one with machinery increases his profit because the cost of production tends to determine price. One might as well forget economics. The rate of profit* tends to be equalized because capital flows to high-profit areas and away from low-profit areas until profit is equalized at the level of the marginal producer. Labor also tends to move until equal labor is paid equally. Machinery is installed because it lowers costs and increases profits, at least until competitors also invest and drive prices down. If labor time alone produced value, the cost of production in the heavily capitalized plant could not be less, and the profit greater; the congealed labor in the capital equipment has already been fully paid for.

This is the genuine contradiction that Eugen von Böhm-Bawerk found between volumes 1 and 3 of *Capital* and that Marx's formula for average profit did not solve.[13] What is, in Marx's account, merely a mysterious and *ad hoc* return of a margin of profit above the cost of production is fully explained by neo-classical marginal analysis—at least in situations in which the real world corresponds to the theory. Furthermore, Marx's treatment of the forces of production—a subject to which I shall return—is reified, and his essentialist definitions fail to account for production.

Logically, neo-classical marginal analysis could be consistent with a declining rate of profit, or, more accurately, return on capital, for industry as a whole. But, except for the fact that the economies of some newly industrialized countries have expanded so rapidly that structural factors tend, in the long run, to bring them back to the world average, the evidence does not support either this or the Marxian arguments for surplus value or the impoverishment of workers. The availability of capital, the demand for it, risk, and so forth, determine its rate of return.

If total national profit is highest in advanced capitalist nations, does it follow, as indeed some modern Marxists argue, that exploitation is greatest when workers are richest and most skilled? Or if the degree of exploitation is the ratio of profit to pay, does it follow that exploitation is greatest when the economy is at its most expansive, employment highest, and wages soaring?

Let us examine some of the consequences of Marx's assumptions. Suppose the managements in a nation poorly arrange their factories so that on the average only four rather than six workers can use a particular space. Now fewer products are made and each product has more exchange value. Is there not something peculiar in the claim that each of the four remaining workers deserves higher pay than any one of the six in a more efficient workspace because each worker produces more value?

Society is poorer and so is the work force as a whole if management is inefficient. By any reasonable measure both the gross national product and the gross national product per capita are lower. Even if we retreat to the argument that the work force as a whole creates less value to account for this fact, the

---

*By profit, Marx means the return on capital, in effect, interest. Genuine profit does not exist in a static and frictionless economy.

imputation to the individual worker of more value per product is unsound. And any plausible system of imputation will reflect this, for competition among workers will force their wages down if management is unable to provide space for more workers. This reveals the fallacy in Marx's use of the categories of labor power and labor value. The market for labor and the productivity of labor have values that function with entrepreneurial skill and the availability of capital.* Labor produces value only as one of several factors in the productive process. The exclusive imputation of value to labor, to land, or to labor and land of the classical economists, within which tradition Marx wrote, produced only static theories of the economy that failed to explain the dynamism of modern economies. These static theories treated both the forces and the relations of production as facts of nature that are external to the economy, thus reifying economic processes, although doing so harmlessly for explanatory purposes as long as entrepreneurial innovation was absent and the concept of rent was employed to account for differences in the bounty of nature.

How can the working class alone produce value, when the employment, income, and productivity of the worker cannot be determined independently of managerial efficiency, whether that efficiency be in the use of space, the flow of work, or in other managerial decisions? If we cannot consider managerial efficiency irrelevant—that is, if management also produces value—how can profit be only surplus value, the reward for exploitation? If these are the results of Marx's definitions, including his technically deficient definition of the value of labor, then we have seen praxically why his entire schema must be jettisoned and why his followers have been driven into other difficulties in the effort to maintain them in some form.

How does neo-classical theory explain profit, exchange value, and the price of labor? Exchange value is set at the price of the marginal seller and buyer of products, labor, capital, and management: in short, for all factors of demand and supply. Labor is a commodity in this sense. If labor sets up a monopoly, it merely changes the equilibrium of the market for labor; it does not permit labor to obtain an average price for a product sold at a marginal price.

By definitional fiat, Marx denied that the capitalist and the entrepreneur are productive; otherwise, he could not claim that wage laborers are always exploited. He turned a truism—that value depends upon human social activity—into a denial of the contribution of both the entrepreneur and the capitalist to the process of production. Thus, on the one hand, he can recognize the productive genius of capitalism; and, on the other, he can deny the entrepreneur a productive role. This is metaphysics in the pejorative sense.

---

*Industrial monopolies and union monopolies change the equilibrium of an economy to their benefit at a price to society as a whole as the United States has discovered. High entry costs are conducive to monopoly (or at least to oligopoly) and close off opportunities for entrepreneurial talent. It is, therefore, not surprising that General Motors and Ford had bad managements until Japanese competition forced change. What was surprising was the apparent management skill of AT&T.

Earlier, as we followed Marx's example of the corn grower and the manufacturer, we saw that he did not treat the labor of the entrepreneur in a genuinely
sociological fashion. Let us now examine that problem.

Marx, as is proper, distinguished labor according to its relations to the means
of production. When he spoke of labor, however, he almost never spoke of the
entrepreneur or of the person who hires or fires. He was speaking of the worker
who makes a product either manually or with a machine. This is the worker
who produces the value of the product, according to Marx. Indeed, even today
the Department of Labor and other sources of industrial statistics measure the
productivity of labor per hour of labor time. Plant and managerial and entrepreneurial activity are treated as givens. Unsurprisingly, when advanced machinery goes into a plant, the productivity of labor rises. When the productivity
of labor in the United States per hour of work ceases to rise, the economists and
the politicians begin to worry.

The measure is a useful tool for certain limited purposes, but, unfortunately,
the underlying concept of labor is a positivistic one that reifies institutions and
social relations. When Henry Ford introduced the assembly line in Dearborn,
Michigan, the productivity of his workers increased and so did their pay. But
did the workers increase the product or did Ford increase it? Ford used capital,
but it was not capital alone that increased productivity, it was his industrial
innovation. Until other industries imitated Ford, and became competitive with
him, Ford reaped monopolistic profits that resulted from his innovation. When
other manufacturers used his innovation—and in this sense, perhaps, exploited
him, for he received no payment—those who benefited, in addition to those
who bought and held Ford and General Motors stock, were the employees who
received higher pay for their work and bought cheaper and better automobiles.
Did labor, in Marx's sense, produce this increase in use value and exchange
value? Obviously not. The entrepreneur cannot be treated as a mere fact of nature
in the productive process, at least not in a genuinely sociological account. Marx
avoided a systematic inquiry into human productivity and his theory was thereby
distorted, misleading, and reified, for it turns a function of human activity into
a thing. The class analysis based on such reification fails to account adequately
for the forces and relations of production.

Marx's problem—and the likely reason one can find at least two different
Marxian accounts—arose from the fact that he was looking for a measure for
value that is independent in the sense of energy in physics and, hence, the
measure of which does not differ with different organizations of the economy
and society.

Robert Nozick has argued, in effect, that the profit of a Henry Ford should
not be taken from him by taxation without his consent because this would unjustly
enrich the public at Ford's expense.[14] However, sociological analysis can be
pushed even further backward. Had Ford lived in the Belgian Congo, would he
have been capable of introducing assembly-line techniques for the production
of automobiles? No. In this sense, we can argue that Ford was the producer of

the additional profits only by virtue of his environment, including the size of the United States, its railroads, its labor force, and so on.

Can we thus save the Marxian argument by saying that production is the product of past and present labor? But change and innovation are always made within organizations and always depend on leaders, at least in part. An amorphous mass of laborers never innovates, although sometimes individual workers do. It may have looked to Marx, in his day, as if machinery bought with money produces more when labor is added to it. However, that machinery had to be invented and ways of using it had to be discovered, which requires creativity and organizational skills. It is only by definition that these talents are unproductive—that is, that they do not produce value—in Marx's account.

In Marx's account, Ford would have to be treated merely as a force of production and, thus, reified. Such an account is neither praxical nor sociological. In effect, it would rob Ford by rationalizing the seizure of his entire contribution to society. But even though Ford, himself, was a producer and thus played a role in the productive relations of society, the entire society can be regarded as a force of production that was transformed by his performance; therefore, his financial rights thereto would have been subject to social regulation just like other rights to income. Our country's laws, for example, regulate access to certain kinds of jobs, ownership, and income. Business and tax laws regulate the citizen's access to and benefits from profits.

Rather than something mysterious, the entrepreneur's profit is a return on the risk that the enterprise will not succeed and a reward for entrepreneurial labor. This fact explains why capitalism is so enormously productive. Even in a socialist society, investment in a means of production or distribution or in a service is a gamble as well as an exercise of entrepreneurial labor. If it is a poor gamble, the investment will be lost, not only to the entrepreneur but to society at large. It is possible to diminish the productive base of a society by unwise investments. Moreover, unless investors and entrepreneurs have a monopoly, they are rarely able to capture the entire net return to society when their activity has expanded the productive base of the society. Motivating and achieving production, although not the only social considerations, are surely among the factors to be enhanced. It is legitimate to ask whether better ways of accomplishing this are possible, but the issue cannot be willed away by definition.

In effect, Marx sought to explain the dynamics of capitalism, and yet he worked with static concepts that failed to account for the real changes in capitalism. Marx neglected the role of credit that is not backed by goods or metal money in economic development and, thus, failed to understand the productive role of capital. In theory, in a frictionless and static economy, there is no profit. It is only the use of capital by an entrepreneur in a dynamic frictionless economy that produces profit. Capital and entrepreneurial profit are the motors of economic development. Only appropriate returns to each permit rational economic development.

As sociology, Marx's treatment of surplus value was strictly mechanical. A quantity of static labor combines with a quantity of static capital, or congealed labor, to produce a static product. The absence of the idea that differences in the form and content of labor produce quantitative jumps in value and a qualitative jump in the productive process—or that the capital the entrepreneur utilizes is not functionally or qualitatively merely congealed labor that has been produced by an ordinary laborer or by other means—shows that Marx has reified his concepts and used them within the terms of a mechanical formula. However useful such devices might be for carrying out particular calculations within a defined structural milieu with the environment held constant, they become, in a more general account, a Maxwell's demon that remains unchanged through all other transformations. They are the unmoved mover: the metaphysical mainspring of a mechanically deductive theory.

THE PROBLEM OF CLASS

Is a class an entity? I know what an organization is because it has structural reality.[15] General Motors and the United Auto Workers, G. M. Division, are entities. They may have some opposed, and some common interests; even then, conflicting interests within these organizations may at times outweigh those between them. They are particular, although collective, entities.

Marx, however, uses the concrete universal to talk of the laboring class as such or for itself; and this is a reification, for it cannot come into existence in this form, except perhaps as a mob. Even a political party would be a more complex phenomenon, although perhaps in a particular case a political party might have a more or less homogeneous membership in terms of, for instance, economic background. However, once organized into a party, its membership would have differentiated, and at least partly inconsistent, interests. In the broad sense in which classes are studied in sociology—e.g., laborer, owner, and so forth—class characteristics exist as qualities of individuals. They may overlap with organizational roles, and social change may produce interest groups with shared or overlapping sociological characteristics; but they cannot coincide, even in principle.

It is the incorrect Marxian account of class that produces so much puzzlement among Marxists when they discover that the nationalization of industry does not produce the results they expected. After the U.S.S.R. nationalized industry, there were still workers and managers. One set of managers did replace another, organizational control shifted, and the character of organizational control changed. All those changes were related to complicated changes of power in the larger system. But the degree of absenteeism and sabotage in the Soviet Union and in other socialist countries suggests that socialism exploits workers.

Changing the ownership of industry does not appear to be a sufficient condition for entering the kingdom of freedom, as Marx urged. There are probably no sufficient conditions, for the complex character of modern industrial organization will always include conditions which will alienate the participants. This is true to some extent even of artisans, who must cope with the resistance of materials, supply, and market. How one ameliorates these circumstances—and whether their amelioration is society's most important need—is a complex problem about which Marx's essentialist analysis tells us little. Certainly that analysis is too faulty, and its solution too mechanical, to inculpate private ownership as a key variable.

NEEDS IN MARX

Although it is true that Marx recognized most reifications for what they are and was developing a methodology designed to avoid reifications, his discussions of the needs of individuals also suffer from reification. As Marx's own methodology would indicate, abilities and needs are not abstractions that are divorced from the concrete conditions of life. However, because Marx argued that capitalism provided workers with only the minimum requirements for human reproduction—and this was not true even in nineteenth-century Europe, as Marx knew from his study of Asian conditions—he failed to take adequate account of the fact that society must provide those rewards, whether economic or of some other kind, that encourage individuals to acquire the skills and engage in the activities necessary to maintain or develop their society, including provision for the needs of others. Marx's own form of sociological analysis should have alerted him—and when he wrote on other issues it did—to this condition: that what is reproduced and developed is not some bare minimum required for biological reproduction, or even that minimum required to produce labor power for industry, but a mode of living. This mode of living is generated by a real social process and, in some systems such as modern industrial society, develops rapidly.

Because Marx's discussion of the price accorded to labor power is conceptually reified, it affects his discussion of estrangement. It is correct that to the extent that labor is paid a wage, labor is treated as a commodity and that the result of this arrangement is at least alienation. But it is not necessarily estrangement, as Marx uses that concept; for this arrangement may be encapsulated within a far larger social process in which the work of the laborer contributes to the quality of human life. This is in part at least what is meant by the dignity of labor; for those who work productively thereby assist in reproducing and developing the social conditions within which their more general and more particular forms of humanity are expressed. Although there is alienation in this process, it is alienation that can be overcome. Whether it is overcome or whether it produces estrangement depends not merely on the economic productive process itself but also on its role in the entire social process, the investigation of which requires a far more complex analytical structure than Marx provided.[16]

CONTEMPORARY VARIATIONS ON THE MARXIAN THEME

A number of sociologists have attempted to adjust Marx's dogmatic concepts to the complexity of social relations under modern capitalism and to treat class structure in a somewhat more complex way than he. They have differed in the elements included in the laboring class and have recognized more complex lines of conflict than Marx. However, they have continued to use all or most of Marx's concepts—such as surplus value, productive labor, a basic conflict between capital and labor, and a transformative solution in socialism—that constitute the core of Marx's evolutionary theory. Thus, their revisions are merely *ad hoc* variations on an unchanged theme. A few illustrations will help me to demonstrate my point.

Jon Elster, who recognized defects in Marx's treatment of surplus value, fell back on a normative justification, rather than an economic analysis, for denying profit to the owners of industry. He wrote:

> It is unjust for one class to appropriate the product of another and to receive an income based on that appropriation without having to work for it, or, at any rate, an income above that justified by work performed.[17]

This formulation is at least as perplexing as Marx's. If the dynamism of modern industry is the result more of the existence of an entrepreneurial class than of a working class—and if even the skills of the working class are the result of entrepreneurial skill—then perhaps it is the price of labor that is now too high. Is this position absurd? I have already mentioned Henry Ford. During World War II, Henry Kaiser reorganized the American shipbuilding industry by reordering tasks in such a way that workers could be trained quickly. The result was an enormous increase in productivity in the absence of which World War II might have been lost. Although few of the workers trained by Kaiser's methods reached a genuine shipbuilder's level of skill, the skill and income of these workers increased. Their own contribution to this process was minimal. It is true that they had to learn some things, but the important innovation was the distribution and scheduling of tasks so that unskilled persons could quickly become relatively skilled workers. In many underdeveloped countries, lack of entrepreneurial activity is a major cause of economic lethargy.

Does a normative consideration of this state of affairs suggest that the entire capitalist class should be rewarded by a tax on labor? Does it suggest that Kaiser alone should be rewarded by a tax? Should we consider the newly skilled workers to be unjustly enriched and distribute their added income to unskilled workers? What is income which is greater than "that justified by work performed," and can we even analyze this question without reifying at least some of the concepts involved in our analysis?

The key question is: What organization of industrial production is best for society? Even in considering the confiscation of inherited wealth on the general grounds of social justice, one must be careful to ask whether one is motivated by just or punitive considerations. Perhaps entrepreneurs are very valuable; if so, the existence of some unproductive heirs may be a small price to pay. The desire of some individuals to create something that will outlive them and that will continue to be associated with their progeny is so strong that we ignore it only at society's peril.

When Jon Elster wrote of working for income, what did he mean? A star basketball player works, but does he really deserve $2,000,000 a year? Is it unjust that he earn so much money when an important physicist earns only $50,000 a year? Is the athlete being enriched at the expense of others? If we talk of worth in terms of exchange value, the question becomes trivial, for the entire complex of economic relationships determines the exchange value of work. But it also does so for the rentier and the businessman.

If, on the other hand, one asks whether one wants to live in a society in which an athlete earns $2,000,000 a year and a renowned physicist earns only $50,000, then one has to ask how to structure a system that weighs things differently. Possibly only a restructuring of the conditions under which the market operates would be involved; perhaps far more radical changes would be required.

If one wishes to examine these more radical changes, then one has to ask whether one is willing to bear all the associated costs, for no restructuring of society can be accomplished without some irrationalities and costs. Personally, I am satisfied to allow the star athlete to keep his $2,000,000 a year; and although I am sometimes less than happy with the thought that he can make more in a year than I can in a lifetime, I doubt that I would be willing to accept the changes that would be required to raise my income and lower his.

Other attempts to reformulate Marxian positions are even closer to Marx's original positions that Elster's are. Nicos Poulantzas asserted, in *Political Power and Social Classes*, that classes cannot be defined outside of "class struggle"; by this term he means outside of the antagonistic, contradictory qualities of the social relations that make up the social division of labor.[18] This social division of labor referred to roles rather than to the individuals who fill them, and, using this criterion, he thrust white-collar employees, technicians, supervisors, civil servants, and so forth into the bourgeois class within advanced capitalism. His basic political criterion was the distinction between supervisory and supervised positions. There was also an ideological criterion: the division between mental and manual labor. He restricted the working class, in a capitalist society, to that labor that produces surplus value

> . . . while directly reproducing the material elements that serve as the substratum of the relation of exploitation; labor that is directly involved in material production by producing use values that increase material wealth.[19]

Non-productive wage workers are also exploited, according to Poulantzas, in the sense that surplus labor is extorted from them, but not in the sense that surplus value is created.

This treatment, which is even more restrictive than Marx's, denies to mental labor any role in the productive process. By this definition, the producer of computer programs that expand the rate of production would be called nonproductive. But, in a fully automated industry, the laboring class would be entirely gone; where would profit come from then? Furthermore, Poulantzas did not include service as productive labor, even though it accounts for an increasingly large segment of the gross national product in the United States.

Erik Olin Wright drew a different distinction between productive and unproductive labor. The clerks who place commodities on shelves, according to Wright, and who "thus perform the last stage of the transportation of commodities,"[20] fall into the category of productive labor that contributes to use value. However, workers who operate the cash register do not contribute to use value and therefore do not create any surplus value.

By this definition, it seems to me, the traffic cop does not contribute to the use value of the roads. Anyone who has driven on a main street during rush hour will doubt this. Although some workers who route goods, and even people, may be costly, no complex system of distribution can work efficiently in their absence, and use value would be diminished.

Arthur DiQuattro recognized that command economies are inefficient and undemocratic. He argued that the advantages of the market can be achieved under socialism in a manner that removes "commodity fetishism."

DiQuattro argued that market socialism can avoid the alienation of the workers whose labor has been embodied in an object and in which that labor therefore exists independently of and opposed to their autonomous power, because under market socialism the workers will

> . . . participate in decision making on the basis of equality . . . The labor of workers is therefore not "forced" and they are able to derive satisfaction both from the work process and from the products produced for the enjoyment of themselves and others in society.[21]

DiQuattro also stated that although in market socialism workers produce for exchange rather than directly for use, this is also true of a planned economy. The important difference is that "since net wages are politically determined . . . labor is not a full-fledged commodity."[22]

DiQuattro was driven to this position by his recognition of the fact that the alternative to the free market is a command economy. Therefore, socialism without a market cannot be a self-managing economic system and it must produce the alienation of which Marx spoke. That estrangement in fact does occur in all extant command economies is obvious to anyone who is aware of the extensive labor sabotage in such economies.

DiQuattro went to this extreme because he also accepted in a fixed form Marx's definitions and axioms pertaining to the forces and relations of productions and classes. He was, therefore, forced away from rather than toward a sociological analysis of the problem of control of production.

What are the organizations through which workers' decisions would be made? How is the agenda to be determined? Who is to control the avenues of access to tasks and functions within the system? Who will control the access to and distribution of information?

If DiQuattro believed that market socialism would be anything other than a system in which social forces and relations are differentiated and structured, he underestimated the complexity of society. His argument that many of the aspects of these processes would not become independent of the will of most of the people who engage in the activities is a myth.

Whether labor is forced or whether workers derive satisfaction from their work and from the products they make is not an either-or matter. It is a more-or-less matter and whether the worker's satisfaction is more or less depends on complex considerations that are, for the most part, partial and local. Moreover, these local criteria are related to a range of others. There are tradeoffs between efficiency and satisfaction at work, and there are tradeoffs between either of these and satisfaction derived from the goods that are produced. It is far from clear that the political decisions of market socialism, whatever these might be in practice, would result in either more income for or less estrangement of wage workers.

We do not begin to understand what might be referred to as the conditions that define Vilfredo Pareto's concept of *optimality*[23]—the convex line at the exterior of a bargaining space which defines the area within which any contestant's benefits may be improved without reducing the benefits to the others—or what they would imply in terms of social or economic organization. The fact is, of course, that no market is insulated from political decisions, whether arrived at by bargaining among owners alone, between managers and workers, between unions and management, or between economic organizations and the state.

It has been argued by one Marxist that the class struggle is a struggle to bring the working class into existence before it is a struggle between classes. But what are the classes that are to be organized? Even the virtues of union organization are not clear.

Although there is debate among economists over whether union organization has in fact raised the wage level of organized workers, one may surmise that some of the workers' interests were best satisfied through the formation of unions, a fact that some capitalists recognized by fighting unions. However, one can also argue that unions serve the interests of union leaders rather than of union members. The demands of the typographers' unions may have forced some newspapers out of business and many typographers out of work. The musicians' unions may have pushed pay levels to the point at which many musicians are out of work and at which many who do work are forced into non-union employment. The organization of building craft workers may have been one reason for the high price of housing and the consequent unemployment of craft workers. It is certainly questionable whether the real interests either of union members or of the public are served by this kind of organization. Nor is it clear that unions in a socialist society would react differently to the gulf between their immediate interests and the larger interests of society.

Because all these Marxian theorists remained wedded to the concept of surplus value and a mechanical view of the value of labor time, they have been forced into various difficulties. One can start with the truisms that value cannot be considered entirely independently of use; that, apart from the gifts of nature, human activity creates value; that human activity can be divided into hours and wind up with the false claim that labor time determines value.

In a correct sociological or economic approach, the value of labor is not considered to be independent of the value of products. Still, these two elements do not alone constitute a valid equation; we must add capital, entrepreneurial skill, and all the other factors of production. In the absence of these other factors, labor is worth much less. It is also incorrect that interests should be organized dichotomously or that the game is virtually a zero-sum one.

Marxists do not deal properly with these problems. They do not ask closely enough how human beings should be organized to pursue their interests, but identify the working class with an over-riding interest in socialism: thus, Marx's distinction between a class of itself, that is, disaggregated individuals who share the same relationship to the means of production, and a class for itself, that is, a class conscious of its own common interest. But "class" in this Marxian sense has never existed nor can it exist as an enduring organization, although it may occasionally be partly integrated into interest organizations or mobs. There are too many interests in common with other elements of society and too many conflicts within the category for this.

Before we turn, in the next chapter, to an examination of the "spirit" of Marx's writings, I wish to show how that spirit is influenced by his class analysis. Even in Jon Elster's intergenerational treatment, the concept of class is reified. In Marx's sense, this form of reification would estrange individuals from their humanity. Why should there be an intergenerational sense of identity among workers? Human beings are not merely members of the laboring class in the Marxian sense. They have other roles in society and life that legitimately help to shape their identifications and self images.

Many wealthy industrialists started out as relatively poor people. John D. MacArthur, for one, started virtually from scratch to become a billionaire. Was this not an intergenerational break?

Individuals, whether contemporaneously or intergenerationally, have a variety of models with which to identify. There is the inventor, the artist, the entrepreneur, the organizer, and so forth. Although Marx foresaw for the human species a future society of pure Communism, in actual practice his followers have identified labor with the least productive segments of modern society. In effect, Communism is the heaven to be prayed for that justifies the meanness of earthly life. One down-to-earth rationalization for this is to say that at least in China or Russia they feed people—even if at the expense of their freedom, which is of interest only to a small number of intellectuals anyway.

It is this conception of the workers as cattle that pervades certain elements of Marxian thought more clearly than it does capitalist thought. It is the foundation of Jean-Paul Sartre's identification with the masses and third-world countries. And Geörgy Lukács, who placed intellectuals at the lever of revolution, merely turned them into a tool for producing revolution.[24]

This tendency, which runs in stronger or weaker forms through all contemporary Marxian thought, is the most powerful producer of estrangement possible. It is a more modest version of the horror I mentioned in chapter 12 of humans hooked up to pleasure machines. But it demeans all real workers by elevating the worst form of their condition to the norm. It does this by attempting to force them to identify with an abstract class rather than with the best human qualities that can be found in their society and to contribute through their human productivity to the generation and development of these qualities. Contrary to the suggestion in Marx that a correct position can be found from the perspective of the worker, the worker's perspective *qua* worker always produces a false consciousness, for in that limited capacity one's most productive human capabilities are not developed.

Only when the worker identifies with the entrepreneur and the entrepreneur with the worker—even if only in part—can a human perspective be developed. Marxian thought turns society into antagonistic groups in which the only hope for the worker is either to destroy the capitalist—and this is a false hope in the more general sense of the capitalist as enterprise leader—or to become a capitalist and to exploit other workers. This aspect of Marxian thought is antithetical to humanism and fortunately is untrue.

Perhaps, it will be argued, Marx knew that the worker *qua* worker would be alienated from the self, but he believed that this alienation would be eliminated under Communism. However, not only would Marx's solution increase the alienation of workers under capitalism—at least if it is imposed—but, as we shall see in the next chapter, it is a philosophically flawed solution.

NOTES

1. Lewis F. Feuer, "Marx and Engels as Sociobiologists," *Survey* 23, no. 4 (Autumn 1977–78), pp. 109 ff.

2. Louis Althusser, *For Marx* (London: Allen Lane, The Penguin Press, 1969), pp. 66–67.

3. Morton A. Kaplan, *Alienation and Identification* (New York: Free Press, 1976), pp. 21 ff.

4. Karl Marx, *Theories of Surplus Value*, translated by G.A. Bonner and Emil Burns (London: Lawrence & Wishart, 1951).

5. See Gerald A. Cohen, *Karl Marx's Theory of History: A Defense* (Princeton, N.J.: Princeton University Press, 1978), pp. 303–304.

6. Karl Marx, *Theories of Surplus Value*, pp. 15 ff.

7. Karl Marx, *Economic and Philosophic Manuscripts of 1844* (Moscow: Progress Publishers, 1974), pp. 21, 26–27.

8. Karl Marx, *Theories of Surplus Value*, p. 305.

9. Karl Marx, *Capital*, vol. 1, translated by Samuel Moore and Edward Aveling (Moscow: Progress Publishers, 1958), p. 39.

10. Ibid., p. 195.

11. Karl Marx, *Theories*, pp. 186–187.

12. Ibid., pp. 227–228.

13. Eugen von Böhm-Bawerk, *Capital and Interest* (South Holland, Illinois: Libertarian Press, 1959).

14. Robert Nozick, *Anarchy, State, and Utopia*, (New York: Basic Books, 1974).

15. See Morton A. Kaplan, *Macropolitics: Essays on the Philosophy and Science of Politics* (Chicago: Aldine Publishing Co., 1969), pp. 28 ff.

16. For an analytical structure that permits such investigation, see Morton A. Kaplan, *Alienation and Identification* (New York: Free Press, 1976).

17. Jon Elster, "The Labor Theory of Value: A Reinterpretation of Marxist Economics," *Marxist Perspectives*, Fall 1978, p. 88.

18. Nicos Poulantzas, *Political Power and Social Classes* (London: New Left Books, 1973), pp. 14 ff.

19. Ibid., p. 216.

20. Erik Olin Wright, *Class, Crisis, and the State* (London: New Left Books, 1978), p. 47.

21. Arthur DiQuattro, "Alienation and Justice in the Market," *American Political Science Review* 72 (September 1978).

22. Ibid.

23. See Vilfredo Pareto, *Manuel d'économic politique* (Paris: Giard, 1927).

24. Morris Watnick, "Relativism and Class Consciousness," in *Revisionism: Essays on the History of Marxist Ideas*, edited by Leopold Labedz (New York: Praeger, 1962).

Chapter 15
The Spirit of Marx's Writing

Although many students of Karl Marx's work make a sharp distinction between his earlier and later writings, I am of the opinion that the philosophical foundations of his thought are to be found in the *Economic and Philosophic Manuscripts of 1844.** Some of the limitations that I believe show up in his substantive comments on the economy and society also appear to have their origin here.

SENSE PERCEPTION AND SCIENCE

According to Marx:

> *Sense perception* (see Feuerbach) must be the basis of all science. Only when it proceeds from sense perception in the twofold form of *sensuous* consciousness and *sensuous* need—that is, only when science proceeds from nature—is it *true* science.[1]

Certainly there is no such thing as science in the absence of observation, that is, of beings who can perceive a world. But this does not make sense perception the basis of science. Nor does it make the senses their own theoreticians, as Marx argued elsewhere, unless this is an obscure way of recognizing the ubiquity of interpretation.*

> But a *non-objective* being is an unreal, non-sensuous thing—a product of mere thought (i.e., of mere imagination)—an abstraction.[2]

However, numbers are objective and they are not merely imaginary—that is, they are not merely abstractions or signs or signs in their role as signs—although there are imaginary numbers in the mathematician's sense. They are not palpable or sensuous, but they function both as abstract signs and as the referents of signs in theories of physics.

---

*The quotations from Karl Marx's *Economic and Philosophical Manuscripts of 1844* in this chapter are used by permission of Progress Publishers, copyright © 1974.

*This is not improbable. The Hegelian distinction between appearances "for self" and "for others" does produce this conclusion. Thus, Hegel's assertion that existential knowledge always contains error. Unfortunately in the search for certainty, and truth with a capital T, Hegel resorts to the Absolute and Marx to the Totality, errors I shall discuss subsequently.

SPECIES MAN AND FREEDOM

Marx argued that

> . . . the whole character of a species . . . is contained in the character of its life activities; and free conscious activity is man's species-character. . . . In creating a *world of objects* by his practical activity, in his *work upon* inorganic nature, man proves himself a conscious species-being. . . . Admittedly animals also produce. . . . But an animal produces only what it immediately needs. . . . Man produces even when he is free from physical need and then he truly produces in freedom therefrom. An animal produces only itself, whilst man produces the whole of nature.[3]

Although the sharp distinction that Marx made between humans and animals is perhaps not fully justified—beavers build dams and squirrels hoard nuts for future needs, for instance—his emphasis is on humans as self-conscious actors who transform the environment through self-conscious activity. There are a number of serious problems, however, with this position as Marx stated it. Is Marx saying that physical need is incompatible with freedom? If so, it would follow that human sexual and feeding activity will occur freely only when physiological needs are least, or even absent. A more modest statement might make some sense: that sex and eating are freer when they are not driven by uncontrollable needs. But if Marx had written thusly, his conclusions would have been different.

Was Marx saying that freedom is the absence of the need to plan for adversity? If that is the argument, would humans engage in philosophical speculation, scientific enterprise, entrepreneurship, or artistic activity if these activities did not bear at least an indirect relationship to possible deprivations? Would someone whose physical needs were fully satisfied in the present and for the indefinite future, as well, engage in any of these activities? But if at least possible physical need is a stimulus to such activities, and if they are desirable, does it follow that freedom is undesirable? Or that the activities are undesirable?

Hegel correctly noted that human freedom, at least in a highly developed sense, was not possible when physical wants could not be satisfied. However, being unable to satisfy physical need, being able to satisfy need with effort, and being free from physical need are quite different conditions.

Marx's position on estrangement seems to follow from his identification of freedom with the absence of physical needs. Of course, Marx's statement may be read as pure tautology. It is true that man "truly produces in freedom [from physical needs if] man produces even when he is free from physical need." However, Marx appeared to regard his statement as more than a tautology. Thus he said,

> . . . similarly, in degrading spontaneous free activity to a means, estranged labor makes man's species-life a means to his physical existence. . . . An immediate consequence . . . is the *estrangement of man* from *man*.[4]

Whereas one would think that it is only animals that characteristically satisfy their physical needs spontaneously, whereas humans plan for the future and to that extent do not act spontaneously, Marx seems to feast on this particularly distinctive human behavior—for animals rarely plan in this extended sense—as the grounds of human estrangement. The musician and the engineer, for instance, must study and plan in order to engage in their individually chosen careers. Moreover, the instrumental role of their careers in society is not an alien quality but a function of their human and moral interest in society. Nature and society both constrain and free human creativity, which does not take place in a vacuum.

However, Marx concluded that if labor is related to external requirements, the product of labor becomes alien:

> If the product of labor is alien to me if it confronts me as an alien power, to whom, then, does it belong? . . . It belongs to some other man than the worker.[5]

However, this is true of the entrepreneur, of the inventor, even of the rentier who lends capital for later consumption. The market, the union, or even stubborn workers, may confront the entrepreneur as alien powers. For reasons stated in Part Three, there cannot be a good society in the absence of rules, that is, of external constraints on individual choices, although in the best societies these rules will be internalized. Can there be civilized life, or life at all, in the absence of estrangement as Marx defined it?

According to Marx:

> Activity and enjoyment, both in their content and in their *mode of existence*, are *social*. . . . The *human* aspect of nature exists only for *social* man. . . . Only here [does] his *natural* existence become *human* existence . . . thus *society* is the complete unity of man with nature.[6]

I have little quarrel with the core of this statement. The penumbra of the passage, however, confounds me. In what sense is society "the complete unity of man with nature"? Can there ever be a complete unity of anything with anything? When Marx said elsewhere that the essence of fish is water, I suspect that language was being used less than precisely. Is not water a source of oxygen? Is swimming not a way of getting to food? Granted that humanity's natural existence is in society, are there not at least residual conflicts between people and society, between society and natural conditions, and between people and society, on the one hand, and natural conditions on the other?

Bertell Ollman, a sympathetic reader, noted that Marx did not use terms consistently. And he doubted that Marx could have used the conception of freedom consistently. According to Ollman:

> Marx . . . says that man's species activity is free, which is additional evidence that he generally locates it in the time of Communism. . . . [However,] freedom of some sort (and therefore in some sense of the term) must always have existed.[7]

Did Marx ever find freedom in actual society?

> . . . the most splendid results are to be observed whenever French socialist workers are seen together. Such things as smoking, drinking, eating, etc., are no longer the means of contact or the means that bring them together. Company, association, and

conversation, which again has society as its end, are enough for them; the brotherhood of man is no mere phrase with them, but a fact of life, and the nobility of man shines upon us from their work-hardened bodies.[8]

This is bad sociology. It probably has more in common with the "Westinghouse effect"—named after an experiment in the United States that showed that the productivity of workers went up whenever the work situation was changed —than Marx could have known in the nineteenth century. There is such a thing as spontaneous activity and it does transform human relationships, even if only for a while. One can note this in lynch mobs as well as among French socialist workers. If the "essence" of humanity lay in continual spontaneity, human evolution would no doubt have stopped at a much earlier stage. The complexities of the world—irruptions from other part systems—eventually intrude on these spontaneous collective acts. And when they do, many of the participants emerge from what sometimes seems to have been madness.

Ollman's conclusion that Marx often used words to mean different things at different times (although without alerting the reader) is correct. If Marx's shifts in meaning merely responded to the requirements of weakly ordered aspects of the world, this would be exemplary. However, the inconsistency of use was essential to Marx for an illegitimate reason. If Marx could not have used the concept of freedom disjunctively, he could not have maintained his other disjunctive positions or have seen Communism as so radically transformative of humanity in a future world in which all signs were coherent and, hence, identical in the totality. This, incidentally, was what made Lenin and Stalin sons of Marx, whatever contradictory positions also may be derived from Marx's writings. If true freedom could exist only in Communism, then who could cavil over the price paid to reach it? Ollman himself said that only in Communism:

. . . can all man's social functions register as free activities; only then, in Marx's words, "is personal freedom possible." Engels goes as far as to maintain that it is impossible even to speak of freedom while classes and the state exist.[9]

Thus, according to Ollman:

Activity in Communism will appear "conscious," "purposive," "concentrated," "physically and mentally flexible," "social," "skillful," and "rational." . . . Given their internal relations to life activity in Communism, the same description will apply to creativity, full appropriation, the satisfaction of human needs, and the fulfillment of human powers.[10]

The exercise of a freedom, however, must always be related to an appropriate constraint.[11] One who wants to exercise one's freedom to think must observe the appropriate rules for thinking: one must acquire the information relevant to the process; one must be physiologically able to exercise one's intellectual capabilities; and one must be emotionally disposed to process information accurately. The character of one's "processing equipment" constrains how one acquires and processes information. Such is the ambiguity of language, however, that we are always free to violate at least some of these constraints. But this signifies only that we can malfunction.

Freedom and constraint are correlatives. The freedom of a ball to roll is related to the character of the surface on which it is placed. And the freedom of humans involves both internal constraints such as have been noted above and external constraints such as social organizations and rules and the availability of goods. It is true that some social systems provide more freedom than others (and some surfaces provide more freedom than others for balls to roll); but no freedom exists or even has meaning in the absence of constraint. The pleasure machine of Part Three "frees" humans from all limitations of nurture but at the price of their humanity. Even short of this extreme, the abstract search for freedom produces distortions of character and mind such as those of the English decadents of the late nineteenth century or of a Marquis de Sade. Moral constraint is the correlative of moral freedom. And social constraint is the correlative of social freedom. External as well as internal relations are intrinsic to the concept of freedom.

The search for some variant of the test-in-principle is, in effect, a search for those social conditions that permit us to exercise some of our more sophisticated moral capabilities. For reasons explained in the earlier parts of this book, the transfinitely stable process, which sharply distinguishes human systems from mechanical systems, produces weakly ordered regimes. Therefore, there is much room for idiosyncratic variation among individuals. On the other hand, these variations respond, in part at least, to the idiosyncrasies of individual histories. Freedom is always of a specific type and is always exercised by individuals. Its constraints always help to determine its specific character.

Although I would agree with many of the adjectives that Marx and Ollman used, notice the important differences in formulation. Without even asking whether the terms that he used had the same meaning in different situations or epochs, Marx interconnected freedom and humanity in a harmonious whole in Communism.

Marx wrote before we were able to recognize that all complex system designs, even the best, involve compromises among the goals to be achieved or restrictions on tendencies inherent in parts of the system. The biological evolution of the human race is no exception to this rule. The human being is not a harmonious whole biologically or psychologically, any more than society is. The attempt to improve a particular element of a system—even of a high-fidelity amplifier—compromises the performance or raises the costs of some of the other elements in optimal systems. Society, including the forces of production and the relations among them, is more complex than Marx was willing to admit.

One can do better with the concept of freedom within a praxical framework. It becomes possible to speak of freedom in a dispositional sense. If they are drugged, for instance, humans are not free to use their intelligence. If a form of the test-in-principle places great stress on this aspect of the personality, then such drugs restrict freedom in an important sense. Freedom, in Marx's writings, is a two-valued quality. With minor exceptions, it exists in Communism and does not exist in the absence of Communism. By idealizing freedom in a hypothetical and undefined Communism, Marx has devalued freedom in all real societies and in all feasible improvements of those societies.

Together with Marx's coherence theory and strongly ordered universe, his concrete universal—species man—has produced the reductionist and determinist conclusions of the Marxian literature. Compare Marx's thesis with the test-in-principle described in Part Three of this book, which relates the phenomenological world non-rigidly to its inherent potentialities. There is a line of intellectual descent in these contrasting positions, but the differences are at least as important as the similarities.

HUMANISM AND NATURE

An objective being acts objectively, and he would not act objectively if the objective did not reside in the very nature of his being. He only creates or posits objects, because he is posited by objects—because at bottom he is *nature*. . . . Here we can see how consistent naturalism or humanism is distinct from both idealism and materialism, and constitutes at the same time the unifying truth of both.[12]

I like Marx's fusing of the humanistic or naturalistic perspective in contradistinction to both materialism and idealism in this passage. On the other hand, most of the passage reads like poor poetry. People do not create because they are nature; they are part of nature and so constituted that within nature they create in certain limited ways. People do not act objectively because objects posit them. Or because they are nature. We breathe without consciousness because it is an autonomic activity. This is, in a sense, in the nature of our being. But whether we paint or build bridges depends not upon our nature alone, but upon our relationships with society and the world, both generally and specifically. My writing of this book is not the externalization of my essential power as an alien object nor is it the subjectivity of my objective essential powers "whose action, therefore, must also be something objective."[13] We can do much better by analyzing such activity dispositionally. A lot of the mystery evaporates when we do.

Marx captured a fundamental theorem of communications theory that I have already noted: structure is more slowly changing process. He wrote:

. . . because this positing of thinghood is only an illusion, an act contradicting the nature of pure activity, it has to be cancelled again and thinghood denied.[14]

However, structure is not an illusion, as Marx suggested; for if it were illusory—if there were no structure that provided a framework for change—there could not be change, either. Change has meaning only in relationship to the unchanged. "Thing" and "process" are correlative concepts. If one is an illusion, then so is the other.

The basic difficulty of Marxian thought stems from Marx's effort to integrate, in a strongly coherent fashion, a metatheory of how we produce knowledge and an evolutionary theory (or perhaps praxical account) of how societies are transformed. The disjunction between the two tasks is so great that they corrupt each other as they interpenetrate.

PRIVATE PROPERTY

Let us see how Marx treated private property:

> Private property has made us so stupid and one-sided that an object is only *ours* when we have it—when it exists for us as capital, or when it is directly possessed, eaten, drunk, worn, inhabited, etc. . . . . The transcendence of private property is therefore the complete *emancipation* of all human senses and qualities. . . . Need or enjoyment have consequently lost their *egotistical* nature and nature has lost its mere *utility* by use becoming human use.[15]

Perhaps this quotation expresses Marx's definition of Communism, which is believed to be absent in his writings except for the apothegm that each should produce according to his ability and that each should consume according to his need. Perhaps I am merely being dense in being unable to understand the relationship between "the *senses* have therefore become directly in their practice *theoreticians*"[16] and his conclusions. Nor do I really see why an eye ceases to be a human eye if private property is present.

If my specially ground lenses are not to be considered my private property, does it mean that such lenses must be freely available wherever I go? If not, by what right do I take them with me and deprive someone else of a lens? What about my shoes? Should I object if a guest with wet shoes takes mine? Must shoes of all sizes be freely available in my house to accommodate guests who come in with wet feet? Is it really profound to say that "to the *eye* an object comes to be other than it is to the *ear*?"[17] What does it mean to say "the specific character of each essential power is precisely its *specific essence*, and therefore also the specific mode of its objectification, of its *objectively actual*, living *being*"?[18] If hearing is different from seeing—and who doubts this?—what does it add to state that the difference is its specific essence? Indeed, what is the difference? And does a difference have an essence? What does it mean to state that the specific essence is the specific mode of an objectification?

To the extent that Marx was prefiguring the pragmaticist position—the production of a phenomenal world through the transactions of human beings with each other and with nature—his intentions were potentially fruitful. To the extent that these arguments can be read as an attack on the copy theory of knowledge, they are important. However, Marx placed these formulations within a framework that made them dense. And they are bound to an attack on private property that is poorly formulated. The relationship of human productivity to access to goods is an extremely complex one. It is unlikely that the legal form of the relationship is the crucial one and, therefore, likely that similar problems will arise in all forms of society.

SOCIALISM

Marx then wrote:

> Socialism is man's *positive* self-consciousness . . . just as *real life* is man's positive
> reality, no longer mediated through the abolition of private property, through *Com-*
> *munism*. Communism is the positive mode as the negation of the negation, and is
> hence the *actual* phase necessary for the next state of historical development. . . .
> *Communism* is the necessary form and the dynamic principle of the immediate future,
> but Communism as such is not the goal of human development, the form of human
> society.[19]

What we see here, as in Hegel, is the substitution of abstract essentialism
—abstract, despite Marx's claim that it is concrete—for concrete praxical analysis; in my opinion, it is this type of abstract and essentialist categorization that
guided Marx's thought throughout his career regardless of the concrete details
of his studies. Abstract alternatives—capitalism, socialism, Communism—are
posed; and social reality is supposed to fit into them. It is Marx's strong coherence
theory that forces this divergence between his abstract categories and his concrete
analyses.

That is not how social science can progress. We can speak of feudalism
because we can relate the concept to concrete human institutions. Even so, many,
including Marx, knew that it was wrong to equate Japanese feudalism with
Western European feudalism despite certain superficial similarities. The respects
in which they are similar and the importance of the differences can be determined
only by praxical analysis. The transformation of feudal into capitalistic societies
depended upon specific institutional developments, not upon negations of negations or even the positive mode of a negation of a negation. What may have
been a useful heuristic device—the posing of socialism as an alternative to
capitalism—to begin the investigation of the transformation of the capitalist
system that existed when Marx lived becomes a straitjacket when used in this
form. Although in practice Marx often rose above these devices—for instance,
he distinguished the Asian mode of production from the European—he, like
contemporary Marxists, always reverted to such formulations at crucial junctures.

ALIENATION

Marx used two terms when he discussed alienation: *Entausserung* and *Entfrem-*
den. *Entausserung*, which Marx's interpreters usually translate as "alienation,"
means the loss of something that still remains in existence. It has the sense of
making something external to oneself. *Entfremden* is usually translated as "estranged" and refers to situations in which one is at odds with something else.

In his *Economic and Philosophical Manuscripts of 1844*, Marx wrote:

> The product of labor is labor which has been embodied in an object, which has
> become material: it is the *objectification* of labor. . . . Under these economic con-
> ditions this realization of labor appears as *loss of realization* for the workers; objec-

tification as *loss of the object and bondage to it*; appropriation as *estrangement*, as *alienation*.[20]

Whether the distinction between the terms is as sharp as most of Marx's interpreters suggest may be doubted from this passage. However, that is not to my present point. Notice that in this passage estrangement stems from the transfer of the products of labor to management. This is a highly specific definition of estrangement, and it is the source of the myth that socialism will end estrangement.

Bertell Ollman claims that Marx's concept of alienation is sociological and quotes Marx to the effect that, in capitalism:

> . . . labor is external to the worker, i.e. it does not belong to his essential being; that in his work, therefore, he does not affirm himself but denies himself . . . and ruins his mind. . . . His labor . . . is forced labor. It is not the satisfaction of need; it is merely a means to satisfy needs external to it.[21]

In the first volume of *Capital*, Marx referred to the physical distortions caused by certain types of work, such as stunted size, bent backs, enlarged bones, and deathly pale complexions. The object of this is to show that the laborers' activity is coerced, that their labor is alienated from them, that their selves are estranged, and that the product of their labor is estranged from them. This, Marx and Ollman wrote, is the result of labor in a capitalistic society, and it prevents people from becoming free, as in a Communist state, in which their labor stems not from need but from an attempt to satisfy themselves.

This concept of alienation and estrangement is neither good economics nor good sociology. Although it is possible to think of some work as inherently satisfying—for instance, the work of the artist or the artisan—society requires the meeting of instrumental needs, whatever the form of the economic system. And even artists and artisans must engage in some irritating activities, e.g., arranging schedules and sending out bills. If coal mining is needed in the state of communism, then, in the absence of technological innovations that would have similar consequences in capitalist societies, coal miners will continue to be stunted.

All ends are related to other ends. There is no end in itself. Part-system analysis of behavior necessarily shifts from consideration to consideration, from rule to consequence, and from consequence to rule. There is a problem here—a problem that stems from Marx's strong coherence theory and his use of signs—because Marx does not have an adequate method of determining what human nature is.

Ollman has written that:

> . . . instead of developing the potential inherent in man's powers, capitalist labor consumes these powers without replenishing them, burns them up as if they were a fuel, and leaves the individual worker that much poorer.[22]

This seems unlikely. There is considerable evidence of great satisfaction in jobs in recent periods of capitalism because they made the role of the worker meaningful in supporting the family and sustaining the children who might do even better. Moreover, the development of the capitalist system, instead of producing "idiocy" and "cretinism," as Ollman stated in referring to Marx's discussion, is producing a society in which many skills are becoming much more sophisticated and refined and much more capable of producing inherent job satisfaction.

I argued in chapter 11 that what is intrinsic and what is instrumental depends on the problems under review and that there is no abstract hierarchy of ends. Indeed, were we ever to find a society in which the amount and variety of food, shelter, and so forth, were truly unlimited and freely available, it is likely that we would either develop more refined needs that required even more training before they could be satisfied or that we would turn on ourselves in sheer boredom or despair. Again, Marx reified his concepts. It requires a comparative series of tests such as those suggested by the test-in-principle to develop an adequate dispositional conception of human nature.

It is surely true that, in particular institutional frameworks, goals are emphasized that can be described only as dysfunctional for humans. Under certain economic conditions, the capitalist emphasis on profit exaggerates the instrumental aspects of human activity. In socialist societies, on the other hand, managers are driven to increase production regardless of need, to falsify figures, and to eliminate bottlenecks by making use of a legally protected black market. Every system produces its distortions, and some may produce more distortions than others. The task of the sociologist is to investigate concrete relationships, not to ascribe them to a set of fixed categories. It is the dichotomous element in Marxian thought that produces the myth that estrangement will be absent under Communism.

In *Alienation and Identification*, I attempted to deal with this problem in a sociological fashion.[23] If we remain at the level of abstract and strongly coherent categorization, as both Marx and Ollman did, we get not sociological analysis but reifications. We lose the significance of activity in context and treat the categories of alienation and estrangement as metaphysical.

Both Marx's analysis and that of most contemporary Marxists, even the so-called revisionists, maintain Marx's definitions and axioms as unchanged categories that determine the reality of the world. Although Ollman, for instance, specifically recognized that Marx employs the term *Wissenschaft* for science, and that this term extends beyond theory to include systematic knowledge, there is not a critical investigation in his book into whether Marx's categories—the forces and relations of production as he described them—match our understanding of the organization of the economy and society. Nor is there an inquiry into whether the concept of *Wissenschaft* is employed at the phenomenological level and driven theoretically by the concept of essence. It is this connection, however, that became the deterministic motor of Marx's thought.

RELATIONS, INNER RELATIONS, AND TOTALITY

There are at least three ways in which we may think of the relatedness among things and processes. One way is trivial: everything affects everything else. A second mode of interpretation is that, in the social sciences and ethics, the basic elements of problems are interdependent. But one important consequence of this view, which is contrary to the Marxian interpretation, is that no rule covers all situations, that no particular outcome can take predominance over all others regardless of context, and that no particular virtue may be regarded as highest regardless of context. A third way of viewing interrelationships is in terms of an articulated interpretation of a problem, of a system, or of a chain of events. This interpretation may produce a theory, which would yield an explanation, or a praxical analysis, which is far more likely, which would yield an assessment.

How did Marx handle relations? According to Jon Elster, Marx borrowed his distinction between essence and appearance from Hegel. To both men, according to Elster, "essence is the totality of interrelated appearances."[24] Elster's formulation almost turns Marx and Hegel into positivists, or at least into phenomenologists. However, essence, in both positions, is what something is as such, truly, and without error or accident. It is this complex relationship between essence and appearance that accounts for the importance of both history and evolution in both positions. Essence is a generative factor—a potentiality or at least a potency—that becomes manifest, but only imperfectly, in appearance. The way in which the concrete universal and a coherence theory of truth bridge the relationship between essence and appearance produces the major unresolved, and unresolvable, problems in both positions.

In any event, Marx's use of essence, let alone Elster's reading of it, posited either too much or too little. Even if, as Marx sometimes did, one distinguishes between the core of the appearances of something and its penumbra, the concept of essence is too embracing and includes too many intrinsically inessential elements. Water is not the essence of fish. It is primarily a medium for swimming and for breathing oxygen. Air is not the essence of humans, although they cannot live in its absence. On the other hand, the concept is too limited; it does not provide a criterion for differentiating important from unimportant aspects of things, for the development of things, or for transformations under complex conditions. This is what eventually reduces Marx's phenomenological worker to a shadow play of internal essence: species man. For Marx, everything is related in a Totality within which things are identical.

It is true that in some sense everything is interrelated. Thus, to make an extremely precise calculation, a scientist studying the movement of the planets might have to take into account the gravitational effects of a galaxy a billion light years distant. However, it would be very difficult to think of a calculation that would require such exactitude.

It is quite true that we cannot understand the eye as an optic organ without some understanding of the sun as a source of light. And if our eyes responded to the ultraviolet range, then we would have to specify its source in the sun also.

Any meaningful set of categories must be adapted to the context in which it is to be used.

If we construct a theory, the meanings of the terms of the theory must be adapted to each other. The concepts of mass and geometry are different in Newtonian and Einsteinian mechanics. It does not follow, however, that every concept relevant to the two theories is different or that we cannot distinguish them experimentally. It is sufficient that there be enough common terms and observations to test the theories against each other. In fact, by making such comparisons, we can even explain why Newtonian theory yields correct information about certain events in the solar system but not about others.

This is not a trivial distinction. The methods of Hegel and Marx imply an extremely strong coherence theory of truth in which all relations, at least in the Absolute or the Totality, are inner, whereas praxical analysis is a reasoning process based on fit, consistency, and so forth. It permits a weak ordering of statements and complementarity. Different types of optic apparatus may be coextensive with the existence of our sun; and indeed they are. They are also coextensive with other lighting systems as well. The meanings of signs differ with their use in different forms and modes of analysis. Correct modes of investigation may be incompatible in terms of the instruments or concepts that they use. There is no single true framework within which the true meaning of signs establishes their identity in a Totality. Although Marx might have granted all these conclusions for appearances, he thought that he could theorize about a Totality to which they were inapplicable.

Let me state the matter in another form. Hegel's Absolute is one in which all elements have an inner relationship to each other. We can interpret Marx's Totality in this same way or, alternatively, and likely incorrectly, we can regard his Totality as limited to particular theories, in which case inner relations are only the relations of meaning within a particular theory. The first interpretation results in the strong order that has been discredited. In the second, the inner relationship loses much of its force, for its validity depends upon theoretical tests, praxical assessments, and external criteria. Furthermore, the lack of a sharp boundary between the concrete area of reality to which a theory would apply and its environment would limit the applicability of Marx's basic definitions. Although passages in Marx can be interpreted in either fashion, the retention of his key categories and conclusions clearly requires the first interpretation.

Marx's Totality can be neither retained nor reformulated. It is a mirror image of Derrida's other, a concept that does not involve the essentialism inherent in Marx's philosophical position. Derrida regarded the Marxian *aufhebung* of Hegel's position as abstract and as partly contaminated by metaphysics, the grip of which, he correctly observed, it did not entirely escape. Yet, in chapter 10, I analyzed the errors in Derrida's effort to make an equivalent concept meaningful even when essentialism and a strong coherence theory are not incorporated in it. In Marx, however, it is the essentialism and coherence of Totality that drove him and his followers into error.

In the most central aspects of most Marxian writings, classes are defined by their legal relationship to the means of production. Therefore, changing legal ownership will change class structure. To a few writers, of whom Gerald Cohen is an example, the dominance of management is the key concept, although Cohen retains Marx's concept of surplus value and his labor theory of value. For some reason, socialism is presumed to eliminate dominance. Still other writers, as we have seen, place various groups of workers into either the capitalist or the working class depending on a combination of similar and conflicting interests, but the conflict remains essentially dichotomous and resolvable only by socialism.

All establish a dichotomy of conflicting categories and reify their analytical tools, for Marxists do not ask whether capitalism and socialism are adequate categories and whether the dichotomy of classes is sufficient to serve as a basis for the analysis of the forces and relations of production. And yet, as has been shown, their general acceptance of the labor theory of value distorts the creative contribution of management. Surely Marx knew this, for he stressed throughout *Capital* the productive power of capitalism. Or did he think that the productivity of capitalism resulted only from finance and the introduction of machinery? Only by calling capital congealed labor and by ignoring the human and contemporary input of the entrepreneur, and even of the rentier, could Marx reach his conclusion.

Much of the ambiguity in Marx stemmed from his use of Hegel's notion of identity. If truth is the whole, if things are more or less identical with the whole that they express, then what can truly be said about the whole can be said about particular things. As Ollman put it:

> Each thing being relationally identical with the whole, all that is true of the latter is its entire truth; and everything short of that—which means all we say about particular things . . .—is partial truth. . . . Identity is clearly a matter of degree; small simple things possess less identity with the whole than large complex ones.[25]

I can understand that similarity is a matter of degree, but identity? And now we are predisposed to search for a total account of society and the economy.

Although Ollman's formulation is not exactly a copy theory, it seems to posit a world that is matched element-for-element in a univocal manner with a completed Totality such that the degree of match between a partial segment and the whole can be determined. Because the emphasis is on a literal matching rather than on the reasons supportive of a hypothesis, the germ of a copy, or at least a correspondence, theory is present, and this explains its repeated occurrence in Marx and his followers (emphatically in Lenin) despite disclaimers or despite attempts to avoid it. The belief in Totality explains the otherwise mysterious recurrence of an end to history in Hegel, Marx, and their followers.

The way in which Marx's position differs from modern systems analysis, apart from the awkward use of the term "identity," lies in the strength of the coherence theory that is adopted, in its symmetry of analysis, and in its failure to recognize that all analysis involves external as well as internal criteria. This is precisely where the gap in the logic that produces the conception of an Absolute or a Totality occurs. And it has similarities to the position of Kripke and Putnam that was criticized in chapter 4. Furthermore, the problems that are raised by the concept of verisimilitude are raised by this position also.

Hegel spoke of contradictions that were to be overcome only in the Absolute, which was the total system in which everything had its coherent role. Communism had a similar significance to Marx. When false consciousness is overcome, antagonistic contradictions will vanish. Each thing has its proper essence. Each essence would have a proper place in the Totality. And thus each individual would achieve satisfaction in the absence of rules and other external constraints. This position entails a classical and incorrect use of signs.

Let us see what is wrong with this position in practical terms. In optimal air raid warning systems, improvements in detection always increase the probability of a false alarm and vice versa. Even if one knew how to build optimal social systems, there would be necessary conflicts among alternative desiderata. Any one particular choice would fall unequally on the members of the system. In biological systems, for instance, white blood cells are sacrificed in fighting disease. There is no theoretical reason to believe that social systems can avoid all harsh results for some members under the best conditions let alone under all conditions. Recognition of the obdurate character of social reality is likely in benign, but not all, circumstances to produce design compromises that minimize irreconcilable conflict.

Belief in metaphysical "identity," on the other hand, is likely to lead to Procrustean and harsh solutions and to the characterization of the undeniable and continuing conflict either as transitional, for it would be perceived as having no legitimate basis in the new social structure, or as non-contradictory. Whereas recognition of the inherent character of conflict at least leaves open the possibility of mutual adjustment—and morally sensitive leaders would seek this—the Marxian thesis legitimizes the war of a revolutionary leadership against the rest of society. It incorporates essentialism, a hierarchical and univocal sign system, and a state of ultimate Truth: positions dealt with in Part One of this book.

Some of what Hegel and Marx viewed as contradiction may be an early insight into what Niels Bohr discussed in terms of complementarity, but forced into an inappropriate metaphysical framework. Other aspects of what they concluded was contradiction may lie in what I regard as the correlative aspects of the real. Morris R. Cohen rejected Hegel's concept of dialectic and the related concept of contradiction, but he noted that language, as a tool, invokes the use of polarities,[26] a concept similar to that of correlatives.

In chapter 4, I pointed out that the qualitative correlative aspects of language are basic to its use. The ordinary qualitative language refers to hot and cold, good and bad, light and dark, free and bound; and I argued that these are intrinsic aspects of praxical assessments and that they cannot be reduced to theory. Although correlative terms may be said to have an inner relationship to each other, as the terms of a theory or as the elements of a system may be said to have inner relationships, it is a misuse of language to apply the concept of identity to them. These terms are inherently relational and they cannot be understood except in terms of their interrelationships. "Internal" and "external" are also correlatives; and hence no world is potentially entirely "internal" as such.

The distinction between intrinsic and extrinsic is one that sociologists have paid a great deal of attention to in a variety of terminologies. The polar distinction between diffused and segmented is a closely related one. Who one is and what one achieves are also polar distinctions.[27] This was the distinction that Ferdinand Tönnies called *Gemeinschaft* and *Gesellschaft*.[28] The Marxian solution to the problem of estrangement rests upon a transformation of society in which one of the polar aspects of these terms—that dealing with diffuseness, spontaneity, intrinsic value, and so forth—becomes the sole measure of Communism.

Although it is possible for certain aspects of the world to which these correlative terms refer to be predominant in some societies or institutions, their polar character implies an inherent tension that is consistent with an unending evolution, as Marx and Hegel sometimes suggested, and that is inconsistent with a millennial ending of history. Nothing can be either of the polar alternatives as such. Had Marx conceived of the referents of these terms as polar asymptotes on a continuum, his conception of sociology would have been richer.

If one recognizes the correlative nature of such concepts and the necessary tension between them, then one inquires into the conditions of life and social organizations to which certain degrees of each aspect of the polarities are appropriate. Then one can investigate sociologically optimal conditions—as in the variance of the test-in-principle—for the transformation of society and the expressions of human nature that occur within it.

One position leads to critical inquiry; the other toward dogma. One position leads toward praxical inquiry within which theoretical constructs, axioms, and definitions are amended; the other leads toward an unchanging motor of history that keeps driving toward a predestined conclusion regardless of variations or uncertainties along the way. Just as the *Geiste* in Hegel drives toward the Absolute despite the fact that Hegel called history the realm of accident, Marx's primitive terms and definitions with respect to labor and the forces and relations of production drive history toward Communism as they remain unchanged and impervious, except in the sense of *ad hoc* emendation, to evidence. Thus, what Marx really promised is not a human future but one that is predetermined by the logic of fixed definitions. It is this failure in the use of sign theory and in distinguishing between theory and praxis that created the fatal disjunction between Marx's abstract concepts* and his concrete historical investigations, which I noted in *Alienation and Identification*.[29]

---

*As did Hegel, Marx finessed the abstract character of his concrete universal by regarding all existents as abstract when detached from the totality.

RAYMOND WILLIAMS AND HEGEMONY

There have been attempts to loosen the concept of Totality. A notable attempt
was made by Antonio Gramsci, who developed the concept of hegemony, and
I shall consider his position in the next section. I prefer to deal first with Raymond
Williams' account because it is contemporaneous and because of its influence
in the English-speaking world. According to Williams, Gramsci's concept of
hegemony is one in which capitalism captures and controls the institutional
developments of modern life. According to Williams, Gramsci believed that

> . . . the reality of any hegemony, in the extended political and cultural sense, is that,
> while by definition it is always dominant, it is neither total nor exclusive. . . . In
> advanced capitalism, because of changes in the social character of labor, in the social
> character of communications, and in the social character of decision-making, the
> dominant culture reaches much further than ever before in capitalist society. . . .
> This in turn makes the problem of emergence especially acute, and narrows the gap
> between alternative and oppositional elements.[30]

Thus, we see, Williams' presentation of Gramsci's account of culture is as
dichotomous as that of Marx in theory; Williams denies only that any real society
entirely fits the model.

Yet is it really true that a capitalist cultural hegemony determines most
important aspects of institutional life? The school system in the United States
does not produce educated people who meet the needs of the capitalist system
in the United States.

The school system, from the elementary through the university, has a strong
autonomous life that is politically strong enough to resist incorporation into the
requirements of industrial capitalism. Whereas industry requires workers who
are sophisticated, who can work without much direction, and who can cope with
complicated jobs, the school system produces many truncated human beings who
are semi-literate. This serves the purposes neither of our economic system nor
of our political system, although it may correspond to the needs of an educational
bureaucracy. If there is some significant way in which capitalism, as distinguished
from the modern economy, specifically affects the school system, it remains to
be shown. In any event, in 1983, a group of large businesses organized an
association in California to raise money for schools and to improve education.

Although Gramsci's concept of hegemony is certainly superior to Marx's
notion of Totality with its Hegelian concepts of inner relations and identity, it
is nonetheless misleading. It implies that the ills of capitalism can be solved by
the social hegemony of a workers' culture. That disjunctive way of looking at
the problem—and the disjunction stems directly from the belief in a strong
order—leads to simplistic formulas.

It will not save the Marxian thesis to argue that the ethos of the school is
itself a product of a capitalist system that encourages egotistical motives. The
knowledge industry, and also the managerial class, are worldwide phenomena
that reflect the enormous importance of these social functions in modern society.
The gulf between the social incentives that sustain these systems and the indi-

vidual incentives that reward progress are at the core of the problem. The Maoist effort to control this gulf, which was based on the dichotomous Marxian view of society, was so dysfunctional that it tended to inhibit recognition of the fact that a genuine problem exists. These social problems are not mere aberrations that result from capitalism or from Stalinist or Maoist doctrines. They are problems inherent in modern society that arise in more severe form in socialist societies because of the need of socialist regimes to maintain total control of society lest they lose control completely. Thus, such regimes tend to oscillate between a professionalism in the absence of which there would be economic, and then political, disaster and a politicization of the knowledge industry that reduces its political subversiveness.

There are undoubtedly better and worse ways to cope with these problems. But knowledge of these ways will not be derived from the dichotomous Marxian perspective that gravely oversimplifies and distorts the problem of relatedness and that in practice exacerbates the consequences of the supposed contradiction.

The pragmaticist movement has always accepted relations as a genuine part of reality. Relationships are not merely abstractions imposed by the mind. And deeper probings into problems usually yield additional important relationships. But what one senses in the contemporary Marxian movement is a metaphysical core that negates its concessions to concrete investigation, lack of inevitability, and so forth. There seems to be a determination to link events in the real world to disjunctive and dichotomous possibilities.

Thus, there is an inclination to dichotomize the alternatives that confront society and to link changes to total packages in ways that are counterproductive. Furthermore, there is usually a failure to examine with sufficient care the relationships that might be produced by transformations of the economy and to assume the coherence of some variant of the original ideal.

Management by workers has been proposed, for instance, as an alternative to state control of the economy. But then one needs to inquire into the extent to which the workers can really participate in management, the consequences of direct participation of this type, the possibility of a new form of serfdom in which the costs of changing jobs become so great that workers become tied to their jobs, and other potential costs to the entire society. Are the consequences really to be feared? I do not know, but the issues certainly ought to be addressed.

On the other hand, the form of co-determination being practiced in the Federal Republic of Germany seems to produce both industrial peace and relative prosperity. Perhaps the German industrialists should be less opposed to it. Is the American authoritarian factory or industry the only valid model? There is some reason to believe that the Japanese form of management is superior and that the Swedish encouragement of worker initiative is more productive.

An interesting example of the way in which Marxist analysts cling to the metaphysical core of doctrine in searching for that body of evidence that will confirm it is provided by revisionist historians who attempt to show that the Marshall Plan was primarily a device for pursuing the welfare of American capitalism. Although the welfare of American capitalism is a legitimate objective of American policy makers, it is a simple distortion of the situation to interpret the Marshall Plan primarily in these terms.

I have asked students to search through the staff papers of the Policy Planning Staff of the State Department to discover why the plan was proposed. The reasons turn out to be the obvious ones: fear that economic disruption in Western Europe would lead to Communist victories in France and Italy and humanitarian concern for those countries even apart from the Communist threat.

However, the revisionists dig deeper to sustain their thesis; and they show, sometimes correctly, that the Marshall Plan established certain advantages for American businesses abroad. Ergo, regardless of the conscious purposes of the planners, the plan was an inevitable outgrowth of the desire to expand American capitalism.

The Congress of 1946 was extremely conservative and very reluctant to approve the huge expenditures required for the Marshall Plan, even though it had been assured that the plan would be good for American business. Some of the provisions added to the plan to gain congressional support made it more advantageous to American capitalists. This establishes only that, in any society, support for a project will be gained by concessions to the interests of those whose support is needed for its adoption. There is every reason to believe that if the United States had been a socialist country, it still would have provided a Marshall Plan for Europe. And in these circumstances the plan would have been adjusted to the needs of American socialists just as the Soviet Union's foreign ventures are adjusted to achieve consensus in the Politburo in that country. The most one can say of the relationship between American capitalism and the Marshall Plan is that a few of the concrete manifestations of the plan were specifically determined by the fact that the American economy is a capitalist economy. The present strength and competitiveness of the European economies, on the other hand, are a tribute to the effectiveness of the Marshall Plan in non-competitive terms.

One could argue that the trade-oriented big businessmen supported the Marshall Plan while the smaller and Midwestern businessmen opposed it, but the argument does not establish a convincing relationship between the plan and the economic structure of society. The foreign market was peripheral to big business at that time, particularly if one took into account the potential profit in domestic pump priming as opposed to foreign investments. It is far easier to assume that the same considerations that moved the policy makers in Washington influenced industrialists whose experience of the world made clear to them the political problems that would ensue from the collapse of Western Europe. Although one cannot ignore, in particular instances, a coincidence of narrow economic interests with the Marshall Plan, such an interpretation strains at a gnat and swallows a camel. The sociological network of interactions and reference groups was a far more powerful predictor than Marxian theory.

Furthermore, not even such broad aims as an increase in trade and reduced controls on trade can be traced to the specifically capitalistic aspects of the

Marshall Plan. The Soviet Union and China also appear to be interested in increased trade.

If my analysis is correct, then I have made my point that the diffuse empirical inquiries of Marxian analysts are consistent with what might be called a commitment to the metaphysical core of Marxian thought: a tight interrelatedness between key categories, simple concepts of class, and most of the bundles of policies that nations pursue.

Everything that I have seen indicates that Marx saw labor and capital as ultimate dichotomous antagonists. Even though his own accounts of society were far more complex than those of most contemporary Marxists, he believed that capitalism necessarily produced this conflict, whatever cross-alliances between groups of capitalists and laborers might form in temporary competition with others. This ultimate conflict was based on the dichotomous relationship of capital and labor to the forces of production. That is the driving determinant that to this day has not been eliminated from Marxian thought by contemporary Marxists.

Even though Marx and Engels, for instance, recognized that officials, during the period of "Asiatic production," constituted a class, this observation was not viewed as contradicting their analysis of the essence of capitalism, their view of historical change in the contemporary period, or their prescription for a socialist revolution. The system would be driven through its complexities until these simple alternatives were realized or stagnation occurred.

With a loosening of the concept of relatedness and Totality, even in Gramsci's sense of hegemony, one can respond to many possibilities that do not fit within Marx's essentialist view of alternatives. The comparative methods suggested by the test-in-principle permit the discussion of inner relatedness from a variety of non-deterministic frameworks. These methods also permit a multi-layered exploration of the concept of identification that does not truncate the conception of humanity.

In *Alienation and Identification*, I discussed in a general conceptual fashion the relationships among alienation, identification, authenticity, creativity, productivity, and style. Identification, rather than authenticity, was shown to be the correlative of alienation. Within this framework, a rich conception of human nature can be developed, one that is related to society as it is produced by the relationships among people.

A NOTE ON GRAMSCI*

It is only fair to note that my treatment of Antonio Gramsci, as Williams presents him, did not do full justice to Gramsci's position. Of all the Marxian writers— and particularly of those holding important political positions—he evinced the

---

*The quotations from Antonio Gramsci in this section are from Luciano Pellicani, *Gramsci: An Alternative Communism*? Copyright © 1981 by Hoover Institution Press, are used by permission of the publisher.

greatest capacity for intellectual growth and the greatest ability to move away from dogma. But because he identifies pragmatism with William James—whose misuse of the term "pragmatism" led Charles Sanders Peirce to coin the term "pragmaticism"—he did not comprehend the strong relation between his concept of praxis and pragmaticism.

It is not clear that Gramsci's concept of hegemony is as dualistic as it appears in Williams' account. To the contrary, Gramsci recognized that positions independent of class can arise. He wrote, for instance, that the fundamental principle of liberalism is the

> . . . separation of powers, and the source of liberalism's weakness then becomes apparent: it is the bureaucracy—i.e., the crystallization of the leading personnel— which exercises coercive power, and at a certain point it becomes a caste.[31]

He also observed that

> Politics becomes permanent action and gives birth to permanent organizations precisely insofar as it identifies itself with economics. But it is also distinct from it . . .[32]

Thus, economics and politics are not simply linked.

Moreover, his definition of the economic in his treatment of catharsis was genuinely sociological. Catharsis, he wrote, is the

> . . . passage from the purely economic (or egoistic-passional) to the ethico-political moment, that is, the superior elaboration of the structure into superstructure in the minds of men . . . the passage from "objective" to "subjective" and from "necessity" to "freedom." Structure ceases to be an external force which crushes man.[33]

Economics, here, refers merely to egoistic motives. This view is compatible with a complete reformulation of the Marxian categories of class. But Gramsci was not able to take this step because his thinking had not become thoroughly praxical. Thus, he wrote:

> In economics the unitary centre is value, alias the relationship between the worker and the industrial productive forces. Those who deny the theory fall into crass vulgar materialism by posing machines in themselves—as constant and technical capital— as producers of value independent of the man who runs them.[34]

And this inability to comprehend the creative function of the entrepreneur led him to further error.

Gramsci believed that the growth of workers' income in the United States was occurring only because the United States had a monopoly of the new means of production and predicted that the growth would end when the rest of the world caught up.[35] There is, however, every reason to believe that Gramsci would have recognized the capacity of modern capitalism to increase income generally had he lived.

Unfortunately, he did not live long enough to take this next step, which would have led him to a more completely praxical analysis. The impulse to do so would have been reinforced by his opposition to physical repression. Although

Gramsci was critical of parliaments and was searching for alternative methods of representation,[36] he consistently opposed repression and in particular was a firm advocate of intellectual freedom:

> In other words . . . who is to fix the "rights of knowledge" and the limits of the pursuit of knowledge? . . . It seems better to leave the task of researching after new truths and better, more coherent, clearer formulations of the truths themselves to the free initiative of individual specialists, even though they may continually question the very principles that seem most essential.[37]

He quickly qualified this liberal position, however:

> Besides, it will not be difficult to expose those initiatives motivated by interests and not by science. For the rest, it is not impossible to imagine that individual initiatives could be disciplined and ordered by passing through the sieve of the academy and cultural institutions of various sorts, and only after having been selected become public.[38]

In other words, those assertions inconsistent with Marxism could be kept from the public by official institutions. The very aspects of Marxian dogma that have been criticized here would control society as soon as the "new religion" had achieved social hegemony.

This interpretation is reinforced by Gramsci's assertion that "Ideological unity is necessary for the communist party to fulfill its function as the guide of the working class."[39] Thus, the specific class reification that moves Marxism toward totalitarianism reappears. It is reinforced by Gramsci's assertion that "The communist party represents the totality of the interests and aspirations of the working class."[40]

Furthermore, the central committee, or the Prince:

> . . . assumes the place of *divinity* and of the categorical imperative. . . . [E]very act is conceived as useful or harmful, as virtuous or wicked, only insofar as its point of reference is the modern Prince himself and it serves to incriminate or hinder his power.[41]

Gramsci does not even hesitate to apply the term "totalitarian" to this process in which objective truth is of indifferent value or even meaningless. His goal is "inner and outer unification" or "the reconstruction of the world" in peace and absence of conflict.[42]

Despite these qualifications, Gramsci longed for human freedom. Who can say where he might have stood on the issue of private ownership were he still alive? Would disbelieving in it have been central to his concept of socialism? Or would Gramsci—who believed that every form of state has the moral function of raising the level of the masses[43]—have viewed socialism as the creation of institutions that fostered nonegoistical motivations as a complement to egoistical ones, thus developing a far more complex and more satisfactory solution?

THE STATE

There are long discussions of what Marx meant by the dictatorship of the proletariat and whether or not his writings justified a political dictatorship in the countries of Western Europe. I cannot pursue an exegesis of Marx's position on this issue here. I shall only adumbrate a position. With respect to the issue of how closely things are connected, I have already criticized Williams' arguments for hegemony. By the same token, I reject the notion that the state is necessarily an organ of the ruling class. And Marx's own view was more complex.

Some states may be the self-conscious agency of a ruling class. In some states, the holders of political power and other privileged groups have such cohesive interests that they are disposed to close cooperation. There is, however, no necessity in this.

The state is obviously responsive, in part, to organized society and in part is independent of it, with imperatives of its own. Power within the state is sought by persons whose relationship to social classes is often quite peripheral. There is within a political system a set of partly autonomous interests that form part of the complex social and political structure. This complex transactional process affects the values of society, the development of institutions within it, and the rewards to individuals and groups.

Moreover, except for Communist states, states that are the agencies of ruling classes are very unlikely to attempt to regulate the bulk of society at large. The great distinction between Communist states and other dictatorships lies in the extent to which they penetrate into the mass of society and create a compradore class whose interests are so tightly tied to the ruling regime that they assist it in suppressing the rest of society in virtually all of its manifestations.

Whereas the authoritarian state sits like a parasite on the back of its prey, the Communist state, like a cancer, spreads its tentacles into all the organisms of society. It is the true ruling state. Of course, even a Communist state does not quite match the ideal structure, but it comes closest of all forms of state. It is worth considering whether the attraction to Marxism for some of the radical African leaders lies not in social justice but in Leninist methods as a means of maintaining control of state and society.

Whatever Marx meant by his analysis of the state and of the dictatorship of the ruling class, these concepts are enormously destructive because they appear to legitimize a political solution of a problem that does not exist in the form described by Marx. Because his fundamental categories—including class, surplus value, and alienation—are mistaken, a state established to solve the problems they represent will impose its solutions on uncomprehending and unwilling subjects. Since these attempts may resemble those of a child to repair a complicated watch, they are far more likely to create unanticipated side effects than they are to mitigate the real problems that Marx sometimes noted in passing.

No doubt we have many destructive muddlers in high office in capitalist societies just as we have destructive muddlers in medicine, the law, and auto-repair shops. The problem with Marxian muddlers lies in the scope of their ambition. Like the doctor who removed the only kidney of a patient because he failed to take an X-ray, the Marxian muddler in his attempt to achieve a total solution may push us past the point of no return. No self-respecting social scientist would claim that we have even begun to understand the profound relationships of humans to society and economy or that we are likely to do well in predicting the effect of change. Social science was incapable of predicting the effect of the automobile on American social life. Marxian predictions deal with the interrelationships of extremely complex systems about which we have only scattered information.

The virtue of Marxian analysis, when contrasted with much of contemporary social science, is that it is focussed on issues that are important. Its defect is that, even at its most sophisticated, it deals with these issues in a simplistic fashion that reverts to true writ when fundamentals come into question.

It is a shame that the important question of the dynamics of the economy, which Marx proposed in provocative form, is neglected by contemporary economists. This neglect occurs partly because the subject is so difficult to deal with, but also partly because Marxian discussions are so dominated by Marx's essentialist theory that the subject is discredited in non-Marxian circles.

There is some merit to the claim that immense political difficulties would arise if the Western economy ceased to grow. As more of the economy is devoted to services, the potentiality for growth may decline. If the estimates of declining natural resources made by the Club of Rome are correct—and I doubt it—or if we fail to develop alternative resources at reasonable prices, then the problem of growth of the economy may become very serious.

This problem will develop in both capitalist and socialist economies. However, the two distribute the cost of the interruption of growth in different ways. In a capitalist economy, the costs are largely decentralized, except in extreme situations. And in modern capitalist economies, social benefits compensate to a considerable extent for some of these costs. But socialist economies cannot escape the problem of investment decisions either, for the cost of capital is a real cost in every system, regardless of the accounting methods used. In a socialist economy, these costs are merely distributed differently.

We need far more extensive study of the problem of growth and decline in the economy as a complex process involving complex feedback loops, and we need better methods of dealing with these problems. It is not a foregone conclusion that growth cannot continue indefinitely, for information revolutions and other types of scientific revolutions may entirely transform the economy. This may make obsolete most of our notions about society and humanity, including both capitalist and socialist notions.

MARX'S SYSTEM

I agree finally with those who see a basic continuity, although perhaps not identity, in the writings of the young and of the mature Marx. The materialistic dialectic and the theory of surplus value are both necessary to Marx's "scientific" account of the supercession of capitalism by socialism. Without the theory of surplus value, other transformations of sociopolitical structures would have as much merit as socialism; without the dialectic, no transformation, let alone the socialist one, could be predicted from the theory of surplus value. Also essential are the concrete universal, in the absence of which Marx's concept of classes would have no foundation, and the concepts of Totality, identity, and essence, in the absence of which Marxian socialism would not be a solution to the problems Marx found in capitalist society. It is because these axioms, theorems, or concepts are the core of Marxian theory that Marx's variable and indeterministic phenomenological accounts never disturb the inner determinism of his system. They are corollary aspects of Marx's theory that serve the same function as Hegel's phenomenology does in his theory. They qualify and complement its inner truths, but they never contradict them. And because contemporary Marxists tend to retain them, they tend toward dichotomous and deterministic conclusions also.

I have no wish to incriminate Karl Marx, who was one of the most seminal intellectual figures of the nineteenth century. Within the philosophical milieu in which he wrote, Marx was a genuinely progressive figure. He pushed forward what might be called a systemic pragmaticist view of philosophy, even though it was not possible for him to do this consistently or ultimately to escape dogma. He opened up essential lines of investigation into the relationship of the polity and the economy, even though he consistently reverted to essences and determinism. Marx denied that he was a Marxist and recognized that his work would have to be transcended. The tragedy of contemporary Marxian thought lies in the fact that it has not transcended Marx in significant ways.

NOTES

1. Karl Marx, *Economic and Philosophic Manuscripts of 1844* (Moscow: Progress Publishers, 1974), p. 98.
2. Ibid., p. 136.
3. Ibid., pp. 68–69.
4. Ibid., p. 69.
5. Ibid., p. 70.
6. Ibid., pp. 91–92.
7. Bertell Ollman, *Alienation: Marx's Conception of Man in Capitalist Society* (Cambridge: Cambridge University Press, 1971), pp. 117–118.
8. Marx, *Economic and Philosophical Manuscript*, p. 109.
9. Ollman, *Alienation*, p. 118.
10. Ibid., p. 120.
11. See Morton A. Kaplan, *On Historical and Political Knowing: An Inquiry into Some Problems of Universal Law and Human Freedom* (Chicago: University of Chicago Press, 1971), p. 147.

12. Marx, *Economic and Philosophical Manuscripts*, pp. 134–135.

13. Ibid.

14. Ibid., p. 136.

15. Ibid., p. 94.

16. Ibid., p. 94.

17. Ibid., p. 95.

18. Ibid., p. 95.

19. Ibid., pp. 100–101.

20. Ibid., p. 72.

21. Ollman, *Alienation*, p. 107.

22. Ibid., p. 138.

23. Kaplan, *On Historical and Political Knowing*, pp. 117–120.

24. Jon Elster, "The Labor Theory of Value: A Reinterpretation of Marxist Economics," *Marxist Perspectives*, (Fall 1978), p. 89.

25. Ollman, *Alienation*, p. 33.

26. Morris R. Cohen, *Perface to Logic* (New York: Henry Holt & Company, 1944), pp. 4 ff.

27. For a fuller treatment of this problem, see Morton A. Kaplan, *On Freedom and Human Dignity: The Importance of the Sacred in Politics* (Morristown, N.J.: General Learning Press, 1973), pp. 46 ff.

28. Ferdinand Tönnies, *Community and Society: Gemeinschaft und Gesellschaft*, translated by Charles P. Loomis (East Lansing, Mich.: Michigan State University Press, 1957).

29. Morton A. Kaplan, *Alienation and Identification* (New York: Free Press, 1976), pp. 17–25.

30. Raymond Williams, *Marxism and Literature* (Oxford: Oxford University Press, 1977), p. 113.

31. Antonio Gramsci, *Selections from the Prison Notebooks*, edited and translated by Quintin Hoare and Geoffrey Nowell Smith (New York: International Publishers, 1977), p. 246.

32. Ibid., pp. 139–140.

33. Ibid., pp. 366–367.

34. Ibid., p. 402.

35. Ibid., pp. 310–311.

36. Ibid., p. 254.

37. Ibid.

38. Antonio Gramsci, *Quaderni del carcere* (Turin: Guilio Einaudi Editore, 1975), quoted in Luciano Pellicani, *Gramsci: An Alternative Communism?* (Stanford: Hoover Institution Press, Stanford University, 1981), p. 10.

39. Antonio Gramsci, *La costruzione del partito communista: 1923–1926* (Turin: Guilio Einaudi, Editore, 1971), quoted in Pellicani, p. 66.

40. Ibid., quoted in Pellicani, *Gramsci*, p. 77.

41. Antonio Gramsci, *Quaderni del carcere*, quoted in Pellicani, *Gramsci*, p. 79.

42. Antonio Gramsci, *L'ordine nuovo*, quoted in Pellicani, *Gramscip*. 81.

43. Antonio Gramsci, *Selections from the Prison Notebooks*, p. 254.

Chapter 16
A Contemporary Social Science: Economics

My colleague, the economist Milton Friedman is, in my opinion, the best contemporary expositor of the neo-classicist position, and I am therefore basing my presentation of neo-classic theory on his work. I shall not restate the position in any detail, for it should be familiar to anyone who has read *Capitalism and Freedom*.*

If the market is free of governmental restraints and monopoly, then according to his analysis it will maximize the satisfactions of people by allowing their preferences to determine what is produced and made available for sale. The decentralization that promotes efficiency, he says, also promotes democracy. Friedman argues that the free-market system is most compatible with democracy because it maximizes the number of influences on decisions and because it serves primarily as a rule maker and umpire in society. Although Friedman considers anarchy the ideal form of government,[1] people, he says, are imperfect. Therefore, absolute freedom is impossible and some minimal level of government is necessary.

The problem is that Friedman attempts to derive too much from the pure theory of competition without assessing the extent to which the theory is relevant to the actual world. The counterfactual assumption of a vacuum in Newton's theory of mechanics is useful because it is possible to take atmospheric friction into account in order to, for instance, predict the path of a missile. In the social sciences, assessments are more difficult and independent measurements are not available. It must be shown that counterfactual premises can be corrected for, as in physics. In any event, in nonmechanical systems comparative theory is the correct approach, for reasons provided in chapter 3. Friedman merely assumes the appropriateness of a single general theory and searches for that set of axioms—e.g., income maximization—that will not conflict with his theory.

Let me consider some particular issues examined by Friedman, for example,

---

*The quotations and summaries from Milton S. Friedman's *Capitalism and Freedom*, copyright © 1962 by The University of Chicago Press, are used by courtesy of the publisher.

his treatment of licensure. Friedman argues that, at first examination, licensing of physicians seems to make sense because citizens should be protected from untrained, incompetent practitioners. However, he then points out that the American Medical Association "is perhaps the strongest trade union in the United States."[2] Its power, he says, lies in its ability to control access to the profession and thereby to maintain high fees. He provides historical evidence that it has done so both by direct control over licensing of doctors and through the licensing of medical schools.

The rationalization of licensure, he says, is that only high-quality medical treatment ought to be available. No one would argue that automobile manufacturers should be prohibited from producing automobiles that do not come to the standard of the Cadillac, but people do defend restrictions on producing physicians. Friedman says that these restrictions do not really work, for the restrictions on the practice of medicine and the increase in its price, among other things, have given rise to the osteopathic and chiropractic professions. Moreover, he says, physicians devote much of their time to activities that could be well performed by technicians.

Friedman argues that

> . . . advances in any science or field often result from the work of one out of a large number of crackpots and quacks and people who have no standing in the profession. In the medical profession, under present circumstances, it is very difficult to engage in research or experimentation unless you are a member of the profession. If you are a member of the profession and want to stay in good standing . . . you are seriously limited in what you can do.[3]

There are, he says, many different routes to knowledge, and orthodoxy tends to cut these off.

Friedman writes that he suspects that many people will still say that licensure is their best way of getting evidence of the competence of a physician. He argues, however, that people do not choose physicians by picking their names at random from a list and that having passed a licensing examination twenty years ago is hardly any assurance of present competence.

Then he speculates about how medicine might have developed and what assurances of quality would have emerged if the profession had not become a monopoly. Suppose, he says, that

> . . . anyone had been free to practice medicine without restriction, except for legal and financial responsibility for any harm done to others through fraud and negligence.[4]

Under these circumstances, the practice of medicine would have been quite different. Group practice in conjunction with hospitals would probably have developed along with medical partnerships or corporations. These groups would have provided central diagnostic and treatment facilities, and probably some form of hospital and health insurance. Other groups would have done things differently. "Department stores of medicine" would have mediated between the physician and the patient. These groups, he says, would have developed their reputations and would have maintained them by controlling the quality of the doctors admitted to the group. Individuals would become more familiar with the reputation of the "department store of medicine" than they could with any individual doctor. Of course, Friedman says, there would still be personal physicians even without a system of licensure.

Friedman has made a case for the abolition of licensure, as he has done in so many others of his arguments, that leaves me willing to reconsider a position that until then I had rejected out of hand. However, his position, although illuminated by his neo-classical theory of economics, is not derived from it. He is forced to make a number of *ad hoc* assumptions about how doctors would be produced and how they would organize under a system in which licensure was absent. Whether or not his guesses are accurate depends upon the milieu. He might be right about the United States, but I doubt even this. I believe that confidence men would reappear faster than they were unmasked and that most would not be unmasked, that life expectancy would decline, that infant mortality would increase, and that the maimed would proliferate. And even if Friedman were right about the United States, there would be other cultures in which things would happen differently.

There are important areas of economic activity that involve processes quite different from those Friedman discusses. For instance, I once speculated that the inefficiency of the American steel industry stems from the fact those who chair the boards and are the operating presidents of companies are usually about five years from retirement and receive very large bonuses for profitable performance. Thus, although they might have been able to predict, from the success of the Prussian steel industry in the late nineteenth century, that similar conditions would arise in Western Europe and Japan after World War II, the personal cost of prudent measures to prevent this development would have been too great.

A distinguished economist, whose position is somewhat similar to Friedman's, responded to this argument by saying that, if it were correct, the price of shares of steel would have adjusted to the managers' lack of foresight and they would have been forced to take corrective measures.

If the stock market really adjusted to the long-term future—even assuming that the ordinary investor knew as much as the top management of the steel industry—one would expect to see this knowledge reflected in the market values of stocks. One of the biggest mistakes I ever made when I was investing in the market was to buy shares in cryogenic companies too long before the new techniques became profitable.

A large number of investors, including the largest institutional investors, make major decisions based on relatively short-term shifts in the prices of stocks. Trading in shares is based far less on expectations about the long run than it is on guesses about what other investors will do over the short or intermediate term. Even if investors think that an industry will collapse in twenty years, they are likely to invest in it and drive the price of shares up if they think it will do well in the next several years. The simple fact is that the behavior of the market does not predict consequences a generation hence, let alone consequences that lie ten or sometimes even two years in the future.

More recently, Milton Friedman argued in the pages of *Newsweek* against imposing a limit on imports of less expensive Japanese steel on the grounds that such a move would increase the cost to the American consumer and that the country is best off under the principle of comparative advantage. Possibly so, but the cost to the average American consumer of a slight increase in the price of steel is relatively small, while the cost to the steel worker of unemployment is large. It very well may be legitimate to protect large numbers of workers against a sudden loss of jobs. One, however, could argue for direct subsidies to the steel workers rather than a quota on imported Japanese steel.

Furthermore, those who are directly hurt will protest politically. Therefore, the refusal to restrict the importation of Japanese steel, rather than reinforcing a situation of comparative advantage, might increase the politicization of trade measures and countermeasures, moving American trade practice toward more rather than fewer restrictions.

In any event, the argument for comparative advantage assumes a world without partitions. In the real world, the Japanese did well to protect their infant industries while they were building control of their own domestic market and achieving efficiencies of scale. The large surplus of dollars they accumulated was a reasonable price to pay for the prosperity that Japan has achieved and that it likely would not have achieved in the absence of those measures.

Furthermore, the neo-classical model is essentially static. The economy is dynamic: it is a complex process in which expectations about the future are politically as well as economically important. Our understanding of the dynamic economy is very limited. Friedman's evidence of the efficiencies of the market seems sufficiently strong to warrant that there be very great reason before interference is permitted. However, in the last analysis, it is necessary to make a praxical analysis in order to discover the relevance of the model to actual situations. There is a dangerous tendency to overgeneralize the methodology and a failure to distinguish between the logic of the model and practical problems.

Politically, Friedman's model of the economy is an ideal that can work only in part. The Manchesterian state, which exercised only security functions, is well behind us, if it ever really existed. Although there is widespread feeling in the United States that government regulation of the economy has reached a point at which it is obstructing economic progress, it seems clear that the hypothesis that the state could be restricted to minimal security functions can be no more than a regulatory idea at best. Any system of taxation or of property rights is a system for structuring incentives and organizational capacities. Many conglomerate businesses are less a response to economic uncertainty than to the tax laws.

The question is not whether government keeps its hands off business, but what it does when it puts its hands on business. Tax laws can be structured to stimulate economic growth, protect the environment, or for almost any other purpose. They can allow business to find its own ways to meet the regulative objectives and pay penalties if it does not. They can bury business in a mass of regulations administered by a government bureaucracy. The government, if it wishes, can insist upon codetermination of large businesses on the German model.* It can regulate the inheritance laws to attenuate the transfer of wealth. It can either outlaw the production of "gas-guzzling" automobiles or tax their purchase heavily. It can even tax automotive companies on the basis of the kinds of automobiles they produce. If the government wishes to pay the associated costs, it can provide tenure to corporation executives. If it wishes to ration gasoline, it can.

Friedman's economic model reifies the concept of desires or wants.** He fails to recognize the extent to which our wants depend upon how the institutions of society process wants. For instance, the dominance in the 1960s of rock music and, in the 1970s, of weird nightclub acts was a response to the fact that most records are bought by teenagers, that those whose records sell appear on TV and receive other publicity, and that teenagers were a large portion of the population. As a consequence, aging corporate and account executives appeared wearing bangs, long beads, and earrings in an attempt to be "with it." Society soirées featured rock groups popular with the young. To argue that this phenomenon maximized the satisfaction of wants, without relating it to the processing of wants by the social system, is to misuse a tautology.

In France today, the small bakery and street food stall are still vigorous, but already under attack by larger businesses. No doubt this is occurring because individuals, offered cheaper and more convenient products, buy them in larger numbers. These individuals do not choose to freeze the small store out of business. The market simply processes their individual demands.

Does the market really maximize the satisfaction of wants? Suppose, for instance, that individuals were permitted to vote on whether the styling of automobiles is to be changed every two years or only every five years? Or on whether some kinds of small businesses, e.g., bakeries, receive tax advantages. Would their decisions be the same as they are when their individual demands are processed?

Perhaps the alternatives to the market's processing of demands without political constraints would be even worse. In the United States, there has been some return to specialized products. Maybe, over a sufficiently long period of time, the negative consequences of the completely free market are reduced or even overcome. At least, this question is one to be decided by complex and detailed investigation rather than by a conclusion derived from a theory.

On the other hand, perhaps the worst aspect of the public debate about the problems of the economy is that it directs attention away from the real problems of the economy. It is possible that large capital-intensive industries, such as

---

*By law, West German unions are represented on the boards of directors of large corporations.

**The concept of wants is reified because it is divorced from the social processes that constrain alternatives and that facilitate the expression of some wants and inhibit those of others.

automobile and steelmaking, are now more suitable for developing economies than for post-modern economies such as the United States and Japan. These vast, bureaucratic enterprises no longer require very skilled workers or creative managers. Even were they better managed than they have been recently in the United States, I doubt that they would remain the prime employers of the vast human resources of the United States.

The most efficient and creative industries in the United States today are the relatively small ones. But relatively little attention is paid by economists to the fact that governmental administrative and purchasing decisions, tax and regulatory laws, and other policies create incentives for corporate mergers and large corporate growth and that they harm small, efficient, and creative businesses. Our neo-classical economists are so bewitched by their formal theories and their quantitative studies that they have little time for comparative and dynamic analysis. The current attempt of President Reagan's administration to reduce federal regulation of business is far too abstract to cut to the core of the actual problem. Although the neo-classical theory of the economy does far less violence to reality than do the Marxian concepts, and although Milton Friedman in particular affords lucid insights into economic questions, neo-classical theory cannot be used in the the absence of a praxical investigation of its relevance.

NOTES

1. For a principled argument against anarchy, see Morton A. Kaplan, *Justice, Human Nature, and Political Obligation* (New York: Free Press, 1976), pp. 194 ff. and 200–202.

2. Milton Friedman, *Capitalism and Freedom* (Chicago: University of Chicago Press, 1962), pp. 149 ff.

3. Ibid., p. 157.

4. Ibid., p. 158.

Chapter 17
International Relations

In the preceding chapters, I made much of the problems of justifying a theory by praxical methods and pointed out that Marxian and neo-classical theories often failed when tested against the evidence. Even a mathematical demonstration of a fit between the predictions of a theory and the circumstances of the real world will not by itself confirm a theory. In an illuminating and ingenious article, "Alliance Behavior in Balance of Power Systems: Applying a Poisson Model to Nineteenth-century Europe," Patrick J. McGowan and Robert M. Rood attempted to justify my theory of the "balance of power" by showing that alliances were stochastically distributed, as the theory predicts; that the time intervals between alliances were randomly distributed, as the theory predicts; that, more specifically, the distribution of interalliance intervals is a negative exponential random variable; and that a decline in the systematic rate of alliance formation precedes system-changing events such as general war. They concluded that my theory "has greater credibility than heretofore."[1]

Within limits, I accept their conclusions, although it must be noted that I did not make an exception of the period just before a war. Moreover, in my terms, World War I was an unlimited war, contrary to predictions derived from my "balance of power" theory under conditions of equilibrium. However, I find the remainder of their results acceptable if, and only if, one can show on the basis of external and internal criteria that the period in question was a period of "balance of power" as I use the term; otherwise, there are no grounds for asserting that the theory explains the behavior. Moreover, even if the system is a "balance of power" type, it is also necessary to scan the environment and to ask whether it is consistent with the environment posited by the theory if equilibrium is to be expected. If it is not, behavior congruent with the theory may be a disconfirmation of some aspect of the theory.

Theories are closed systems, while the real world in which they are to be applied is an open system. On the basis of the "balance of power" theory, one would expect, under equilibrium conditions, alliances to be short-lived, based on immediate interests, and neglectful of existing or previous alliances.[2] The progressively rigid alliances developed by European countries between 1871 and 1914, and the relatively unlimited nature of World War I, are superficially at least, inconsistent with the prescriptions of the "balance of power" theory. One could resolve the problem by viewing the period from 1871 to 1914 as a rigid "balance of power" system. This type of solution, however, would require the use of a different systems theory for every characteristically different set of relations among international actors, thus depriving the concept of "system" of much of its theoretical meaning and turning it into a descriptive device. The alternative procedure is to decide whether the underlying theory of the "balance of power" system can be used to explain the discrepancies.

If the theory of the "balance of power" system can account for the rigid alliances of 1879 to 1914 and the unlimited character of World War I if boundary deviations from equilibrium are taken into account, it does not thereby become *the* explanation of the deviant behavior. Other factors undoubtedly played important roles in producing both the specific sequence of events and their general form. I will merely have established that the so-called irregular or deviant behavior does not invalidate the theory and that, using it, we may be able to relate a wider range of phenomena than we could without such a theory. This may increase the confidence that can be placed in the correctness of the theory and its explanatory power.

The praxical reconciliation of theory and events follows. If one recognizes, as Bismarck—who was constrained by German domestic politics to conduct a dysfunctional foreign policy—foresaw, that the seizure of Alsace-Lorraine by Prussia would provoke revanchism in France, the theory would lead one to expect events like those that did occur. As long as Germany was unwilling to return Alsace-Lorraine to France, France would be Germany's enemy. Thus France and Germany became the poles of ultimately rigid and opposed alliances, as neither would enter—or at least remain in—the same coalition, regardless of other common interests. The chief motive for the limitation of war against enemy actors, according to the theory, is the need to maintain them as potential allies. For the foreseeable future, however, France and Germany were not potential allies. Consequently, neither had the incentive—as they normally would in a "balance of power" system—to limit its war aims against the other as the essential rules of the system prescribe. What had been an incentive for limitation became instead a disincentive. The theory is consistent with the seemingly discordant behavior when we take into account the changed environment.

Many historians explain the breakdown of the historical "balance of power" system in 1870 as caused by nationalism. This is misleading. Although it is true that nationalism interfered with the Dual Monarchy's ability to function as an essential national actor, nationalism accounts only for the deviant behavior of the Dual Monarchy and, thus, is an environmental consideration rather than an element in a theory of international politics. To the extent that nationalism prevented Bismarck from acting rationally in the matter of Alsace-Lorraine or that it led to an inappropriate French response, again it affects only an environmental or boundary condition. It did so for reasons that were accidental in terms of a theory of the system. That is, in principle, all the actors could have been nationalistic without creating instability. It was only as they applied their policies that conflicts arose between the internal problems of the regimes and rational foreign policy. In principle, nothing required, in a real but nationalistic world, a problem like Alsace-Lorraine or a state like the Dual Monarchy. That is why the effect of nationalism on the breakdown of the balance of power system was indirect, and even accidental, from the standpoint of a theory of international politics. Nationalism, in combination with other factors, explains why a boundary change occurred. It does not identify the particular boundary change as inconsistent with international equilibrium in the absence of a theory of the international system nor explain why it affected the system as it did. Only a theory of the international system permits the identification and explanation.

The European system after 1870 is also a good example of how praxical analysis can be applied to a particular situation. Bismarck's effort to build a Germany that would be a major, and even possibly the most important, nation in the international system was not in itself destabilizing. However, the domestic support that enabled him to block the emperor's policies after Sadowa and to pursue his other foreign policy objectives made it impossible for him to allow France to keep Alsace-Lorraine even though he was aware of the problem its seizure would cause. The reinsurance treaties were part of Bismarck's effort to shore-up a system that he knew had lost some degree of stability. However, in the crucial instance of Alsace-Lorraine, his need for a domestic base of support precluded the rational foreign policy that is a condition of stability in the model. French public opinion then made it impossible for France to react rationally. What occurred thereafter is consistent with what the theory predicts under this set of boundary conditions. A complete praxical assessment, however, would require, in addition, an examination of the stability problems of the Dual Monarchy, the character of the mobilization system of the pre-World War I period, and of many other conditions.

The method just used is merely a variant of the normal testing of a theory. International theory sketches can be tested as theories are supposed to be tested. That is, seemingly discordant behavior can be explained through praxical application of the theory or theory sketch, as I have just done.

On the other hand, seemingly concordant information is not in itself confirmatory, for one must be able to show that the situation corresponds with the conditions under which that behavior is expected. Thus, for instance, Winfried Franke's analysis of Italy's city-state system showed that, in its first phase, the behavior of the system was consistent with the essential rules of the "balance of power" system. However, further analysis showed that this consistency depended upon boundary conditions such as the absence of a state apparatus and, hence, of a bureaucracy that could continue hegemonic policies after the death of a duke, deficient logistics, and other external reasons.[3] Hence, the theory does not account for the system's rule-congruent behavior in that phase of the system.

In the absence of international theories and theory sketches and praxical analysis, it would not be possible even to conduct such an investigation. Moreover, when such theory sketches are used, it is possible to search more systematically and more coherently for the circumstances that produce or reinforce various states of equilibria or disequilibria. Thus, praxical analysis is not open-ended; seemingly concordant behavior can fail to confirm a theory; and seemingly discordant behavior can turn out to be consistent with a theory. Praxical reasoning is subject to the same community activity of science as theoretical reasoning.

The reader will see from the previous section that theory sketches in international relations (and also in the other social sciences) are not merely descriptive, that they do give some power in analysis. But because of the greater variance at the boundaries of the social systems, for reasons discussed in chapter 3, the correct method of analysis is to use comparative theories that deal with different types of similar systems.

NOTES

1. Patrick J. McGowan and Robert M. Rood, "Alliance Behavior in Balance of Power Systems: Applying a Poisson Model to Nineteenth-Century Europe," *American Political Science Review* 69, no. 3 (September 1976), p. 870.

2. See Morton A. Kaplan, *Towards Professionalism in International Theory* (New York: Free Press, 1979) pp. 134 ff, for a statement of "balance of power" theory, of its three types of equilibria, of boundary conditions, and of the rationale for limited wars and shifting alliances. Donald L. Reinken, in "Computer Explorations of the Balance of Power," in *New Approaches to International Relations*, edited by Morton A. Kaplan (New York: St. Martin's Press, 1968), pp. 459–482, discusses a computer realization model of a "balance of power" system.

3. Winfried Franke, "The Italian City-State System as an International System," in *New Approaches to International Relations*, edited by Morton A. Kaplan (New York: St. Martin's Press, 1968).

Epilogue

By this time, even the perceptive reader may be thinking: "I understand Kaplan's philosophy of science, his use of signs, his epistemology, his value theory, and his objections to alternative positions. However, what is his justification for asserting that his position restores the human race to its place in a natural universe?"

For the same reasons that I did not attempt to sketch a systematic position on the nature of humanity and on a schema of values, I cannot present in this book a systematic position on the place of humanity in a natural universe. Such a discussion would fall in the realm of praxis. Because of the weak relationships among a multiplicity of perspectives, both first and second order, any attempt to state a systematic position would divert attention from the philosophical positions I wish to emphasize, and emphasize instead the quarrels over particular hypotheses.

My aim, in discussing the realm of values, is to establish the legitimacy of a claim that values are objective and perhaps common. My claim for the place of the human race in the world is equally limited. I wish to establish only that the concept is legitimate and that at least partial answers to the inquiry are possible.

I would not be entirely unjustified in saying that an outline of an answer has already been sketched in the book. In the first place, whatever the order of the world, it is not the strongly coherent, univocal, and hierarchical order of classical sign theory. The impressive arguments against that world view do not defeat the contention that the human race has a natural place in a natural universe. Beyond this, I have shown, in contradistinction to Derrida, for example, that the concept of potentiality is valid. This enables us to support the concept of evolution—and not merely of biological evolution—although not in a univocal or fully determinate fashion. In cosmological terms, for instance, we can understand that the world of galaxies and solar systems likely evolved out of a primal bang, even as we can argue legitimately over alternative hypotheses as to how this happened. We can understand that evolution produced not merely inorganic but also plant and animal life. We also can understand that intelligence evolved in this process. Rather than being a purely random process in a cold and foreign universe, as Jacques Monod asserted,* we can see that these developments likely

---

*Jacques Monod, a French Nobel Laureate in biology, argued that evolution is a matter of chance and that there is no purpose in the world.

are inherent in the universe, although not foreordained, uniquely determined, or derived from the inner relations of a theory. By deciphering the DNA code, we can see the intimate linkage between humans and their evolutionary precursors.

But the case for a hospitable cosmos may be stronger. In *Macropolitics*, I speculated:

> If all organic material were multistable, or at least ultrastable, then all organic material would have regulatory components. If this were so, it would be possible for the systems to regulate not only to maintain the value of some essential variable but also to increase some aspect of it.[1]

The hypothesis of molecular drive accounts for speciation. However, molecular drive is internal to molecular processes and not external, as are mutation, adaptation, and genetic drift. There may be other drives we have not yet anticipated.

Although the ordinary arguments in favor of design that are based on the improbability of life are not interesting—in the game of bridge, for instance, any hand is just as improbable as thirteen spades—there are arguments different from mine that deserve consideration. Hiroshi Nagai, for instance, argued that for chance to produce the dominant L-type configuration of amino acids, it would take 10^{100} different types of protein. "The weight of all these proteins would amount to 10^{75} tons. . . . When one considers the fact that the weight of all matter in the universe is roughly estimated at 10^{40} tons, even if the universe were wholly composed of amino acids alone it could not satisfy the demand to produce the required protein of 100 amino acids in accordance with a certain designed order in only a mechanistic way."[1] Sir Fred Hoyle and Chandra Wickramasinghe, two eminent scientists, have made careful calculations that show, they say, that evolution, as we know it, could not have occurred in the absence of externally-supplied information.

Hoyle and Wickramasinghe have shown, rather convincingly I believe, that neither chance nor any current evolutionary hypothesis can account for the evolution of the species. Their hypothesis that external intelligence (divinity?) produced the evolution of the species is not necessarily wrong. Yet, despite the good fit between modest changes in the molecular structure of DNA and the carbon-dating of the origins of individual species, it would require us to believe that external intelligence modified the DNA structure of individual species at widely spaced intervals of time. It would seem more reasonable to believe on the basis of what we know about natural events that some as yet undiscovered natural process was at work.

Moreover, the extreme sensitivity of life to the narrow range of conditions that make it possible is at least suggestive of fine tuning. To speak of design is to use a metaphor that depends on an ant's-eye view. To suggest, however, that the cosmos is a mystery that we do not begin to understand and that the mechanistic views of the universe that are so popular are equally naive is reasonable. Life, including conscious, moral, and rational life, may be inherent potentialities of our universe, toward which its components have a tendency to move. That hypothesis may be wrong, but it is not absurd.

When we turn to social evolution, we can see it not merely in the relativistic terms used by most anthropologists, but as involving conscious as well as non-conscious choices in which values come into play. These values are understandable in their circumstances and subject to second-order modification as the realm of knowledge enlarges. Thus, the choices that people and societies make are determined not merely by environmental circumstance or unique histories, but at least in part by the mental capacity to rise to a second-order level of consideration and to develop conceptions of justice on a broadly comparative basis.

We can understand how second-order forms of reasoning, and not merely environmental factors of scale, have helped to widen the range of human identification from family to tribe to state to mankind and even to animals and to nature. Thus, although I cannot assert with the classical social evolutionists that societies must go through particular stages in a particular order or that any particular stage of social evolution has a unique content, neither do I see the process as only a chance one.

There is still another way in which we can see an outline or hint of the nature of humans and of their relationship to their world. And this manner of doing so may help to bridge the gap between Eastern and Western philosophy. Scientific theory, which has been the motor of economic and political development in the West, has produced an abstract and manipulative approach to nature.

Praxis, however, has more in common with the intuitive, pragmatic, and communal qualities of Eastern philosophy. In praxical reasoning, closer attention is paid the similarities and differences that individualize persons, things, events, and processes. Particularly in areas in which there is a strong interdependence between the internal variables of a field and their environment—in the social sciences, the key role of identification was noted—we are brought close to the sensible, the individual, and the unique aspects of life. The theoretical and the praxical are correlative techniques; each is misleading in the absence of the other. Thus, it may be that we have reached the stage in social, scientific, and philosophical development at which we recognize the onesidedness of either approach and at which we may be ready for a cultural reorientation in which they are blended.

In *Alienation and Identification* I developed this theme, investigated the aspects of being, distinguished the role of identification from that of authenticity, and related creativity, productivity, and style. This is not the place to recapitulate that discussion, but it complements my previous remarks about reconciling Eastern and Western ways of looking at the world.

Literary critics have sometimes noticed a disjunction between philosophical novels and novels dealing with events in the lives of individuals. In this respect, Thomas Mann's *Magic Mountain* may be instructive. In the first part of the novel, Herr Naphta and Signore Settembrini engage in a lively and seemingly enthralling intellectual controversy about rationalism versus faith. Later in the book Peeperkorn comes on the scene, and the sheer force of his personality dwarfs them. We can think of Naphta and Settembrini as Western models *par excellence*. Their theoretical depth is the obverse of their existential aridity. Peeperkorn, on the other hand, despite his life and vigor, lacks deep meaning. If he is something more than a lively mechanism, the life of his mind is deeply buried.

Individual human life is characterized in large part by its uniqueness, by its details, by its feel, its smell, and its look. That is why our interest is maintained primarily when such details are present. When these details are detached from a knowledge and awareness of what it means to be human, or a member of the community, or a tailor, or a doctor, not merely in a particular society but also comparatively, then the book is only half-written. This insight need not be explicit; it may be brought to awareness by detail. Yet it is a part of the human drama that deepens and sustains its meaning.

In *Alienation and Identification*, I distinguished the sensual from the theoretical and the sacred, the latter two being varieties of timeless structure. Although these categories are not identical with theory and praxis, they fill similar roles in understanding the character of human being and society. The drama unfolds, and it can be understood. It takes place in a universe that is favorable to it and in the absence of which it could not be understood. That alternatives are present and that things might have gone differently does not rupture the web of relatedness. It does determine its weakly ordered character and accounts for its richness, its ambiguity at the edges, its inherent tragedies, and its potential sustenance.

Most of the method and substance of this book has constituted a defense of science and of literal language. Clearly, I wish to sustain that position. Scientific knowledge is genuine and the concept of absolute knowledge is misleading. Nonetheless, two important distinctions must be made. We may be limited in the types of transactions we can participate in and, therefore, in the forms and types of knowledge we can produce. We may have only an ant's-eye view of the world and of our place in it.

In the second place, we do know things that we cannot prove. Some things we can learn to prove, as in the logical demonstration that the heads of horses are the heads of animals. It may even be that we know some things that we cannot communicate verbally, for we may perceive them too dimly to do so. Mysticism, as Josiah Royce pointed out, gets into trouble only when it enters the kingdom of reason. As a natural exercise that is intended to put us in touch with an inexpressible reality, scientists can have no objection to mysticism, however much they may be disinclined to accept it. Science is not antithetical to mystery, but only to systems of mystery, for these make claims that cannot be defended.

When an attempt is made to use metaphor to state what cannot be made literal, it is an illusion. When metaphor is used to put one in touch with the incommunicable, it may have a function, but one that is not susceptible to public judgment. When it is used to adumbrate the limitations and relativity of knowledge, its content can be conveyed better at the literal level.

Some physicists have attempted recently to reinterpret physics in the light of Albert Einstein's and Boris Podolsky's thought experiment, Bell's theorem, and related experimental evidence. That experimental evidence now strongly calls into question realism as it relates to local space. An alternative interpretation of the evidence might be that communication between quanta occurs at speeds faster than that of light. Some of these physicists and their interpreters now claim that Hinduism, Buddhism, particularly Zen, and other Eastern religions and philosophies are closer to the truths of physics than classical Western cosmologies and sign systems: particularly those of the seventeenth and eighteenth centuries, although there are some elements of continuity going back to classical Greece.

I think they go too far. If, for instance, Zen koans are considered as instructional devices, it can be argued that they open the mind better to contemporary concepts of quantum physics than do more traditional Western metaphors. But they do this only as metaphors. Physicists understand these hypotheses in literal language. When their interpreters use concepts such as "illusion," "higher degree of reality," or the "basic identity of everything," they are misusing signs and sign systems.

Buddhism rejects all concepts of the absolute. All things are impermanent and relative. And the only way to salvation is through emptying the self of desire and attaining nirvana. This, Buddha said, meant emptying oneself of *samsara*, the endless progression of existence and one's attachment to it. However, this state of nirvana also emptied one of sympathy for others, he also said, and, hence, in a sense is a false opposite. True nirvana, thus, must combine *samsara* and the limited nirvana. Perhaps this is an early version of my transcendentally stable system. Surely Hegel must have been influenced by this philosophy, for his concept of false opposites seems similar. The resemblances to Heidegger and Derrida also seem clear, for they both deny the absolute "whatness" of any existent. The search for absences and presences is but a short step. I certainly do not wish to deny what I have in common with these figures. But I believe that they present their conclusions in a metaphoric language that hides truths that best can be expressed in literal language. My view of the correlative character of language, I believe, permits the expression of what is true in what they assert without losing what science has to offer.

Unlike the Buddhists, who regard the real world as empty, I have taken the position that references to kinds, events, and processes are limited truths. Gautama Buddha, anticipating Hegel, argued that the opposites of objectified discourse—e.g., the self and its world, consciousness and objects—are false opposites. There is an element of truth in this view. But if one views them as correlatives employed in producing and understanding experience, the metaphysical problem that he perceived and that he solved by metaphor ceases to exist.

Metaphor leads to communicable knowledge when it facilitates the use of literal language. It may help us to break out of our tendency to simplify signs and to put the universe in a straitjacket. Yet this use of metaphor is at best a prelude to literal analysis, but one that no longer posts a univocal true order in the world.

NOTES

1. Hiroshi Nagai, "A Philosophical Conception of Finality in Biology," in Gunnar Andersson, editor, *Rationality in Science and Politics* (Dordrecht, Boston, Lancaster: D. Reidel Publishing Company, 1985), p. 213.
2. Roy Abraham Vargese, "Science and the Divine Origin of Life," *The World & I*, July 1987; vol. 2, no. 7, pp. 182–187.

Appendix I
A Note on the Phenomenological Movement

I am aware that some of my readers may be wondering if my critique of intentionality in chapter 7 really responds to the claims of the major figures in the phenomenological movement and, if so, how. Because these writers are difficult to interpret, and because there are so many controversies over their interpretation, it is not possible to satisfy these doubts. Nonetheless a brief outline of my understanding of the main positions of the major figures in the phenomenological movement may convey to the reader my interpretation of these writers. In any event, the bulk of the book, with the exception of the chapter on Derrida, deals with the Anglo-Saxon and Popperian positions. Thus, this appendix, even though it only adumbrates the main issues, is useful.

HUSSERL

Edmund Husserl is generally viewed as the founder and perhaps leading figure in the phenomenological movement. Although not as convoluted a writer as Martin Heidegger, Husserl shifted the traditional meanings of terms. Husserl was not a systematic writer, and the reader must contend with a number of serious ambiguities. Moreover, his position, as is perhaps natural, seemed to shift with time. The only elements that remained relatively consistent were his ideal of a rigorous science (although not one modeled on natural science) and his belief that he could get to the core of philosophical problems through rigorous subjective inquiry. According to Husserl, science requires true premises. Although he believed that there was a crisis in science and doubted that deductive certainty could be found in physics, Husserl attempted to reach true foundations that would provide certainty through a phenomenological reorganization of philosophy. In doing this, however, he was determined to avoid what he regarded as an unphilosophical study of mere facts, or a naturalism that could not reveal ultimate truth. Thus, he refused to identify norms with natural facts or to derive them from observed facts.

Although Husserl insisted upon rigor, it is not clear what he meant by that term. Perhaps what he meant was the deeper and deeper delving into mind, or at least into mind as related to phenomena. At any rate, he asserted that "transcendental subjectivity" was the foundation of this rigorous method. By *tran-*

scendental subjectivity, he meant a form of reflection that, beginning with a phenomenon that is held in mind, soon leaves it far behind by purging it of all the presuppositions that experience brings to it. The framework of experience would not be discarded; rather, it would be subjected to the most rigorous and radical examination.

There was, Husserl said, such a thing as pure ego and pure consciousness. He did not regard this ego or "I-ness" as an entity, either transcendental or phenomenal. In its pure form, according to Husserl, it established only a relationship to a body of experiences.

Husserl was a radical *anti-relativist*, as that term was then understood. He rejected the notion that the rules of thinking could be derived from psychology or that logic found its basis in psychology. Feelings did not determine truth, in Husserl's view. Logic was divided into two levels: the first was the study of propositions according to the logic of statements and involved meanings and their combinations; the second was the study of the things to which statements referred. Husserl, however, did not develop his logic rigorously: logic interested him as a way of studying its subjective correlates. Thus, he strove to find the ideal types of logical experience that corresponded to ideal logical laws. Real thinking was merely the entry point for this study. Ultimately, the application of thought to empirical experiences led to what he regarded as the pure types of the essences of the experiences.

Husserl's method led him directly to the concept of *universal essences*. From thinking about experience, whether actual or imaginative, of particular colors, one could reach the essence, color. Husserl did not consider this an abstraction, for abstraction, he said, cannot be universalized. Universal propositions could be satisfied only by general essences. Even if he never argued that essences were eternal or changeless, he did insist that they were concrete.

Another important, even vital, aspect of Husserl's thought was the concept of the *intentionality of consciousness*. By this he meant that consciousness was directed toward an object of consciousness, not that the object existed within consciousness. Such objects were the focus of intentions. He did not claim that all psychological phenomena had intentionally, only those that could be called acts. Thus, data are merely raw material within a complex structure and the same object of intention may be referred to from a variety of intentional frames of reference. Moreover, it is this intentionality that relates objects to each other and that brings coherence to experience.

Husserl distinguished between mere *intention*—the vague generation of an orientation toward intentional objects—and *intuitive fulfillment*, which characterizes the intention in concrete form. In this sense, Husserl eventually called fulfillment the constitution of the intentional object, for its concrete form results from the complex task of intentional analysis. The test of knowledge, for Husserl, ultimately resided in a scientific intuition that presents intentional objects in their most adequate and self-evident form, a form that cannot be described in terms of sensory data: for example, he wrote that sensory data cannot directly present concepts such as "number" or "similarity." Things become self-evident when one penetrates to the universal or general essences, which then become the basis of discourse. At this point, one has penetrated to authentic reality. On the other hand, it is not clear that Husserl was willing to accept any claim concerning what is self-evident; and there seems to be an ambiguity either in his thinking or in his presentation of this matter.

According to Husserl, the phenomenological process involves the initial seizing of the object of experience, its initial explication by descriptive categories, and eventually the seizing of the concept or percept in relation to other objects. This is worked out in what he calls the *reduction*. This is not simplification or reduction to anything else; it apparently means going back to the origins. The *eidetic reduction* involves a reduction from particular facts to universals or general essences. For instance, the sensory knowledge that three apples and two apples are five apples is intuited in terms of a pure immanent essence—that 2 + 3 = 5—when all the sensory evidence is set aside.

The *phenomenal reduction*, on the other hand, refers to the suspension of the belief that a transcendent reality produces passive experience. The subject, not the subjective, perceives something that is universally valid; for instance, that pain is evil. Although some pain may be good—it may warn one of an injury—pain as a transcendent essence is the negation of life and therefore evil. There is, however, no way to test such claims through an appeal to experience, nor can we know, with any clarity, what he meant by saying that pain is the negation of life.

Science, according to Husserl, involves the ultimate intuition in experience of both immanent and transcendent essences. It is the belief in pure essences that reinstated an outdated metaphysics in Husserl's philosophy in the form of certain truth. An alternative method that I advocated in chapter 1 is to tentatively bracket aspects of experience while accepting other aspects as tentatively given, thus permitting the exploration of experience in different contexts. My method is inconsistent with a concept of pure essences with univocal meanings and the strong metaphysical order to which such conceptions give rise.

Husserl referred to phenomenalism as an idealistic philosophy. He did not mean subjective idealism by this, however. Basically, he argued that Being derives its meaning from consciousness and that the very concept of a reality that is not related to consciousness is self-contradictory.

Husserl responded to the perceived inadequacies of the philosophy of science of the twentieth century. However, he still accepted the definition of theory that lay at its base and, in addition, Aristotle's assumption that one must start from premises known to be true in order to arrive at true conclusions.

If one understands that theory is bounded by praxis, then all assumptions are accepted or bracketed only tentatively. Because his concept of science did not permit him to accept this, Husserl never could achieve a statement of logic or a method of reduction that would validate his statements about essences, Being, or consciousness.

SCHELER

Max Scheler carried the concept of essence further than Husserl. His approach ultimately differed from Husserl's in important respects, however. He had no interest in rigor; he was far more interested in solving what he regarded as the key crisis of the modern age by a reconstruction of moral thought. Scheler argued that phenomenology refers to the way people intuitively entered into relationships with the objects they experience. Thus, he differentiated natural facts, scientific facts and phenomenological facts. *Natural facts* incorporate the preconceptions of the time, whereas *phenomenological facts* are experienced immediately in a pure form.

Scheler's *phenomenological reduction*, or stripping away, was an attempt to move back from symbols to the things themselves, to what they are, and to the connections between them and other things. Scheler dispensed with self-evidence. And, unlike Husserl, who used the phenomenological reduction to understand reality, Scheler used it to free humanity from what he regarded as the grasp or hold of reality. Still, like Husserl, he wanted to go back to essences, to the true universals that one could grasp intuitively whatever one's actual experience with things. Thus, Scheler could argue that we might incorrectly categorize a particular act as generous, but that we can still understand that generosity is more valuable than meanness.

Scheler also studied cognitive emotion and attempted to use phenomenology to break down the sharp boundary between reason and emotion, reasoning that many emotions have external reference and thus relate to intentional acts.

Although Scheler, unlike Husserl, did not insist upon a true set of assumptions as a basis for reaching scientific conclusions about data, his assertion of people's ability to recognize differences in essences is neither justified systematically nor based on a method that others can replicate. He merely asserts that people can make these judgments.

If, however, one starts with the distinction between praxis and theory, there is no need for a concept of essences. Intensionality, in the praxical frame of reference, is merely a characteristic of a particular system that can be subjected to as public an examination as any other aspect of reality.

HEIDEGGER

Whether we view Martin Heidegger as an existentialist or a phenomenologist, he is regarded by many as the foremost modern philosopher. If there are difficulties in understanding Husserl's language, they are multiplied a thousandfold by Heidegger. Indeed, some have argued that Heidegger was neither an existentialist nor a phenomenologist, but a mystic who denied the value of articulation. He is certainly not easy to understand. Heidegger insisted that psychology cannot become a positive science of subjective experience in which the transcendent ego can find itself. Unlike both Husserl and Scheler, Heidegger was primarily concerned with explaining the world of objective Being. However, his explanation of the history of objective existence of the human race is based largely on human failure to ask fundamental questions about human Being. The meaning of this Being, according to Heidegger, is the fundamental question that alone can serve as the subject of a fundamental investigation. And because only human existence can be with or without meaning (a statement that is clearly false in respect to some animals), that fact fundamentally distinguishes human Being from other Being.

The great failure of modern science, according to Heidegger, lay in the lack of distinction between things that have Being and those in which Being is used (''how'' questions). Thus, Being, must be studied independently of things-in-being. Being even has a kind of active role, in that it can hide itself from or partially reveal itself to people. Therefore, Being can have its own history. It can have a unity that articulations only distort.

How can we summarize Heidegger? Being is itself. It is its own truth. It has a tendency to hide and withdraw. On the other hand, its revelation of itself and its truth is its own doing and is, therefore, something that is active. Being is temporal, neither timeless nor eternal. It therefore develops. Although ground-less, it is the source of all things-in-being. It is essential to the human race. It is a non-symbolic fact the interpretation of which depends upon hermeneutics. Hermeneutics, according to Heidegger, also permits the investigation of being-in-the-world. Since human Being, in particular, cannot occur except within the framework of the world, there is therefore a close relationship between Being and being-in-the-world.

Heidegger never showed how hermeneutics operates or how its conclusions are validated—for instance, how Being is related to being-in-the-world—or even why hermeneutics is necessary if truth, after hiding, reveals itself.

There is an alternative interpretation of Heidegger that mitigates his mysticism and relates his position to my own. In this interpretation, Greek thought, and modern Western thought based on it, is metaphysical because truth is seen as permanent, distanced from Being, and independent of consciousness. Further-more, in separating subject and object as radically as we do, we lose both the element of caring, which unites the past with the future and us with others, and a sense of anxiety as we contemplate the emptiness (true nothingness?) of a world in which all things are transient and relational. Here again we see a relationship backwards in time with Buddhism and forward with Derrida, for the later Heidegger also talks of presences. We also find in his later writings a description of modern thought as dominated by *techne*, a lack of *sorge* or caring, a theme that reemerges in Habermas. These failings, he said, are the metaphysical and technological foundation of modern Western thought. Thus, the things-in-being are reified, obscuring the temporal variability of things, their development in time, and their capacity to surprise us.

If this is what Heidegger meant by hiddenness, the non-being of Being, and the spontaneity even of the inanimate, I believe that the position developed in Part One and my use of it to criticize Derrida in chapter 10 is a clearer, more coherent statement, without the mysticism into which Heidegger retreats. The synthesis of Western and Eastern philosophies that he attempts, in my opinion, can be developed better by distinguishing between theory and praxis.

We learn what science is by observing what scientists do. We distinguish techniques that permit fruitful investigation from those which do not. We learn what works, and we do this in an increasingly rich fashion. As the history of science demonstrates, we continue to learn not merely about the substance of science but about its methodology as scientists cope with problems. We do not make this advance by studying the essence of science, the Being of science, or, except peripherally, the original meaning of words. If we wish to learn what science is, we do it by investigating scientific behavior. We make distinctions which eventually create new problems for us. We look for comparative evidence. This leads us to make still other distinctions and to offer reasons for these distinctions. We do not investigate the essence of science; we engage in a praxical analysis that helps us to weave the tapestry of the realm of knowledge. We can learn to distinguish good science from bad science, courage from foolhardiness, and generosity from profligacy.

SARTRE

Jean-Paul Sartre reacted to Husserl's work by accusing him of a Berkeleyan idealism in his concept of Being and with a form of immanentism that maintained the "thing-illusion." According to Sartre, Husserl's philosophy remained permanently on the level of mere appearances, and he thus became unable to move toward existential dialectics. Husserl, wrote Sartre, could not move beyond the present into the past and future, and confused phenomenology with Kant's concept of a "transcendental subject." He did not take sufficient account of immediate experience. According to Sartre, the fundamental task of philosophy is the objective discussion and investigation of the Being of consciousness.

Sartre accused Heidegger of pseudo-idealism and of using rhetoric to mask the obvious. He accused him of eliminating the Being of consciousness from his *Dasein*. And he asserted that Heidegger's inappropriate use of hermeneutics led him to ground the phenomenological concept of Nothing on the experience of anxiety rather than on the negative element in human spontaneity. Heidegger, wrote Sartre, did not understand humans as active Beings who project themselves upon the world.

Sartre juxtaposed freedom and Being, but he seemed able to express these concepts only in his literary works. Thus he was able to assert that never had the French been freer than under the German occupation, for the very repression of freedom brought out its meaning. Although it is certainly true that a period of deprivation may enrich experience by forceably demonstrating the value of something that is absent, one wonders whether Sartre was not engaging in the same kind of rhetoric of which he accused Heidegger.

Was Sartre really able to reconcile Being and Nothingness and the "for-self" and "in-self?" To Sartre, everything seemed to depend on choice, the pride of choosing. This meant rejecting what the universe thrusts on one and replacing it with a projection that one imposes on the world. Can one achieve the pure spontaneity that Sartre called for? Can one reject one's own past and one's biological nature? Can one accept the manner in which Sartre attempted to overcome solipsism: by reducing the structure of the self to a position in which it no longer takes precedence over other selves?

For Sartre, Being was the whole world outside of consciousness. Time, which for Heidegger constituted the main property of Being, in Sartre was paralleled by Nothing. Whereas Heidegger's concept of Being constituted an attempt to approach an understanding of Being, Sartre's Nothing is the great enemy of Being. Consciousness is only for itself and it refers to being-in-itself against Being; for unless one questions Being, there is no place for Nothing.

There is a form of pure activity that is the foundation of human existence, according to Sartre. Absolute freedom and responsibility are the foundation of this activity, and people derive their Being from it. But if freedom determines human nature, as Sartre claimed, then how can we determine what is a free act and what is not? Whereas skepticism enables us to challenge preconceived ideas, Sartre reduced everything to an objectively meaningless flow of events upon which people arbitrarily impose their own meaning. Although there is reason to believe that Sartre accepted the independence of facts-in-the-world from particular consciousnesses, he appears to define freedom as our unconstrained transformation of facts: it is not merely that our choices are not uniquely determined, but that all constraints seem to be gone.

Like Heidegger, Sartre believed that the analysis of concepts such as Being and Nothing permit the analysis of experience. While Heidegger argued that Nothing, as distinguished from simple negation, is based on anxiety, Sartre found it in the absence of things in our daily experience. Although his concept is certainly more practical than Heidegger's, there is nothing in it that permits it to serve as a key philosophical concept except for Sartre's insistence that it has a status of its own in the absence of which Being cannot be understood.

MERLEAU-PONTY

Maurice Merleau-Ponty rejected all forms of idealism. He argued that existence is essentially interpenetrated with meaning or sense. Thus, he did not regard the world as meaninglessly opaque. Unlike Sartre, he did not find meaning merely in choosing. Furthermore, Merleau-Ponty did not distinguish as sharply between people and things as did Sartre, but regarded them as interrelated. Merleau-Ponty believed that the subjective and objective aspects of the phenomenal world could be reunited in a higher dialectical synthesis. He argued that they are constantly reunited in actual life.

Merleau-Ponty, thus, was much closer to my own position than was Sartre, for he rejected Cartesian subjectivity and accepted modern science. He saw the difference between sense and nonsense, not as absolute but as one of transition and degree. Unlike Sartre, he did not accept irrationalism; he understood much of the ambiguity of experience. He viewed philosophy as an interrogation of nature and attempted to unite the objectivism of the traditional sciences and a reasonable form of subjectivism.

Some phenomenological reduction remained, for Merleau-Ponty attempted to discover the uniqueness of facts before any linguistic information. Thus, he retained the concept of essence. This brought him closer to existentialism, but essence had a metaphysical content in his philosophy. Although it is true that we sometimes gain fresh insight by studying the root of a word, I believe that the methodology outlined in chapter 4 for examining the whatness of phenomena is a more valid method. It can be enriched by the evidence provided by the roots of words—or by any other conscious or preconscious evidence that permits us to make useful distinctions—but praxical methods are not based on the assumption that facts imply essence, that they have a unique existence, or that their meaning is best revealed by stripping away their context. Context is essential to meaning, particularly in comparative analysis.

In practice, Merleau-Ponty retreated from his own approach; in his philosophy of nature he considered the physiological, the biological, and the human in terms of different configurations and thus approached both a systems and a contextual analysis. He did not, however, get rid of his conceptualist approach. Instead of recognizing subjectivity as the field within which concepts are held, perceptions organized, and theoretical and praxical reasoning employed, he considered it an independent subject of investigation.

Of all the phenomenologists and existentialists, Merleau-Ponty was perhaps the most amenable to a modern scientific approach. However, the fundamental concepts he used, such as "being-in-the-the-world," cannot be used to develop scientific propositions. It is true that people are in the world and that their understanding of the world is the framework within which they make statements about it. But this is a mere truism that does not facilitate any practical investigation. Although Sartre's existential anxiety, which he says arises from the perception of Nothingness, may be one of the major determinants of his writing and his political positions, I believe that psychology and sociology will permit us to describe and analyze anxiety in a practical and objective language. And although Merleau-Ponty kept shying away from such excesses, he remained within a tradition that continues to exploit them.

FINAL COMMENTS

All the philosophers discussed in this appendix wrote during the period in which some form of positivism dominated the intellectual framework of Europe. They were either unfamiliar, or insufficiently familiar, with Peircean pragmaticism. Rather than viewing mind as employing a code that is transformed through experience and that validates these transformations through successful use, Husserl, like most of the other writers, dichotomized concept and fact and merely inverted the positivistic method. It is no accident that he also called himself a positivist.

Most phenomenologists retain a concept of a pure or, alternatively, of a transcendental ego. There is no pure or transcendental ego. The illusion that there is arises from the fact that one level of thought is treated reflexively as the object of another level of thought and that this reflexive process can continue indefinitely, at least in principle. There is a great deal of evidence to suggest either that not all thought is self-conscious or that the thoughts we designate as self-conscious arise from functions of the dominant cortical system: a system that is without direct access to some other thinking processes. It is also possible that what we regard as conscious thought involves a heightened process within the cortex that fuses thought and feeling. Self-consciousness would then involve the treatment of feeling and thought as objects of cognition. Self-consciousness is neither temporal nor spatial; it is the field within which are presented the objectified reflexive elements to which time, space, and qualitative judgments apply.

Information, as a state of the organism, triggers action and self-conscious thought. But the state of information that is part of the self-conscious data bank is not the informational element that has done the triggering—the latter can never be held in consciousness—but only the reflexive handling of it, just as the symbols of the scientist are not the real world but their reflexive abstract treatment. Thus, feeling would not be a product of the neurons but a heightened state of their activity.

Apart from the other difficulties I have found in these so-called phenomenological positions, their investigations were concentrated on what can only be called epiphenomena: an abstract set of true meanings. The actual field of knowledge, whether of the person or the world, presents problems within an informational context. It is the world of science. Husserl, Scheler, and even Heidegger, despite his supposed rejection of metaphysics, were pursuing a ghost: a consciousness or ego that is differentiated from both the reflexive process of knowing and thinking and the real entity—that is, the manifest entity plus its potentialities—that knows and thinks.

SELECTED BIBLIOGRAPHY

Husserl, Edmund. *Cartesian Meditations: An Introduction to Phenomenology*, translated by Dorion Cairns (The Hague: M. Nijhoff, 1960).

———. *The Crisis of European Sciences and Transcendental Phenomenology: An Introduction to Phenomenological Philosophy*, translated by David Carr (Evanston: Northwestern University Press, 1970).

———. *Experience and Judgment: Investigations in a Genealogy of Logic*, edited by Ludwig Landgrebe, translated by James S. Churchill and Karl Ameriks (Evanston: Northwestern University Press, 1973).

———. *Formal and Transcendental Logic*, translated by Dorion Cairns (The Hague: M. Nijhoff, 1969).

————. *The Idea of Phenomenology*, translated by William P. Alson and George Nakhnikian (The Hague: M. Nijhoff, 1970).

Scheler, Max. *Formalism in Ethics and Non-Formal Ethics of Values: A New Attempt Toward the Foundation of an Ethical Personalism*, (5th edition), translated by Manfred S. Frings and Roger L. Finch (Evanston: Northwestern University Press, 1973).

————. *Man's Place in Nature*, translated and introduction by Hans Meyerhoff (New York: Noonday Press, 1961, 1973).

————. *On the Eternal in Man*, translated by Bernard Noble (Hamden, Connecticut: Shoe String Press, 1960, 1972).

————. *Problems of a Sociology of Knowledge*, translated by Manfred S. Frings, edited and introduction by Kenneth W. Stikkers (London: Routledge and K. Paul, 1980).

Heidegger, Martin. *Existence and Being*, introduction by Werner Broch (Chicago: H. Regnery Company, 1949).

————. *Identity and Difference*, translated and introduction by Joan Stanibaugh (New York: Harper and Row, 1969).

————. *An Introduction to Metaphysics*, translated by Ralph Manheim (New Haven: Yale University Press, 1959).

Sartre, Jean-Paul. *Being and Nothingness; An Essay on Phenomenological Ontology*, translated and introduction by Hazel E. Barnes (New York: Philosophical Library, 1956).

————. *Critique of Dialectical Reason, Theory of Practical Ensembles*, translated by Alan Sheridan-Smith, edited by Jonathan Ree (Atlantic Highlands, New Jersey: Humanities Press, 1976).

————. *Existentialism*, translated by Bernard Frechtman (New York: Philosophical Library, 1947).

————. *Of Human Freedom*, edited by Wade Baskin (New York: Philosophical Library, 1966). Collected Essays.

————. *The Psychology of Imagination* (New York: Philosophical Library, 1948).

Merleau-Ponty, Maurice. *Consciousness and the Acquisition of Language*, translated by Hugh J. Silberman (Evanston: Northwestern University Press, 1973).

————. *In Praise of Philosophy*, translated with preface by John Wild and James M. Edie (Evanston: Northwestern University Press, 1963).

————. *Phemenology of Perception*, translated by Colin Smith (New York: Humanities Press, 1962).

————. *Sense and Non-sense*, translated and preface by Hubert L. Dreyfus and Patricia Allen Dreyfus (Evanston: Northwestern University Press, 1964).

Appendix II
Equilibrium and Self-Organizing Change

This body of material was not included in the main text because it would have interrupted its progression. Insofar as I shall argue that the study of dynamically stable and self-organizing systems entails considerations of equilibrium—because "system," or "structure," are correlatives of "process"—this brief section qualifies the discussion of equilibrium in chapter 3. Insofar as I introduce considerations relevant to transfinitely stable systems, it expands the discussion of values in Part Three.

Ilya Prigogene has made important contributions to the study of dynamic self-organizing transitions in thermal kinetic systems in a state of inequilibrium that are irreversible, that do not respond to the law of large numbers, and that are responsive to global features of the system in which they occur and to initial conditions. He also has called attention to possible analogies in social systems: genetic processes, processes involving competition for resources, cooperative regulation, and migration.[1] Some social scientists believe incorrectly that this mode of analysis is either the only alternative to the analysis of equilibrium and stability, or that it is preferable to it. Although Prigogine's non-equilibrium thermodynamic analysis accounts for irreversible (and hence historic) change at the level of molecular biology, it is not an exclusive alternative to equilibrium analysis of social systems.

In simple mechanical systems, for which independent measures exist, it is possible to construct complex Markoff-chain equations—that is, equations expressing probabilities that produce transitions between successive states—for gross aspects of dynamic processes and to derive transitional states of equilibrium from them if the initial conditions are given. In such systems, the transitional states can sometimes be understood better in terms of the dynamic processes than as individual stages.

When we move to more complex physical systems under fluctuating conditions or to social systems—for which independent measures do not exist and the terms of which vary in meaning with context, as we observed in chapter 3 —the use of dynamic chains is not likely to be useful, except to sketch an analytically distinctive part of a concrete system. Even then, we must depend on the relative stability of boundaries as when we study suicide or the use of beaches, and the analysis of equilibrium remains of great importance to our understanding of these dynamic processes.

Let us consider some examples. In doing so, I shall distinguish between system-dominant and subsystem-dominant conditions. In a static and perfect market, the system is dominant: although the market is constituted by the universe of individual decisions, the state of the market functions as a boundary condition for those decisions. Thus, the market is dominant and the system determines individual decisions and continuously reproduces the static structure of the market.

Let us now vary the market so that economies of scale can enhance some initial advantages. Now there will be a continual, not continuous, transition to a subsystem-dominant oligopoly in which the state of the market is no longer a mere boundary condition; rather its equilibrium interacts complexly with individual decisions to establish successive states of equilibrium. Our understanding of the transitions of such systems is illuminated at least as much by the before-and-after states of equilibrium as by an understanding of the process of transition. Moreover, the transitions can be related to the system meaningfully only if the equilibrial conditions of the successive stages—and particularly of the type of market—are understood. Because these may produce genuine novelty, as Prigogene is careful to emphasize, they may in principle be unpredictable, although it may be possible to understand them after the event.

C. H. Waddington coined the term *homeorhesis* to distinguish a system that maintains not a particular value of a variable but a direction of flow in a system.[2] I coined the term *transfinite stability* to account for a type of stability that involves intentional transitions in values and structures.[3] These concepts are important to the analysis of changes in stable or transitional equilibria.

In the real world no state of a system is permanent. And transitions may affect not merely the type of market (or of other systems) but also types of industry within a market. Thus, there may be dynamic processes that make the production of energy more important than the production of automobiles or the production of information more important than energy. However, to make decisions that will help or hinder transitions involves reflecting not merely upon environmental change but also upon the transitional possibilities of the system —that is, if the decisions are to be good ones. Otherwise, injurious short-term advantages may be pursued. Thus, even though the open world is characterized by self-organized changes—in some of which the system dictates the individual decisions, in some of which individual decisions dominate, and in some of which there is a strong interaction between the two—the key to analysis lies in the understanding of equilibrium conditions. The concepts of transfinite stability and the test-in-principle discussed in chapters 11 and 13 represent such a dynamic self-organizing principle at the level of human and social values.

It is important not to try to do everything at once and not to attempt to develop a total theory that accounts for everything. In international relations, for instance, it may be possible to study some aspects of an international system and transnational processes that help to explain some of the system's characteristics. But the price in terms of scientific understanding is too high if an attempt is made to unite such separate studies or to substitute one for the other. For instance, one can make relatively independent analyses of such processes as the spread of nuclear weapons, increases in cooperation in international trade, the growth of multinational corporations, and so forth. One can then ask how this growth will alter the international system and how the system will function at its new stage. One can also ask how the system will affect these processes.

Perhaps the most controversial aspect of Prigogene's position lies in his contention that these irreversible transitions are probabilistic and, hence, in principle unpredictable: that the universe in its non-equilibrium aspects—and these are the standard case according to Prigogene—produces genuine novelty. This accords with my view that the universe is largely weakly ordered, that there is no implicate order that deterministically flows from what is. However, it may be possible to argue for a potentiality in what is. If this potentiality can be triggered non-deterministically by relatively small changes in intitial conditions in non-equilibrial dynamic circumstances, it will not be predictable. This is a position I argued for in chapter 7.

NOTES

1. Ilya Prigogine, "Order through Fluctuations: Self-organization and Social System," in *Evolution and Consciousness: Human Systems in Transition*, edited by E. Jantsch and C. H. Waddington (Reading, Mass.: Addison-Wesley Publishing Co., 1976).

2. C. H. Waddington, *Tools for Thought* (New York: Basic Books, 1977), pp. 104 ff.

3. Morton A. Kaplan, *Justice, Human Nature and Political Obligation* (New York: Free Press, 1976), pp. 19–20.

Index

Abortions: claims and, 207; praxical inquiry on, 205

Absolute: Hegel's concept of, 134, 237*n*, 248, 250; the Relative and the, 200–201

"Acts of force," 131

Agency, concept of rational, 172–174

Alienation, Marx on, 244–246

Alienation and Identification (Kaplan), 246, 251, 255, 275, 276

"Alliance Behavior in Balance of Power Systems: Applying a Poisson Model to Nineteenth-Century Europe" (Mc Gowan and Rood), 269

Alliances, characteristics of, 269–270

Alsace-Lorraine, 270, 271

Alter ego, 136

Althusser, Louis, 218

American Medical Association, 264–265

American Political Science Review, 58

Analysis, varying foci of, 179–180

Analytical pragmatism, *xiv*

Anarchy, 263

Anti-relativist, Husserl as, 280

Appearance and Reality (Bradley), *xvii*

Appearances, consciousness, realism, and, 81

"Appears," "is" and, 151

Aristotle, 33, 65

Ashby, W. Ross, *xvii*, 155

"Asiatic production," 255

Assessment, 9–11; critical experiments and, 69; explanation and, 50; realism and, 67–82

Assymetric bargaining games, 41

Balance of power, theory of, 269–270

Base, superstructure and, 217–218

Basketball, 58

Being: Derrida's transcategorical use of, 137, existence and, 138; Heidegger on, 283; "other" and, 136–141; Sartre on, 284–285

Belief: as complex concept, 123; knowledge and, 104–105

Blanshard, Brand, 45, 189–190

Böhm-Bawerk, Eugen von, 224

Bohr, Neils: complementarity principle of, 38, 250; on reality and information, 89–90

Bolce, Louis H., 59

Bootstrap theory, 72–75

Born, Max, 14, 34

Boundary conditions, as essential, 95

Burt, Cyril, 54–55

Buddhism, influence of, 277

Bushido, ethical code of, 156

Capital, relationship of labor and to forces of production, 255

Capital punishment, 185, 186

Capitalism: dynamics of, Marx on, 227; Marx's account of, 219–221; productive power of, Marx on, 249